GAY BERLIN

GAY BERLIN

Birthplace of a Modern Identity

ROBERT BEACHY

Alfred A. Knopf | New York | 2014

Boca Raton Public Library

THIS IS A BORZOI BOOK
PUBLISHED BY ALFRED A. KNOPF

Copyright © 2014 by Robert Beachy

All rights reserved. Published in the United States by Alfred A. Knopf,
a division of Random House LLC, New York,
and in Canada by Random House of Canada Limited, Toronto,
Penguin Random House companies.

www.aaknopf.com

Knopf, Borzoi Books, and the colophon
are registered trademarks of Random House LLC.

Library of Congress Cataloging-in-Publication Data
Beachy, Robert.
Gay Berlin : birthplace of a modern identity / by Robert Beachy.
pages cm
ISBN 978-0-307-27210-2 (hardback) — ISBN 978-0-385-35307-6 (ebook)
1. Gay men—Germany—Berlin—Identity.   2. Gay culture—Germany—
Berlin.   3. Homosexuality—Germany—Berlin.   4. Gender identity—Germany—
Berlin.   I. Title.
HQ76.2.G42B43 2014
306.76'60943155—dc23   2014004986

Jacket images: (top, left to right) transvestites, Eldorado nightclub, 1929, akg-images; *Die Freundin*,
1928; cabaret poster, Berlin, 1920; (middle) Berlin at night, 1928, akg-images; (bottom) Eldorado
advertisement, c. 1920s; game of tug-of-war, anonymous photographer, 1930s
Jacket design by Evan Gaffney Design

Manufactured in the United States of America

First Edition

For Ada

(1925–2005)

Contents

Introduction   ix

CHAPTER ONE   The German Invention of Homosexuality   3

CHAPTER TWO   Policing Homosexuality in Berlin   42

CHAPTER THREE   The First Homosexual Rights Movement
and the Struggle to Shape Identity   85

CHAPTER FOUR   The Eulenburg Scandal and the Politics of Outing   120

CHAPTER FIVE   Hans Blüher, the Wandervogel Movement,
and the Männerbund   140

CHAPTER SIX   Weimar Sexual Reform and the Institute
for Sexual Science   160

CHAPTER SEVEN   Sex Tourism and Male Prostitution
in Weimar Berlin   187

CHAPTER EIGHT   Weimar Politics and the Struggle
for Legal Reform   220

Epilogue   241

Acknowledgments   249

Notes   251

Sources and Bibliography   275

Index   297

Introduction

"Look at me!" blared the capital of the Reich. "I am Babel, the
monster among cities! We had a formidable army: now we
command the most riotously wicked night life. Don't miss our
matchless show, ladies and gentlemen! It's Sodom and Gomorrah
in a Prussian tempo. Don't miss the circus of perversities! Our
department store of assorted vices! An all-out tale of brand new
kinds of debauchery!"

—KLAUS MANN, *The Turning Point* (1942)

In October 1928, Wystan Hugh Auden, aged twenty-one, moved to Berlin, ostensibly to learn German. The following March he was joined by
his friend Christopher Isherwood, who visited for about a week. Later
Isherwood also settled in Berlin, and resided there until the spring of
1933. As Auden explained, Isherwood's arrival prompted him to begin
keeping his Berlin journal. In the very first entry, under the heading
"Saturday getting tight," Auden outlined the introductory tour he conducted for his friend: "It begins with the Hirschfeld museum. We waited
in an eighteenth century drawing room with elderly ladies and lovely
young boys." The "Hirschfeld museum" was part of the famous Institute
for Sexual Science, located at the northern edge of the Tiergarten Park,
which the pioneering homosexual rights activist Dr. Magnus Hirschfeld
had founded in 1918. In addition to its "museum" of sexual artifacts and
colorful displays, the institute housed medical exam rooms, a lecture

hall, offices, a library, and lodging for staff. It not only attracted curious tourists but also served as a social venue for locals. Only later did Auden and Isherwood realize that those they encountered in the waiting room were not "elderly ladies" but men in drag.[1]

From the institute Auden and Isherwood went to eat in a restaurant just south of Unter den Linden, the main thoroughfare of Berlin's historic center. After the meal, they made their way to Auden's hangout—the Cosy Corner—best known for its male prostitution. Auden had moved to a nearby apartment a few months earlier, simply to be closer to his favorite pub. The southeast neighborhood surrounding the Cosy Corner, Hallesches Tor, was proletarian and considered very rough. As Auden described frankly in various correspondence, "I've moved to a slum . . . 50 yrds from my brothel." In another letter written soon after that he reported, "I spend most of my time with Juvenile Delinquents. . . . Berlin is the buggers daydream."[2]

Though few have left written traces as candid as Auden's, there can be little doubt that Weimar Berlin was an astonishing revelation for many first-time visitors. After discovering the city for themselves, Auden and Isherwood became apostles for Berlin's uninhibited sexuality, luring a wide circle of English authors, poets, and curiosity seekers. In his own autobiographical account, Isherwood described how Berlin's openness freed him not only to explore his homosexuality but ultimately to accept and embrace what he came to think of as a sexual orientation and identity. This was a freedom, moreover, that Isherwood—like his compatriots—never felt in London. Writing about himself in the third person, he described the revelation that was Berlin: "[H]e was embarrassed because, at last, he was being brought face to face with his tribe. Up to now, he had behaved as though the tribe didn't exist and homosexuality were a private way of life discovered by himself and a few friends. He had always known, of course, that this wasn't true. But now he was forced to admit kinship with these freakish fellow tribesmen."[3]

Isherwood's recollection of this apparent "coming out" was composed decades after the fact, of course, and possibly romanticized his experience. But Auden's Berlin journal offers immediate, contemporary evidence, showing clearly how Berlin shaped sexual identity. In a remarkable entry from April 6, 1929, the aspiring poet described a seemingly trivial event. Rushing to the train station to meet his current boyfriend,

Gerhart, for an excursion to Hamburg, Auden had a brief encounter on the tram with a young woman. He describes how she made eye contact, approached him, and flirted: "She—came and stood beside me till I got out. I wanted to make an 18th century bow and say 'Entschuldigen Sie, Madam, aber ich bin schwul.'" The best translation of Auden's imagined reply would be "Excuse me, Madam, but I am gay." And what an incredible statement that would have been! Instead of disdain for his admirer, or bemusement, Auden believed her flirtation to be based on a misperception; she mistook Auden for a man who was attracted to women. And although Auden's command of German—by his own admission—was never great, he formulated an appropriate response that his German admirer would have understood.

Auden's use of this particular word, *schwul*, is especially striking. An etymology identifies the word as Berlin vernacular and traces its origin to the German for humid, *schwül*, suggestive presumably of the expression *warme Brüder* (warm brothers), which was also German slang for men who loved other men. The word was also associated with criminality, and one 1847 publication by a former Berlin police commissioner, *Die Diebe in Berlin* (The thieves in Berlin), defined a *Schwuler* as a crook "who loves certain immoralities."[4] Despite this pejorative association, the word was also adopted by self-identified homosexuals. In the third edition of a medical study devoted exclusively to homosexuality—and based on ethnographic research in Berlin—psychiatrist Albert Moll claimed in 1899 that members of Berlin's homosexual subculture (both men and women) used the word *schwul* to describe themselves.[5] (By the late nineteenth century a section of the Tiergarten Park, where men had long cruised for sex, had a small path that acquired the nickname *schwuler Weg,* or path.[6]) Although the written documentation is somewhat obscure, the term clearly had neutral or even positive connotations by the 1920s for younger homosexuals, who commonly described themselves and each other as *schwul.*[7] It appears as well that there was something of a generational divide. Historian Manfred Herzer recounts in his biography of the pioneering sexologist and homosexual rights activist Magnus Hirschfeld how Hirschfeld chided a homosexual youth for using the word, although it was clearly a feature of the young man's Berlin dialect.[8]

Emerging from Berlin vernacular, the term is the best translation for the English word "gay." Had Auden had a similar experience in London, however, there would have been no English counterpart. Indeed, his 1928 vocabulary included English-language words such as queer, bugger, pederast, sodomite, molly, queen, fairy, and pansy. Some were clearly used for self-identification—Auden described Berlin as "the buggers daydream," after all—but they were also pejorative. A few months later, during a brief visit home, Auden broke off his long-term engagement with a woman. "Never—Never—Never again," he recorded in his journal.[9] Auden's Berlin awakening is striking, and in the late 1920s he could describe his sexuality more articulately even in halting German than he ever could in English.

The experiences that helped Auden to make this dramatic transition are significant, of course, but of equal interest are the contours of the terminology that evolved to describe the sexual minority to which he now felt he belonged. A central argument of *Gay Berlin* is that the emergence of an identity based on the notion of a fixed sexual orientation was initially a German and especially a Berlin phenomenon. This makes the Berlin etymology of *schwul* that much more significant, since language can help us to chart the growth of a new group identity.

The word *schwul* was neither the first nor the only German term, however, that shaped modern notions of sexual orientation. The word "homosexuality" was itself a German invention, and appeared as *Homosexualität* for the first time in 1869 in a German-language pamphlet that polemicized against the Prussian anti-sodomy statute.[10] An odd amalgam of Latin and Greek, *Homosexualität* became the enduring appellation for same-sex erotic love. Its precise definition varied, certainly, and while sympathetic doctors or homosexual rights activists used the word in a more neutral fashion to suggest the condition of having a fixed sexual orientation, others felt that the word suggested that same-sex desire was caused by disease or degeneration.[11]

The claim of German originality does not deny, of course, that there have always been men and women who pursued erotic love with their own sex.[12] Certainly gay history has identified entire networks of premodern men who sought sex with other men. Fifteenth-century Florence created a special office to police male prostitution.[13] Early modern Spain and Germany interdicted and severely punished the crime of sodomy.[14] Some historians have even argued that the origins of modern homosexuality can be traced to the early *eighteenth* century, when premodern same-sex subcultures allegedly fostered minority identities distinct from a "heterosexual" majority. In the decades after 1700, certain London taverns or "molly houses" became exclusive venues for men ("mollies") seeking sexual contact with other men.[15] The eighteenth-century Netherlands witnessed a similar phenomenon of male "sodomites" who established secretive networks based on erotic same-sex attraction.[16] Enlightenment Paris also harbored large groups of male "pederasts" who sought the sexual companionship of other men and developed, arguably, the identity of a sexual minority.[17] Certainly these Dutch, English, and French subcultures have been well documented with contemporary printed materials as well as police and trial records. But whether they influenced or even conditioned modern sexual identities remains an open question.[18]

The nineteenth century has served as the more common focus for locating the origins of a modern homosexual identity. Since Michel Foucault's *The History of Sexuality: An Introduction* in 1976, many historians have argued that a hetero/homosexual binarism developed only after 1869 following the coinage of the term "homosexuality," which, according to Foucault, introduced the homosexual as a new "species" of being. Some interpretations of Foucault's work have emphasized the precise moment when the "homosexual" created a radical rupture in Western understandings of sexual deviancy. According to this view, the social and cultural identities based on an exclusively same-sex erotic attraction were virtually impossible before the nineteenth century.[19]

Other historians of sexuality have supported Foucault's periodization but questioned his exclusive emphasis on medicalization. In his study of Sweden, Jens Rydström identifies a "paradigm" shift that began to distinguish sodomy from bestiality—effected without the influence of psychiatry—and accompanied the growth of an urban same-sex-oriented subculture in Stockholm beginning in the 1880s.[20] Dan Healey's work on Moscow and St. Petersburg documents a shift in same-sex relations around 1900 from an earlier model of adult men patronizing younger male *and* female prostitutes to a subculture of men who desired exclusively other men.[21] Recent studies of Victorian London and Paris demonstrate, similarly, the growth of erotic same-sex subcultures in which groups of men pursued erotic and social relationships in established venues with other same-sex-desiring men.[22] Whether these late-nineteenth-century networks can be traced back to the "molly houses," "sodomites," or "pederasts" of the eighteenth century is theoretically debatable, but there are few demonstrable continuities.

Certainly the cosmopolitan culture and anonymity fostered by nineteenth-century European urbanization permitted the emergence of minority sexual communities. If we concede a qualitative shift, however, and not just numerical growth, we must also consider the kind of conceptual transformation addressed by Foucault. A central—if not *the* central—element that has characterized modern homosexuality is the understanding of erotic same-sex attraction as a fundamental element of the individual's biological or psychological makeup. Homosexuality has thus been defined and constructed around the debate over the innate character of sexual identity, whether governed by nature or nurture, biology or culture, genetics or environment. The history of this debate, moreover, suggests that the idea of (homo)sexual personhood has a fairly recent origin.

This book will argue that the homosexual "species" took root in Germany after the mid-nineteenth century through the collaboration of Berlin's medical scientists and sexual minorities. This confluence of biological determinism and subjective expressions of sexual personhood was a uniquely German phenomenon, moreover, and it clearly underpins modern conceptions of sexual orientation.

Foucault failed, however, to consider the *German* context of his own observations. Although he emphasized the word "homosexuality" and the work of the Berlin psychiatrist Carl Westphal, he never identified the urban context sources that gave rise to the neologism and its science as specifically German. Foucault's apparent oversight is even more glaring when we consider that homosexuality was only one in a series of German terms invented to describe erotic same-sex love as a fixed condition and social identity. Those who created this German-language terminology were advocates for legal reform, doctors who studied same-sex erotic behavior, and their subjects; all participated integrally in elaborating a science of homosexuality. The image Foucault has offered of a laboratory test tube in which medical professionals concocted new sexual identities is completely one-sided and misleading.

My purpose therefore is to historicize the invention of the homosexual and place this sexual identity firmly within the German milieu in which it appeared. In my analysis, I adduce four broad vectors of German history: the criminalization of male same-sex eroticism and the inclusion of the Prussian anti-sodomy statute as Paragraph 175 in the new German imperial criminal code after 1871; the research methodologies of nineteenth-century German forensic and psychiatric professionals; the public engagement of literate middle-class Germans who openly protested Paragraph 175; and, finally, a relatively free press. The Prussian anti-sodomy statute and Paragraph 175 prompted both public avowals of sexual difference (by self-identified sexual minorities), and theories elaborated by German psychiatrists that sexual orientation was somehow congenital or "hardwired."[23] Scientists such as Berlin's chief medical officer Johann Ludwig Casper, who studied Berlin's sexual "deviants" in the 1850s and '60s, concluded that same-sex love was a natural, inborn characteristic, and not merely the perversion of a "normal" sexual tendency.

By 1908 the authoritative, broadly circulated, German-language encyclopedias *Meyers* and *Brockhaus*—which provided reliable, up-to-date references for Germany's burgeoning middle classes—included entries for *"Homosexualität."* The *Meyers* article explained that male and female homosexuals suffered from an "inborn and perverse feeling" and that they could be found in all social classes.[24] The *Brockhaus* entry cross-referenced *"Homosexual"* with *"conträre Sexualempfindung"* (inverted sexual feeling).[25] The encyclopedia entries suggested directly or implicitly that same-sex eroticism was a naturally occurring, if uncommon, phenomenon that affected a small percentage of the general population. Whether neutral or negative, the neologism "homosexuality" helped to suggest that same-sex love was caused by a fixed condition not amenable to treatment or cure.

We might reject the linguistic determinism of Foucault, yet it is clear that the word had far greater circulation in German than in any other language. Although it appeared in French, English, and Italian transla-

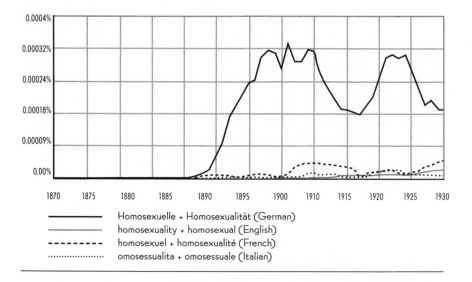

0.0004%

0.00032%

0.00024%

0.00018%

0.00009%

0.00%

1870   1875   1880   1885   1890   1895   1900   1910   1915   1920   1925   1930

———————— Homosexuelle + Homosexualität (German)
———————— homosexuality + homosexual (English)
- - - - - - - homosexuel + homosexualité (French)
·················· omosessualita + omosessuale (Italian)

tions by about 1900, its usage in these languages remained somewhat rare and extremely uneven. The pioneering work of German sexologists and activists made the term far more common in German texts. Here the Google Books project, which has digitized millions of volumes from the world's major research libraries, provides an enormous database for measuring linguistic usage. Based on the database, the Ngram chart (above) demonstrates how much more frequently "homosexuality" and its derivatives appeared in German (from 1870 to 1930), as a percentage of the German-language publications entered in the database, when compared to French, English, and Italian.

This is not surprising, perhaps, since the word was a German invention. Moreover, it demonstrates how German-language publications emanating from Berlin and Leipzig popularized the term among German speakers. The application of new labels and the frequency (or infrequency) of their usage is certainly one form of evidence for measuring the growth of an incipient identity.

Chapter 1 of this book examines the life and career of Karl Heinrich Ulrichs (1825–1895), a German activist described by some as the world's first open homosexual. Ulrichs began an extremely public if solitary campaign in the early 1860s to overturn the Prussian anti-sodomy stat-

ute. In the process he examined and theorized his own sexual constitution in a set of published pamphlets, arguing that his erotic attraction
to men was inborn. Coining the word *Urning* to describe this identity,
Ulrichs claimed that men with his sexual instincts had the soul of a
woman trapped in the body of a man. Although Ulrichs ultimately failed
to effect legal reform, his campaign sparked the interest of Richard von
Krafft-Ebing, who pioneered the study of sexuality (and homosexuality) and helped to launch the discipline of sexology. Though difficult,
the relationship between Ulrichs and Krafft-Ebing exemplified the
"feedback loop" that connected the "homosexual street" and medical
professionals, a circuit of subjective self-avowal and medical study that
fashioned a new sexual identity.[26]

Chapter 2 considers Berlin's homosexual subcultures and their relationship to the police. Under the leadership of an innovative commissioner, the Department of Homosexuals and Blackmailers, a special
taskforce of the Berlin police department, found creative methods for
enforcing the German anti-sodomy statute, Paragraph 175. Since only
specific sexual acts and not homosexual association were formally
criminalized, Berlin police monitored, observed, and ultimately permitted the operation of same-sex venues and entertainments. The very
existence of the law inspired sexual blackmail, however, so the Berlin
police targeted male prostitutes and attempted increasingly to provide
support to blackmail victims. This passive enforcement of Paragraph
175 had an equal if not greater significance in the way it gave visibility
and definition to what had formerly been a shadowy, indistinct group
of sexual minorities. By tolerating erotic same-sex sociability, the Berlin
police permitted same-sex-loving men and women to congregate and
forge a community. Access to this community was facilitated in turn
for medical professionals, literary figures, and journalists who described
and broadcast this incipient identity. In short, Berlin's policing strategies
played a critical role in the creation of a homosexual milieu and identity,
which became an established feature of prewar Berlin.

Chapter 3 examines the 1897 founding of the world's first homosexual rights organization in Berlin, the Scientific-Humanitarian Committee (SHC). Under the leadership of pioneering sexologist Dr. Magnus
Hirschfeld, the SHC combined innovative methodologies to study

human sexuality with full-throated advocacy for legal reform. Through the publication of scientific research—as well as popular literature on homosexuality—the organization hoped to educate and enlighten the German public. This activism ultimately popularized many of the SHC's own theories about homosexuality and sexual orientation.

Chapter 4 considers the role of a major sexual scandal beginning in 1907, which placed the court of German Emperor William II under the cloud of suspected "perversion." As it eventually became clear, some of the Kaiser's closest friends and courtiers were homosexual (or bisexual). This had long been known or at least suspected among elite political observers and was eventually exploited by an influential, muckraking journalist, Maximilian Harden, who made targets of specific political operatives. In the extended libel and perjury trials that followed Harden's accusations, Magnus Hirschfeld and other prominent sexologists provided expert testimony on homosexuality. Although the scandal incited a powerful and destructive backlash—at least for homosexual rights activists—it also made homosexuality, in Germany if nowhere else, a household word.

Chapter 5 considers how competing paradigms of male-male eroticism were popularized before, during, and after the First World War. Inspired by so-called "masculinist" dissidents from Hirschfeld's SHC, Hans Blüher elaborated a German-nationalist and anti-Semitic theory of the homoerotic Männerbund, based in part on his own adolescent experience in Berlin's fledgling youth movement. In the 1920s, Blüher's notion of the Männerbund became a pervasive pop-sociological theory and cultural trope for explaining all-male sociability, including adolescent as well as adult clubs and associations, political parties, and militia groups. For some anti-Semites and nationalists, Blüher's Männerbund offered a right-wing alternative to Hirschfeld's explanation of homosexuality, which was presumed to be "effete" and "Jewish."

Chapter 6 considers the founding and activities of Hirschfeld's Institute for Sexual Science in 1918. The first establishment of its kind, the institute promoted the sexological studies of the prewar SHC, while expanding that organization's purview to promote not only legal reform for sexual minorities but also progressive education about "straight" sexuality, including marriage, birth control, and abortion. The institute also pioneered theories of transsexuality, applying Hirschfeld's "adaptation" therapy for sexual minorities and performing some of the world's first sex-reassignment surgeries.

Chapter 7 explores the sexualized culture of Weimar Berlin in the 1920s and early '30s by considering the city's male prostitution and sex tourism. Even before the arrival of the Auden-Isherwood circle in the late 1920s, Berlin had developed a reputation for its hedonistic nightlife and party culture. The relatively open homosexuality of the German capital was purveyed by an extensive homosexual club culture based on same-sex bars, entertainments, and other forms of sociability. This club life was also supported by a broad cultural establishment that included not only gay-themed film, theater, and pulp fiction, along with dozens of periodicals, sold openly at newspaper kiosks, but also popular cultural figures who imbued Weimar culture more or less discreetly with a "queer" sensibility. This spectacle, along with male prostitution, promoted a sexual tourism consisting of curiosity seekers and voyeurs as well as homosexuals who indulged their sexual appetites.

The eighth and final chapter considers more narrowly the political strategies, activism, and infighting of Berlin's three major homosexual rights organizations. The oldest of these, Hirschfeld's SHC—under the institutional umbrella of the Institute for Sexual Science—continued to pursue its prewar agenda of legal reform, allied, as before, with the left-wing Social Democratic Party. Under the erratic leadership of Adolf Brand, the literary organization the Community of the Special (CoS) joined initially with the SHC, but then veered toward an anti-Semitism that slandered Hirschfeld as a Jewish outsider, before finally adopting an unaffiliated stance. A new outfit, the Human Rights League (HRL), which quickly became the largest homosexual organization, steered a centrist course, flirting at times with the fascist parties of the radical right. Although collectively these groups nearly overturned the anti-sodomy statute in 1930, the parliamentary stasis that led to the downfall of the republic in 1933 impeded a final Reichstag vote that might have reformed or eliminated the law. With the electoral successes of the Nazi or National Socialist German Workers' Party beginning in 1930, and Hitler's appointment as chancellor in January 1933, the fate of the world's first homosexual rights activism and open, urban culture was sealed.

GAY BERLIN

CHAPTER ONE

The German Invention of Homosexuality

When considering the questions "What is natural?" and "What is unnatural?" it is paramount to apply a standard that is not foreign to one's own nature.

KARL ULRICHS, "Vindex: Social and Legal Studies on Man-Manly Love," 1864

On a bright Thursday morning in late August 1867, the German lawyer Karl Heinrich Ulrichs, a former member of the civil service in the kingdom of Hanover, approached the Odeon concert hall in Munich. Since the beginning of the week, the Association of German Jurists had been assembling in this magnificent neoclassical structure to present papers and discuss the legal issues of the day. The professional group included lawyers, officials, bureaucrats, and legal academics from the thirty-nine states and cities of the former German Confederation, a loose association created at the Congress of Vienna in 1815. This imposing body of Ulrichs's colleagues made up the government establishment of the nascent German Empire. Dressed formally even in the midst of summer, they had first met in 1860 to facilitate great tasks of statecraft. As ardent nationalists, they hoped to promote German legal unification, even before the emergence of a nation-state.[1] Although the jurists' political program would have important consequences for the incipient German state, Ulrichs's appearance at the Odeon marked a revolution all its own. He was preparing to address his professional colleagues on an unmentionable subject, same-sex love, and to protest the various German anti-sodomy laws that criminalized it.[2]

Ulrichs had celebrated his birthday the day before, and now, at the age of forty-two, he hoped to deliver a speech for which he arguably had spent most of his adulthood preparing. As a university student, he had recognized that he was attracted to other men. This sexual peculiarity and rumors of his intimate affairs had forced him to resign the only professional position he had ever held, as a government official. Finally, in an act of enormous courage, he disclosed his secret to his closest kin. Raised in a pious Christian family whose extended members included numerous Lutheran clergy, Ulrichs struggled for years with heart and intellect to make sense of his seemingly unacceptable feelings. Were they unnatural? Had he somehow caused them himself, through actions of his own? He examined carefully his own motivations and desires; he scoured legal and scientific publications on the topic. Following the tradition of the great Protestant reformer Martin Luther, Ulrichs countered prevailing beliefs and developed a theory of his own selfhood—though defined in sexual, not spiritual, terms—forming the conviction that he must face down an established authority and counter centuries of prejudice. To that end, since 1864, Ulrichs had published pamphlets under a pseudonym, arguing his case that sexual deviance was an endowment of nature and must be respected.[3]

But on that morning in August, crossing Munich's imposing Odeonsplatz, framed by government and cultural buildings, past the grand loggia of the Field Marshals' Hall and the baroque spires and dome of the Theatine Church, Ulrichs felt his heart palpitate almost audibly as he neared the Odeon hall. As he would later recount, an inner voice whispered, "There is still time to keep silent. Simply waive your request to speak, and then your heart can stop pounding." But Ulrichs also remembered those "comrades" who were anticipating his protest—"Was I to answer their trust in me with cowardice?"—and he recalled a desperate acquaintance who had committed suicide to escape criminal prosecution for sodomy and the public humiliation that would have followed. "With breast beating," Ulrichs entered the building, mounted the speaker's platform, and began reading his text to more than five hundred professional colleagues. "Gentlemen," he intoned, "my proposal is directed toward a revision of the current penal law" to abolish the persecution of an innocent class of persons. "It is at the same time," Ulrichs continued, "a question of damming a continuing flood of suicides." The victims, he said, were those sexually drawn to members of their own sex.[4]

Expressions of outrage and scattered cries of "Stop!" began echoing through the chamber. Alarmed by the voluble hostility, Ulrichs offered to surrender the floor, but others in the audience urged him to continue, and he again took heart. This "class of persons," he went on to say, suffered legal persecution only because "nature has planted in them a sexual nature that is opposite of that which is usual." Raucous shouts now emanated from the audience; Ulrichs heard hooting, catcalls, and cries of "Crucify!" from groups on his left and directly in front. On his right stood those who were not prepared for the content of his address and out of curiosity demanded that he finish. But the cacophony overwhelmed Ulrichs and forced him to descend from the podium without finishing his speech, while the assembly chairman attempted to reestablish order. The Association of Jurists refused to press Ulrichs's agenda after the meeting concluded. Within five years member states of the new German Empire had adopted a full penal code in which the punitive Prussian law making a crime of sodomy prevailed over the more liberal law codes of the other German states. But standing at the podium in Munich, Ulrichs had started something important with the first public coming-out in modern history.[5]

Just how much courage did this take? By August 1867 Ulrichs had already forfeited his career and exposed himself to potential rejection by family members. He had little left to lose and later described his appearance before the jurists at the Odeon as the proudest moment of his life. Freed now to go on making a public case for his cause, he continued publishing pamphlets after 1867, but under his own name, not a pseudonym. And although he failed to avert the imposition of an anti-sodomy law throughout the newly unified German nation after 1871, his writings and actions helped inspire the world's first movement for homosexual rights, launched a generation later in Berlin, in 1897.[6]

The truly remarkable aspect of Ulrichs's brave initiative was the important contribution he made to the redefinition—indeed the *invention*—of sexuality (and homosexuality) in nineteenth-century Europe. Traditional medical "science" explained "sodomy" as a willful perversion and the product of masturbation or sexual excess. "Sodomites" were understood to be oversexed predators who had simply grown bored with women. The established science of sexual "perversion" viewed same-sex erotic activity as that which it seemed to be and nothing more, an isolated genital act. It was possible to imagine, in fact, that almost anyone might succumb to the crime of sodomy, either through seduction or by willful decision, but ultimately as a result of moral weakness. Sexual desire was considered a fluid and malleable drive that might easily be warped and perverted. Only in the 1850s did the first medical doctor, a German in Berlin named Johann Ludwig Casper, question this received wisdom and argue that some "sodomites" had an innate, biological attraction to the same sex. By 1900 a progressive school of German psychiatry had formed around the belief that same-sex attraction might be congenital, and somehow an integral feature of a small sexual minority. It became possible now to imagine that certain individuals were attracted innately to their own and *not* the opposite sex. Indeed, German speakers—both self-identified same-sex-loving men and medical doctors—invented a new language of sexual orientation and identity that displaced the older understanding of perversion and moral failure. Invented terms such as *Urning* (Ulrichs's own coinage) or "homosexual" first entered the German lexicon and later other European languages as well. Ulrichs's pamphlet propaganda played a critical role in this development: his theories of an inborn *Urning* sexuality and character coupled with his outspoken activism helped not only to influence the incipient sciences of sexuality but also to mobilize an imagined community of homosexuals. Concretely, Ulrichs spearheaded a conceptual revolution that transformed erotic, same-sex love from an idea of deviant acts into a full-blown sexual orientation with its own distinct quality and character.

Ulrichs was an improbable innovator, and certainly an unlikely activist for the civil rights of a sexual minority. Born in 1825 in Aurich, a typical small-town German community located in East Friesland, which became part of the kingdom of Hanover in 1815, the young Ulrichs was sheltered from the cultural and intellectual life of nineteenth-century Europe. His father was a district engineering official and civil servant, and his mother's clan included numerous Lutheran pastors. From infancy, Ulrichs's conservative family trained him for academic study and a professional career, either as a bureaucrat or a clergyman. This early preparation endowed him with a restless intelligence, however, and the independence to follow his own calling.[7]

Ulrichs's family must be seen as elite—despite its small-town origins—and typical of a wider German class of educated professionals, *Bildungsbürgertum,* a group that enjoyed significant social prominence throughout the German territories. What anchored their elite status was education: most attended *Gymnasium,* the Latin high school that prepared its graduates for university study. Talent was a necessary but rarely sufficient qualification for *Gymnasium.* Germany's educated elite shared a class background of social and cultural—if not financial—capital, provided by families that could prepare sons for rigorous training and the connections to navigate social and government networks. Higher education was the credential that guaranteed a civil service career as jurist, teacher, cleric, or official in any one of Germany's city, state, or church bureaucracies.[8] Many such families boasted a long string of church or state officials, often stretching back generations. The Ulrichs family was no exception.

As his parents' only surviving son—an older brother died in infancy in 1824—Ulrichs enjoyed the attention and encouragement that prepared him well for academic study. He later described this as a happy childhood: "From loving motherly care, I received in part my first education and in part a whole series of other intellectual impressions and influences."[9] Ulrichs's mother also imparted the conservative piety of traditional Lutheranism, teaching her son devotional exercises, scripture, and prayers. After the death of his father in 1835, Ulrichs and his family moved to live near his maternal grandfather and a married sister in the Hanoverian town of Burgdorf, where he was confirmed in the Lutheran Church by his grandfather on Easter Sunday in 1839, a religious and social milestone marking a new stage of his life. Young Karl then attended *Gymnasium,* first in Detmold, home of his mother's brother (likewise a Lutheran pastor), and then in nearby Celle. The close structure of Ulrichs's family—infused with conservative Protestant religiosity, loving attention, and careful social control—served the boy well. At nineteen he completed his *Gymnasium* exams with excellent results in Latin and Greek, the subjects required for university entrance.[10]

That fall, he began legal studies at the University of Göttingen. Founded in 1734 by George II, ruler of Hanover and also king of Great Britain, Göttingen was just one of the twenty-odd German institutions of higher learning established before 1800. Unlike the centralized states of England and France, which had no more than a handful of universities at this time, the semi-sovereign states of the Holy Roman Empire maintained their independence, both culturally and—to some extent—politically. The size and character of these territories varied tremendously, and counting the tiny estates of the imperial knights numbered above eighteen hundred.[11] The largest, including Brandenburg-Prussia, Austria, Bavaria, Saxony, and Württemberg, often had the trappings of sovereign states. Since the High Middle Ages, the rulers of these largest German territories founded universities in their competition for cultural distinction and to train those who served in state and city bureaucracies. This political fragmentation also explains best the tradition of a *Bildungsbürgertum* in German central Europe: the many small and medium-sized states, each with its own princely court and administrative bureaucracy, required both literate staff and the institutions to educate them. Ulrichs was fortunate to live in the Hanoverian state, since Göttingen had established itself very quickly as one of the premier German universities. The law faculty was particularly prominent and trained numerous statesmen and scholars, including Austrian prime minister Clemens von Metternich; Wilhelm von Humboldt, who founded the University of Berlin in 1810; and Otto von Bismarck, first chancellor of the German Empire when it was formed in 1871. By the first decades of the twentieth century, more than twenty-five Nobel laureates had Göttingen affiliations, either as onetime students or professors.[12]

It was as a student at Göttingen that Ulrichs first identified the issues that would inspire him to take up his activism. He identified his own sexual peculiarity, and also embraced the ideal of *großdeutsch,* or greater German statehood, a nationalist ideology that promoted the idea of a unified German state that would incorporate all German speakers, including denizens of Austria and the Habsburg crownlands. Although these two strands of political action were seemingly unconnected, Ulrichs's human rights activism and his nationalism were curiously intertwined. By promoting "greater German" statehood, Ulrichs hoped to counter the influence of Prussia, and, in turn, the likelihood that Prussia's anti-sodomy statute might be imposed on the other German territories.

After five semesters in Göttingen, Ulrichs transferred to the University of Berlin, where he studied for one year. His decision to move was on its face of no particular note; many German students attended several universities before taking a degree. Ulrichs had a special motive, however, for coming to Berlin. In his second year at Göttingen, he had become self-consciously aware of his attraction to men. As he divulged later in a family letter, "Approximately half a year . . . before I went to Berlin, I was at a dance. . . . But among the dancers there were about twelve young, well-developed and handsomely uniformed forestry pupils. Although at earlier dances no one caught my attention, I felt such a strong attraction that I was amazed. . . . I would have flung myself at them. When I retired after the ball, I suffered true anxieties in my bedroom, alone and unseen, solely preoccupied by memories of those handsome young men."[13] Clearly this sexual awakening jolted the young Ulrichs, but it also underscored the loneliness he felt in Göttingen. As far as he could see, there was no one else there like himself.

Ulrichs almost certainly had an awareness of Berlin's reputation. With a population of nearly 400,000, the city was bound to be more exciting than the sedate university town of Göttingen. But there was something more specific. As a garrison city, Berlin had been known for its male prostitution since at least the eighteenth century. As early as 1782 one guidebook devoted a short chapter to Berlin's "warm brothers" and the prevalence of male prostitution as an income source for garrisoned soldiers.[14] This reputation was well established by the time Ulrichs moved to the city. One telling account, an 1846 volume on Berlin prostitution, identified the areas where men sought sex with other men. These included the city's main thoroughfare, Unter den Linden, the large, forested Tiergarten Park at the western edge of the city center, and a grove of chestnut trees just north of the neoclassical Guardhouse, designed by the architect Karl Friedrich Schinkel.[15] An anonymous informant, corresponding with Berlin's chief medical officer Johann Ludwig Casper in the 1850s, described his sexual initiation as a youth when, on the promenade of Unter den Linden, he encountered a gentleman, who then accompanied him to the Tiergarten for a tryst.[16] Both Unter den

Linden and the Tiergarten Park remained prominent locations—well into the twentieth century—for male prostitution and men cruising for sex with other men. Whether Ulrichs took advantage of the city's soldier prostitution and clandestine sexual networks remains unclear. But his later writings make plain that he was keenly aware that in Berlin he would be far more likely to find congenial company.

After just one year, however, Ulrichs returned to the town of Burgdorf, where his mother, sister, and uncle still lived, and studied for the Hanoverian civil service test. The aspiring jurist had already distinguished himself as a student and legal scholar. First in Göttingen and then following his stint in Berlin, Ulrichs wrote prize-winning Latin-language legal essays. With these awards in hand and his rigorous education completed, he sat for the exhausting three-day examination with a "very good" assessment. This impressive result allowed him to assume his first position as a Hanoverian bureaucrat in the entry-level post of "auditor." The career path Ulrichs had chosen began with positions in local government but held the promise of promotions leading to service in the Hanoverian state administration. After four years of service, he was permitted to take the next examination, for which he again received a "very good" rating, qualifying him for promotion to the next level, "assessor." By this time, though, Ulrichs had grown disillusioned with government administration, and he asked for a transfer to the Hanoverian Ministry of Justice. This was a plausible lateral move within the structure of the state civil service, particularly for a talented jurist. His request was granted, and he received the title of assistant judge.[17]

Ulrichs's promising career was cut short by the threat of scandal, however, which followed him from his earlier posting and forced him to resign in late 1854. A report submitted by the superior court in Hildesheim informed the Justice Ministry in Hanover about Ulrichs's alleged sexual activities: "Ulrichs is said often to be seen in the company of lower-class persons under circumstances that allow one to conclude a closer connection. . . . [T]here came to my attention a rumor that Ulrichs practices unnatural lust with other men."[18] Although Ulrichs's superior was skeptical initially, the rumors were soon confirmed by a police official. The report also noted that Ulrichs was suspected of similar indiscretions in his previous posts, but it further conceded that Ulrichs had broken no law, strictly speaking, because the Hanoverian penal code did not make a crime of same-sex love. Still, Ulrichs's alleged behavior was unacceptable, since the Hanoverian law included the provision that "[w]hoever is guilty of unnatural lust under circumstances that cause public offense, shall be punished with imprisonment."[19] Since he was a state official and public personage, mere rumors of disreputable private conduct made Ulrichs liable to disciplinary action. As a result the report called for his dismissal from office. Although he was technically innocent of any crime, gossip about his same-sex affairs, particularly with "lower-class persons," cost him his position and his career.

Aware of the gossip, Ulrichs tendered his resignation within weeks of assuming the new post on November 30, 1854. Ulrichs's abrupt decision to give up his career was certainly influenced by the dawning realization that he could not accommodate his private life to his public status as a state official. While he was able to preempt disciplinary procedures, his superiors refused to grant him a formal certificate of service, which limited his ability to find future employment. Almost overnight, his professional training had become virtually worthless, and now he was left—as he approached his thirtieth birthday—without prospects for employment.[20]

Soon after his resignation Ulrichs fled Hildesheim, venturing first to Burgdorf, "for religious considerations," as he later explained, "where my pastor lived," and then to a small town near Göttingen, where he lived with his sister and her Lutheran-pastor husband. To them Ulrichs revealed the reasons for the demise of his career and explained that he found himself sexually attracted to men. Against the protests of his brother-in-law, he began to question conventional morality. In the most painful fashion, Ulrichs was forced to confront the fact that even the liberal Hanoverian law—which did not make a crime of same-sex eroticism—was an oppressive instrument. Indeed, if his sexual attraction to men was innate, inborn, and, by extension, God given, as he increasingly believed, what law or human custom should censor that?

Ulrichs now faced the quandary of finding a new vocation and the more pressing task of supporting himself. Having returned to Burgdorf, he lived with family members. The death of Ulrichs's mother in Burgdorf in 1856 was a significant blow, which he recalled sadly in later writings. An inheritance of 2,800 florins, as well as a share of his mother's house, satisfied his immediate material needs. As a university-trained lawyer, Ulrichs hoped to augment this nest egg with the small fees he collected from clients. His fledgling legal practice was stymied, however, when he was fined for "unauthorized practice as an advocate" and for using the title of "former Assessor." The report explaining the penalty cited "a not unfounded suspicion that he [Ulrichs] is guilty of the crimes of unnatural lust . . . [which] are said to have led to his resignation from Royal Service." Ulrichs protested the fine, which was ultimately pardoned in 1860. Though never convicted of breaking any law, Ulrichs was forced once again to contend with the rumors surrounding his resignation from public office.[21]

Humiliated for his private affairs, Ulrichs was determined to find a way of living so that he would never again need to fear exposure. He soon found himself caught up in the nationalism that so animated German public sentiment. While the nationalist revolutions of 1848 had sparked hopes for German unification, the failure of the Frankfurt Parliament that convened later that year to establish a viable constitutional system left the question of statehood unresolved. The Frankfurt lawmakers were divided by the overarching difference between those who promoted a großdeutsch (large German) state and those favoring a kleindeutsch (small German) solution to the national question. While großdeutsch partisans hoped to forge a federal state that would include Austria, the proponents of a kleindeutsch solution favored a German state led by the Prussian Hohenzollern dynasty. Of course, the rivalry between Hohenzollern Berlin and Habsburg Vienna had dominated intra-German politics since at least the eighteenth century, and neither dynasty was prepared to cede influence to the other. As the Frankfurt Parliament dithered, the German princes reestablished their control, and when the bourgeois nationalists finally offered an imperial German crown to the king of Prussia, Frederick William IV, in May 1849, their opportunity had passed. The Prussian king spurned the offer contemptuously, and claimed that he would never accept such a title from a representative assembly; he ruled, in his own view, by the grace of God. The nationalist project was defeated, at least for a time. In the wake of this failure, German rulers vigorously repressed nationalist agitation and unleashed the forces of political reaction.[22]

Although the repression of the 1850s inhibited more direct political action, German nationalist sentiment gained expression through literary and cultural associations. As a staunch supporter of *großdeutsch* unification, Ulrichs fervently promoted this broader movement, and he joined nationalist literary and cultural associations, including the German Association of Jurists, to whom he would later make his epochal appeal for legal reform. He also began writing articles for the *Allgemeine Zeitung,* a daily paper with a pan-German readership issued by the prominent Cotta publishing house based in Augsburg, Bavaria. Perhaps the most important German political newspaper of the nineteenth century, the *Allgemeine Zeitung* developed an international reputation and supported correspondents around the globe. The paper also maintained strong ties to Austria and a *großdeutsch* editorial perspective.[23]

Pan-German newspapers and cultural associations were not the only forces that promoted German unification after 1848. Commerce and transport played a powerful role in gradually knitting together the disparate regions that would eventually form the new empire. In 1834 Prussian officials had organized a customs union (Zollverein), which, by 1842, embraced more than half of the thirty-nine members of the German Confederation. This seemingly neutral commercial association was more effective in breaking down the barriers of import taxes, varied currencies, and disparate systems of weights and measures—which had stifled intra-German trade for centuries—than any overt political initiative. But the effect of forming a closer union among its members was indeed unintended. Prussian rulers remained completely dismissive of German nationalism, and supported the Zollverein simply to promote their commercial advantage, particularly over Habsburg Austria. Significantly, Austria was banned from joining the union.

German railway construction was another critical force that promoted exchange among the German states. Two long-distance rail lines were completed in the 1830s, the first in Bavaria and a second in Saxony. Into the 1860s, more than half of the German railways remained in private corporate hands, since there was no centralized state that could initiate, plan, and construct a national system. Public excitement over the first successful railways sparked a flurry of projects, however, and by 1852 investors had created more than 4,000 miles of track, a figure that increased sixfold, to 24,000 miles, by 1873. Between 1850 and 1875, some 25 percent of German industrial investment flowed into developing railways, stimulating collateral industries such as coal mining, steel production, and manufacturing. The railways also lessened bulk transport costs, while opening markets and improving distribution. Of course, the trains reduced travel time, creating a dramatic increase in both commerce and communications.[24]

Ulrichs belonged to that generation of Germans who experienced this transportation revolution firsthand. He could travel from Hanover to Berlin in 1846 in less than a day, a trip that had taken three days by horse-drawn coach. In the 1850s Ulrichs traveled widely outside of his native Hanover—to the German cities of Bamberg, Würzburg, Darmstadt, Mainz, and Wiesbaden, as well as to the Netherlands, Belgium, Bohemia, and Switzerland—trips easily compressed into short periods with the benefit of trains. Thus the convenience of rail transport also made Ulrichs's work as a freelance journalist easier.[25] Cheaper and faster distribution also increased the circulation of a pan-German paper such as the *Allgemeine Zeitung* and lowered the cost of its European-wide coverage. In the years 1862–63, Ulrichs wrote more than one hundred articles, many of which required significant travel.

In the summer of 1862, Ulrichs reported stories for the *Allgemeine Zeitung* on a pan-German shooting festival held in Frankfurt. The German sharpshooting clubs were yet another manifestation of the infectious nationalism that animated a wide spectrum of educated and working-class Germans after 1848. (Equally popular were the pan-German choral and gymnastics societies, which sponsored hundreds of local societies and also organized regular festivals, drawing thousands from throughout the German states.) The sharpshooting festival captivated Ulrichs, but not merely for its promotion of *großdeutsch* nationalism. At the beginning of August, Johann Baptist von Schweitzer, a club official and event organizer, was arrested and imprisoned for allegedly molesting an adolescent boy. Ulrichs was outraged by the uncorroborated charges and supported Schweitzer with a pair of lengthy legal defenses. These briefs were little help, and in September Schweitzer received a two-week jail sentence: he was not convicted of committing a sexual crime, however, but of provoking public offense. The youth with whom Schweitzer was alleged to have had sexual relations disappeared before the trial; no witnesses appeared who could swear that a crime had been committed. The only "evidence" provided in court was the account of two women who reported overhearing the boy's description of his encounter with Schweitzer. This testimony alone proved sufficient to convict Schweitzer of offending public decency. Curiously, the witnesses who recounted the story—and not the youth—were themselves considered the injured parties.[26]

The apparent injustice of Schweitzer's imprisonment inspired Ulrichs to begin his public campaign. The centerpiece of this project was a series of publications on same-sex eroticism and the implications of the various German anti-sodomy statutes. By turning to print, Ulrichs hoped to provoke open debate and ultimately win support for legal reform. Print culture, he felt, would also provide an important medium for fostering identity and community. This was a daring initiative with little precedent, and it exposed Ulrichs to ridicule or worse. But working alone and without models, Ulrichs proved to have a remarkably sophisticated ability to garner publicity and also to support men—and likely a few women—who lacked other information or resources.

Ulrichs explored the character of same-sex love by drawing first on his own experience. The drive to understand himself was unquestionably a product of his Lutheran background. Like the great Protestant reformer Martin Luther, who defied pope and emperor, Ulrichs was driven by his own stubborn reason and a personal integrity that would not allow him to turn away from the truth, as he perceived it. This need to explain himself required first that he confront his family. In the months following Schweitzer's conviction Ulrichs wrote a series of circular letters, explaining both his attraction to men and his writing campaign. Although only four letters from this extended correspondence survive, the character of this discussion is clear. In a letter to his sister dated September 1862, Ulrichs dismissed her claim that he might simply "make the decision to change"; his nature, he told her, was "inherent." The inclination to love men, Ulrichs argued, was as natural for him as the attraction most men feel toward women. Ulrichs also rejected his sister's charge that his study in Berlin had somehow "perverted" him. "To believe that this tendency was at some time assumed is an error," he wrote; "it came about exactly at the time of my puberty." Ulrichs closed by asking his sister to circulate the letter among their closest family members.[27]

In a second letter from November, addressed "Dear Loved Ones," Ulrichs shared the basic insight that would shape his ultimate theory of sexual identity. Men who loved men, he ventured, represented a third sex, characterized by a feminine nature trapped in the physical body of a man. The chief evidence for this claim came from Ulrichs's recollections of his own boyhood and adolescence: "How often did my dear mother complain, 'You are not like other boys!' How often did she warn me, 'You will be an odd one.' Coaxed or by force, nothing could bring me up to the standard of boys. It was not in me. I was already an odd one, namely by nature. Because of my feminine nature even as a boy I was unjustly mistreated and set apart." The lack of appropriate "boyishness" that Ulrichs identified in himself was also something he claimed to have observed in other men attracted to their own sex: "a so-called feminine mannerism, can be observed since childhood in the inclination to girlish preoccupations, in shyness, in play, in not scuffling, or throwing snowballs as boys do, in manners, gestures, and in a certain gentleness of character." It was unjust, however, Ulrichs declared, that he be expected to live a life of celibacy. Sexual gratification was a God-given right, "on the assumption that the means of gratification is achieved in the way which nature intended for the individual." To demand, as his closest family members did, that he and those like him lead a life of sensual deprivation was "an extreme abuse, since we are justified to exist in human society, just as you are."[28]

In two additional letters, both dated December 1862 and addressed "Dear Uncle," Ulrichs elaborated his views, emphasizing the "hermaphroditic" identity of those who loved their own sex. The occurrence of hermaphrodites in nature offered positive proof, Ulrichs claimed, that sexual drives did not always correspond to sexual organs. Not only human hermaphrodites born with male and female genitalia but also "hermaphroditic" animal species such as snails confirmed for Ulrichs the natural character of same-sex eroticism. Since nature endowed individuals and entire species alike with ambiguous or even paired male and female sexual organs, Ulrichs reasoned, it followed that same-sex eroticism was similarly a natural, if fairly uncommon, phenomenon. Ulrichs marshaled additional support for his claims, citing his own interviews with like-minded men as well as a range of medical and biological sources, including anatomy textbooks and medical journals. This evidence was likely drawn from a manuscript that Ulrichs mentioned in the second letter to his family members.[29]

Ulrichs's siblings, uncle, and aunt could not accept easily, if ever at all, his extraordinary arguments. Their resistance was clear not only from his labored attempts to refute their objections, but also from the postscripts they added to his circulated letters. One brother-in-law attempted to dissuade Ulrichs from publishing his tracts, arguing that they would tarnish the family name. Ulrichs's uncle scribbled the note "I am unable to judge to what degree your detailed information is substantiated, but I am saddened, dear Karl, that you continue to excuse yourself of that which is, according to my conviction, unpardonable." (Despite his censure, however, this skeptic signed off, "Love you dearly, Uncle.") One comment in the margins of the first letter—written perhaps by Ulrichs's older sister—conceded, "I have always believed to have noticed just such a feminine mannerism about Karl." But the remarkable, indeed marvelous result of this difficult correspondence was the simple fact that Ulrichs's beloved family members never explicitly disowned or rejected him: he remained forever welcomed into their homes. The family support that Ulrichs had always enjoyed was not compromised, even after divulging a radical, disturbing truth about his private sexual urges. The ability to come out into the open and find that he was still loved surely bolstered his confidence.[30]

Now Ulrichs pursued his mission with growing assurance and purpose. His first pamphlet, titled "Vindex: Social and Legal Studies on Man-Manly Love," appeared under the pseudonym Numa Numantius—in deference to his family's wishes—in April 1864. Here he introduced new terms for describing innate sexual identities: the word *Urning* named the identity of those men who love their own sex; *Dioning* denoted the heterosexual majority. Ulrichs took inspiration for these neologisms from his classical schoolboy training. He derived *Urning* from the Greek god of the heavens, Uranus, whose solitary parentage of Aphrodite, the goddess of Eros or sexual love, symbolized same-sex eroticism in Plato's *Symposium*. In Plato's dialogue, the discussion of Eros (sexual love) mentions two contrasting accounts of Aphrodite's birth. The first Greek myth claims that Aphrodite was parented by Uranus, a birth in which "the female played no part." The second identifies Aphrodite as the offspring of Zeus and Dione. While the single-parented Aphrodite of the first story was invoked in the *Symposium* to symbolize the Greek masculine love of male youths, or same-sex attraction, the second represented the more common sexual attraction of a man to a woman. Ulrichs introduced the term *Urninden* in his second pamphlet to describe same-sex loving women or lesbians.[31]

With this inventive nomenclature, Ulrichs was able to frame the specific identity of men who loved men, and in so doing to address their characteristics, interests, and the persecution they experienced as a group or class. Same-sex eroticism was no longer simply a collection of disembodied sexual practices, but rather the innate sensuality that defined, at least in part, a significant, if tiny, sexual minority. The pamphlet's title, "Vindex," or "Vindicator," signaled Ulrichs's purpose: he presented himself as the defender, indeed emancipator, of all *Urnings* who suffered under the prejudice and persecution of a *Dioning* majority. His central thesis was that Uranian love was inborn or natural, caused neither by pathology nor willful perversion, and as such its expression could not be criminalized. Ulrichs suggested that at least 25,000 adult *Urnings* resided in the German states. Nothing could justify the denial of fundamental rights to such a large group.[32]

Ulrichs's second pamphlet, "Inclusa: Anthropological Studies on Man-Manly Love," appeared just one month later, in May 1864. In this work Ulrichs presented evidence for his argument that *Urnings* were psychological hermaphrodites—in short, biological men with a feminine character. By way of example Ulrichs asserted that when *Urnings* formed social networks, they frequently gave each other feminine nicknames, or referred to one another as *Schwester* (sister) or *Tante* (aunt). Myriad historical figures demonstrated the timelessness of an *Urning* identity, Ulrichs offered, and urban ethnographies of Berlin and Rome, among other cities, would illustrate the persistence of this minority.[33]

Ulrichs was prolific, and he issued the third, fourth, and fifth pamphlets in 1865. These installments continued his passionate advocacy for tolerance and the decriminalization of same-sex love. Titled "Vindicta: Battle for Freedom from Persecution," the third volume described the legal ramifications of German anti-sodomy laws: many people were imprisoned under these laws, and more than a few of those accused and convicted committed suicide. Although many German states did not formally punish same-sex acts, including Ulrichs's native Hanover, popular prejudice and public decency laws, as Ulrichs understood so well, remained sources of harassment and discrimination. Equally pernicious was the threat of blackmail by male prostitutes, a threat, Ulrichs claimed, that was "growing rapidly in the dark streets of the largest cities." The fourth volume, "Formatrix: Anthropological Studies on Man-Manly Love," broadened Ulrichs's earlier analysis and suggested a wide continuum of sexual identities. Now Ulrichs recognized that some male *Urnings* had a very masculine demeanor, while female *Urninden* might very well exhibit feminine character traits. For the first time, Ulrichs also described an identity of *Uranodionism,* bisexual individuals attracted to both sexes.[34]

In the fifth volume, "Ara Spei" ("Refuge of Hope"), Ulrichs considered the traditional Christian condemnations of same-sex eroticism, perhaps his thorniest challenge. Of course, this had been an important issue for him when he confronted his imposing Lutheran family. As he had in that earlier argument, here he asserted that "Christianity has a place not only for Dionian but also for Uranian love." The larger issue was that congenital Uranian love had been unknown to Christianity; how then could the religion possibly have developed a coherent theology about the question? While the Bible condemned same-sex male prostitution or those who perverted their nature, it said nothing about an inborn *Urning* nature. "There is simply an omission," Ulrichs wrote. And since Uranian love could not produce children, he reasoned, neither the institution of marriage nor sanctions against extramarital sex had any particular bearing for *Urnings.* This line of argument conveniently ignored the traditional Christian teaching that sex was meant only for procreation, perhaps the greatest barrier for Christians in accepting same-sex eroticism. The Christian principle of charity, Ulrichs declared optimistically, would promote the acceptance of Uranian love as well as its open expression.[35]

In late-nineteenth-century Europe, these arguments were extremely provocative, even explosive, and surely enough to stir up the censors. Commissioned by Ulrichs, the publisher Heinrich Matthes, based in Leipzig, printed just under fifteen hundred copies each of the first two volumes and was responsible for distributing them at the annual Leipzig book fairs and through postal orders. But six weeks after they were first printed, officials in Leipzig seized the remaining copies of the first two titles from Matthes's shop. At the trial conducted later in the month, the prosecutor charged both author and publisher with "degradation of family and marriage" and the advocacy of "illegal behavior." These charges were hardly surprising, since the kingdom of Saxony, where Leipzig was located—unlike Hanover—had a particularly oppressive anti-sodomy statute.

Ulrichs's great advantage, however, was the influence of the Leipzig publishers, who dominated the German-language book trade. This powerful industry was represented by a well-organized professional group, the Association of German Publishers and Printers (also based in Leipzig), which influenced Saxon censorship laws, their application, and press freedoms more generally. Saxony's liberal standards for censorship also shaped the print culture of the rest of the German-speaking world, which remained relatively open as a result. Honoring the interests of the Leipzig publishers, the court rejected the prosecutor's claims and cited the "scientific value" of Ulrichs's first two publications: "It seems they have been published without the intention of eliciting immorality." As a consequence, the ban was lifted and the confiscated copies were returned to Matthes on the same day. The court's decision discouraged the Leipzig prosecutor from filing charges against Ulrichs's subsequent publications, which were distributed without difficulty, at least from Leipzig. This early victory for freedom of expression was also an important harbinger of the relative tolerance that later German activists and sexologists would enjoy. Officials in Prussia were less tolerant, and Ulrichs's first two volumes were banned there in September 1864. Certainly this prevented Berlin booksellers from displaying Ulrichs's works openly, but it was always possible for private individuals to order them from Matthes directly or from other book dealers outside of Prussia.[36]

The print run was limited for the first five pamphlets, but their distribution was wider than anyone could have expected. Ulrichs certainly achieved one of his primary goals: stimulating debate about the legal treatment of same-sex eroticism. Moreover, the mere threat of censorship seemed to enhance the sale of his pamphlets. In his introduction to the third volume, "Vindicta," Ulrichs reported that the first two works, "Vindex" and "Inclusa," had nearly sold out. While most of the copies were purchased in Saxony, Baden, the western Rhine provinces, and Austria, there were also orders from outside the German-speaking world, including Italy, France, the Low Countries, and England. Because Ulrichs published under the pen name Numa Numantius, most correspondence was addressed to the publisher, Matthes, who then forwarded it to Ulrichs. Many missives came from grateful *Urnings,* who saw themselves reflected in Ulrichs's analysis. There were letters from some sympathetic *Dionings* as well, and Ulrichs reported proudly that the Frankfurt municipal library had placed his first two volumes in its collection. Others condemned Ulrichs, however, for his "perversions" or "moral turpitude." Newspapers and journals in Hanover, Berlin, Vienna, and the Rhine region included notices of Ulrichs's publications and the controversy they provoked, most with scorn but a few with guarded tolerance. The volumes also inspired attacks in the Leipzig press, which reported that officials had confiscated the first two volumes. All three Leipzig dailies condemned the court's original decision and acquittal. Ulrichs rebutted the papers' editors, and two, including the pan-German *Deutsche Allgemeine,* printed his response: "By publishing these writings I have initiated a scientific discussion based on facts. This should interest doctors and jurists. Until now the treatment of the subject has been biased, not to mention contemptuous. My writings are the voice of a socially oppressed minority that now claims its rights *to be heard.*"[37]

The scientific interest that Ulrichs hoped to inspire had become a reality. Ulrichs's claims about the congenital character of same-sex desire seemed—in fact—to converge with and confirm the arguments of recent German medical scholarship. From the outset, Ulrichs had sought medical accounts of *Urnings* and hermaphrodites, both to educate himself and to corroborate his views; he began citing these articles in his very first volume. One of his most important medical sources was the forensic pathologist Johann Ludwig Casper (1796–1864). While serving as Berlin's chief medical officer, Casper had been responsible for investigating sexual crimes and providing evidence of them in court. In this capacity, he examined both victims and defendants. He also founded and edited a prominent scientific journal, as well as an influential medical manual. Long after his death, the journal continued publication, and the forensics manual was reissued in multiple new editions.[38]

In 1852 Casper published the first scholarly analysis of same-sex eroticism based on the case studies he encountered in his official duties. The article—cited for generations by psychiatrists and medical researchers— broke with older stereotypes by arguing that same-sex love might stem from a congenital condition. Casper began his analysis of "sodomy" or "pederasty," as same-sex love was then labeled, with a powerful critique. The relevant scientific literature, Casper claimed, provided no empirical evidence and simply repeated the unsubstantiated claims of older sources. For example, the traditional, nineteenth-century forensic manuals predicted that a "sodomite" might be easily identified based on physical symptoms, including a broad range of debilitating viral and venereal diseases that were often observed to afflict prostitutes. This literature also predicted that while a "passive" sodomite would exhibit flaccid buttocks and a funnel-shaped sphincter, an "active" sodomite could be detected by his narrow, arrow-headed penis. Among Casper's eleven case studies introduced in his 1852 article, however, not one suffered a venereal disease or exhibited such physical characteristics.

The most startling of Casper's subjects introduced in the 1852 article was Count Alfred von Maltzan-Wedell (1792–1858), a Berlin aristocrat who was tried and incarcerated under the Prussian anti-sodomy law. In addition to interviewing and physically examining the count, Casper also read his personal journals, which gave detailed information about his sexual exploits and a broad network of Berlin sodomites.[39] Casper never published Maltzan-Wedell's journals, which are now lost, and he provided little specific description of their contents. "I can only hint," Casper claimed, "at the depictions of orgies that are given in these diaries." Although clearly disturbed by the count's sexual activity, Casper approached his subject with open-minded curiosity. Maltzan-Wedell,

Casper wrote, had engaged in passive pederasty for nearly thirty years, but showed no awareness that his sexual activities were even illegal. Endowed with a "feminine-childish essence," the count responded openly, "without inhibition," to every question. Casper marveled at the man's heartfelt feelings: the "love and longing" with which he remembered his first affair; the "effusive nicknames" he used for his lovers; and the "jealousy" he experienced when competing for affection.[40]

Not only the count's dramatic emotional life but also the results of his physical examination undermined the conventional wisdom on sodomy. Based in part on Maltzan-Wedell's physical condition, Casper determined that pederasts could not be identified with certainty by any external signs; those diagnostic markers of sodomy asserted by most forensic physicians were without any basis in fact. But Casper's most contentious assertion was that the "sexual inclination of man for man among many of these unfortunates, though I presume only among a minority, is innate."[41] In 1858 Casper argued more radically that "for most who are given to this [pederasty], it is innate and at the same time a form of mental hermaphroditism."[42] This revolutionary claim refuted decades of traditional medical opinion that viewed same-sex love as an acquired perversion, caused by masturbation, overwrought desire, or extreme sexual activity.

The similarities between Casper's innate "mental hermaphroditism" and the characteristics that Ulrichs ascribed to the *Urning* are certainly striking. Yet Ulrichs appears to have developed his own explanation for same-sex eroticism before he ever encountered Casper's scholarship. It was only in his second volume, "Inclusa," that Ulrichs cited Casper on hermaphrodites, and still later in the fourth and fifth volumes that he considered Casper's claims that same-sex love stemmed from an innate predisposition. In the fourth pamphlet, "Formatrix," Ulrichs lauded Casper's research under the heading "Dioning Testimony That Uranism Is Natural." However, he also scolded Casper for his expressions of scorn and pity for *Urnings*. In contrast, Casper likely never learned of Ulrichs's campaign, and his death in 1864 prevented Ulrichs from initiating any direct correspondence with one of the pioneering investigators of same-sex love.

Ulrichs did find an interlocutor in Richard von Krafft-Ebing (1840–

1902), the Austrian physician who became a leading late-nineteenth-century sexologist. In his second pamphlet, "Inclusa," Ulrichs cited one of Krafft-Ebing's first essays, published in 1864, and heralded his commitment to the scientific scholarship that could displace ignorant prejudice. "The protectors of justice should not shun the results yielded by natural science," Krafft-Ebing claimed, "but rather they should conform to them." Ulrichs sent Krafft-Ebing his first five pamphlets in 1866, when the young physician was just finishing an internship at the University of Vienna. The inspiration was mutual, and Ulrichs in turn shaped Krafft-Ebing's views of same-sex love. Krafft-Ebing's first article to address same-sex eroticism explicitly appeared in 1877. And in 1886 the first edition of Krafft-Ebing's *Psychopathia sexualis*, the perennial best seller that appeared in multiple expanded editions, cited Ulrichs's pamphlets.[43] Krafft-Ebing also expressed his appreciation in a letter to Ulrichs: "The research in your writings on love between men has interested me in a high degree. . . . From that day on when you sent me your writings, I have given my full attention to the phenomenon. . . . [I]t was the knowledge of your writings alone, which gave rise to my research in this highly important field."[44] This glowing encomium from one of the world's most celebrated psychiatrists, at least before Freud, illustrates the impact of Ulrichs's publications.

By publishing his experiences and theories of same-sex love, Ulrichs offered himself as both subject and muse for medical doctors who studied the subject. German psychiatrists such as Carl Westphal, Albert Moll, and Iwan Bloch discussed Ulrichs and cited his tracts. Ulrichs's writings were also important for prominent French, English, Italian, and Russian specialists of "perversion" and same-sex love, including Havelock Ellis, Paolo Mantegazza, and Marc-André Raffalovich. Ulrichs reached many educated laymen, as well, who read his writings for personal reasons or from sheer curiosity. In 1870 even Karl Marx and Friedrich Engels exchanged letters—albeit disparaging—about Ulrichs and his first pamphlets.[45]

Of course, German speakers searching for some affirmation of their same-sex attraction read Ulrichs's work most avidly. The letters and notes published by Krafft-Ebing in later editions of *Psychopathia sexualis* offer the best evidence of this influence. As one of Krafft-Ebing's correspondents claimed, "When I was thirty years old, I found the work of Numa [Ulrichs's pseudonym], and I cannot describe what a salvation it was for me to learn that there are many other men who are sexually constituted the way I am, and that my sexual feeling was not an aberration but rather a sexual orientation determined by nature. . . . I no longer attempted to fight this orientation, and since I have given my Urning nature freer reign, I have become happier, healthier, and more productive."[46] Ulrichs was also the source of youthful self-discovery. "When I was about 24," one man wrote to Krafft-Ebing, "I learned by reading Ulrichs that I am not the only man of this persuasion."[47] Another credited Ulrichs with solving the riddle of his existence: "I encountered a few books by Numa Numantius and from these I was enlightened about my condition, which up to this point had been completely inexplicable."[48] Sadly for a few, reading materials, including the publications of Ulrichs and Krafft-Ebing, took the place of human contact. "Even though I have never met another Urning," one reader admitted, "I am very familiar with my condition because I have been able to read almost all of the relevant literature. Recently I was confronted by your work *Psychopathia sexualis.*"[49] The most striking evidence of Ulrichs's impact was the rapid and widespread adoption of the *Urning* name for those inclined to love their own sex. By 1900 the term was commonly used in German to describe same-sex attraction, and not only in specialized psychiatric literature. Both German-language encyclopedias, *Meyers* and *Brockhaus,* included entries for "homosexuality" that either cross-referenced *Urningsliebe* (the love of Urnings) or used the term *Urning.*[50] Ulrichs's nomenclature likely influenced the English language, as well, though this is disputed by some.[51]

Since the German criminal codes varied greatly—a legacy of political fragmentation—the continued existence of laws punishing same-sex eroticism remained an open question and one that could be resolved only with unification. By the early nineteenth century, however, all of the German territories had eliminated the death penalty as a punishment for same-sex sodomy. The striking counterpoint was Britain, where sodomy convictions remained punishable by death until 1868. In contrast, the French Revolution had established the liberal principle of shielding private, consensual, sexual relations from state control, and revolutionary France chose not to include an anti-sodomy law in its criminal code of 1791. France influenced much of Europe's legal culture, in turn, and other states adopted this progressive element of the new French law: Spain, the Netherlands, Belgium (after 1830), and most Italian states rescinded their laws punishing sodomy.

Bavaria was the first German territory, in 1813, to exempt same-sex eroticism from criminal prosecution (except in the application of force or with youths under the age of twelve). Baden and Württemberg in southwestern Germany, where the Napoleonic Code was also imposed for a short period, eliminated laws against sodomy after 1815.[52] By the 1820s Hanover and Brunswick had followed suit, albeit with minor variations. An important caveat in considering more progressive penal codes—including the French—was the persistence of public decency laws, which were often applied to harass and imprison men for offensive public behaviors. This helps to explain the threat that compelled Ulrichs to resign his Hanoverian post even though he had violated no law. Of course, several German states maintained their laws punishing private sexual acts between adults, including Prussia, Austria, Saxony, and the city-republics of Hamburg and Bremen. Austria's anti-sodomy statute deserves special mention since it was unique in German central Europe for criminalizing sexual acts between women.[53]

Because Prussia led the unification of Germany, its criminal code and punishment of sodomy had a profound influence in the new empire after 1871. As Bismarck predicted in the wake of the failed 1848 revolution, the "German question" would be resolved through "blood and iron" (or warfare), not through the idealism of bourgeois nationalists. The first of the three wars of German unification was fought in 1864, when Prussia joined with Austria and defeated Denmark for control of the northern duchies of Schleswig and Holstein. Like most Germans, Ulrichs applauded the Austro-Prussian collaboration, something he had called for in a short pamphlet published in 1862.[54] The Danes quickly sued for peace, but the precise status of the duchies remained unresolved. Bismarck had little use for nationalism—kleindeutsch or großdeutsch—and hoped instead to increase Prussia's control over all of northern Germany.

The second war of German unification was fought between Prussia and Austria in 1866, when Bismarck maneuvered to exploit the Danish conflict and further limit Austrian influence. The unresolved status of Schleswig and Holstein provided Bismarck with a pretext for goading Austria to war. Prussia alienated most of the middling German states, the so-called "third Germany" of Hanover, Saxony, Bavaria, and Württemberg, which had consistently promoted Habsburg influence in German affairs, since they viewed Austria as a necessary counterweight to Prussian strength and the guarantor of their own independence.

Before the outbreak of the Austro-Prussian War, Prussia demanded neutrality from Hanover. When the king of Hanover, George V, refused, Prussia invaded, and George V was forced to capitulate and cede his property to Prussia. The terms of the armistice stipulated that Hanoverian troops remain neutral for the remainder of the conflict. Within two weeks, on July 3, 1866, Prussia defeated Austria at the Battle of Königgrätz, ending any hope that King George might regain his realm. By formal decree, Prussia annexed Hanover in September, leaving the Hanoverian dynasty stateless. The Prussians returned the personal property of King George, but the dethroned monarch was forced into permanent exile in Austria. Ulrichs, as a proud Hanoverian patriot, declared himself a Prussian adversary and attempted to rally support for his king. The Prussians monitored Ulrichs—always skilled at attracting attention—and imprisoned him twice during the first half of 1867. They interrogated him during both periods of detention, and then banished him permanently from Hanover. These detentions also gave Prussian officials the opportunity to search Ulrichs's home in Burgdorf, where they confiscated a collection of his manuscripts and correspondence. The letters and other documents they seized proved to be very sensitive, and one file listed the names of 150 prominent Berlin residents alleged to be *Urnings*.[55]

Ulrichs petitioned for the return of his property and also for damages suffered from the detentions, which he claimed were unlawful. Except for a few papers forwarded to his new address in Bavaria, he was never able to recover these materials. As it turned out, Bismarck himself had taken a personal interest in Ulrichs, and ordered that his papers be delivered to his own desk. Undoubtedly, the shrewd Prussian minister president was not going to miss an opportunity to collect information that might allow him to manipulate allies or blackmail enemies. Ulrichs's dossier—more than seventy pages—was eventually deposited in the Prussian state archive, but only after the sensitive list of alleged *Urnings* had been removed.[56]

Prussia quickly consolidated the gains from its victory over Austria and established the North German Confederation in 1867. This truncated version of the former German Confederation excluded Austria, as well as the southwestern states of Bavaria, Baden, and Württemberg. This outcome deviated widely from the *großdeutsch* solution hoped for by Ulrichs and many others, and forced a rapid reorientation by German nationalists of every perspective. But if some *großdeutsch* partisans despaired of Prussia's growing influence, others began to view Bismarck as a kind of savior who might succeed, where the bourgeois nationalists had failed, in creating a unified Germany. The anticipation of unification also encouraged the activity of those cultural associations that intended to support the needs of an emergent Germany. The nationalist Association of Jurists had sponsored congresses since its inception in 1860, and its sixth congress was scheduled to be held in Munich in August 1867.

It was at this meeting that Ulrichs publicly demanded an open debate on the legal status of same-sex love and recommended a dramatic revision of the remaining German anti-sodomy statutes. The path leading to Ulrichs's historic appeal was a complicated one and required significant wrangling. Two years earlier he had submitted his first five volumes on *Urning* love to the planning commission of the German jurists along with the following resolution for discussion at the sixth congress:

I. That inborn love for persons of the male sex is to be punished under the same conditions under which love of persons of the female sex are punished; that it is, therefore, to remain free of punishment, so long as: neither rights are violated (through application or threat of force, misuse of prepubescent person, the unconscious, etc.) nor public offense is given;

II. That, however, the present, often thoroughly unclear requirements for "giving public offense by sexual acts" be replaced by such as preserve legal guarantees.[57]

The committee attempted to suppress the petition, dismissing it as "unsuitable." Ulrichs was undaunted, and he wrote the congress chairman demanding an opportunity to protest "the exclusion of an agenda proposal" at the closing plenary session. The request was granted, and Ulrichs prepared for this unprecedented opportunity. Although silenced by jeering and tumult, Ulrichs managed to present the subject of *Urning* emancipation, which introduced his cause to the leading legal minds of the German world. The five hundred lawyers, officials, and legal scholars who attended the closing meeting would certainly remember Ulrichs and his impassioned appeal.[58]

Despite his dispiriting Munich reception, the unflappable Ulrichs pressed ahead with his writing campaign. In 1868 he published the sixth and seventh pamphlets in his series, and for the first time under his own name. The sixth volume, "Gladius Furens" ("Raging Sword"), gave a detailed account of his Munich experience and a stinging rebuke to the congress for his treatment there. Ulrichs also identified the larger significance of his seemingly quixotic effort: "I raised my voice in free and open protest against a thousand years of injustice. Unbiased, oral, and open debate of man-manly love has been until now kept under lock and key. . . . Hatred alone has enjoyed freedom of speech. These barriers I have forcefully broken through—broken through without having offended thereby my duties to uphold public morality. By so doing I gave the impetus to restore to the other side the freedom of scientific public debate." This was only one aspect of Ulrichs's struggle. He also explained how even his lone voice would empower those too inhibited to act on their own. "The present battle situation has totally changed," Ulrichs claimed. "We were a scattered body of defenseless weaklings, persecuted and mangled." But now, he wrote, "We have found courage! Henceforth we shall take a decisive stand and face these persecutions. We shall be steadfast. We refuse further persecution."[59]

The printed word, Ulrichs believed, was the medium that would drive this collective action. Public interest in the pamphlets bolstered Ulrichs's confidence, and he was also heartened by the correspondence that followed each new volume. Ulrichs began most installments, including the seventh, "Memnon," with a description of the responses to the previous publication. This usually included notes from anonymous

Urnings, as well as from officials, lawyers, and doctors, who were variously contemptuous, supportive, or, at a minimum, intrigued enough to write him. The immediate influence of Ulrichs's campaign is difficult to gauge. Many jurists rejected his ideas, and dismissed him as a misguided eccentric or worse. His rapport with physicians and psychiatrists was equally problematic. While Krafft-Ebing praised Ulrichs effusively, many others described him as unscientific and took greater interest in his status as an *Urning* and potential case study than as a professional researcher.

All the same, Ulrichs managed to place himself at the center of an unfolding legal and medical debate that gained increasing relevance with the march toward unification. The North German Confederation was governed by a new federal constitution and hoped to create a uniform penal code with jurisdiction over all member states. This marked an important departure from the much weaker constitution of the former German Confederation, which had left intact—from 1815 to 1866—the individual law codes of its thirty-nine members. Prussian officials wanted to "homogenize" the German penal codes, using their own legal system as a template. But the prospect that Prussia would replace the more liberal Hanoverian treatment of private sexual behavior with its own anti-sodomy statute was in Ulrichs's view an especially grave threat.

In June 1868 Bismarck ordered the preparation of a revised code by the Prussian minister of justice, who commissioned the Prussian Medical Affairs Board to study the anti-sodomy statute. The board chairman was Berlin pathologist Rudolf Virchow (1821–1902), one of the most famous doctors of his age, who also served—as cofounder and member of the German Liberal Party (Deutsche Fortschrittspartei)—in the Berlin City Council, the Prussian Diet, and later the German Reichstag.[60] The other board members were prominent physicians and psychiatrists with academic posts in the medical faculty at the University of Berlin. Under Virchow's leadership, the board submitted a formal report in March 1869 recommending *against* the anti-sodomy statute. The group argued that male-male sexual relations were "no more injurious than other forms [of illicit sexuality]," like fornication or adultery. They claimed further that they were unable "to offer reasons why sex between men should be punished by law when other forms of illicit relations are not."[61] Surprisingly, perhaps, the board's recommendation reflected the liberalism of its members, who largely supported free trade, minimal government interference in the lives of private citizens, and, not least of all, the determinations of modern science. No doubt the French decriminalization of sodomy also influenced their thinking.

While considering the anti-sodomy statute, the Justice Ministry received nearly one hundred petitions—from jurists, medical doctors, and private individuals—most arguing against the anti-sodomy statute. Ulrichs initiated this chorus for legal reform by submitting his first of five petitions in September 1868, along with two of his published pamphlets. "The hermaphrodite [*Urning*] is not only a human being," Ulrichs pleaded; "he is also a competent citizen of the constitutional state and as such he may demand, so long as he neither harms the rights of others nor gives public offense, that he too not be punished for the expression of his sexual love."[62] The Medical Affairs Board announced its conclusions in March, and newspapers reported that officials had determined to exclude the anti-sodomy statute from the new penal code. Ulrichs took this satisfying victory as an opportunity to send one last petition, this time requesting pardons for those convicted or incarcerated for sexual crimes related to their *Urning* identity.

One significant result of this legal review was the invention of the word *Homosexualität*, homosexuality. The man who coined this influential neologism was the enigmatic author and journalist Karl Maria Kertbeny (1824–1882), who introduced his terminology in two short publications protesting the anti-sodomy statute. Submitted anonymously to Prussian minister of justice Leonhardt in 1869, Kertbeny's self-published pamphlets were also circulated by booksellers in Leipzig and Berlin. As the anonymous author, Kertbeny maintained in the two pamphlets that he was sexually "normal" but argued passionately—based on the conclusions of Virchow's board, as well as the findings of other psychiatric authorities, including Casper—that "homosexuality" was an inborn condition and that the anti-sodomy statute violated the fundamental civic and constitutional rights of "homosexuals." Kertbeny rejected Ulrichs's *Urning* theory of psychological hermaphroditism, but he clearly took inspiration from Ulrichs's public campaign, and the two had corresponded since 1865. Kertbeny never made public his support for homosexual emancipation, however, and so guarded was he that even Ulrichs was unaware—until much later—of his identity as the anonymous author.[63]

Ulrichs's campaign to end the punishment of same-sex love appeared poised to succeed. Like Kertbeny, many of those sympathetic to Ulrichs and his cause took inspiration from his public stance while remaining skeptical of his theories. Stimulating open debate among legal and medical professionals—and perhaps influencing their views—was a critical achievement. But what Ulrichs could not easily control was entrenched prejudice, nor the brutal, unsolved sex crimes that enraged popular sentiment in Berlin in the late 1860s. In early 1867 the mutilated body of a sixteen-year-old apprentice was found in a Berlin park. According to the coroner's report, the boy had been constrained by one assailant and anally raped with a stick-like object by a second. His colon and stomach cavity were perforated, and blood loss from these wounds caused his death. His attackers also severed and removed the boy's testicles. Whether he was castrated before or after his death remained unclear.

Only a censored version of this vicious and sadistic attack was published in the papers. The motive suggested was theft and the cause of death given as a fatal blow to the head. Although the press also reported the mutilation, this was explained as an attempt to cover the true nature of the crime and to mislead the police. Rumors circulated quickly, however, that the attack was of a more demented and sinister nature. Located on Berlin's northwestern periphery, the Invaliden Park, where the assault occurred, was known for its male and female prostitutes. Newspaper reports soon claimed that the police had identified suspects among criminal circles, including pimps, prostitutes, and their patrons. The police raided locales and outdoor areas where men cruised for sex with other men and also interviewed those with prior sodomy convictions. The investigation was unsuccessful, despite a substantial reward, and no plausible perpetrator could be found. This failure had political repercussions. Prussian king William I demanded daily reports on the status of the investigation, and according to court reporter Hugo Friedländer, the king held the Berlin police president, Otto von Bernuth, accountable for not bringing the culprits to justice. In April 1867 Bernuth was dismissed and replaced by Günther Karl Lothar von Wurmb.

The failure to solve the crime also heightened public anxiety. Within the calendar year (1867), Berlin residents provided the police with more than fifty anonymous tips—all of them fruitless—that identified men presumed to be "perverted." Public outrage reached a boiling point with the discovery of another mutilation victim. In January 1869 a five-year-old boy was discovered whimpering in pain in the attic of his apartment building, located in the eastern working-class neighborhood of Friedrichshain. The youth was delivered to the nearest police precinct and then taken to a hospital. His doctors discovered a wound in his anus and tears in his rectum. Like the first victim, the boy had been anally penetrated with an object and then possibly raped by his attacker. He was also the victim of mutilation: most of his foreskin was severed and he suffered bite marks on his neck. The attacker had also strangled the youth, and assuming him to be dead, deposited the body in a chimney flue. The boy was able to free himself, however, and neighbors responded to his pitiful cries.

In his initial police statement, the delirious boy seemed to accuse his father, a poor laborer, who was subsequently arrested and questioned. The boy's mother provided her husband with an alibi, however, and the man was released the following day. In a second statement, the boy described a bearded man as his assailant, who had lured him to the attic with the promise of books. He was unable to provide additional details, and the only other clues were a white walking stick and red handkerchief found at the crime scene. Once again, King William took a personal interest in the crime, placing the investigating officers—as well as the entire police administration—under tremendous pressure. Despite extensive interviews with neighbors, the police were unable to identify a suspect.

A break in the case came when a neighborhood tailor reported seeing a man, Carl von Zastrow (1821–1877), loitering in the area several days before the attack. The man who fingered Zastrow, Ferdinand Müller, had worked as a police informant and knew Zastrow personally, and he demanded the five hundred taler reward after Zastrow's arrest. (Later, at trial, Zastrow claimed that he had once had a sexual relationship with Müller and that the denunciation was an act of vengeance.) A onetime Prussian officer, the forty-eight-year-old Zastrow had a significant record of sodomy charges. He had been arrested or detained in Dresden, Kassel, and Berlin for suspicious behavior. Zastrow's "Herculean form" made him a striking figure, and he was known in Berlin—at least by police—for propositioning strange men on his evening jaunts. He is also believed to have belonged to a group of homosexual men who congregated at the old Berlin National Theater, an august cadre that included the court actor Hermann Hendrichs, Prince Georg von Preußen (a relative of King William), and Johann Baptist von Schweitzer, whose arrest in 1862 was the initial spur for Ulrichs's campaign.

The police had interrogated Zastrow once before in relation to the unsolved 1867 murder, so the denunciation for the new crime was especially compelling. When officials presented Zastrow to the victim, still recovering in the hospital, the young boy responded with shock and muted crying. Press reports on the investigation brought public reaction to a fever pitch, and there were popular demonstrations in front of the Berlin town hall. Even the distinctive Berlin dialect incorporated his name, both as verb and subject: "Zastrow" became synonymous with homosexual, and the verb zastrieren meant to commit homosexual rape. The evidence itself was hardly compelling. A plaster cast of the teeth marks in the boy's neck appeared to match Zastrow's mouth. But neither handkerchief nor walking stick could be tied with certainty to Zastrow. The alleged culprit also had witnesses who placed him in a café in the western suburb of Charlottenburg at 3 p.m. Reaching the crime scene on the other side of town by 3:30, when the attack was estimated to have taken place, was impractical, although carriage drivers were able to demonstrate that it would have been possible.

The investigation concluded in April, and the trial opened in July 1869. The press and public were usually excluded from the courtroom when cases involved sexual crimes. The Berliner Gerichtszeitung protested this successfully and gained access for its own and other reporters. This helped to fuel public interest and sell newspapers, but it also preserved a detailed trial record. At the point of his arrest and throughout the trial Zastrow maintained his innocence. He also admitted freely his sexual attraction to men, and identified himself with Ulrichs's definition of a congenital Urning. He denied vehemently, however, any attraction to boys or adolescents. Zastrow's open admission that he was homosexual complicated the prosecution, so the court summoned three Berlin psychiatrists as expert witnesses. The physicians were unable to provide immediate testimony, claiming inadequate time and opportunity to examine the defendant.

The judge halted the proceedings until the three doctors could conduct their own assessments. In short, they assumed the same role that Casper had played during the trial of Count Alfred von Maltzan-Wedell in 1849. The three expert witnesses were familiar with Casper's published research, and accepted Zastrow's sexual orientation as innate and fixed. Explaining same-sex eroticism as a congenital trait had eclipsed traditional medical theories that stressed masturbation, excessive sexual activity, or acquired perversion. In this connection, Zastrow's own assertions—that he had always felt "that way" and that he embraced Ulrichs's writings—reinforced the doctors' diagnosis.

But the experts reached widely differing conclusions. One physician determined Zastrow to be mentally unbalanced, and therefore incompetent to stand trial. The second agreed that Zastrow was clinically insane, but felt all the same that he was morally accountable for his actions. A third emphasized Zastrow's congenital homosexuality and concluded that the sexual assault and mutilation conformed to Zastrow's unnatural sexual urges as a "pederast"; he also agreed that Zastrow was competent to stand trial. Most striking was the extent to which all three physicians explained homosexuality within the context of disease or pathology, which influenced them to conflate it with pedophilia, rape, and sexual mutilation. At this early date in the development of sexology, there were no distinct categories for "homosexual," "pedophile," "sexual predator," or "sadist." If Ulrichs had helped to introduce the identity of a congenital homosexual or *Urning*, this "creature" was also believed to be psychologically diseased, at least by most medical professionals.

Precisely these views determined Zastrow's fate. The trial finally resumed on October 25, and four days later the jurors delivered a "guilty" verdict. The judge sentenced Zastrow to fifteen years imprisonment. During this final stage of the trial, the judge permitted the testimony of a new witness: a woman came forward and declared that Zastrow had given her two packets, one containing a severed penis, the other a woman's breast. These absurd claims were completely unsubstantiated, and the judge asked a single question: "It was really flesh, what he showed you?" It appears unlikely, in fact, that this outrageous story had any influence on the trial's outcome. It does illustrate, however, the tenor of the proceedings—the gullible willingness of court officials to entertain incredible stories and baseless slander. Although the 1867 murder remained formally unsolved, the two attacks were virtually conflated in the mind of the public. For police and politicians alike, a conviction for the second crime conveniently mollified demands to find the perpetrator of the first. Until his death in the Berlin Moabit Prison in 1877, however, Zastrow always maintained his innocence.[64]

The same ignorance and popular prejudice that condemned Zastrow also derailed Ulrichs's campaign to end the legal persecution of *Urning* sexuality. On November 7, little more than a week after the conclusion of the Zastrow trial, Prussian officials announced their decision to include the anti-sodomy statute in the revised law code. Prussian cultural minister Heinrich von Mühler, citing "the people's sense of right and wrong" (*Rechtsbewusstsein des Volkes*) that held homosexual conduct to be a crime and not just a vice, rejected the counsel of his own leading medical advisers.[65] A draft of the North German penal code was published in December, and the section addressing same-sex eroticism reproduced the language of the Prussian penal code from 1851. Sodomy was defined as the sexual penetration of one man by another, as well as "sexual contact between man and beast." The draft code was debated in the Reichstag of the North German Confederation from February to May 1870, and during this period Ulrichs petitioned again, requesting that lawmakers, if the sodomy paragraph were preserved, also insert the following qualification: "The preceding does not pertain to a person who commits sexual acts that correspond to his innate sexual drive." The only significant change, however, was the assignment of a new paragraph number, which provided the nickname—Paragraph 175—for the statute criminalizing sex between men. The North German penal code was finally promulgated as law on May 31, 1870.

The precise machinations that led Mühler to overrule the recommendation of the medical board are not clear. Kertbeny argued that the Zastrow affair had an inordinate influence on the process of legal codification. Ulrichs held the same view, and he devoted his tenth pamphlet, "Argonauticus," to Zastrow's trial and alleged crime. While avoiding pronouncements about Zastrow's guilt or innocence, Ulrichs complained that "for the opponents of the cause I champion, the Zastrow case was a plum fallen into their laps."[66] It may be unfair to claim that the trial was directly responsible for the inclusion of the anti-sodomy statute in the new criminal code. The timing suggests clearly, however, that the publicity surrounding Zastrow's trial strengthened proponents of the sodomy statute. The obverse dynamic is equally probable: public hysteria about a sadistic pedophile might easily have weakened the resolve of influential progressives like Rudolf Virchow, as well as other medical and legal experts, to oppose its inclusion.

It is almost certain that those with access to conservative Prussian cultural minister Mühler lobbied forcefully to include the sodomy paragraph. Later Ulrichs reported receiving a letter in early 1870 from a sympathetic Berlin university professor who wrote, "[T]he decisive reason for certain influential persons, even if they never say so, is this: they want to make a concession to the orthodox religious tradition." Others speculated that Mühler was unduly influenced by his own wife, Adelheid, who had access to the Hohenzollern court and direct contact with King William I. It bears noting that her brother Gustav Gossler was appointed to her husband's post as cultural minister in 1881. This clash of Prussia's conservative officials and churches with a progressive medical establishment was a perennial tension that would characterize the life of the German Empire after 1871.[67]

The third and ultimate war of unification was a crushing political denouement for Ulrichs (and the other German opponents of Prussia). Once again, Bismarck outmaneuvered a weaker and less capable adversary, Napoleon III, emperor of France, by deftly manipulating his French rival into declaring war. The immediate cause was the candidacy for the Spanish throne of a distant Catholic cousin of the Prussian king, Prince Leopold von Hohenzollern-Sigmaringen. Napoleon III feared the prospect that his neighboring states, Prussia and Spain, might be ruled by members of the same Hohenzollern dynasty, and he pressed the Prussian king to pledge never to support Leopold's candidacy. In June Bismarck allowed the press to publish a version of the Prussian king's dispatch, the so-called Ems telegram, which described the king's discussion of the Spanish throne with the French ambassador. Bismarck did so without royal permission, however, and he also edited the telegram with the intention of inflaming both French and German public opinion. He succeeded spectacularly, and on July 20 Napoleon III declared war. At the Battle of Sedan in early September, superior German forces—which included not only Prussians and North Germans but also the armies of the southern German states—defeated the French and captured the French emperor. French republican forces regrouped and continued the fight, but the Germans besieged Paris successfully from October to January, forcing the new republican government to sue for peace. Before the armistice was even signed, the German Empire was declared, on January 18, 1871, from the Hall of Mirrors in Versailles. Here the Prussian king was crowned German Emperor William I.

The new German Empire incorporated the core states of the North German Confederation, as well as Baden, Württemberg, Bavaria, and the territories of Alsace and Lorraine, which had been annexed from France. The exclusion of Habsburg Austria from a unified German nation-state was now absolute. The empire was broadly federalist, allowing its member states wide latitude in cultural affairs (including the regulation of religion and education). Prussia dominated the new national institutions, however, including the judiciary. One central challenge was to forge a uniform imperial law code that would simplify jurisprudence across former state boundaries. While the German Civil Code required nearly thirty years of careful planning and was only promulgated in 1900, the criminal code proved less difficult to introduce. The Prussian or North German penal code served conveniently as a template. Although the individual states formally "adopted" the Prussian penal code, the benefits of uniformity created both pressure and incentive to accept the existing North German law. In his eleventh pamphlet, "Araxes," Ulrichs described Bavaria—since eliminating laws against sodomy in 1813—as "the oldest asylum for *Urning* nature in Germany." Ulrichs urged Bavaria to resist Prussian pressure, and opined optimistically that the state "might yet continue, thanks to destiny, to offer an asylum in the heart of Germany to a persecuted nature, a place of refuge where martyred and hunted human beings can breathe." This hope was misplaced, and at the beginning of 1872 Bavaria also adopted the penal code and with it the Prussian anti-sodomy statute, Paragraph 175.[68] Ulrichs's worst-case scenario had effectively come to pass. Not only were the Berlin medical proponents of decriminalization ignored but the Prussian unification of Germany served to reintroduce an anti-sodomy statute in those German states that had long ceased to punish sodomy as a crime.

Although the foundation of the empire thwarted hopes for *Urning* emancipation, at least in the near term, Ulrichs continued his public campaign. In 1879 he completed his twelfth and final pamphlet, "Critische Pfeile" ("Critical Arrows"). In this tract, Ulrichs tacitly conceded the unlikelihood of eliminating the sodomy statute, and instead emphasized the need for additional research and study. He also argued again that the fundamental disposition of an *Urning* was both congenital and natural—not acquired through "perverse" actions or the product of mental disease or physical degeneration. His assessment of the *Urning* character had grown more complex than in his earlier publications and allowed for a broad and rich spectrum of intermingled sexual and gender attributes spanning the stereotypical extremes of masculinity and effeminacy for *Dionings* and *Urnings* of both sexes.[69]

In 1880 Ulrichs traveled to Italy, crossing the Alps on foot. Italy had become the home to immigrant German and English homosexuals—increasingly throughout the nineteenth century—who fled the persecutory laws of their native countries. This was Ulrichs's first trip to Italy, and he anticipated an extended visit. Although he had plans to return to Germany, ultimately he remained in Italy for the rest of his life. Ulrichs's itinerary took him to Ravenna, Florence, and Rome, and he finally settled in Naples. After three years there, Ulrichs moved to L'Aquila in the Abruzzo region, where he favored the colder climate and mountain air. Although Ulrichs befriended the local notabilities in L'Aquila, he led a largely solitary life. His writing projects were varied, but he no longer pursued his erstwhile dream of *Urning* emancipation. In 1889 Ulrichs began publishing *Alaudae,* a small Latin-language literary journal consisting of his own poems, translations, and reviews. Within a few years, Ulrichs had garnered subscribers from throughout Europe and North America. Initially, the journal appeared in some twenty issues annually, but it was published less frequently later on. The last installment was produced in February 1895, five months before Ulrichs's death from a kidney infection on July 14, at the age of seventy-four.[70]

The struggle of this brave and lonely soul appeared all but forgotten at the point of his death. Sadly, Ulrichs's fundamental goal of achieving legal reform went unrealized. With his stubborn conviction and activism, however, Ulrichs established a powerful legacy. He was arguably the first man in modern history to acknowledge openly his sexual attraction to other men. By outing himself, he also became the first public activist for the legal emancipation of *Urnings*, or homosexuals. His pamphlets, petitions, and public pronouncements were frequently reviled, but they also ignited debates about the character of same-sex eroticism that still echo today. Although his theories were largely spurned by the German medical establishment, he influenced a group of progressive psychiatric and legal professionals to accept the idea that same-sex love was an inborn phenomenon, not simply a vice, a perversion, or a traditional sin.

Ulrichs also developed the first vocabulary for describing modern sexual identities. If eclipsed in the twentieth century by words like "homosexual" and "heterosexual," his terminology gained wide popular currency in the German-speaking world. His theories also supported others struggling to understand their sexual urges, and helped to forge— largely with the printed word—an incipient community of like-minded persons, including many of Krafft-Ebing's correspondents. Perhaps Ulrichs's greatest contribution to the cause he championed was his serving as the inspiration for the founding of the Scientific-Humanitarian Committee (Wissenschaftlich-humanitäres Komitee) in Berlin, just two years after his death in 1897. Led by the Berlin medical doctor Magnus Hirschfeld, this group represented the world's first homosexual rights organization. Their raison d'être, like Ulrichs's own, was the scientific study of homosexuality and an end to legal discrimination. The Prussian anti-sodomy statute, Paragraph 175, which had incensed Ulrichs, was the very spur that prompted Hirschfeld and his colleagues. The work of the Scientific-Humanitarian Committee would soon help to make Berlin a center of sexology research and the capital of homosexual rights activism. The German anti-sodomy statute called forth a reaction, in short, that both Hegel and Marx would have immediately understood. The demand for emancipation was a dialectical response to legal discrimination. The committee honored Ulrichs by conducting systematic research to reconstruct his life and biography, and in 1898 they also republished his twelve revolutionary pamphlets.

CHAPTER TWO

Policing Homosexuality in Berlin

From the evening hours till early the next day
Through the Friedrichstraße we make our way
We've been doing this for quite some time
We prowl the strip arm in arm
As always we are dressed to the nines
Since modest garb does the business harm

This is the dollboy's first rule
Appear always chic and elegant
The second is to be assertive and cool
Never shy or reticent
And finally if one hopes to inherit
Blackmailing a john is the surest bet

—"Berliner Pupenjungen" (Berlin dollboys), Berlin folksong,
first published in volume 3 of *Lieder aus dem Rinnstein* (Berlin, 1905)[1]

It was the visibility rather than the mere existence of a homosexual
and lesbian subculture that was important, for London and Paris
also contained such a culture, but in Berlin it was more readily
inspected, photographed, and written about.

—GEORGE MOSSE, *Nationalism and Sexuality: Respectability and
Abnormal Sexuality in Modern Europe* (1985)

On a dark winter evening in February 1885, police officers descended on Seeger's Restaurant, a small bar located in central Berlin at 10 Jägerstraße, just south of Unter den Linden. Although close to government offices and cultural institutions, the pub was surrounded by a quiet residential neighborhood, dotted with small stores and businesses. Located on the ground floor of a middle-class apartment house, the non-descript locale might never have attracted the attention of neighbors—if not for the police raid. The simple interior was typical of many Berlin taverns: the front door faced the street and opened into a small room with an oak bar, tables, and chairs; from there a doorway led into a second, larger room, where more tables, chairs, and a sofa were arranged. The owner, Carl August Seeger, had opened his establishment in 1881 and always made sure that the bar and its clientele were orderly, discreet, and respectable.

Neither Seeger nor his patrons had done anything to attract attention. As one newspaper later reported, the police, upon entering, identified few "incriminating factors."[2] The men in the bar—there were no women—came from all walks of life and included tradesmen, merchants, and professionals. They lived in a range of neighborhoods; the city's *Stadtbahn,* the elevated railway system inaugurated in 1882, extended in all directions from the urban center, like spokes on a wheel, hastening travel to Berlin's new suburbs. Possibly a few were from Berlin's eastern working-class districts, but most resided in the historic city core or in the expanding townships of Schöneberg, Wilmersdorf, and Charlottenburg. Despite varied social backgrounds, the bar patrons were all in their prime, most between thirty and fifty years old. What drew them to Seeger's Restaurant was the opportunity to meet men who preferred men, for love or sociability, and to do so in a safe environment. Seeger cultivated this security together with his barkeep, Paul Block, who answered to a feminine nickname, "the shrew" (*die Fuchtel*). We know nothing about the family situations of Seeger's patrons, but some might have been in committed same-sex relationships. Others were likely single and alone, or perhaps married with children. In any case, as Berlin residents or out-of-towners, they met lovers and friends or made new acquaintances in this modest pub, albeit one with a very special profile.[3]

Seeger's Restaurant had been investigated several weeks before the raid, when Berlin police commissioner Leopold von Meerscheidt-Hüllessem responded to an anonymous tip. In late January a plainclothes officer—accompanied by an acquaintance—visited the bar and later described the patrons to Hüllessem as *warme Brüder*, "warm brothers." On this initial visit, the two interlopers had been heartily welcomed, and they claimed to have observed anywhere from twenty to fifty men. Commissioner Hüllessem required more information before authorizing the raid, however, so the officer returned the following week, this time alone.[4] When questioned where his "lover" (*Verhältnis*) was, the undercover investigator responded that the friend was sick. This second report prompted Hüllessem to order the raid for Sunday, February 25, confident that the evidence would stand up in court. With officers stationed in the street, the undercover agent and his colleagues forced their way into the bar, and then turned on the patrons, arresting twelve men, including Seeger and his employee. The group was trundled in a horse-drawn paddy wagon to Berlin's old police station, and then charged with creating a public nuisance and jailed.

Neither the investigating officer nor the second witness had observed any *illegal* sexual acts. Yet their testimony was the only evidence presented in court. As the police official claimed, the bar patrons had flirted with salacious bonhomie during his undercover visits; the twelve accused men "kissed and caressed one another, patted each other's bottoms, sat on each other's laps, addressed each other with women's names, and fondled one another in the crotch."[5] One man had announced loudly that he "wanted to f-ck" that evening but his sexual partner "needed to have a powerful cock."

The defense questioned whether these homosexual flirtations represented a public disturbance, and countered that the bar patrons never *perceived* any discomfort on the part of the officer. If the undercover officer and his companion appeared to fit in, how could Seeger or his patrons be accused of creating a public disturbance? Seeger argued that the establishment was not truly public since his clientele sought out the pub for its distinctive character. He also denounced the police and their methods: the surveillance was illegitimate and the arresting officers were aggressive and rude. Neither the undercover investigation nor the raid, Seeger maintained, was customary or acceptable.[6]

The court ruled against Seeger, however, since the repulsion expressed by the two police informants satisfied the charge that the bar patrons had created a "public disturbance." After all, the police had no difficulty entering the bar where they observed the "offensive" behavior. Therefore the bar could not be considered a private club at all but was indeed a public accommodation. Moreover, the second room with the sofa where the most offensive behavior took place was visible through the un-curtained doorway from the smaller room in front. Based on this reasoning, the judge convicted Seeger of "procurement" and inciting illegal activity: Seeger and his barkeep received eight- and four-month prison terms, respectively. The patrons—merchants, artisans, a man of independent means (*Rentier*), and a manservant—were given three- to four-month prison sentences for disturbing the peace. Only one fellow, a schoolteacher, already dismissed from his position, was allowed to go free.[7]

Commissioner Hüllessem might have taken great pride in the success of his investigation and raid: twelve arrests and the prosecution of eleven men was impressive indeed. Only a few years earlier in 1881, Hüllessem had closed a similar pub on nearby Brüderstraße, just south of the Hohenzollern Palace. In that case, however, no one was charged or imprisoned.[8] It now appeared that the commissioner was preparing to clamp down on the "warm brothers" of Berlin and stem the growth of the homosexual bar scene.

Certainly the problem had become acute by the early 1880s. We know from published sources that Seeger's was clustered within a few blocks of several small taverns serving a homosexual clientele. This group appears to have been anchored by the most prominent venue, the Pariser Keller, a club inside the French embassy complex next to the Brandenburg Gate, which had gained its reputation by about 1880 and was protected from German officials as property of the French state. Hugo Friedländer, an habitué of this early subculture, named more than fifteen other locales that had been popular with homosexuals in the 1880s and '90s. Like Seeger's Restaurant, most of the bars were "primitive," as Friedländer described them, and quite small, located in larger apartment buildings, usually at street level, in basements, or in interior courtyards.

Friedländer also mentioned the raid of Seeger's Restaurant, but reported—incredibly!—that at least five new bars opened within a few blocks soon after Seeger's was closed.[9] How was this possible? If Hüllessem had just embarked on a policy of zero tolerance, why did new bars open soon after the raid?

Although it appears that the police commissioner was considering a more draconian enforcement policy, this was arguably quixotic. The "homosexual" fraternization of Seeger's bar patrons was *not* a crime, and therefore police and court officials confronted an enormous challenge in closing down such an establishment. Illegal sexual acts were committed in private or under cloak of darkness, so Paragraph 175 was highly impractical for controlling alleged homosexual behavior. Consider that only sexual practices between men that simulated heterosexual intercourse (as well as bestiality) could be prosecuted. For this reason the charges of "procurement" or "creating a public disturbance"—not violations of Paragraph 175—were leveled against Seeger and his guests, based entirely on eyewitness testimony of the officer and his friend. In short, Hüllessem faced the impractical task of investigating dozens of small bars where homosexuals might congregate, a nearly impossible task in a large, sprawling city.

An additional explanation for Hüllessem's mysterious about-face might have been political. In the same year as the raid on Seeger's establishment, Bernhard von Richthofen received a royal appointment as the new police president, making him Hüllessem's formal superior. Richthofen, who never married, was widely rumored to have been homosexual himself. Allegedly, his own underlings had to monitor his sexual escapades to prevent public disclosure and scandal.[10] A newspaper profile and portrait of Richthofen published in 1893 suggested that the man had little public presence and that he remained enigmatic and obscure despite his high office.[11]

Although few internal police sources survive from this period, the reports of contemporary observers make it clear that Hüllessem adopted a policy of tolerating homosexual bars and entertainments. A study published in 1886, just one year after the Seeger's raid, *Die Verbrecherwelt von Berlin* (The criminal world of Berlin), claimed that the police had come to accept Berlin's homosexual haunts: "[Homosexuals] have their own specific locales where they meet for beer and to socialize."[12] It creates a feeling of "togetherness for pederasts [*Päderasten*]," the author continued, and even allows them "to imagine that their activities are sanctioned." Arguably, the writings of Ulrichs and others had begun to undermine the law's perceived legitimacy, which encouraged the more lenient policy. "There's no shortage of jurists and doctors," the author claimed, "who demand exemption from punishment [*Straffreiheit*] for this vice." As long as there are no public disturbances, "the police are tolerant, even if they monitor closely."[13] This account implies that Hüllessem had resigned himself sometime soon after the raid to the growth of a homosexual milieu. The author of *Die Verbrecherwelt* also suggested that the implicit policies of Hüllessem and his subordinates actually fostered the growth of Berlin's homosexual community: the sociability of an undisturbed bar culture created a feeling of "togetherness" as well as the sense of official sanction. Certainly, as we will see, Hüllessem was aware of the innovative medical and psychiatric assessments of homosexual behavior. The recent "invention" of homosexuality—as an inborn condition with a corresponding identity—shaped the attitude that homosexual conduct, at least among consenting adults, was a victimless crime.

The enlightened self-interest of Hüllessem's enforcement policy is counterintuitive, perhaps, yet an important if underappreciated factor in the history of gay Berlin. It helps to explain the rapid growth and incredible visibility of Berlin's homosexual scene after 1890. Of course, Hüllessem inaugurated this new approach only after staging the raid on Seeger's Restaurant, which itself offers an amazing glimpse of Berlin's same-sex sociability. While the fate of Seeger and his friends was atypical, the raid itself was a watershed moment in Berlin's enforcement policy, and marked the beginning of an era in which same-sex bars, clubs, and other entertainments would multiply and thrive. As we will see, Hüllessem's approach played a powerful role in fostering Berlin's emergent homosexual community.

·   ·   ·

The challenge of policing a sexual minority was even more daunting if we consider the speed with which Berlin expanded in the late nineteenth and early twentieth centuries. At the time Karl Heinrich Ulrichs studied in Berlin in 1846–47, the city was the provincial capital of Brandenburg-Prussia with a population of 400,000. As the new German capital in 1871, Berlin's population stood at 865,000, reaching the 1 million mark within a few years. By 1905 this figure had doubled again to more than 2 million. Including the population of the independent suburban townships, *greater* Berlin reached nearly twice this size in 1914, with over 3.5 million inhabitants. When the city incorporated its neighboring communities in 1919, Berlin's population stood at 3.9 million. Driven by explosive growth, Berlin's development was sudden and wildly disorienting, creating one of the most modern cities in Europe, if not the world.[14]

The contradictory observations of foreign visitors document well the speed of Berlin's dramatic transformation. Among those who visited before the city's abrupt development was Harvard student Henry Adams, a member of the American political dynasty and a prominent historian, who described Berlin in 1858 as "a poor, keen-witted, provincial town, simple, dirty, uncivilized, and in most respects disgusting."[15] British diplomat Frederick Hamilton, stationed in Berlin after unification, remarked on the city's strained effort to wear the mantle of a national capital: "Berlin of the 'seventies was still in a state of transition. The well-built, prim, dull, and somewhat provincial *Residenz* was endeavoring with feverish energy to transform itself into a world city, a *Weltstadt*."[16] Throughout the 1870s, foreign and German visitors commented on Berlin's backwardness—unlit streets, the stench of open sewers, and the crude manners of city residents.[17] "Berlin is not a lively nor even a particularly bustling city," London journalist and publisher Henry Vizetelly wrote in 1879. "It altogether lacks the gay, kaleidoscopic life of a great metropolis."[18]

A dramatic shift in these travel reports appeared through the course of the 1880s, as Berlin became known for cleanliness, savvy urban administration, and an extensive transportation grid.[19] This new reputation for urban modernity was shaped most powerfully by Mark Twain's travel report "The German Chicago," published in 1892. Berlin has "no resemblance to the city I had supposed it was," Twain opined: "a dingy city in a marsh, with rough streets, muddy and lantern-lighted, dividing straight rows of ugly houses all alike." No, Twain continued, "[i]t is a new city; the newest I have ever seen . . . as if it had been built last week." The most striking feature, claimed the American sage, "is the spaciousness, the roominess of the city. There is no other city, in any country, whose streets are so generally wide." Perhaps the amenities of urban modernity offended Twain: "Gas and the electric light are employed with a wasteful liberality, and so, wherever one goes, he has always double ranks of brilliant lights stretching far down into the night." According to Twain, Berlin was "the European Chicago."[20]

It was the Franco-Prussian War and German unification that guaranteed Berlin's future growth and helped to elevate the city in the estimation of foreign observers. For one, Prussia's victory had netted an indemnity of 5 billion francs, extracted from France, which spurred investment in Germany and especially in Berlin. The boom years of the *Gründerzeit,* the "era of foundation," came to a standstill in 1873, however, following a stock market crash in Vienna and the onset of a worldwide depression. But Berlin remained the capital, with all that implied, housing Germany's new federal administration, as well as the German Kaiser, his court, and the government, dominated by Chancellor Otto von Bismarck. According to the new constitution, Berlin hosted Germany's houses of parliament: each of the twenty-five federal states sent delegates to the upper house, the Bundesrat (Federal Council), and the members of the lower house, the Reichstag (National Assembly), were elected by universal male suffrage.[21]

National unification was also the decisive fillip for the city's many industries and their founders, which not even the crash of 1873 could undermine. The Borsig ironworks, established by Berlin blacksmith August Borsig in 1837, had supplied most of Germany's railway stock since the 1840s, and emerged after 1871 as an industrial behemoth with its factory complex northwest of the city. Prussian army officer Werner Siemens, who studied in Berlin, invented a process to insulate overhead wires that could be used along railways. His innovation was first tested along the Berlin–Potsdam line in 1847. The firms that Siemens founded and controlled also helped to lay the first transcontinental and submarine telegraph cables, and in the 1880s he electrified Berlin—quite literally—

with the world's first electric streetcars and streetlights. Siemens's great rival Emil Rathenau studied engineering and worked in the Borsig firm before founding the German Edison Company in 1883—later renamed AEG (Allgemeine Elektricitäts-Gesellschaft)—to manufacture Thomas Edison's inventions in Berlin. Rathenau produced lightbulbs and also built Berlin's first municipal electricity works. The rivalry of Siemens and Rathenau spurred innovation and industrial growth, and helped to create Berlin's reputation—reinforced by Mark Twain—as the "city of light."[22]

As urban historian Peter Hall has claimed, Berlin in the late nineteenth century was "the Silicon Valley of its day."[23] Much of the basic research conducted in the physical and natural sciences at the University of Berlin had direct practical applications for the city's burgeoning industries. The German chemical and pharmaceutical industries grew out of the collaboration of entrepreneurial "lay scientists" and their academic counterparts. Ernst Schering, the son of a Berlin pub owner, opened a small pharmacy in 1852, which expanded quickly by producing chloroform and eventually medicinal cocaine and by pioneering the manufacture of synthetic drugs, inspired and assisted by Berlin professors of medicine. Chemical production was another major industry: in 1867 the chemists Paul Mendelssohn Bartholdy and Carl Alexander von Martius founded a firm for the production of aniline, used to create synthetic dyes. The German chemical giant AGFA emerged from this concern, and led German output in photographic materials, optical tools, and other precision instruments. AGFA also relied on academic chemists—many trained at the University of Berlin—to produce medical supplies and precision machine tools. Its manufacture of synthetic dyes supported the city's fashion and garment industries—including ready-to-wear clothing for men, women, and children—which employed thousands of unskilled sweatshop laborers in the city's southeastern neighborhoods.[24]

Jobs created by Berlin's burgeoning industries lured workers from throughout the German Reich, all the more so after 1873 as smaller manufacturing centers suffered from the economic downturn. Berlin had coped with a housing shortage since the 1860s, but the situation became acute after unification. Speculators invested fortunes to develop new suburbs, which would soon ring the city. East and west of the historic center, manorial estates were purchased for housing developments; potato farmers in Schöneberg retired on the windfall profits from the sale of their small plots. State and city officials attempted to regulate growth with a plan for rectilinear streets and uniform apartment buildings. But the drive to create housing units (and maximize profits) led to the construction of massive five-story complexes that could occupy an entire city block. This dynamic produced the infamous Berlin tenements or "rental barracks"—*Mietskasernen,* a Berlin architectural vernacular—pervasive in the poorer suburbs to the north and east of the city but found throughout the capital. External units had street access, but the cheaper, darker apartments inside could be reached only through a warren of cavernous courtyards. A single apartment complex might have a hundred or more units with a thousand occupants, including small retail stores, taverns, and artisan workshops. The internal courtyards within a Berlin rental barracks formed a small dark universe where children played, women hung laundry, grocers tended their produce, and independent craftsmen plied their trades. Needless to say, these quarters were squalid, poorly lit, and disease ridden.[25]

Not only the poor, however, suffered from the effluences of cramped urban life. Indoor plumbing and running water were rare indeed, and most residents relied on public pumps for drinking water. August Bebel (1840–1913), leader of the German Social Democratic Party, described how Berlin's streets "emitted a truly fearsome smell," lined with open gutters for household waste and raw sewage.[26] Not until the late 1870s was Berlin able to develop a modern sewage system. The impetus to address public hygiene came from Berlin medical professor Rudolf Virchow (the same man who chaired the Prussian Medical Affairs Board that recommended against maintaining the Prussian anti-sodomy statute in 1869). As a Berlin council member, Virchow presented research in 1872 that demonstrated a *climbing* mortality rate among Berlin residents. In response, city officials authorized a commission to study the sewage systems of London and Paris and then undertook a comprehensive project to build a vast web of underground soil lines, which channeled household waste to pumping stations and from there to farms far outside the city's perimeters.

Once underground sewers were in place, extensive indoor plumbing and outdoor public toilets became practical. Although the city had opened its first crude outdoor public facility just south of Unter den Linden in 1841, public accommodations became common only much later. The first ladies' toilets were built in 1879—after significant council debate on the propriety of public restrooms for women—and by 1901 more than a hundred enclosed water closets and pissoirs, including fourteen for women and children only, had been opened, primarily within the old city center.[27]

City fathers also introduced measures to improve hygiene and living conditions for the working poor: municipal utilities outfitted tenements with indoor plumbing and eventually gas and electric power sources. New city regulations eliminated basement apartments and set strict limits on the number of residents permitted to occupy a single flat. By 1892 the city had built a dozen public bathhouses, mainly for the poor, with many more projected for the future.[28] Berlin's emergence by 1900 as one of the most hygienic cities in Europe—after decades of frenzied construction and a population explosion—is truly astonishing. French illustrator and travel writer Charles Huard praised the cleanliness of not only wealthy residential districts but also Berlin's working-class neighborhoods and slums: in comparison to Berlin, Huard wrote in 1907, "Paris is a stable, London a sewer, and New York a pigsty."[29]

Berlin's fearsome expansion was accompanied by the development of one of the world's best urban transportation networks. The city's first long-distance terminals were built well before 1850—at Potsdamer Platz and Schlesisches Tor—but only in the 1870s did they begin to offer more amenities for travelers, including enclosed waiting areas, kiosks, and public toilets. By 1900 twelve railway lines transported visitors from all points in Germany and Europe to the ten long-distance stations that now ringed the city. In 1867 city planners demolished the city's old fortifications (nearly a decade after Vienna's had been torn down), creating the path for an elevated circular or "beltway" train connecting the long-distance railway stations. Initially horse-drawn, the circle line or *Ringbahn* was powered soon after by steam engines. Berlin also maintained public horse-drawn carriages, and provided thirty-six separate tramlines in 1871. These were increased throughout the 1870s and finally replaced by the world's first electric streetcars in the early 1880s. By 1882 the elevated *Stadtbahn* connected the inner city with the expanding suburbs. In 1902 Berlin opened the first leg of what would become an extensive underground subway, two years ahead of New York City.[30]

If Berlin emerged as a model of urban modernity within just a few decades, one of the institutions responsible for this reputation was the police force. To explain the position and role of Berlin's constabulary we must consider the German concept of *Polizei*, a term with broader connotations than its English counterpart. During and after the Protestant Reformation—beginning in the sixteenth century—secular rulers increasingly assumed authorities that had once rested with the Catholic Church; the princes of the disparate German states, including Berlin's Hohenzollern rulers, bolstered their territorial control through the meticulous regulation of their subjects' lives. This meant in practice that state officials, or *Polizei*—in *addition* to general law enforcement— regulated most everyday, urban activities: commerce and exchange; rights of residency; morals violations including adultery; censorship; and even street cleaning. German notions of "policing" preserved elements of this premodern understanding, conferring greater authority, and responsibility, on modern municipal officials. In short, a German police unit did much more than simply apprehend criminals. Shoring up public order demanded constant vigilance and creative innovation, especially in the face of exponential urban growth and the emergence of a new industrial order.

Berlin was also the *Residenz,* or court city, of the ruling Hohenzollern dynasty, heightening the autocratic legacy of the early modern *Polizei.* As such, the city served as an urban military base: some 20 percent of the 100,000 residents in 1780 had been soldiers; in 1900 greater Berlin was still dotted with more than one hundred military institutions and barracks. And Berlin's *royal* police force, the Königliches Polizeipräsidium, was a seamless extension of Prussia's military establishment. Most police officers and all higher-ranking commissioners were both Prussian aristocrats and military officers who began their careers in the elite Prussian officer corps. At the pinnacle of the city's law enforcement pyramid stood Berlin's police president, who received his appointment from the interior minister and served as a member of that department. Drawn from the military elite of Prussia's aristocracy, the Berlin police president and his commissioners represented the Kaiser and his government, not the municipal government or Berlin's citizenry.[31]

Into the twentieth century, Berlin's police presidents exercised office with expansive powers, conferred by the grace of the German Kaiser. As the American lawyer Raymond Fosdick explained in a 1915 study of European constabularies (commissioned by John D. Rockefeller), "[T]he German citizen is always confronted by newly adopted police regulations. Thus in Berlin, the police president has recently issued ordinances regulating the color of automobiles, the length of hatpins and the methods of purchasing fish and fowl. He has decreed that a prospective purchaser shall not touch a shad in order to determine whether there is any roe and shall not handle a fowl to verify the market woman's praise of its tenderness. Each such ordinance provides a penalty for violation."[32] These officious and petty regulations illustrate well the tremendous authority, for better or ill, that the police president and his underlings maintained over all aspects of the everyday conduct of Berlin's residents.

As undemocratic as they were, such extensive powers gave Berlin's police great flexibility for dealing with intractable problems, including the enforcement of Paragraph 175. A perfect illustration of this was Berlin police commissioner Hüllessem's initiative to create the "Department of Homosexuals" (Homosexuellen Dezernat) in 1885, just after the raid of Seeger's Restaurant. There was little precedent for this new department, and its creation suggests the extensive character of Berlin's homosexual subculture. Hüllessem was able to use it, moreover, to formalize older policing strategies and to introduce a general principle of tolerating homosexual bars and entertainments. We know that the police had monitored men considered to be habitual violators of the anti-sodomy statute since at least the 1860s. The alleged murderer Zastrow, who was convicted of sexual assault and sodomy in 1869, had been known to police long before his arrest; reportedly his name was entered on a special *Päderastenlist* (list of pederasts). The man whose denunciation led to Zastrow's arrest had been a paid police informant. These tactics were applied more vigorously throughout the 1870s—as memories lingered of the sadistic murders ascribed to Zastrow—and the suspects of same-sex "perversion" were kept under close watch, often with the assistance of spies. By about 1880, the police introduced plainclothes investigators, who patrolled public parks and actively entrapped suspected homosexuals.[33]

Hüllessem knew firsthand the difficulty of policing Berlin's public spaces and recognized that the proliferation of homosexual locales might actually simplify his job. The introduction of the Department of Homosexuals was almost certainly intended to help pursue a policy of qualified toleration, following as it did the raid of Seeger's Restaurant and corresponding likewise to Berlin's rapid growth. As the city expanded geographically, a policy of monitoring every park and public space was no longer cost-effective or even realistic. So instead of aggressively interdicting *potentially* illegal sexual activity—which would drive it underground and out of view—the new approach was to tolerate homosexual fraternization within certain limits.[34]

Hüllessem's response to Paragraph 175—arguably quite progressive— reflected his creative approach to law enforcement more generally. An aristocratic, Prussian army lieutenant, he had joined the police in 1873 at the age of twenty-four. Throughout his career, his interests in science and in the application of new policing methods were important factors in his professional success. In 1876 Hüllessem organized Berlin's first mug shot albums (*Verbrecheralbum*), organized by crime, to identify and apprehend repeat offenders.[35] Before photography, detectives relied on crude physical descriptions; now mug shots allowed victims to identify their assailants, which assisted the investigation of crimes. Only in its infancy as a tool of law enforcement, photography had recently been adopted by police departments in London and Paris; New York would soon follow.[36] Hüllessem trumpeted other novel investigative techniques, including anthropometry—the failed science of measuring a criminal's physical features—which was pioneered by the famous French criminologist Alphonse Bertillon (1853–1914), whose tutelage Hüllessem sought in Paris in 1895. Although anthropometry was soon abandoned, in Berlin and elsewhere, Hüllessem also spearheaded the application of a more useful science, dactylography, or fingerprinting, which proved to be far more effective for investigating crimes and their perpetrators.[37]

Even before he founded the Department of Homosexuals in 1885,

Hüllessem had augmented the collection of mug shots with a special volume devoted to "pederasts." This album was an extension of the special lists of suspected homosexuals kept since at least the 1860s.[38] The pederast label was ambiguous, of course, and the police included male prostitutes, men who had sex with men, men who wore women's clothing, and men who preyed sexually on children. At its inception, the photo volume included thirty-four images. This number grew sixfold by 1890, and by a factor of nearly ten by 1895, with more than three hundred images. The number of photos increased dramatically into the twentieth century, reaching nearly a thousand on the eve of the First World War. Police officials photographed most men detained under suspicion of violating Paragraph 175. A majority of those arrested were involved in prostitution or other criminal activity, and of course the number recorded in the *Verbrecheralbum* greatly exceeded those who were ever successfully prosecuted.[39]

What the *Verbrecheralbum* represented above all was a system of surveillance that helped Hüllessem and his subordinates to monitor individuals within Berlin's homosexual community. If we consider Hüllessem's approach more carefully, we can begin to appreciate how the Department of Homosexuals contributed to the *creation* of Berlin's community of sexual minorities. Hüllessem knew and used the term "homosexual," a neologism from 1869, as we have seen, that was just entering German psychiatric literature (although not the popular idiom). This suggests that he had some familiarity with the most recent medical literature and that he might have adopted the view that homosexuality was inborn or congenital. In this sense the Department of Homosexuals actually gave life to a theoretical construct—the theory of the inborn homosexual—by projecting it as a social and cultural identity and allowing it to develop within a network of bars and same-sex entertainments.

Hüllessem helped further to create this milieu by making it an object of study. He literally gave tours of the city's homosexual nightspots and escorted visitors to same-sex costume balls. Berlin came to serve as a kind of laboratory of sexuality, made available for investigation to a range of psychiatrists, sexologists, journalists, and popular writers. The experience of playwright August Strindberg (1849–1912) at the Café National in February 1893 illustrates this brilliantly. Accompanying other friends who had been invited by a Berlin "Police Inspector" (presumably Hüllessem), Strindberg described his astonishment (and disgust), always referring to himself in the third person as "the author":

> It was the most horrible thing he had ever seen. In order that a better check might be kept on them, the perverts of the capital had been given permission to hold a fancy-dress ball. When it opened everyone behaved ceremoniously, almost as if they were in a madhouse. Men danced with men, mournfully, with deadly seriousness. . . . The one playing the lady's role might have the moustache of a cavalryman and pince-nez, he might be ugly, with coarse, masculine features, and not even a trace of femininity. . . . The Police Inspector and his guests had seated themselves at a table in the centre of one end of the room, close to which all the couples had to pass. . . . The Inspector called them by their Christian names and summoned some of the most interesting among them to his table, so that the author could study them! . . . In the female section, where women danced with women, the most noteworthy person was a stately lady. . . . Her eyes followed a radiant young blonde. The Inspector informed them that the two were bound together by a passionate love for each other, and that, as the elder woman was poor, the younger one supported her by selling herself to men she abhorred.[40]

Apart from his visceral repulsion, Strindberg's strongest reaction was to the ball's openness and the official surveillance. The "Police Inspector" did not even disguise his presence and actually knew and greeted the participants by name.

Simply *allowing* the growth of a homosexual culture contributed to the burgeoning science of sexology. In one pathbreaking work, the first of its kind, published in 1891, Berlin psychiatrist Albert Moll thanked Hüllessem for helping him with his urban ethnography and for allowing him to view internal police and trial documents on cases related to Paragraph 175.[41] The illustrious Richard von Krafft-Ebing thanked Hüllessem for his assistance in the 1893 edition of *Psychopathia sexualis*.[42] These examples illustrate a seeming paradox of Hüllessem's policies. The self-serving strategy of tolerating bars and other entertainments was intended to enhance surveillance and control; all the while it raised the profile of Berlin's same-sex milieu, giving it far greater publicity and significance than it would have otherwise enjoyed. Although Hüllessem's brilliant career was cut short by a scandal, which implicated him in a massive cover-up to protect a powerful friend accused of rape—leading to the commissioner's suicide in 1900—Hüllessem's legacy survived his premature death. The investigative techniques he introduced—and more significantly for our interests, his attitude toward Berlin's sexual minorities—played a tremendous role in establishing a modern homosexual identity.[43]

The published medical, literary, and popular accounts that Hüllessem facilitated are also some of the most important sources for reconstructing the evolution of same-sex sociability in Berlin before the First World War.[44] Unlike earlier literature, many of these publications mentioned the many venues of Berlin's homosexual nightlife. Albert Moll's 1891 study, for example, described numerous public venues, including small pubs, restaurants, and Bierkeller. Moll relied on Hüllessem, and also enlisted the expertise of a Berlin editor, Adolf Glaser, whose bona fides included his arrest in 1878 on Paragraph 175 charges. Moll even alluded to Seeger's Restaurant and the policy of toleration that had since been adopted, explaining that raids "happen seldom now in these locales." Although pubs opened and closed with relative frequency, according to Moll, decorum "in comparison to early times" had improved, allowing the establishments to operate without police interference. Overtly sexual behavior was not tolerated, Moll claimed, but there was no mistaking the homosexual character of the clientele and their interactions. At some bars the patrons appeared in drag, and many adopted female nicknames—most used the labels "sister" (Schwester) or "aunt" (Tante) to refer to friends and lovers.[45] Another work, Die Enterbten des Liebesglückes oder das dritte Geschlecht (Those dispossessed of love or the third sex), appeared in 1893 under the pseudonym Otto de Joux. Unlike Moll, the author claimed to be homosexual himself, and—with an insider's access—used oral testimonies, journals, memoirs, and creative works from a wide circle of homosexual friends and acquaintances. In addition to bars, clubs, and costume balls, "de Joux" described homosexual marriages (*Urning-Ehen*), clandestine gay societies with secret codes, and privately printed *Urning* almanacs.[46]

One of the most important chroniclers of Berlin's homosexual milieu, sexologist and homosexual rights activist Dr. Magnus Hirschfeld, cooperated closely with Hüllessem and with his successor, Hans von Tresckow, who directed the Department of Homosexuals after Hüllessem's death in 1900. In his *Berlins drittes Geschlecht* (Berlin's third sex) from 1904, Hirschfeld identified fifteen bars and taverns, and he claimed in 1914 to know of at least thirty-eight Berlin establishments that catered primarily to homosexuals and lesbians.[47] Like Hüllessem before him, Tresckow supported the investigations of other psychiatrists, journalists, and popular authors. Both psychiatrist Paul Näcke and sexologist Iwan Bloch were given expert tours of Berlin's homosexual clubs for their scholarly studies. French and Swiss journalists Oscar Méténier, Octave Mirbeau, Henri de Weindel, and F. P. Fischer reported on Berlin's increasingly notorious, public homosexual culture in the decade before the First World War to Francophone audiences. Even American sociologist Abraham Flexner received a tour for his study of European prostitution published in 1914.[48]

These sources document not only a surprising number of homosexual establishments but also their remarkable longevity. Clearly this reflected the tacit toleration established by Hüllessem after 1885. Although the oldest bars—contemporaneous with Seeger's and located just south of Unter den Linden—disappeared by about 1900, at least one, the Krause Kasino, which had opened in a cramped basement in the 1870s, remained in business as late as 1910.[49] After about 1890 new locales opened in Berlin's southern and eastern neighborhoods, along Potsdamer Straße to the southwest, and even in the north. Most of these were neighborhood affairs that catered primarily to their immediate communities. For example, the Hannemann Bar, named for its manager, Gustav Hannemann, opened in 1892 at 123 Alexandrinenstraße. The tavern attracted a crowd of "respectable" older men and enjoyed the "best reputation" with police and neighbors, who never "took offense that homosexuals came and went." One source reported that Hannemann's was "one of the oldest bars in Berlin and thrived for decades without complaint."[50] Around the block at 62 Brandenburgstraße was the Schöne Müllerin, the feminized nickname of owner Otto Müller, who ran his bar from 1906 until it closed in 1921. An accomplished pianist, Müller entertained his guests in drag. "The entire neighborhood knew *what was up with her* [Müller]," according to the insider's guide *Das perverse Berlin*, "but she [Müller] was nevertheless a popular presence."[51] Restaurant Frohsinn had a similar profile at 4 Willibald-Alexis-Straße, a few blocks further south, where the Bavarian Peter Sonnenholzer opened for business in 1903. Although the management changed several times, the Frohsinn endured as a same-sex venue into the 1930s.[52]

By 1900 several distinctly working-class locales had opened in the city's eastern neighborhoods. One tavern along Müncheberger Straße in the blue-collar district of Friedrichshain was staid and respectable, patronized by laborers. "The majority of the same-sex-oriented men who flirt with each other there come from the working class," according to one observer. "They slave away the entire week so they can enjoy a Sunday evening indulging their tendencies. . . . And when they go to the voting booth, they vote as workers, always and without exception— Social-Democratic." The tavern had such a respectable reputation that "the police do not consider it necessary to impose their 11 pm closing."[53] By contrast, a second working-class bar on nearby Weberstraße was subjected to constant surveillance. Hans Ostwald reported in 1906 that the venue was rowdy and "the police keep a sharp and watchful eye." With an uncommonly large backroom, the bar also served as a dance hall for same-sex costume balls.[54]

At least two locales had opened in northern Berlin by the early 1900s. An establishment on Kleine Hamburger Straße just north of the Museumsinsel was run by a former soldier, *"der dicke Franz"*—the fat Franz— assisted by his male piano player "Rita" and a "large-breasted waitress named Minka," who was actually a man in woman's garb. Regulars played skat at small tables, and the bar sponsored youth dances on Saturday and Sunday. Further north a small locale along Ackerstraße served middle-aged and older men who lived in the neighborhood.[55] Although most homosexual venues after 1900 were located south of the center city, the bars in northern Berlin—like their southern Berlin counterparts and the working-class taverns of Friedrichshain—were integrated into their immediate neighborhoods, where they offered local homosexuals the sociability and entertainment of a same-sex-oriented milieu.

The upscale homosexual cafés of Wilhelmine Berlin served a more exclusive public of professionals, businessmen, and aristocrats, who likely lived in the burgeoning western suburbs. The Café Dorian Gray opened its doors in 1905 on Kleiststraße, close to Nollendorfplatz. It was one of the first bars in a neighborhood that—by the 1920s—would become a center of Berlin's homosexual nightlife. An obvious reference to Oscar Wilde, the name would have been recognized only by insiders, since Wilde's novel had only just been published in German translation.[56] The Mikado, at 15 Puttkamerstraße, just south of central Berlin, was perhaps the most stylish homosexual bar before 1914. Fashioned after a "Japanese Teahouse" with "Oriental" silk screens and paper lanterns, the Mikado was considered especially reputable: the bar's proprietor took the men's bathroom door off its hinges so that no one—especially the police—could claim that "indecent activities took place there."[57] Opened in 1907, the Mikado drew a late-evening crowd and became a hangout for members of Berlin's homosexual rights movement, including the author and activist Adolf Brand. In 1896 Brand had begun publishing Der Eigene, described as the world's first homosexual journal, which was offered for sale at the Mikado. A member of Hirschfeld's Scientific-Humanitarian Committee, Baron Willibald von Sadler-Grün, known as "the Baroness," was also a regular and played piano there, usually in drag. The avant-garde art critic and journalist Emil Szittya recalled that "the homosexuals have a great affection for Christmas." The Mikado, Szittya explained, would plan its Christmas Eve festivities throughout the year so that these "sentimental, rejected men," without other family, could sing "religious songs" dressed in women's clothing "under the Christmas tree."[58] (By the 1920s, the Mikado had become one of Berlin's best-known transvestite bars and therefore was an immediate target of the Nazis in 1933.) Two nearby venues along Potsdamerstraße, Café Continental and Café Imperial, attracted a "mixed" public of homosexuals and others, but like the Mikado they were considered well-heeled.[59]

·   ·   ·

In addition to bars and cafés, large same-sex costume balls held in concert halls, theaters, and private clubs became a signal feature of Berlin's
homosexual culture. The earliest account of these events came from
Karl Heinrich Ulrichs, who described an "Urning costume ball," sponsored by a rich Polish count and held in a Berlin restaurant: "Ten handsome soldiers, all Dionings [heterosexuals] were selected to attend, and
among the Urnings, six wore women's clothing."[60] Hugo Friedländer
confirmed this, claiming that homosexual and transvestite balls had
been common since the 1860s.[61] As early as 1886, *Die Verbrecherwelt von
Berlin* (The criminal world of Berlin) reported that elaborate same-sex
costume balls, or *Puppenbälle* (from *Puppe,* the Berlin slang for male prostitute), were held in prominent public venues, lasting late into the night,
with half of the male participants attired in women's evening gowns.
Moll, Hirschfeld, Krafft-Ebing, and many others attended these events
and described them as well-organized, seasonal affairs held in the most
prominent Berlin theaters and banquet halls, often attracting five hundred or more participants.[62]

The homosexual balls of Wilhelmine Berlin were generally open,
and required official permission like any public entertainment, including concerts or theater productions. Throughout the prewar period,
Berlin's individual police precincts were responsible for reviewing per-
mit requests, which required a detailed description of time, venue, the
character of the event, and an application period of two days. Owners
of the largest theaters and dance halls were able to apply for annual permits allowing them to rent their spaces to event planners. Since bar and
restaurant concessions generally disallowed dancing, and owners faced
fines if they failed to enforce this prohibition, the formal permits for
dancing events were especially coveted and often quite lucrative.[63]

Although rarely identified, the impresarios who organized the balls
were likely owners or managers of other homosexual bars. Hugo
Friedländer mentioned the balls planned by "N" in the "Dresdener
Kasino" and those of "L." held in the "Central-Theater" as especially
popular.[64] The frequency of the "Homo-Balls" is difficult to determine,
although by 1900 they appeared to follow the patterns of the conventional ball season, commencing in November and continuing into the
spring with specially themed balls. The venues included Berlin's most
prestigious addresses: the Deutschen Kaiser, the Philharmonie, the

Orpheum, the Buggenhagen Theater, and the König von Portugal, in addition to the Dresdener and Central. The largest of these spaces accommodated more than a thousand people. Particularly opulent evenings might begin with a sumptuous buffet dinner, followed by all-night dancing and an early-morning breakfast. The expense must have been formidable, and a large costume ball also generated significant demand for hospitality services, musicians, tailors, and even coach drivers.[65]

These same-sex costume balls established a reputation that extended well beyond the homosexual community. As Berlin journalist Konstantin Grell explained, "If one goes, perhaps in the company of a well-known police official, one is astonished to encounter many familiar faces, who of course only want to witness the scandal first hand but were able all the same to acquire tickets through an acquaintance. The tickets are nowhere on offer, and the promoters sell them only to insiders. Of course there are no announcements for such original entertainments."[66] Whether the many acquaintances Grell surprisingly encountered were merely "slumming" tourists, as they claimed, or more intimately involved in Berlin's homosexual nightlife is unclear. Grell implied that admission tickets were sold directly by the event planners, perhaps in the homosexual locales that they owned or managed. The events were not advertised, as Grell claimed—and only when censorship laws were relaxed after 1918 was such promotion possible—though *accounts* of the balls were sometimes published after the fact in the Berlin press. As early as 1894, the *Berliner Zeitung* included a lengthy description of a same-sex costume ball (*Maskenball*) under the heading "Ball for the Enemies of Women" (*Ball der Weiberfeinde*).[67] A report on another ball was printed in the *Berliner Morgenpost* in 1899. According to this piece, the event got under way on a Friday evening a little before midnight in the main hall of the hotel King of Portugal, attended by several hundred men, roughly half of whom wore women's clothing.[68]

Grell suggested likewise that the balls were a magnet for journalists, authors, and other urban ethnographers. Like Grell himself, Oscar Méténier, a naturalist author and former Parisian police officer, explored Berlin's homosexual subculture for a French-language work published in 1904. Naturally Méténier's study required the requisite visit to a homosexual ball:

> We were deposited in front of the brilliant façade of a theater known as the Dresdener Casino. In a broad vestibule the bouncer took our coats, and another determined that we had the necessary invitations. Finally we were admitted through double doors into an enormous, richly decorated hall flanked by columns. I remained standing, dazzled and stupefied. Before me was a crowd of four or five hundred, dancing to an orchestra—excellent like all German orchestras—hidden behind a platform. All or nearly all the dancers were wearing costumes. Only here and there in the swirl of color could one detect the black jacket of the police officers. We slowly made our way to an unoccupied table not far from the buffet. Many of the dancers were wearing women's clothing.[69]

Certainly Méténier had been briefed before attending and had some idea what to expect. But his astonishment is palpable: not even the rumors in Paris could convey adequately what transpired in Berlin.

The costume balls drew obvious curiosity seekers—without psychiatric or literary interests—who rarely recorded their impressions. However, one retired Prussian officer, Paul von Hoverbeck, described an early-twentieth-century visit to a *Balllokal* in eastern Berlin in his 1926 memoir: "I'll never forget the scene. Hundreds of men and women of all ages, most made-up, many of the men attired as women and many of the women as men. As we entered the brightly lit hall, the entire crowd knew that we were curiosity seekers accompanied by police officials."[70] The impression Hoverbeck conveys is that regular ball participants—namely, homosexuals and lesbians—had come to expect, like the animal inmates of a municipal zoo, both curious outsiders and official surveillance. Indeed, the common element in all these accounts, strikingly, beginning with Moll's 1891 study, was a police presence, which facilitated in turn the visits of uninitiated observers and helped to make known this distinctive, eccentric sexual minority of imperial Berlin.

Commissioner Hüllessem was far less tolerant of male prostitution, for which Berlin had a notorious reputation. As early as 1782 one scurrilous travel guide described "boy bordellos" and furtive networks of "warm

brothers."[71] Nineteenth-century accounts of crime in Berlin often mentioned the young men and especially the soldiers who sold themselves
for sex. Lacking the specialized knowledge of "homosexuality," internal
police reports from the 1840s and '50s sometimes hinted at male prostitution, using expressions such as "depravity" or "moral turpitude" to
describe the activities in certain city taverns that attracted both adolescent and adult male patrons. Published accounts describe the outdoor
locations where men sought illicit contacts: the Tiergarten Park, Unter
den Linden, and the copse of chestnut trees just north of the university. Such established sites for prostitution and cruising were augmented
in the second half of the nineteenth century with newly opened public
toilets, the canals, the expanded railway stations, and other commercial centers. When the Friedrichstraße train station opened in 1882, it
served as the northern terminus of the north-south Friedrichstraße,
which formed a T with Unter den Linden just east of the Brandenburg
Gate before conducting traffic to the Hallesches Gate. This thoroughfare gained notoriety as an all-purpose market for male and female
prostitutes who congregated in the Passage, a six-story corner structure
completed in 1874 with a covered market full of shops, cafés, and eater-
ies.[72] Berlin's particular reputation for male prostitution extended well
beyond Germany: in his authoritative comparative study of European
prostitution, published in 1914, American sociologist Abraham Flexner
described Berlin as Europe's "main mart" for homosexual hustlers.[73]

Into the twentieth century, Unter den Linden and the Tiergarten
Park remained Berlin's best-recognized cruising locations for men seeking erotic male companionship, as well as for those prepared to buy
or sell it. The southwest corner of the park, in the area surrounding
the Goldfish Pond, was especially well trafficked, accessed along the
so-called *schwuler Weg,* or gay path.[74] It was here in 1904 that a young
Kurt Hiller (1885–1972), the communist author and homosexual rights
activist, reported meeting an older male prostitute whom he paid for his
first homosexual encounter.[75] In 1911 the police president, Traugott von
Jagow (1865–1941), requested that this section of the park be outfitted
with gas lighting. Jagow wrote the Berlin City Council, "I have received
many complaints, also from those who manage the Tiergarten, that certain sections of the Park have become meeting places at night for male

homosexuals. . . . But we are unable to take significant action unfortunately, because no punishable crime [under Paragraph 175] is committed there, and instead the rendezvous are arranged for elsewhere." Within a year the city had managed to install some three dozen "efficient" gas lanterns, and "without damaging tree roots or other foliage."[76]

The relationship between male and heterosexual prostitution was complex and variable, not only within Germany but also throughout Europe, depending on national, regional, and even local ordinances. Germany had no federal statutes governing male prostitution, since Paragraph 175 criminalized "sodomy." The criminal code was ambiguous, however, on the question of female prostitution; although federal law banned "procurement" (Kuppelei), it likewise authorized the police to register female prostitutes and force them to submit to medical exams, a formal if implicit sanctioning of the world's oldest profession.[77] In 1888 the German Supreme Court interpreted the prohibition on heterosexual procurement as a ban on pimping and brothel keeping. The application of the law after this decision varied dramatically from place to place, however, reflecting the independence of urban and regional officials. A few German cities continued to tolerate brothels, despite their proscription by the supreme court ruling, notably Hamburg and Leipzig. Others, such as Bremen, adopted an "internment" policy (Kasernierung), which required that prostitutes live and work within a restricted area, creating de facto red-light districts. Property owners in these districts often received formal municipal licenses allowing them to rent to prostitutes. Most German cities adopted registration policies, though these were also applied with great variation. In some locations prostitutes were required to register with the police, while in others registration was voluntary. The specific Berlin regulations included a prohibition on brothels (in place since the mid-nineteenth century), and a free-will or voluntary registration. While prostitutes were allowed to live throughout the city, streetwalking was banned on main thoroughfares such as Unter den Linden.[78] These rules were enforced by Berlin's morals police, the Sittenpolizei, which had extensive personnel for monitoring the heterosexual demimonde.

The Department of Homosexuals was under a different administrative unit—a subdivision of the criminal police—and lacked the resources to monitor male prostitutes with the same diligence.[79] As boys or young men, moreover, male prostitutes had greater freedom of movement and could cruise most public areas with relative impunity. Male prostitutes were also spared the degrading scrutiny of forced medical exams, despite posing a public health risk as potential agents of venereal disease. Male prostitutes were generally less recognizable than their female counterparts, though there was significant variation. Kurt Hiller described his Tiergarten contact as "masculine," "muscular," and "mature," meaning a man in his mid-twenties. Soldier prostitutes actually solicited in uniform, which signaled strength and virility. But many adolescent male prostitutes rouged their cheeks, plucked their eyebrows, wore lipstick, and assumed feminine nicknames. Some even appeared in public attired as women, although this could attract police attention or incite the anger of some unsuspecting heterosexual john. More conspicuous manners and attire subjected male prostitutes to greater surveillance, of course, and their photos were typically entered in the *Verbrecheralbum* after an initial arrest.[80]

It was also common for male and female prostitutes to share working and living quarters; sometimes they were even coupled or married. The newspaper account of a 1904 police raid offers an evocative portrayal of one milieu: "The area around Oranienburger Gate houses a large number of dive bars, most located in rear courtyards, where business only begins in the early morning hours. When the *Variétés* and the evening cafés close, then the big-city night owls flutter to this spot. Here in the wan lamplight and thick tobacco smoke the night is lengthened. Often only with the street noise that penetrates an open door comes the warning that a new day is dawning outside."[81]

This was the scene of the raid of a bar located off Novalisstraße, remarkable only for its location *directly across* from the police precinct house in north-central Berlin. The area was noted for its large tenement buildings and labyrinthine courtyards. Neither noise nor alleged prostitution prompted the bust-up, however. Rather, a thousand marks had gone missing from the precinct house earlier in the day and was presumed stolen by an occupant of the all-night tavern. According to the newspaper account, police herded some two dozen female *and* male prostitutes into the street, demanded identification, and transported those without papers to the central station at Alexanderplatz.[82] Clearly female prostitutes and rent boys not only formed close associations and even rented common quarters but also shared work spaces that served men of every sexual persuasion. In some cases married couples pursued prostitution as a family business. The male barkeep of the Haase-Ausschank, a small tavern that attracted male prostitutes and was located conveniently at the southern edge of the Tiergarten near the city's foremost homosexual cruising area, was himself a prostitute who pimped for his wife, likewise a prostitute.[83]

Although Hüllessem's policies prevented most male prostitutes from plying their trade indoors, at least before the 1920s, a few particularly disreputable bars—such as the Haase-Ausschank—served male prostitutes and their clients. One of the best known was the Katzenmutter, along the Waterloo Canal just east of Hallesches Gate. The bar was likely named for its numerous pet cats, or for the cat motifs on the walls, or possibly for the catlike appearance of Wilhelmine Techow, who managed the place. Exactly when the bar opened is unclear, but Techow had lived in the building since before 1885. Located close to several military barracks, the area was notorious for soldier prostitution, and the canal was popular for homosexual cruising. The bar itself served both soldiers and homosexual johns, facilitating assignations. Psychiatrist Paul Näcke described it as two small rooms on the ground floor, packed with men, half of whom were soldiers. "Here is the main place," according to Näcke, "where one can *have* soldiers, and although most are heterosexual, they are always keen to earn something on the side." Another observer claimed that "a significant portion of the history of homosexuality had unfolded at the Katzenmutter in the last two decades." Not only military personnel but also "blue-blooded, landed aristocrats with endless genealogies, workers with calloused hands—all sat together in the small, lowly restaurant of the Katzenmutter." The bar's profile changed dramatically, however, in the wake of the Eulenburg scandal (discussed in detail in chapter 4), when, in 1908, army officials placed the Katzenmutter on a list of bars prohibited to soldiers.[84]

Hüllessem and his successors were especially diligent in thwarting pimping and brothel keeping, neither of which was tolerated among heterosexuals. There are many examples that illustrate this priority. One would-be pimp, an out-of-work actor named Gustav Haupt, formed a partnership with the merchant Karl Moscholl and then opened for business in a dingy apartment at 21 Mohrenstraße, located a few blocks south of Unter den Linden. Recruiting male prostitutes straight off the streets, Haupt and Moscholl cultivated a wealthy clientele and enhanced their profits by robbing their disrobed johns. Of course, these victims of theft avoided the police for fear of a second and more figurative exposure. By the time an anonymous tip led to the apprehension of the pimps in 1902, they had operated the boy brothel for nearly two years.[85] The enterprising merchant Fritz Geßler, a tobacconist who specialized in cigars, used the backroom of his shop as a boy bordello. A newspaper account of his arrest described the reaction of neighbors, who had marveled at the apparent uptick in his business and the boisterous traffic in and out of his small store. Geßler was finally arrested in May 1905, but only because he and his rent boys had become greedy and begun blackmailing the customers.[86] Another procurer, a young man named Wittenberg, abducted a fourteen-year-old in Hamburg, brought him to Berlin, pimped him on Friedrichstraße, and then blackmailed his patrons. Until Wittenberg's arrest in May 1906, the two lived comfortably in a small hotel in central Berlin.[87] Prostitution was only one line of business for these pimps and brothel keepers, who likely earned much more from robbing and extorting their clients.

As in most cities, Berlin's prostitution often had links to the city's criminal underworld. According to Hans Ostwald, the popular author and lay sociologist of the Berlin demimonde, prostitution was a symbiotic feature of organized crime. Magnus Hirschfeld claimed that "prostitution and criminality go hand in hand; thefts and break-ins, blackmail and extortion, and violent acts of every kind."[88] A gang of eight thieves arrested in March 1898 embodied this all-purpose deviancy. Employed as house servants, butchers' apprentices, grill cooks, and barkeeps, according to one newspaper report, these youths appeared to earn their pocket money as rent boys and shoplifters, and they spent much of their free time dressed in women's garb. They were apparently successful passing themselves off as women, for they descended on department stores, en masse, where they stole large quantities of merchandise, which was later recovered from the ringleader's apartment. In drag they used nicknames like "Die Schöne" (the pretty one), "Schminkjuste" (Juste in makeup), and "Seiden-Guste" (Gustav in silk), and solicited sex at the Katzenmutter.[89]

The relationship between female prostitution and homosexual sub-cultures is especially important since policies regulating prostitution—in most times and places—generally shaped early homosexual milieus. In most cities the first identifiable homosexual neighborhoods tended to border or even overlap with heterosexual red-light districts. Consider Montmartre in Paris, Soho in London, or the Tenderloin in San Fran-cisco. In the German cities of Munich, Hamburg, Frankfurt, Cologne, and Leipzig, the oldest homosexual venues were likewise opened in and around areas designated for the heterosexual demimonde. Berlin's policies had a more tenuous impact, however, on the city's homosexual scene. For one, the prohibition on brothels and the rejection of "intern-ment" policies prevented the emergence of any single red-light neighbor-hood. As a result, Berlin's same-sex bars, entertainments, and outdoor cruising areas were geographically diffuse.

Even more significant than the policies that regulated prostitution in Berlin was Hüllessem's tacit toleration for "respectable" taverns and pub-lic drag balls. By permitting "homosexual fraternization," Hüllessem and his successors fostered safe, separate spaces, apart from the sexual underworld of street solicitation or an established red-light district. The boundaries of Berlin's more staid homosexual club culture were never impermeable. Male prostitution venues such as the Haase-Ausschank or Katzenmutter attracted "criminal elements," certainly, and skirted the limits of official toleration. Yet the open character and longevity of so many homosexual taverns fostered a new homosexual eroticism that was liberated from the shadow of a semi-criminal sex trade.

The men who did patronize male prostitutes made themselves particu-larly vulnerable to blackmail, a crime that was clearly not victimless. Because of both Paragraph 175 and the social stigma of homosexual-ity, same-sex-loving men faced far greater risk of scandal. By contrast, nineteenth-century bourgeois ideology tacitly sanctioned straight pros-titution to "absorb" the surfeit of male sexuality and "preserve" the more delicate sexual natures of elite and middle-class women. This double standard endorsed male promiscuity and tended to shield heterosexual johns. Of course, the customers of male prostitutes risked not only exposure as homosexuals but also arrest and possibly jail time. The young men and boys who prostituted themselves understood the vulnerability of their patrons. As historian Angus McLaren has argued, sexual blackmail in the nineteenth century was nearly synonymous with homosexual scandal and was largely a product of the increased awareness of erotic same-sex love.[90]

Hüllessem had confronted the problem throughout his career, and finally in 1896 he renamed his unit the Department of Homosexuals and Blackmailers.[91] The curious pairing of two seemingly incongruous phenomena—blackmail *and* homosexuality—demonstrates well the extent to which blackmail threats accompanied illegal sexual acts. Long before this, of course, Hüllessem's mug shot album had subsumed sexual blackmail under the rubric of crimes related to Paragraph 175; it was an article of faith that most rent boys also blackmailed their clients. Under the new title, the department was formally responsible for policing "pederasty and the offenses related to this, including blackmail or the creation of public disturbance through exhibitionism."[92]

Middle-class and elite men—those able to pay and motivated to preserve a social reputation—were at greatest risk. This helps to explain Hüllessem's concern, of course. But it oversimplifies to describe the pursuit of blackmailers as little more than a form of class-based justice. Indeed, elites and bourgeois men who had sex with other men or boys were also closely monitored; Hüllessem had maintained a collection of index cards with the names of aristocrats, military officers, and business leaders suspected of homosexual liaisons. Since 1885 Hüllessem had apparently safeguarded the reputation of his own superior, Berlin police president Richthofen, who allegedly caroused with young men. Hüllessem feared, presciently, that the exposure of Richthofen (or others like him)—a risk heightened by the threat of blackmail—could directly affect affairs of state. Shortly before his suicide in 1900, Hüllessem asked a friend to deliver some one hundred of these index cards to the emperor. William II refused to open the packet, afraid of finding names of associates or even family members, and sent it unopened to the police president.[93] Hüllessem's index cards represented the new reality that aristocrats and other elites could no longer indulge their "perversions" indiscriminately. In this respect blackmail proved a powerful leveling force. Wealth or title offered little protection, since even those with great resources might one day be branded homosexuals.

One of the most jarring scandals involved Germany's wealthiest industrialist, the "Canon King," Friedrich Alfred Krupp, and led to his apparent suicide in 1902 at the age of forty-eight. Long before Krupp's alleged escapades came to light, Hüllessem and Tresckow had cataloged the magnate's interests in adolescent boys. Although the palatial Krupp villa was located near Essen, Krupp spent much of his time on the island of Capri, in the Gulf of Naples, or in Berlin, both sites for pursuing his greatest passion. When visiting the capital, Krupp always stayed in the Bristol Hotel, where he was attended by Italian boys recruited from Capri. Disturbed by Krupp's interference with his management—namely, Krupp's insistence that his young friends be employed by the hotel, albeit at Krupp's own expense—hotel owner Conrad Uhl, fearing a scandal that might besmirch his own good name, approached Tresckow to discuss the problem. At this point Tresckow also learned that Krupp's wife and two daughters lodged in a different hotel when accompanying him to Berlin.

Though unrelated to blackmail, Krupp's downfall was clearly the result of newspaper reports about his alleged homosexual activity. Italian officials banished Krupp in the spring of 1902 for having sex with minors. The great irony was that Italy did not otherwise have an anti-sodomy law; technically Krupp's crime was sex with minors, not homosexuality. Italian papers reported on the affair, and *Vorwärts,* the official organ of the Social Democratic Party, decided to torment the class enemy by publishing the story, on October 20, 1902. Krupp, in turn, considered bringing charges of libel. Before taking this step, however, he sent his personal secretary to confer with and sound out Tresckow. The commissioner recommended that Krupp take legal action only if his "conscience were clear," since Krupp otherwise risked perjuring himself in court, which could create even more trouble. The day after this interview, on November 22, Tresckow learned that Krupp had died under mysterious circumstances.

Krupp's funeral was attended by the Kaiser himself, who blamed the Social Democratic press for the defamation that led to Krupp's "heart failure." The consensus of most contemporaries, including Commissioner Tresckow, however, was that Krupp chose to end his life rather than explain the accounts published in *Vorwärts*.[94] A telling and extended postscript to the story was that there were repeated attempts to blackmail Krupp's widow with alleged evidence of her deceased husband's homosexuality. The first such attempt was mentioned in the *Berliner Tageblatt* in September 1905: a young man posing as a former associate of Krupp's claimed to possess incriminating letters, which he offered the widow for an exorbitant price. She balked and managed to have the young man arrested, although he was later released.[95] In 1910 a fifty-seven-year-old writer received a thirty-month jail term for attempting to extort Mrs. Krupp by threatening to publish a salacious tell-all book about the alleged exploits of her husband.[96]

After the press began publishing stories about the sexual scandals of prominent figures, would-be blackmailers gained even greater leverage over potential victims. The only way to hinder or discredit a blackmailer required criminal charges of either blackmail or libel. Either scenario required a trial, which might disclose even more sensitive personal information. The extortion and eventual suicide of the forty-year-old Berlin department store owner Hermann Israel illustrates precisely this risk. A leader in the Berlin Jewish community, Israel also bore the honorific title *Kommerzienrat* (commercial counsel), which signaled his standing with the imperial government. Israel was the victim of blackmail in 1904 when a former Prussian officer, Ernst Ohm, described as Israel's "travel companion," threatened to create "difficulties" if Israel failed to pay him a certain sum of money. Israel turned Ohm's letters over to the public prosecutor in Berlin, and Ohm received a two-month jail sentence for blackmail.[97]

In his trial testimony against Ohm, Israel, a bachelor, swore under oath that his "orientation" (*Veranlagung*) was not homosexual. This inspired Ohm—after completing his short jail term—to charge Israel with perjury. Forced to appear in court again but this time as a defendant accused of perjury, Israel faced a parade of boy prostitutes, all claiming to have had sexual relations with him. The credibility of most of these witnesses was compromised by police records, which included jail sentences for blackmail. Israel also argued that his sworn testimony in the original trial—his claim that he was not homosexual—was made in reference to Paragraph 175; *technically* he had never broken the law. Arguably, Israel was mistaken and *had* perjured himself: German discourse distinguished increasingly between a fixed homosexual "orientation" and same-sex erotic acts. A man (or woman) might be deemed "homosexual" without having violated Paragraph 175. The case was initially dismissed, but then was appealed by Ohm and reopened. When Israel learned that the perjury trial would continue, he shot himself in November 1905 on his yacht on the Rhine River, exactly three years (to the day) after the death of Krupp.[98]

Israel's legal travails were reported in the press, almost simultaneously with the unfolding scandals of two prominent public officials. In December 1904, August Hasse, a judge and director of the regional court in Breslau, traveled to Berlin, where he shot the man whom he had paid some forty thousand marks over the course of two years. In 1903 Hasse had responded to the sexual overtures of a nineteen-year-old who exposed himself to Hasse in a public toilet in Breslau. Hasse then became the victim of an orchestrated blackmail campaign conducted by two older ringleaders who manipulated him into a liaison with the attractive teenager. After he was no longer able to pay, Hasse arranged to meet one of the extortionists in a darkened churchyard in Berlin, apparently with the intention of killing him. After firing a small pistol, Hasse turned himself in to local officials, believing that the man lay dying. Hasse's tormenter was only grazed, however, and sent another threatening letter a few days later from his home in Hamburg. This was intercepted by Hasse's grown son, who managed to have the man arrested. The other two were quickly apprehended as well, and the three were tried in Berlin. The man Hasse attempted to kill was condemned to ten years imprisonment; the other two were sentenced to four and five years, respectively. Hasse himself was allowed to go free. As determined by the Berlin judge, Hasse did not contravene Paragraph 175, and he was deemed "not responsible for his actions" (*Unzurechnungsfähig*) at the point when he fired his gun.[99]

Hasse's real punishment, of course, was the loss of a substantial fortune and the public humiliation that ended his career and forced him into retirement. In this regard, his fate was similar to that of Dr. Paul Ackermann, a prominent fifty-five-year-old jurist and Saxon state official, who received a two-month prison sentence in March 1905 for violating Paragraph 175. Ackermann was released immediately following the trial, however, for time served during the four-month investigation. Once again, the villains were three male prostitutes *cum* extortionists, who acted in concert to blackmail Ackermann for several thousand marks. The main culprit was a twenty-three-year-old Berliner, Heinrich Wallmann, known in prostitution circles as "Revolver-Heini." Ackermann had traveled to Berlin repeatedly in the summer and fall of 1904 for trysts with Wallmann in a Berlin hotel along Friedrichstraße near the train station.

On one of these visits, in October 1904, Ackermann and Wallmann were "discovered" by Wallmann's partner, the twenty-one-year-old barkeep Wilhelm Dupke. Together with a third accomplice, Wallmann and Dupke opened what the newspapers described as a "blackmail campaign" (*Erpressungsfeldzug*). After making two substantial payments, Ackermann balked. When the three hoodlums surprised him with a visit to his Dresden apartment, the frightened jurist turned to the Berlin police, who arrested his tormentors in early November. During the investigation that followed, Ackermann was committed to a psychiatric facility for six weeks of "observation." The suspension of Ackermann's two-month sentence for time served reflected a general sympathy for his "condition" and the exploitation he had suffered at the hands of the extortionists, who received prison sentences ranging from fifteen to thirty months. Like Judge Hasse, Ackermann's real punishment was the disgrace of exposure and the blemish he brought to his family's name. Although married and the father of one son, Ackermann, according to newspaper accounts, had been known in elite circles as someone with "punishable tendencies."[100]

The cases of Ackermann, Hasse, Israel, and Krupp were only the proverbial tip of the iceberg. The timing of these scandals and the publicity they garnered functioned as a catalyst, moreover, for the hundreds of blackmail cases that seemed to plague the city in the following decade. Berlin's popular press not only increased the impact of blackmail on potential victims, it also spurred copycat extortionists, who recognized a lucrative and seemingly risk-free crime. These newspaper stories document the evolving practice of extortion, and they provide intriguing access to the otherwise invisible lives of the people who inhabited the seamy underbelly of Berlin's homosexual milieu.

The press published stories of egregious, brazen blackmail threats: after dark, men were accosted by adolescent hustlers, who would threaten to report solicitation to a nearby police officer unless paid a sum of money on the spot. One late-night reveler, "merchant K.," was tailed by seventeen-year-old Reinhold Kroll while returning home through the Tiergarten. Kroll approached the man and demanded that he pay him or face arrest by a nearby police officer. The merchant managed to alert the officer himself, who arrested Kroll instead.[101] Another near victim, a wine steward returning home from his place of employment, noticed that he had been followed into the public bathroom at the Lehrter train station, just north of the Tiergarten; twenty-one-year-old August Schäfer then demanded twenty marks. The wine steward managed to clobber the male prostitute, who fled on foot. With the help of a police officer, the man chased down and captured Schäfer, who had hidden between tombstones in a neighboring cemetery.[102]

One common tactic for extorting money was to gain access to the apartment or hotel room of an intended victim. This gave the blackmailer's account greater credence: private quarters afforded the opportunity for sex, and why else would two male strangers spend time together? One fellow, making his way home through the Tiergarten alone at night, innocently offered his lit cigar to a young man who requested a light for his own cigarette. When the hustler, Joseph Bieneck, suggested that they venture out for just one more beer, the cigar smoker assented. Hours later, Bieneck explained that his own building was locked by now and asked if he might spend the night. In the morning the hustler threatened to describe the sexual molestation he had been subjected to and demanded one hundred marks. The victim, badly hung over, paid the sum but then reported his experience to the police. With the help of the *Verbrecheralbum*, the blackmailer was identified as a prostitute and picked up within a few hours.[103] A dentist from Charlottenburg had a similar experience returning home late through the Tiergarten. Upon meeting twenty-two-year-old Bruno Müller, the dentist agreed to give the apparently homeless young man temporary lodging. In the morning the dentist faced a blackmail threat and also agreed to pay the hush money demanded of him. But he then enlisted help from the police, who intercepted Müller soon after, when he returned to the dentist's apartment to demand yet more money.[104]

Of course, extortion attempts more often involved letter writing than face-to-face confrontation. Over and over again, apparently innocent men turned to the police after receiving threatening letters from complete strangers. The young factory worker Karl Rieloff received a three-year prison sentence for sending threatening letters to a man whom he had never even met.[105] The unemployed "worker" Ernst Nentuez sent letters to a Prussian aristocrat who lived outside of Berlin demanding one hundred marks. According to the newspaper report, the aristocrat had never had any interaction at all with his would-be blackmailer. Nentuez admitted his deception and received a one-year prison sentence.[106]

That homosexual blackmail had come to be considered a lucrative specialization among a class of convicted criminals is clear from some of the schemes that came to light. Indeed, time spent in prison often led to new "opportunities." While serving a five-year sentence for extortion, Gustav Rohde solicited information from fellow inmates to compile a list of suspected homosexuals, and upon his release in Berlin in 1905, he sent a series of letters demanding hush money (*Schweigegeld*). Rohde confused names and addresses, and his misidentified targets submitted the threatening letters to the police. Soon after, Rohde was arrested at the post office as he collected his mail, and at trial he received a six-year sentence.[107] Similarly, restaurant waiter Heinrich Schön learned the name and identity of a wealthy German aristocrat—"Freiherr von D."— from a fellow inmate while serving a three-year sentence for homosexual extortion. After his release for the initial charge, Schön was arrested again for the attempted blackmail and given an even longer sentence.[108] The prostitute Willi Scheib, after serving a six-month sentence for blackmail, trolled for victims in the corridors of the police headquarters at Alexanderplatz, where he presented himself as a private detective and offered to investigate blackmail threats. Instead of helping his "clients" to exonerate themselves, however, Scheib used the information he could glean to engage in his own blackmail, at least until he was arrested again and brought to trial.[109]

Although any man who seemed to be wealthy was a potential target, tourists appear to have been especially vulnerable. Several Americans were featured in press stories on homosexual extortion. One man, staying with his father-in-law in one of the city's nicest hotels, met several youths in Café Kranzler at the corner of Friedrichstraße and Unter den Linden, a location notorious for its various prostitutions. The American escaped extortion, though he was relieved of his pearl chest pin and a thousand marks. He never recovered his property, and his story made the morning paper.[110] Another more fortunate American—likewise "unfamiliar with local conditions"—brought home a hustler whom he had met at the symphony. In his hotel room, the tourist was forced to hand over his valuables and cash. The American reported the theft to the police and identified his blackmailer in the *Verbrecheralbum*. The hustler was quickly apprehended, and the watch and chain were returned to the owner before he left the city.[111]

Out-of-town Germans were also frequent victims. One visitor from western Germany, described as a "big industrialist," came to Berlin for a family celebration, but wound up in a dive motel after bar hopping in the Friedrichstaße. In the morning, unable to recall details of his evening, the man simply reported his wallet and cigarette case missing. Soon after returning home, the industrialist received a visitor who claimed to be the cousin of the young man who had not only accompanied the out-of-towner on that Berlin evening but had also had sex with him. In return for his silence, the visitor demanded six thousand marks. The industrialist notified Berlin officials, who monitored a scheduled meeting between the industrialist and his blackmailer in a Berlin café. Ultimately, four members of an extortion racket were arrested.[112] In a similar case, a group of eight "youthful" blackmailers successfully targeted affluent visitors, including a university professor and an out-of-town military officer.[113] While seriously inebriated, another visitor to the capital was approached by twenty-year-old Kurt Ostberg, who accompanied him to his hotel, threatened him with blackmail, and then stole his wallet. With the help of local officials, the man identified Ost-berg the very next day prowling Unter den Linden.[114]

As American sociologist Abraham Flexner acknowledged, Berlin gained a reputation for male prostitution well before the First World War. It comes as no surprise, therefore, that the city had begun to attract male tourists seeking assignations with other men; Dr. Acker-mann and Krupp—visitors to the capital—were not the only ones. Like Ackermann, Austrian merchant "Georg M." was stalked at home—in this case Vienna, not Dresden—by blackmailers he had encountered in Berlin. In December 1906, the Austrian paid male prostitute Heinrich Hampe for sex, but continued to pay when Hampe and his accomplice Marcus Katellaper extorted first one hundred marks and then additional sums. Once "Georg M." alerted the Berlin police, the two were quickly arrested. Nineteen-year-old Berlin prostitute Hans Schwaiger met an aristocrat from the Rhineland on Friedrichstraße in the autumn of 1904. Schwaiger was able to extort a cool two thousand marks before his john departed Berlin. Following in pursuit, Schwaiger secured another eight hundred marks, and demanded still more. "Georg M." finally turned to Berlin officials, who were able to identify, track down, and arrest Schwaiger within a period of days.[115] The case of the young ophthal-mologist Dr. Gumprich, a professor at the University of Halle, was especially tragic. The unmarried twenty-eight-year-old doctor had a reputation for hard work and withdrawn modesty. Berlin's male prosti-tutes were his apparent vice and ultimately his downfall. When Berlin police arrested a twenty-year-old named Kurach loitering along Frie-drichstraße in April 1908, they discovered Gumprich's business card in the young man's possession. Initially, Kurach denied any connection to the doctor, but eventually he admitted to a sexual tryst with him in a Berlin hotel over the Christmas holidays. During the investigation, Gumprich denied committing acts that violated Paragraph 175, but the judge brought charges all the same. After receiving the court summons, Gumprich grew despondent, and finally fled to Amsterdam, where he committed suicide.[116]

From many reports, however, blackmail victims clearly intended to pay for sex. "Merchant G.," for example, only reported his tormenter after months of harassment. In this case, the blackmailer, Paul Lemke, was a well-known rent boy who plied his trade in the Tiergarten and on Friedrichstraße and went by the nickname "Schmus-Anna" ("sweet-talk Anna"). Whether "merchant G." was punished is unclear, but "Schmus-Anna," for his crime, received two and a half years in prison. The young "worker" Willi Haß similarly accompanied "merchant R." to his apartment, and then returned several times throughout the following week—always demanding more money—until "merchant R." finally found the courage to call the police.[117] One older fellow was threatened and robbed by a new acquaintance brought home from Friedrichstraße. Upon arriving in the apartment, the blackmailer had demanded payment and promptly left with the old man's cash. The sorry victim admitted that his understood purpose was a sexual assignation with the young man, but he denied—improbably—that the sex involved a monetary exchange.[118]

Some cases of homosexual blackmail appeared to spring from ongoing sexual relationships, animated perhaps by genuine affection. In 1912 an employee of the American Express office in Berlin managed to embezzle 100,000 marks. As it turned out, the money was a "nest-egg" for fleeing Berlin and settling overseas with the rent boy and heterosexual pimp Alex Thomas, know in prostitution circles as "Matrosen-Alex" ("Sailor Alex"). Whether "Sailor Alex" shared the dreams of his "friend" is unclear; he had successfully blackmailed the American Express employee for an extended period and regularly "garnered" half of his wages.[119] In another case, the merchant "Kasparin K." invited the nineteen-year-old Max Minuth to his "elegantly appointed bachelor's apartment," initially just for the night. Minuth was allowed to stay, however, and soon began to steal his patron's possessions. Periodically "Kasparin K." would pay local pawnbrokers to recover his things. After Minuth sold all of the household furnishings to an estate agent, the police were finally notified, although this was only because "Kasparin K." thought that his apartment had been burgled. In the resulting criminal trial, Minuth received a two-year sentence, while "Kasparin K." was jailed for one month on Paragraph 175 charges.[120] Another remarkable story involved "Dr. B." in Wilmersdorf, who faced blackmail after firing his manservant and masseur, "Franz N." When "Dr. B." refused to pay his former employee a ten-thousand-mark "settlement," "Franz N." barricaded himself in the apartment. After police finally "liberated" the domicile, "Franz N." was arrested and then sentenced to eight months in prison.[121] Another wealthy merchant, based in Kassel, allowed nineteen-year-old Ewald Schäfer to move in, but fled to Berlin after the young man began to steal from him. Schäfer located his erstwhile lover in Berlin and began to harass him with blackmail threats. The merchant finally reported Schäfer, who was arrested and brought to trial. After the judge imposed a fourteen-month prison sentence, however, the merchant pleaded for clemency for his former lover and tormenter and asked that the charges be dropped.[122]

The success police had in tracking down suspected blackmailers—at least those cases reported in the papers—suggest that the Department of Homosexuals and Blackmailers was especially efficient. Many accounts mentioned the positive identification of a suspect, often in conjunction with the use of the *Verbrecheralbum*.[123] The department also offered advice and counsel to the victims of blackmail: Commissioner Tresckow actually received an annual stipend during his tenure as director for the separate office in his apartment where he counseled victims between 5 and 6 p.m. Krupp, for one, had sought Tresckow's advice in 1902—via his personal secretary—although the commissioner's frank warning to avoid perjury might have hastened the steel baron's suicide. Beyond simply identifying suspected blackmailers, Tresckow and his men helped victims entice their tormenters to meet them in public places, where they might be arrested by officers in hiding. They accompanied other victims on tours of homosexual cruising areas to identify and arrest a suspected blackmailer.[124]

It appears that Berlin officials earned and maintained a positive reputation within the city's homosexual milieu. One newspaper report explained in 1905, "[W]e have been informed that the number of blackmail cases is not multiplying, rather blackmailed persons have the trust now to turn to the police. Earlier they either accepted the ongoing extortion or 'for unknown reasons' ended their lives."[125] Whether greater trust in the police explains the increase in the number of reported cases is impossible to determine, though victims of blackmail were certainly reassured by the relatively sympathetic treatment they received in court. A prison sentence for a violation of Paragraph 175 was rare and, when imposed, only nominal. Dr. Ackermann was deemed to have violated Paragraph 175, but was released after trial for "time served" during the investigation. Judge Hasse attempted to kill his blackmailer, but went unpunished due to "incapacitation." By contrast, the men who blackmailed Ackermann and Hasse received up to ten-year prison sentences. The merchant "Kasparin K." was imprisoned for a month, but his erstwhile companion, Max Minuth, was locked up for two years. When it came to contradictory testimonies, elite and bourgeois blackmail victims almost always had the upper hand. In 1914 a medical student reported two alleged blackmailers, whom the police quickly identified as prostitutes with a long string of convictions. The blackmailers accused the student, in turn, of violating Paragraph 175, a charge the public prosecutor decided to pursue. After a city judge rejected the blackmailers' countercharge, the prosecutor appealed to a district court, but the initial decision was upheld.[126] Despite their apparent leverage with potential blackmail victims, prostitutes were deemed to have very little credibility when blackmail cases were brought to trial.

In Magnus Hirschfeld's estimate, nearly 30 percent of Berlin's homosexual community was blackmailed at some point.[127] This might have been exaggerated, although published crime statistics always indicated many more prosecutions for blackmail than for violations of Paragraph 175, often by a factor of four or more. Berlin's annual statistical almanacs only began tabulating figures for blackmail in 1906. This also reflected the perception that there were many more incidents than before. Denunciations for homosexual blackmail peaked in 1910 (477 in that year alone), as did the number of resulting arrests (106). Particularly telling are the corresponding figures for denunciations and arrests for sodomy—359 and 20, respectively. While fully one in four and a half blackmail denunciations led to an arrest, only one out of eighteen Paragraph 175 denunciations resulted in arrest.[128]

What demonstrates most clearly the enforcement priorities of Berlin officials are the city's criminal statistics.[129] Published annually beginning in 1876, arrests for sodomy remained remarkably low throughout the imperial period (likewise during the Weimar Republic). Before 1890 the greatest number of arrests recorded for a single year was only eleven (in 1882), and 1911 set the record with just thirty-five. The difficulty of enforcing the law is underscored further by the rapidly growing number of denunciations. While the tips given to police of suspected homosexual activity increased fivefold from 1890 to 1910 (from 67 to 359), the number of arrests increased only modestly. This figure—the number of denunciations—also suggests the increasing visibility of homosexuals in Berlin. If we consider the city's significant population growth, from 825,000 inhabitants in 1871 to just over 2 million in 1914, the per capita number of arrests remained virtually constant.

As Hirschfeld claimed, it was "not the act, but rather bad luck" that was punished.[130] Hans Ostwald observed more cynically that "now and then the police seize one from the thousands on the *Päderastenlist*. . . . [T]hey maintain their respect and 'significance' with an occasional arrest."[131] In 1920 the Berlin police commissioner Dr. Heinrich Kopp, who had worked in the Department of Homosexuals and Blackmailers since 1904, reported that the beat officers in his division "had only once in sixteen years happened upon a situation that actually represented a violation of the law." In other words, only once between 1904 and 1920 had two men in Berlin been caught in flagrante delicto in a sex act that violated Paragraph 175.[132]

Of equal significance was formal police toleration of same-sex locales. After 1885 there were no recorded cases in greater Berlin—except those involving flagrant prostitution, or criminal activity unrelated to Paragraph 175—where police raided a same-sex male or lesbian bar, at least not before the Nazis came to power.[133] As late as 1932, Berlin officials articulated the policies that Commissioner Hüllessem had implemented forty-five years earlier. In March of that year members of a men's club from the provincial city of Bautzen, after visiting Berlin for an annual convention, submitted a letter to the Prussian minister of the interior in which they complained bitterly about the "locales" where "young men appear in women's clothing." The letter continued, "It undermines respectable, German manners when our officials tolerate such a thing. . . . We consider it a pressing matter that state officials counter this immoral mischief [*Unfug*] with all available means."[134]

Whether these concerned citizens received any response is unclear, but the internal correspondence between the Berlin police president and ministry officials is highly illuminating. In a note dated April 29, 1932, the police president explained that

> the general toleration of locales with a homosexual public corresponds to an old practice of the Berlin police that was established already in the last century. . . . The existence of these locales has two practical advantages: it simplifies the observation of these circles for the criminal police, and it keeps them from causing public disturbances in the streets. . . . Although the complainants appear to suggest that such pubs contribute to the spread of homosexuality, this view is mistaken. There are still differences of opinion about the cause of a same-sex orientation, but no serious scientist today has the view that this perversion of the sexual impulse can be influenced from outside.[135]

This enlightened response to a diverse community of sexual minorities helped to define and eventually entrench an incipient identity. What Hüllessem, Tresckow, and their colleagues accomplished was nothing less than the creation of a homosexual milieu in which same-sex-loving men and women were permitted to drink, dance, and socialize without fear of arrest. Hüllessem and others also facilitated access to this exotic world for medical and media professionals who theorized and broadcast the emergence of a new urban culture, the representations of which became an integral feature of Berlin in the first decades of the twentieth century.

CHAPTER THREE

The First Homosexual Rights Movement
and the Struggle to Shape Identity

Within the larger world, the homosexual portion of humanity creates a world of its own, small in relationship to the rest but large enough to be studied in its own right. Whoever correctly recognizes and assesses this *terra incognita* will resemble a research traveler who sojourns in foreign territory to study from the ground up.

—MAGNUS HIRSCHFELD, *Die Homosexualität des Mannes und des Weibes* (1914)

When Magnus Hirschfeld welcomed a few acquaintances to his Berlin apartment in May 1897, he had grand designs, bolstered by the energy of youthful optimism. The young medical doctor had just turned twenty-nine the day before, on the fourteenth, and was now embarking on a brash plan to establish the world's first homosexual rights organization. Hirschfeld's guests included the publisher Max Spohr, the journalist and editor Adolf Glaser, the railroad official Eduard Oberg, and the Prussian officer and colonial administrator Franz Josef von Bülow. Hirschfeld also invited Berlin police commissioner Leopold von Meerscheidt-Hüllessem, known within the homosexual community as the official who had first tolerated gay bars and costume balls. Though Hüllessem likely did not attend, Hirschfeld's invitation indicated the close cooperation that Berlin's homosexual rights activists would enjoy with the police. Oberg and Bülow never played significant roles in the fledgling organization, yet both were able to make generous contributions. Adolf Glaser was a prominent personality who also gave tours of Berlin's homosexual nightlife (sometimes together with Hüllessem). Based in Leipzig, Max Spohr had established his own publishing niche with avant-garde works on the occult and homeopathic medicine. Happily married with children, Spohr recognized the popular interest in sexual minorities—after publishing his first work on the subject in 1893—and functioned as Hirschfeld's muse.[1]

Hirschfeld embodied a new approach to political and social reform. What he proposed was the coupling of media-savvy activism with modern medical scholarship to ameliorate the plight of German homosexuals. The new organization that Hirschfeld founded that day in his Charlottenburg apartment was christened the Scientific-Humanitarian Committee (Wissenschaftlich-humanitäres Komitee), and the group adopted the motto *"Per scientiam ad justitiam"* ("Through science to justice"). As the motto suggested, Hirschfeld and his fellow members expected that scientific research (together with public education) would effect a dramatic cultural reassessment of homosexuality within Germany, leading eventually to acceptance and legal reform.[2]

The proposed research objectives of the SHC also provided a pretext for those who might otherwise have resisted associating themselves with such an organization. Hirschfeld was single himself and remained so, although he never publicly admitted his homosexuality. (He entered a relationship with a life partner, Karl Giese, soon after 1918.) The son of a Jewish medical doctor, Hirschfeld was born in 1868 in the Prussian spa resort of Kolberg on the southern coast of the Baltic (now the Polish town of Kołobrzeg). One of seven children, Hirschfeld, like his two brothers, studied medicine, matriculating first in Breslau, then Strasbourg, Munich, Heidelberg, and finally Berlin, where he completed his medical degree in 1892. After his studies he traveled in the United States and western Europe before opening a practice in Magdeburg, which he moved to the elite neighborhood of Charlottenburg on the western edge of Berlin in 1896.

Hirschfeld's direct motivation for founding the SHC was the suicide of a homosexual patient, recounted in his first sexological publication on the topic, *Sappho und Sokrates: Wie erklärt sich die Liebe der Männer und Frauen zu Personen des eigenen Geschlechts?* (Sappho and Socrates:

How do we understand the love of men and women to persons of their own sex?), which he published with Spohr under the pseudonym "Th. Ramien" in 1896. Hirschfeld described the fate of a young military officer who, when pressured by his family to marry, killed himself instead (on the very eve of his wedding). The young man entrusted Hirschfeld with a farewell letter explaining that Paragraph 175, the anti-sodomy statute, would follow him throughout life, always threatening disgrace. For Hirschfeld, the young man's suicide was a jarring epiphany, revealing the legal and social discrimination experienced by homosexuals. The pamphlet was also an opportunity to offer a theory of homosexual orientation, which Hirschfeld explained as the inborn mental and physical condition of a small minority. Like someone suffering from a harelip or cleft palate, Hirschfeld argued, homosexuals had a congenital defect and deserved to be tolerated, even accepted and embraced.

Although Hirschfeld developed his theories significantly throughout his career, *Sappho und Sokrates* expressed the fundamental view that he embraced and consistently promoted: sexual orientation was biological. Under his own name, Hirschfeld released a second work with Spohr, *Der urnische Mensch* (The uranian person), in 1903, which reiterated his view that homosexuality was congenital. While Richard von Krafft-Ebing and the Berlin psychiatrist Albert Moll had come to share Hirschfeld's position—or at least accepted that *some* homosexuals had an inborn condition—others, including two of Hirschfeld's most ardent naysayers, the Berlin sexologist Dr. Iwan Bloch and the professor of medicine Albert Eulenburg, continued to argue that a homosexual orientation was "caused" by seduction or even poor parenting. Hirschfeld argued from his by-now-extensive clinical experience that most of his homosexual patients not only exhibited characteristics of the typical "uranian Person" but also had experienced a typical "uranian childhood." Within a short time Hirschfeld managed to convert both doctors to his view, a significant accomplishment that early on helped to establish his reputation. It was Hirschfeld's familiarity with such a large number of homosexual men and women and with Berlin's same-sex club scene—he provided both Bloch and Eulenburg with tours—that appears ultimately to have won them over.[3]

A third Hirschfeld publication from 1910, *Die Transvestiten* (*The Trans-*

vestites), was the source of yet another German neologism. Hirschfeld coined the term based on his experience of Berlin cross-dressers, including professional actors and especially male and female impersonators. Hirschfeld not only contributed a new word for an otherwise unnamed phenomenon but also was the first to argue that cross-dressing had no direct relationship to sexual orientation: the "transvestites" Hirschfeld featured in his study were heterosexual. Hirschfeld's *Transvestites* also provided the earliest full account of his theory of "sexual intermediacy" (*sexuelle Zwischenstufenlehre*). This convoluted expression was sometimes explained as a "third-sex" theory. However, this simplification was (and is) misleading. With the publication of *Die Transvestiten*, Hirschfeld no longer asserted that there was a discrete "third gender" comprising homosexual men and women, but claimed instead that human sexuality could be mapped on an intricate spectrum from "absolute woman" to "absolute man," reflecting a set of four central criteria. Of course, the "absolutes" were ideal types and existed nowhere in reality. The four criteria that Hirschfeld identified included genitalia, other physical characteristics, sex drive, and emotional characteristics; these four variables, he believed, explained the enormous range of sexual minorities—physical hermaphrodites (individuals with ambiguous genitalia), homosexuals, bisexuals, asexuals, cross-dressers (transvestites), effeminate men who loved masculine women, the reverse, and so on. Admittedly, Hirschfeld's specific assessment of any one of these criteria—except perhaps genitalia—was extremely subjective and more a reflection of his own views and culture, dictating what "men" and "women" should be. All the same, the schema, as Hirschfeld worked it out, allowed for no fewer than 43 million distinct combinations. In short, Hirschfeld endorsed an infinite range of orientations and a wild diversity of human sexuality. What undergirded his analysis was the central belief that sexual expression was also somehow congenital. This biological determinism animated both the scholarship and the activism of the SHC.[4]

From its inception the SHC pursued direct political action, scientific research, and popular education, usually all at the same time. What supported these activities was the print production of Max Spohr and his Leipzig publishing house. Spohr had released his first work on homosexuality, *Die Enterbten des Liebesglückes oder das dritte Geschlecht* (Those dispossessed of love or the third sex) by Otto de Joux (Otto Podjukl) in 1893. In 1896 Spohr published Hirschfeld's *Sappho und Sokrates,* and a second work by de Joux, *Die hellenische Liebe in der Gegenwart* (Hellenic love in the present day), which proposed the idea of an organization that would promote the rights of homosexuals. This inspired Spohr to introduce Hirschfeld and de Joux. Hirschfeld was the one to take up the idea, however, and pursued it with Spohr's support. In 1898 Hirschfeld edited and Spohr republished all twelve pamphlets authored by Karl Heinrich Ulrichs, who had died in Italy a few years earlier, in complete obscurity. (These had been released originally between 1864 and 1879.) A year later Spohr issued the first volume of Hirschfeld's *Jahrbuch für sexuelle Zwischenstufen* (Yearbook for sexual intermediaries), a scientific journal of sexology devoted largely to the study of homosexuality. The very first of its kind, *Jahrbuch* received positive critical reviews from the German medical establishment, and appeared in twenty-three editions, surviving to the Great Inflation of 1923. Some issues of the journal exceeded one thousand pages, in editions of five hundred or more, which were provided to SHC members at a reduced rate or sold to institutional subscribers and in bookstores.[5]

It was not only Spohr's academic publications but also the popular SHC "propaganda" that allowed Hirschfeld to combine scholarship with homosexual rights advocacy. This commitment to public agitation was so great, in fact, that by 1903 the SHC had elected a "Propaganda Commission," responsible solely for popular education. At least since Ulrichs's lonely campaign in the 1860s and '70s, the dispelling of false stereotypes about homosexuality had become a central objective. When the Prussian minister of the interior adopted the anti-sodomy statute as Paragraph 175 in 1871—against the recommendations of Rudolf Virchow and the Prussian medical commission—he justified his decision as a necessary measure to preserve the "popular feeling of the nation." Krafft-Ebing decried this conservatism in 1894: "If it were possible to popularize the findings of medical science," he opined, "Paragraph [175] could no longer be maintained."[6]

To that end the Spohr Verlag also produced dozens of small monographs and pamphlets on homosexuality, legal reform, and related topics. From 1898 to 1914 the Spohr house (led by Max Spohr's younger brother after Max's death in 1905) published more than one hundred titles on homosexuality, making up 40 percent of the firm's list. By producing such a wide range of brochures and studies, many authored by lay activists, the publishing firm helped to undermine the monopoly of medical, psychiatric, and juridical scholars on the public discussion of homosexuality.[7] Hirschfeld's own publications alone, beginning with *Sappho und Sokrates,* were produced in multiple editions running to tens of thousands of copies. The most popular SHC title was *Was Soll das Volk vom dritten Geschlecht Wissen?* (What should the [German] people know about the third sex?). This eighty-page booklet had a print run of eighteen thousand copies in 1901, and a total of no fewer than fifty thousand had been published by 1911.[8] Not all or even most were sold, but instead were distributed at SHC meetings, lectures, and other events. Members were encouraged to leave copies on Berlin trams, in train stations, and in bars and restaurants.[9]

This pamphlet literature was a critical element in the SHC's petition drive to reform Paragraph 175. After organizing the SHC, Hirschfeld solicited and won the support of August Bebel (1840–1913), leader of the German Social Democratic Party (whom Hirschfeld had befriended while still a student). Bebel signed the petition and introduced a measure in 1898 to overturn the anti-sodomy statute, sparking a full debate on the floor of the Reichstag. The initiative failed, but the SHC pressed ahead. The brochure, *Eros vor dem Reichsgericht* (Eros before the imperial court), authored anonymously by a jurist (and published by Spohr), was sent—along with the petition—to officials, attorneys, and legal scholars. Methodically, the SHC targeted professional groups—7,500 Catholic priests in Bavaria, Baden, and the Rhineland in 1899, for example, and 28,000 German doctors in 1904. A "yield rate" for these mass mailings is impossible to determine, but by 1902 the committee had collected 4,500 signatures, mostly public figures, medical doctors, and other professionals. That number had grown to more than 6,000 by 1906.[10] In his monumental 1914 study, *Die Homosexualität des Mannes und des Weibes,* Hirschfeld claimed that nearly 100,000 "enlightenment brochures" had been mailed to the press; to local, state, and federal officials; and to politicians, attorneys, medical doctors, university professors, religious figures, and school teachers.[11]

The freedom with which Hirschfeld, Spohr, and the SHC pursued their public campaign is astonishing, especially in light of counter-initiatives to increase censorship and curb pornography. Since the early 1890s, the "Lex-Heinze" ("Heinze Law"), a restrictive censorship law proposed by the Kaiser and named for a convicted pimp and murderer, was hotly debated, dividing social conservatives and free-press advocates. The version promoted by the Catholic Center Party would have preempted most of Spohr's publications on homosexuality and limited the advocacy work of the SHC. But in 1895 the German Publishers Association organized a successful campaign to temper the bill. The version proposed in March 1900 elicited significant resistance from artists, writers, academics, and public intellectuals, who organized themselves in so-called Goethe Leagues, named to suggest the freedom necessary to inspire the creativity of Germany's poet laureate. Within a few months a compromise was reached, and the new law, dramatically watered down from earlier drafts, did little more than criminalize the sale of blatant pornography.[12] Works on homosexuality with any scientific or educational merit, according to the historian Mark Lehmstedt, were almost never censored: "[T]he books on (hetero) sexual enlightenment were more often the focus of court proceedings and Spohr was rarely directly affected."[13] Certainly censorship remained a genuine threat, and not until the Weimar Republic were Berlin activists and publishers able to establish a vibrant homosexual press. Still, the climate in Wilhelmine Germany was strikingly liberal, particularly in contrast to the rest of Europe.

Britain offers the most striking counterpoint. Like Germany, England maintained a punitive anti-sodomy statute. But unlike Germany, there was no tolerance for advocating homosexual emancipation or even for scientific publications on the subject. The Oscar Wilde trial in 1895, which condemned the Irish wit to two years hard labor, certainly poisoned public and official views. But Wilde's spectacular downfall was more a symptom than a cause of English intolerance. Publishing the work of an outspoken English activist similar to Ulrichs would have been inconceivable. Both John Addington Symonds (1840–1893), an Oxford-trained classicist, and Edward Carpenter (1844–1929) asserted the innate character of homosexual love and called for legal reforms: Symonds's *A Problem in Greek Ethics, Being an Inquiry into the Phenomenon of Sexual Inversion; Addressed Especially to Medical Psychologists and Jurists* and *A Problem in Modern Ethics* were produced in 1883 and 1891, respectively, and Carpenter had two hundred copies of his *Homogenic Love* printed in 1894.[14] But these works were published privately—none was advertised, reviewed, or sold openly in bookstores in Britain.[15] Even the works of Krafft-Ebing received a tepid English reception. When an English-language translation of his *Psychopathia sexualis* appeared in 1892, the "objectionable" sections were rendered in Latin. The *British Medical Journal* opined that the entire text should have been "veiled in the decent obscurity of a dead language."[16]

The most egregious English censorship case, the so-called Bedborough Affair, banned Havelock Ellis's *Sexual Inversion,* published in 1897. (Significantly, Ellis's work had already appeared without any difficulty in German translation a year earlier under the title *Die Homosexualität,* although not published by Spohr.) The leading English psychiatrist of his age, Ellis was inspired by his *Sexual Inversion* collaborator, Symonds, who died in 1893 before the volume had been completed. Ellis's relationship with Symonds can be compared to that of Krafft-Ebing with Ulrichs, or Moll with Adolf Glaser, and Ellis cited French and especially German authors, including Casper, Ulrichs, Westphal, Krafft-Ebing, and Moll, arguing like the more progressive German psychiatrists that "inversion" was inborn and should not be criminalized. In May 1898 the London bookseller George Bedborough was arrested for stocking the volume. After Bedborough decided to plead guilty, there was no effective defense; both he and Ellis's publisher were fined. The London *Daily Chronicle* reported approvingly that "the courts of the law and the criticisms of the press are the responsible organs of public opinion in such a matter and we cannot take the view that the book has any scientific value whatever. . . . [I]n the discharge of our duty to the public we feel bound to say that the book in question ought never to have been written or printed . . . even if the science it professes to advance were worth studying."[17] Although Ellis later published the title with a Philadelphia press—which also released the other five volumes in his series *Studies in the Psychology of Sex*—the stultifying effect of the case on British sexology can scarcely be exaggerated. In 1906 the Edinburgh doctor James Burnet commented, "It is a great pity that medical men in this country, with almost unanimous consent, have agreed to ignore the study of sexual science in its bearing on practice."[18]

The mildness of censorship in France was a legacy of the French Revolution.[19] Certainly French psychiatric and sexological literature was direct and often explicit. But French publications lacked the empirical documentation of bourgeois and elite case studies that characterized most German scholarship.[20] There were no influential French autobiographical works comparable to Ulrichs's pamphlets, published to inform popular opinion, mobilize a homosexual community, or influence political debate. Nor was there a French equivalent of the Scientific-Humanitarian Committee, since, of course, adult same-sex erotic relationships had been fully decriminalized in France. The collaborative relationship between medical science and bourgeois subjects that characterized German sexology—and the activism it inspired—was largely missing in France. The limited contact of French medical professionals to non-institutionalized homosexuals—in short, their ignorance of the French homosexual subculture—also accounts for the paucity of ethnographic description in French studies.[21]

It was precisely the open, public agitation of the SHC that distinguished Germany from other European countries. In the name of popular enlightenment the SHC sponsored dozens of public lectures, primarily in Berlin but also in other major German cities. This work was supported by a number of SHC auxiliary groups or "subcommittees" that were organized in Munich, Leipzig, Frankfurt, and Hamburg. Most often Hirschfeld was featured as speaker, although medical doctors and sexologists who belonged to the committee gave lectures as well. Hirschfeld's research fascinated a broad swath of Berlin's educated and economic elites, and the SHC received many requests to stage lectures: elite all-male clubs, groups of businessmen, private associations, and student organizations solicited speaking engagements. Some of these events targeted large working-class audiences with up to one thousand people in attendance. For "mass" meetings (*Volksversammlun-*

gen) the SHC rented large "class-appropriate" locations: the Ahrendt and Patzenhofer breweries in the northern working-class neighborhood of Moabit were frequent venues, both large enough to host an audience of a thousand or more.[22]

The practical planning of SHC activities was accompanied by discussions of a more theoretical bent. Though united in their goal to eliminate the German anti-sodomy statute, SHC activists discovered that they were divided by profound philosophical and strategic differences, which would soon split the movement. By no later than 1902, the biannual board meetings, held initially in Hirschfeld's cramped apartment, had been moved to a prominent hotel. The surviving minutes of a meeting held on July 5, 1903, document the attendance of a range of activists from throughout Germany, as well as observers from the Netherlands, Switzerland, Italy, and Russia.[23]

The most important initiative had been and remained the lobbying for legal reform. Since the failure of Bebel's 1898 initiative to abolish Paragraph 175, the Reichstag had commissioned eight leading law professors to undertake a comprehensive revision of the German criminal code. The SHC had already targeted these eight with their materials: two had responded positively and four had promised to review the issue carefully, but the two most conservative members of the Legal Reform Commission had ignored the SHC entirely. At the July board meeting, the avowedly heterosexual anarchist Eric Mühsam suggested making yet another appeal to the jurists on the Reform Commission. The SHC attorney, Joseph Fraenkl, countered that only the two liberals, Adolf Liszt and Alfred Blumenthal, at the universities of Leipzig and Berlin, respectively, would ever support eliminating the anti-sodomy statute. The other six, he argued, were simply too conservative. Hirschfeld agreed, adding that, anyway, the SHC lacked any new materials to send to the conservative members of the commission.[24]

The publisher Adolf Brand spoke repeatedly in favor of a more aggressive strategy, one that would enlist the support of other progressive groups, including the Goethe League, which had played such a prominent roll in minimizing the impact of the Lex-Heinze censorship law in 1900. Brand also suggested that the SHC send the petition to any potential supporters in the Reichstag, requesting that they issue public statements condemning Paragraph 175. Several board members spoke against Brand's suggestions, however, including Hirschfeld, the anarchist Johannes Holzmann, and the Munich physician Ernst Burchard, who argued that such a "premature action could be damaging." Echoing Hirschfeld's position, Mühsam chimed in and warned that the SHC needed to avoid appearing to be politically engaged and should maintain its more neutral profile as a supporter of scientific study. The attorney, Dr. Albert Jakobs, also derided Brand's suggestion and stated presciently, "I'm a pessimist, and I believe it will take 100 years before we achieve this."[25]

As the last agenda item, Hirschfeld described his plan to prepare and distribute popular surveys to determine the percentage of the German population that was "homosexual." Discussion turned quickly to the difficult issue of definitions. Who was a "homosexual," and who defined it? Was it a matter of sexual acts or some intangible orientation? These questions had never been asked before, and certainly never debated and discussed, at least not in a systematic fashion, based as it were on empirical evidence. Of course, the ability to enumerate the size of the homosexual population in a city such as Berlin—or in Germany, for that matter—would provide an important and critical statistic for lobbying against the law. Hirschfeld, for his part, argued that the survey should measure sexual practices statistically, since the primary objective was to create a sexual profile of a given demographic. This, in Hirschfeld's view, would provide the raw data to begin to define the size and character of a given population. Inspired by a recent study completed by Dutch psychiatrist Lucien von Römer—who was in attendance at the SHC board meeting—Hirschfeld hoped to question members of a Berlin metalworkers' union as well as a cohort of students at Berlin's Technical University. Römer, for his part, had surveyed some six hundred Dutch university students in Amsterdam and had estimated based on a 50 percent return rate that some 2 percent of the Dutch male population had sexual relations exclusively with other men. [26]

Many in the meeting reacted to Hirschfeld's proposal with skepticism. Some questioned whether survey participants would have the courage to divulge information about illicit sexual acts, even with the guarantee of anonymity. The attorney Rudolf Schulze argued that most homosexual men were completely "cowardly." "They will never acknowledge that they are homosexual," Schulze claimed, based on his experiences living in France, England, and different regions of Germany. "Considering the difficult legal situation, they do not have the strength to make such admissions." Berlin merchant Georg Isaaks agreed that it would be impossible to establish a clear picture based on a voluntary survey, but for a very different reason: "[M]any young men between seventeen and twenty," Isaaks argued, "imagine themselves to be homosexual, but they are mostly inclined to masturbation. . . . How many of these [youths] have confessed their homosexuality, when in reality they are not at all?" The Munich activist Ernst Burchard agreed with Isaaks, claiming that the misleading responses of seventeen- to twenty-year-olds would actually discredit the study, making it fairly useless and even a source of ammunition for "our enemies."[27]

The more contentious issue, however, revolved around the precise meaning of homosexuality. The entomologist Dr. Benedict Friedlaender, an independent scholar who also contributed generously to the SHC, opined that a statistical study was completely impractical and would account only for those who had "a completely extreme orientation." Men who practice a kind of "bisexuality," he argued, would never even be detected by such a study. The author Edwin Bab complicated the issue by demanding that homosexual inclination and not just practice should provide the critical measure. As Bab argued, "It doesn't matter who has had homosexual experiences, but rather who has already detected in himself a homosexual orientation." Mühsam concurred that the critical factor to measure was "the number of those who *felt* themselves to be homosexual." Friedlaender responded that the best survey study would somehow measure both "orientation" and actual sexual practice.[28]

Hirschfeld reiterated his view that the most important index of orientation was sexual practices and that the critical first step in assessing Berlin's homosexual population was to establish "how high might be the percentage of those who are completely homosexually oriented, that is those who can only have intercourse with the same sex." Clearly not all accepted Hirschfeld's assumptions. Board members agreed, however, to elect a special commission to consider a statistical study, composed of Friedlaender, Römer (in Amsterdam), Burchard (in Munich), and Hirschfeld himself.[29] The study was begun in 1903 and completed in 1904. Hirschfeld published his results in *Jahrbuch,* and, extrapolating from the two polling samples, estimated that roughly 2 percent of German men were exclusively homosexual. Hirschfeld also claimed to prove, definitively, the existence of bisexuality.[30]

Although the study received generally positive reviews, Hirschfeld's greatest publicity came inadvertently from a libel lawsuit. Four of the students who received the questionnaire successfully sued Hirschfeld, who was defeated on appeal, and then a second time as well. The nominal fine that the judge imposed was well worth the additional positive publicity that Hirschfeld received; critics of the guilty verdict praised the quality and care of Hirschfeld's sexological research and his broader project of developing a science of human sexuality. Indeed, Berlin's liberal press lionized Hirschfeld, condemning any attempt to muzzle free expression or the pursuit of science. Science, it would seem, was truly the path to justice.[31]

The SHC owed much of its early success to Hirschfeld's astute instrumentalization of positivist research and his savvy exploitation of Berlin's liberal press. Both the organization and its leader were heavily indebted to Germany's cultural climate at the turn of the century. For one, the powerful publishing industry together with prominent literary figures defeated the most draconian version of the new censorship law passed in 1900, which allowed the SHC to establish a broad public platform for its various projects. This continued a liberalization that had begun already in 1890, when the anti-socialist laws of 1878 were finally allowed to expire. Once the nominally Marxist Social Democratic Party was permitted to organize openly, it quickly became Germany's largest political party. Certainly parliamentary government was hobbled in Germany. There were no democratic constraints placed on the imperial cabinet, which served at the pleasure of the emperor, for example, and at the state level, a three-class suffrage system all but eliminated the influence of salaried workers, who otherwise comprised an electoral majority. Still, Germany's Social Democrats created a haven for opponents of the conservative industrial and aristocratic establishments. Moreover, much—if not all—of the party leadership embraced Hirschfeld and the SHC, making homosexual rights a progressive cause. Not only the party leader August Bebel, but also the leading party theoretician Karl Kautsky and the important theorist of "evolutionary reform" Eduard Bernstein, who represented the party's right wing, were among the first to sign the SHC petition.[32]

The movement for homosexual rights was bolstered as well by imperial Germany's cultural avant-garde. Despite the conservative political and social views that emanated from the Hohenzollern court, Germany's creative classes enjoyed surprising latitude. If the emperor dictated foreign policy, he had great difficulty dominating or even influencing the arts, despite his pretentions and significant efforts to do so. Under the leadership of Walter Leistikow and Max Lieberman, for example, German impressionists forged the Berlin Secession movement in 1898, breaking with the tradition of academic art (and the implicit patronage it enjoyed from the Hohenzollern court). Both men were early supporters of the SHC and its petition.[33]

Germany's broad and diffuse counterculture was yet another wellspring of support and activism. The so-called life reform movement (*Lebensreform Bewegung*) included a hodgepodge of vegetarians, teetotalers, nudists, free-love proponents, clothing reform activists, anti-immunization zealots, advocates for alternative medicine including homeopathy and naturopathy, and the back-to-nature Wandervogel ("wandering bird") hiking groups that formed the backbone of the incipient youth movement.[34] Hirschfeld was himself a proponent of alternative medicines, an avid nudist, and an apostle for sobriety. In 1907, for example, he published a short study, *Die Gurgel Berlins* (The Throat of Berlin), which analyzed consumption patterns—food and drink—and the deleterious effects of alcohol on the city's working classes. Hirschfeld was also personally acquainted with the leaders of many of Berlin's *Lebensreform* groups.

Of greatest significance was the fact that several prominent *Lebensreform* figures actively supported homosexual rights and even joined the SHC. The prominent Wandervogel leader Wilhelm Jansen was not only an active SHC member but also director of the SHC subcommittee based in Frankfurt. Jansen was forced to relinquish his leadership position in the Wandervogel when exposed as a "homosexual" in 1910—the Jansen "scandal" provoked a crisis among the Wandervogel about the propriety of homoeroticism, creating a rift in the organization. Another Wandervogel figure with ties to the SHC was Hans Blüher, an adolescent member of the original Wandervogel troupe, organized in the Berlin suburb of Steglitz in 1896. His accounts of the Wandervogel and his full-blown historical sociology of the Männerbund, imbued, as he theorized it, with a constitutive homoeroticism, gained him tremendous notoriety (this is considered in greater detail in chapter 5).

One important bastion of early SHC support was the community of writers, painters, intellectuals, and nudists who established an artists' commune in 1890 in the village of Friedrichshagen on the outskirts of Berlin. By the 1880s the electrified train network of greater Berlin had connected Friedrichshagen with the city proper, making it a practical resort for bohemians fleeing the city. Many of Germany's leading naturalist writers, including Frank Wedekind and Gerhart Hauptmann, were Friedrichshagen residents. Swedish playwright August Strindberg was a frequent guest and also one of those who toured Berlin's homosexual nightlife with Hüllessem in the early 1890s. Hirschfeld was personally acquainted with Wedekind and his brother Donald. Significantly, adolescent homosexual self-discovery was an important theme in Wedekind's most famous play, *Spring Awakening,* which he completed in Friedrichshagen in 1891. It comes as little surprise, then, that both Wedekind and Hauptmann were signatories to the anti–Paragraph 175 petition. A number of other prominent German writers—some, though not all, with ties to the German naturalists, symbolists, or expressionists— were early supporters as well, including Detlev von Liliencron, Max Nordau, Rainer Maria Rilke, Hermann Hesse, Richard Dehmel, Ernst von Wildenbruch, Heinrich and eventually Thomas Mann, Franz Werfel, Max Brod, and Stefan Zweig.[35]

Anarchism was another ideological current—nurtured by the Wilhelmine counterculture and by Friedrichshagen particulary—that fostered supporters of homosexual rights. As one resident and chronicler described the colony, "[I]t satisfied all the conditions of an actual *Bohème,* an anarchistic community."[36] The number of early SHC members and supporters who were either resident at Friedrichshagen in the 1890s or occasional visitors is remarkable: Peter Hille, Else Lasker-Schüler, Erich Mühsam, Wilhelm Bölsche, Bruno Wille, Johannes Holzmann, Fidus (Hugo Höppener), Adolf Brand, Benedict Friedlaender, and John Henry Mackay. The leading theoretician for many of the German anarchists was left-Hegelian Max Stirner (1806–1856), author of *Der Einzige und sein Eigentum* (literally "the individualist and his own," and published in English as *The Ego and Its Own*), which first appeared in 1844.[37] The Scottish-born John Henry Mackay, who joined the German movement of literary naturalism in the 1880s, made his name within and beyond anarchist circles in the 1890s with an intellectual biography of Stirner as well as with literary accounts of the German anarchist movement. Mackay was also a self-described "boy lover," and produced, under the pen name "Sagitta," a large collection of pederastic novels and poetry, including his most famous, *The Hustler* (*Der Puppenjunge*), in 1926. Ulti-mately, his eccentric individualism prevented him from joining any of the Berlin homosexual rights organizations, although he remained a ubiquitous (if enigmatic) figure in Berlin through the end of the Weimar Republic.[38]

A common feature of the anarchists was a commitment to individu-alism and the freedom of sexual expression, an obvious motivation to support homosexual rights. For this reason Paragraph 175 came to sym-bolize much of what was considered insupportable about Wilhelmine culture. As a result, the emancipation of homosexuals and the work of the SHC—at least for some anarchists—was more of an ideological mis-sion or even a cause du jour than a commitment motivated for personal reasons. Some if not many of the initial anarchist supporters, including Erich Mühsam, claimed to be heterosexual. Many short-lived anarchist journals and papers published around 1900—*Neues Leben* (New life), *Der freie Arbeiter* (The free worker), *Der arme Teufel* (The poor devil), or *Der Kampf* (The struggle), *Die Kritik* (The critique), or *Magazin für Literatur* (Magazine for literature)—included articles and essays that promoted legal reform or reported on the SHC and the homosexual rights move-ment more generally.[39]

One well-documented example of the nexus of anarchism and the struggle for homosexual rights was the League for Human Rights (Bund für Menschenrechte), founded in Berlin in 1903 by Johannes Holzmann, a veteran of Friedrichshagen and SHC activist who also published *Der Kampf.* As an anarchist organization, the group was carefully monitored by Berlin police officers, who filed detailed reports on the fortnightly meetings, sometimes attended by fifty or more people. The freedom of sexual expression and the rights of homosexuals were frequent topics of discussion, and Magnus Hirschfeld addressed the group in September 1904.[40] It is unfortunate from the historian's perspective that there are no similar, detailed police reports on the SHC. But, of course, Hirschfeld invited Commissioner Hüllessem to the SHC's founding meeting, and cultivated a close working relationship with him and with his successor, Hans von Tresckow. Clearly state officials were far more exercised about the activities of an anarchist outfit than they ever were about the doings of homosexual rights activists.

The principle of sexual self-expression, promoted by anarchist philosophy, did not always jibe, however, with Hirschfeld's biological determinism. In this regard, the counterculture fostered alternative communities of sexual minorities as well as competing theories of same-sex eroticism. Hirschfeld's greatest intellectual challenge came from dissenters eventually identified as the "masculinists," many of whom had been among his first supporters. One of the leading masculinist figures, Adolf Brand, was also, like Hirschfeld, a pioneer. In 1896, Brand published the first issue of a literary journal, *Der Eigene,* which is now considered the first homosexual magazine. The name is difficult if not impossible to translate—either "The self-owner" or perhaps "The self-possessed"— and was inspired by Max Stirner's philosophy. Brand was also influenced by the residents of Friedrichshagen, due in part to geographic proximity. The son of a village blacksmith, Brand was raised and spent his life in Wilhelmshagen, another Berlin village that neighbored the artists' commune. Like the Friedrichshagen Bohemians, Brand rejected the traditional morality of church and state. He had met Hirschfeld by no later than 1896 and attended SHC meetings, at least for a time. But Brand also came to disdain the classifications of the medical profession, especially those of the incipient disciplines of sexology and psychiatry.

The earliest issues of *Der Eigene*—which were published erratically and in various formats—emphasized Stirnerian anarchism. By 1898, however, the journal was also explicitly homosexual. Brand was especially interested in promoting a revival of Greek "pederastic" love— the idealized relationship of an older man who befriends (and takes as his lover) a male adolescent. The journal established a reputation for its homoerotic illustrations and aesthetics, and Brand was one of the first to publish the nude male photography of Wilhelm von Gloeden, for example, who lived and worked in Italy. Today, von Gloeden's portraits of Italian adolescents are considered key works in the shaping of a modern gay male aesthetic. Early editions of *Der Eigene* also included drawings by the important symbolist artist Fidus (Hugo Höppener), who was resident in Friedrichshagen in the 1890s. Fidus was an illustrator for the Munich magazine *Jugend* (Youth), and contributed to the development (and labeling) of German Art Nouveau or Jugendstil. By the time the last issue of *Der Eigene* appeared in 1932, more than 450 authors had contributed to the journal.[41]

The nudity in Brand's publications was a source of significant trouble, and *Der Eigene* was confiscated and censored on numerous occasions. Brand's legal entanglements were legion, and his living quarters and press were routinely subject to police searches. He was, in fact, the perfect counterpoint to Hirschfeld, who cultivated strong relations with police and municipal officials. Unlike Hirschfeld, Brand was short-tempered, abusive, and often violent. For example, in 1899 he struck a Reichstag deputy in central Berlin with a dog whip. In 1903 Brand was arrested for *Der Eigene*'s "lascivious content" and imprisoned for two months on immorality charges. Max Spohr had published the confiscated issue—the only time he worked together with Brand—and for his part was fined two hundred marks (approximately a month's salary for a skilled tradesman).[42]

After serving his short sentence in 1903, Brand founded a literary society, Gemeinschaft der Eigenen (Community of the Special, or CoS), which offered an alternative of sorts to the SHC. Brand's initial motivation, however, was to elude the censors. Now subscribers were required to join the CoS, which allowed Brand to characterize the journal as a "manuscript," privately printed for the limited membership of a closed association. Member-subscribers were also forced to sign a declaration promising not to be shocked by the journal's images or content. Although the number of members probably never exceeded fifteen hundred, Brand attracted an elite readership, including residents of the Friedrichshagen literary circle and several classical scholars. An avid nudist himself, Brand also drew in early leaders of the FKK (German nudist) movement, including Heinrich Pudor and Karl Vanselow, who edited the first nudist journal, *Die Schönheit* (Beauty), beginning in 1903.[43]

The society was more than a pretext for publishing the journal, however, and was run by Brand as a kind of symposium—styled on the ancient Greek model—which he also compared to a Masonic lodge. Weekly meetings were held in Brand's home in Wilhelmshagen, where he organized outings and nature hikes. The printed announcement that Brand distributed as a membership application listed the ten principles of the CoS. These included a pledge to "promote the rebirth of friend-love [*Freundesliebe*] and strive for the social recognition of its natural and moral justification in public and private life as it existed during the period of its greatest estimation in ancient Greece." Brand also supported a "closer connection of the man with the youth and of the youth with the man."[44] Implicit in this formulation, of course, was the endorsement of an erotic relationship between adult men and adolescent boys, or ephebes, in the language of the ancient Greeks. Fundamentally Brand embraced and promoted his own understanding of the sexuality of elite men in ancient Greece. Adolescents would be mentored by older male patrons until old enough to marry and begin their own families. As adult family patriarchs they could then patronize a male adolescent lover of their own. The so-called *Freundesliebe* expressed in these relationships or in those of adult men transcended any romantic ties forged between men and women. Brand managed to live out his ancient Greek fantasy, in fact, and actually married sometime around 1900. Although he never fathered children, Brand resided with his wife and several generations of his extended family (and serially, several younger lovers) in Wilhelmshagen until killed in an Allied bombing raid in 1945.[45]

If Brand's views seem idiosyncratic (or worse) today, they were less unusual in fin-de-siècle Germany. The so-called "tyranny of Greece over

Germany" expressed the extent to which Greek aesthetic and political models pervaded and influenced—at least superficially—imperial German culture.[46] The genealogy of this love affair with the classical world reaches back to the seminal work of Johann Winckelmann (1717–1768) and follows a rich trajectory of scholarship in art history, political history, and philosophy. Winckelmann, whose sexual relationships were exclusively with other men (and who allegedly was killed by a male prostitute in Trieste in 1768), completed his German *Gymnasium* training, steeped in the classics, before studying medicine at universities in Halle and Jena. In 1755 he first traveled to Italy, where he spent most of the rest of his life. Published in 1764, Winckelmann's *History of Ancient Art* is a foundational text for both scientific archaeology and art history. Historian and Nobel laureate Theodor Mommsen (1817–1903), a founder of the subfield of ancient history, is considered one of the greatest classicists of the nineteenth century, based in part on his four-volume *History of Rome,* which he published in the 1850s. The philosophy of Friedrich Nietzsche (1844–1900), a brilliant classical philologist, was inspired by his (re)interpretation of ancient Greek literature (he published *The Birth of Tragedy* in 1872), and had an outsized influence on Brand and his entire generation.

Several of Brand's early supporters were friends from Friedrichshagen (and refugees from the SHC), including the physician Edwin Bab, Peter Hille, and Benedict Friedlaender. In 1903 Bab delivered a lecture to the CoS—a part of which was later published under the title *Die Gleichgeschlechtliche Liebe* (Same-sex love) with a dedication to Brand—which rejected Hirschfeld's assertion that homo-sex reflected some kind of psychological hermaphroditism or that it sprang from a congenital difference confined to only a minority. Like Brand, Bab contended that most men were capable of loving men and women alike—therefore essentially "bisexual"—and that it was misleading to identify "homosexuals" either as a minority or as somehow sexually distinct from the larger population.[47] Benedict Friedlaender offered a complementary view in his monographic study *Renaissance des Eros Uranios* (Renaissance of uranian eros), which he published in 1904. Like Brand, Friedlaender was married, and he was also the father of a young child. Unlike Brand, however, Friedlaender remained—at least until 1906—a member of both the

CoS and the SHC. He was a major source of financial support, in fact, not only for the SHC but also for some of Brand's publications, including *Der Eigene*; a number of anarchist papers, including Johannes Holzmann's *Der Kampf*; and the pederastic literature of "Sagitta," John Henry Mackay.[48]

Even if the differences between Hirschfeld and the masculinists undermined a fleeting unity that might have aided the cause of legal reform, their wrangling fostered a range of theories about (and sensibilities toward) same-sex erotic love that proved in its own right tremendously productive. One of the important achievements of this struggle was the creation of a homosexual cultural canon.

A practice that proved irresistible—and still proves so today—was the naming of famous historical figures alleged to have been homosexual. The political utility of a "pink" pantheon is not difficult to imagine: "If we judge homosexuality to be immoral," one *Jahrbuch* contributor opined in 1902, "must we not also then agree that the great and noble figures who manifested this orientation be excluded from the ranks of humanity? . . . Should the love of a Michelangelo, a Shakespeare, or Frederick the Great be considered immoral?"[49] Of particular interest were powerful political and military figures, including King David (and his friend Jonathan), Alexander the Great, Emperor Hadrian (and Antinous), Valois king of France Henry III, Frederick the Great, or Bavarian king Ludwig II. Arguably, Henry III and Ludwig II lacked the virile qualities of the others, yet the allegation of homosexuality made any political ruler worthy of study.[50] Most popular among these, and naturally so in Berlin, was Frederick the Great, who never cohabited with his wife and died childless. It is clear that Frederick attempted as a young prince to escape his cruel father, King Frederick William I, by fleeing Potsdam with his friend (and presumed lover) Hans Hermann von Katte. After they were apprehended, the king forced his son to witness Katte's beheading.[51]

A perhaps surprising candidate for membership in the order of heroic homosexuals was the philosopher Friedrich Nietzsche, who had died only in 1900. By this date his reception was in full swing and he had become the philosophical guru—across the entire political spectrum—of the German cultural avant-garde. Certainly both wings of the homosexual rights movement were votaries of the incipient cult. In the pages of *Jahrbuch,* Hirschfeld paraphrased Nietzsche approvingly (without providing any clear citation): "The degree and kind of a man's sexuality reaches up into the topmost summit of his spirit."[52] Brand and other masculinists were no less adulatory. Like the anarchist Max Stirner, whose work (*Der Einzige und sein Eigentum*), we recall, inspired the title of Brand's journal, Nietzsche was one of the key philosophical guides of the masculinist movement. *Der Eigene* advertised Nietzsche's publications in its very first issue, and frequently published aphorisms from Nietzsche's *Thus Spake Zarathustra,* as well as excerpts from his other published works.[53] Popular understandings of the "Dionysian" or the "transvaluation of values"— the rejection of traditional Christian morality—seemed to endorse non-normative sexuality. But the pious devotion of all of Berlin's homosexual activists was also due to Nietzsche's rumored homosexuality; at least one theory ascribed his insanity (and incarceration in an asylum for the last ten years of his life, beginning in 1890) to tertiary-stage syphilis, which he allegedly contracted in a boy brothel in Italy.[54]

The early publications of Hirschfeld, Brand, and the Spohr Verlag also helped to create what was arguably the first "gay" literary canon. Brand's Community of the Special was essentially a reading and literary circle, after all. And Hirschfeld's SHC also sponsored cultural events, including dramatic readings and musical performances; in 1904 the SHC announced the formal organization of a lending library, collecting quality scientific works as well as German and world literature to "serve the enlightenment" of the members and donors granted borrowing privileges.[55] This "enlightenment" aided the construction of an identity, transcending time and place, as well as the formation of a cultural community, which allowed at least some to identify with a collective "we." All of this was made possible, of course, by the necessary though not sufficient condition of imperial Germany's (relatively) liberal censorship. An equally important element was the middle-class readership that consumed these publications and provided the commercial support for an incipient homosexual press. The process of canon formation was dynamic and unsteady, moreover, and relied intrinsically on a stream of

Portrait of Hirschfeld in France from 1934

Adolf Brand

Both photos: Schwules Museum, Berlin

Jap. Chin. Teehaus u. Café „Mikado", Berlin SW. 48, Puttkamerstr. 15.

ABOVE: Picture postcard of Mikado (Puttkamerstr. 15), which was opened from 1908 until 1933
Schwules Museum, Berlin

LEFT: Photo portrait of Hermann Freiherr von Teschenberg (1860–1911), active member of the Scientific Humanitarian Committee who published the first German translations of several of Oscar Wilde's plays
Magnus Hirschfeld, Geschlechtskunde, *5 vols. (1926–1930), 5: 642*

BELOW: Picture postcard of Zauberflöte (Kommandantenstr. 72), which was a popular café and dancing venue for homosexuals and lesbians before the First World War
Schwules Museum, Berlin

Gruss aus dem Dresdener Casino. ⊞ Berlin S., Dresdener Strasse 96.
Inh. A. Muxfeldt ○ Fernspr. Amt 4, 8666

Säle für Vereinsfestlichkeiten, Hochzeiten, Commerse, Versammlungen usw.

Berlin, den _29.–30.12.16,_

ᴏᴠᴇ: Picture postcard of Dresdener Casino
ʀᴇsdener Str. 96), a popular venue for
ᴛᴀnsverstite balls in the prewar period
ᴀwules Museum, Berlin

ᴳʜᴛ: Graf Kuno von Moltke depicted as Dorian
ᴀʏ: When Moltke examines his own portrait,
ʜ is mortified to discover a youthful Maximilian
ᴀʀden, his nemesis. Oscar Wilde's novel had been
ʙlished in German translation only in 1902.
ᴜstige Blätter (Berlin), 22, 28 (9 July 1907): 1

ʟᴇꜰᴛ: "Greetings from the Scientific
Humanitarian Committee." Hirschfeld in a tutu,
with his signed greeting: "Long live Science!
Always Your Dr. Magnus Hirschfeld."
Simplicissimus (Munich) 13, 1 (6 April 1908): 5

A typical Berlin *Pissoir* (now used by a fast-food vendor), located under U-Bahn Line number one

Photo by author

"Transvestite Pass" allowing Berthe Buttgereit to appear in public wearing men's clothing, issued May 3, 1918

Landesarchiv Berlin, A Rep. 341-04 Nr 1087

Film still from *Anders als die Andern* (*Different from the Others*) showing the protagonist confronting his would-be blackmailer

Magnus Hirschfeld, Geschlechtskunde, 5 vols. (1926–1930), 5: 644

w of the main villa of the
titute for Sexual Science
vules Museum, Berlin

e museum in the Institute for Sexual Science
la 3, 145 (30 December 1933): 11

Karl Giese (Magnus Hirschfeld's lover) giving visitors to the Institute for Sexual Science a tour of the museum
Schwules Museum, Berlin

Hirschfeld sitting with two transvestites outside the villa of the Institute for Sexual Science
Voila 3, 119 (1 July 1933): 6

Newsstand at Potsdamerplatz, displaying prominently the gay newspapers (center of photo) *Die Insel, Die Freundschaft, Freundschaftsblatt,* and *Eros* (1926)
Landesarchiv Berlin, A Pr. Br. Rep. 030, No. 16935-1

Newsstand at Friedrichstraße Train Station with the gay newspaper *Die Freundschaft* and the lesbian journal *Frauen Liebe* displayed openly for sale (1926)
Landesarchiv Berlin, A. Pr. Br. Rep. 030, No. 16935-2

Unsere Geschäftsstelle

Friedrich-Radszuweit Verlag

Berlin S 14, Neue Jakobstraße 9. — Tel.: Moritzplatz 16945.

Aufruf an unsere Mitarbeiter und Freunde!

Der Verlag der „INSEL" hat sich, dem Wunsch vieler seiner Leser entsprechend, entschlossen, ein Gedicht- und Novellenbüchlein herauszubringen. Es soll, den Ansprüchen unserer Zeit Rechnung tragend, einfach, billig, gediegen und geschmackvoll sein. Wir brauchen aber dafür die Mitarbeit aller, denn es soll eine Sammlung von Arbeiten vieler Autoren werden, also ein Sammelwerk.

Viele sind berufen, viele können ausgewählt werden. Senden Sie uns Ihre Gedichte, Skizzen oder Novellen ein. Wir werden sie prüfen und veröffentlichen! Die Einsendungen müssen das Kennwort: „Gedichtband!" tragen. Jeder kann sich beteiligen, jeder erhält vom Verlag umgehenden Bescheid.

Alle Zuschriften sind zu richten an den Verlag „DIE INSEL", Berlin, S 14, Neue Jakobstr. 9.

Preisfrage

Homo- oder Heterosexuell

Für die richtige Beantwortung unserer Preisfrage haben wir folgende Preise ausgesetzt:

1. **Jahresabonnement** auf „Das Freundschaftsblatt"
2. **Jahresabonnement** auf „Das Magazin der Ehelosen"
3. **Jahresabonnement** auf die „Blätter für Menschenrecht" und
20 **Trostpreise**

Bei der Preisverteilung entscheidet das Los. Die Bekanntgabe erfolgt im Oktoberheft dieses Magazins.

Nummer 3 — Preis 30 Pf.

Frauen Liebe und Leben

ABOVE, LEFT: Bookshop of the Friedrich-Radszuweit Verlag. From *Die Insel*, October 1927, first page after p. 28. Published by Friedrich Radszuweit.

ABOVE, RIGHT: "Preisfrage / Homo- oder Heterosexuell" (Contest / Homosexual or Heterosexual)

Free magazine subscriptions for correctly identifying the sexual orientation of the men and women depicted in the photos. From *Die Insel*, September 1926, first page after p. 16. Published by Friedrich Radszuweit.

LEFT: Cover illustration of *Frauen Liebe und Leben* (Women's Love and Life), 3, 1928. Published by Freiderich Radszuweit.

All photos: German National Library, Leipzig

Die Insel

PREIS 50 PFENNIG

Männer zu verkaufen

Näheres siehe Seite 31 „Die Insel"

Garçonne
Junggesellin

Preis 30 Pfennig · Mit den Beiblättern: „Femina", Blätter für somatische Veredelung und Schönheitspflege. — Der Transvestit. — Die Romanbeilage · 1. Dez. 1930, Nr. 4

Herbstweh

Der Traum des Sommers ist entschwunden
Und kühle Herbstwinde weh'n.
Das Lied der Liebe uns entwunden,
Die Hoffnung ist im Untergeh'n.

Kalt grüßet jeder Baum und Strauch
Zerpflückt vom Laub der Zeit.
Und Wald und Flur bekleidet auch
Das graue Winterkleid!

Nicht anders geht's dem Menschenherz
Auf dieser bunten Welt;
Denn alles ist nur Rausch und Scherz
Hier unter'm Himmelszelt!

Wie's draußen ist, so ist's auch innen.
Bald sonnenhell, bald finst're Nacht.
Die schönsten Stunden, sie zerrinnen —
— Das Glück zerstört des Schicksals Macht!

„Denn war es gestern noch dein eigen,
Heut weilt's an einem andern Ort!
Dich grüßt das Leid von kühlen Zweigen —
Und suchend, hoffend lebst du fort!"

An. Ha.

Aus dem Inhalt:

Prof. Karsch-Haack: **Junggesellin und Junggeselle** (4. Teil mit Illustration)
Elisabeth Holtenau: **Deine Hände.**
Ikarus: **Die Frau und die Gewohnheit**
Roman-Beilage: Honoré Balzac: **Das Mädchen mit den Goldaugen.** Bearbeitet von Karen

Helga Wolff: „Chanson triste"
Der Transvestit, geleitet von Maria Weiß. Die Aufgaben der Vereinigung „D'Eon"
Femina-Kosmetik, geleitet von Fr. Scott. Wie ist das mit dem Pudern — Es kostet viel Zeit — Massage in der Schönheitspflege

ABOVE, LEFT: Cover of *Die Insel*, December 1930, advertising serialized installment of *Männer zu verkaufen* (Men for Sale). Published by Friedrich Radszuweit.

ABOVE, RIGHT: Cover of *Garçonne—Junggesellin* (Flapper—Bachelorette), no. 4, December 1, 1930. Published by Friedrich Radszuweit.

RIGHT: Advertisements in *Die Freundschaft*, including a medical doctor specializing in "sexual disturbances," a Pinkerton Private Detective Agency (offering to investigate blackmail threats), and a gay- and lesbian-friendly tobacconist photos: *German National Library, Leipzig*

Erasmus-Diele
Berlin NW 87
Erasmusstraße 17   a. d. Beußelstraße
Autobus 11, Straßenbahn 3, 11, 13, 14, 44, 45

Sonnabend, den 4. Oktober
zur
Eröffnungsfeier
Venezianische Nacht
*
Große Gratis-Tombola
Saalpost
Große
Confetti-Schlacht
Unter neuer Leitung

Traviata
Passauerstr. 5   am K. d. W.

Neu eröffnet

Treffpunkt der eleganten Welt

*

Täglich ab ½ 8 Uhr:

Künstler-Konzert
Stimmung

Neu eröffnet   Neu eröffnet
RESTAURANT PLATON
Moabit, Sickingenstr. 9, am Bahnhof Beusselstr.   Tel. Hansa 3667
═══ ZUR ERÖFFNUNG ═══
am Sonnabend, d. 4. Oktober ladet alle Freunde und Bekannten ein
Lothar Lenz
Kalte und warme Küche   Straßenbahn: 3, 14, 44, 45, 13, 113   Streng solide Preise

---

Von der Reise zurück
Dr. med. Schneidler

Dr. Iwan Bloch
Facharzt für Haut- und Sexualleiden,
insbesondere Störungen der Sexualsphäre
Institut f. Sexualforschung
Berlin W 15
Joachimsthaler Straße 9
(Sprechstunden v. 10-12 u. 4-7 Uhr)
Poliklinik
BERLIN-WILMERSDORF
Berliner Straße 38
Sprechstunden v. 12-1 u. 7-8 Uhr

Homosexuellen
die der Erpressungsversuchen ausgesetzt sind,
wird dringend geraten, sich vertrauensvoll an
G. GERHARDT
Direktor der
Pinkerton-Gesellschaft
BERLIN W. 9, Schellingstraße 2
oder Privatwohnung, Charlottenburg, Grolmanstraße 31-33
(Telefon: Kurfürst 1344 und 3173) zwecks Befreiung von
verbrecherischen Elementen
zu wenden. Erfolg garantiert.

Gleichgesinnte kaufen
Zigarren, Zigaretten,
Rauch-, Kau- und
Schnupftabake
bei
Claire Splettstösser
Berlin W. 57
Culmstrasse 20
zu billigsten Preisen
Die „Freundschaft" liegt aus.

Verlag: Karl Schultz-Verlagsgesellschaft m. b. H., Berlin NW 87, Darother Str. 1. — Verantwortlich für den gesamten Inhalt sowie für den Verlag der Zeitung „Der Merkur":
Fritz Flotig, Berlin SW 61 — Druck: H. Wilgenkow, Berlin N. 20

ELDORADO
MOTZSTR. 15
WAS SIE WO ANDERS NICHT SEHEN
INTERNATIONALER BETRIEB
DAS INTERESSANTE LOKAL
EINTRITT FREI ! BIER · KAFFEE

osite, top left: Hansi Sturm, winner of
Miss Eldorado transvestite pageant in 1926
vules Museum, Berlin

osite, top right: Advertisement for Eldorado
he mainstream cultural journal *Queerschnitt*:
'hat you won't see elsewhere / International
ntele / The interesting locale"
erschnitt, March 1932

osite, bottom: Photo of transvestites in
orado, from the early 1930s
a 3, 119 (1 July 1933): 6

ve: Berlin gay bar Marienkasino with
nsvestite prostitutes
*gnus Hirschfeld, Geschlechtskunde, 5 vols.
6–1930), 5: 590*

HT: Picture postcard of the gay club
iouette, which was popular in the late 1920s
l early 1930s
vules Museum, Berlin

"SILHOUETTE"

W. H. Auden, Stephen Spender, and Christopher Isherwood, on vacation at the North Sea on the Island of Rügen, summer 1931

Huntington Library, CI, Box 92, 3113, p. 34

LEFT: Christopher Isherwood posing with his boyfriend "Otto" (name unknown but the inspiration for Otto Nowak in *Goodbye to Berlin*) in the Tiergarten (Berlin), autumn 1931
Huntington Library, CI (Christopher Isherwood), Box 92, 3113, p. 6

BELOW: Christopher Isherwood's boyfriend "Otto" sunbathing on the Island of Rügen, summer 1931
Huntington Library, CI, Box 92, 3115, p. 39

Christopher Isherwood's working-class "friends," who were likely habitués of the Cosy Corner and occasional prostitutes

Huntington Library, CI, Box 92, 3113, p. 27

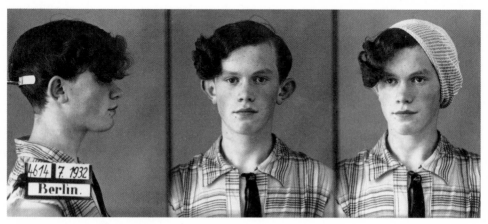

Police mugshots of Berlin prostitute Johann Scheff, arrested July 1932

Landesarchiv Berlin, A Rep. 358-05 Nr 56643

...zi officials sort "un-German" and "perverted" materials in the debris of the Institute for Sexual Science, ...sacked on May 6, 1933, for the book burning four days later on May 10 (undated photo, May 6–10, 1933).

...agentur für Kunst, Kultur und Geschichte (Berlin)

ABOVE: Hirschfeld and Giese
together in France
Schwules Museum, Berlin

LEFT: Hirschfeld in exile in France
sometime after spring 1933
Voila 3, 145 (30 December 1933): 11

original literature as well as literary and cultural criticism served up by both *Der Eigene* and *Jahrbuch*.

The compiling of homoerotic writings, however, was not original to the late nineteenth century. By the Renaissance, humanist scholars had begun collecting classical texts documenting "Greek love." Borrowing from these models, *Eros oder die Männerliebe der Griechen* (Eros or the male-male love of the Greeks) was one of the earliest anthologies of classical Greek texts that explicitly celebrated same-sex eroticism; it was published by the Swiss-German author Heinrich Hößli in 1838.[56] Pioneering activist Karl Heinrich Ulrichs also published excerpts of homoerotic literature in two of his pamphlets, "Ara Spei" (1865) and "Memnon" (1868). In 1896 the Spohr Verlag published *Der Eros und die Kunst: Ethischen Studien* (Eros and art: Ethical studies), under the pseudonym "Ludwig Frey." This was arguably the first volume devoted entirely to "gay canon formation." As the author "Frey" argued—with a prescient, AIDS-era sensibility—"Silence is death" (*Stillschweigen ist der Tod*). "The spirit through which the knowledge of the essence of *Urningtum* is spread exerts itself," according to Frey, "and will not rest until its idea has achieved victory."[57] Other anthologies followed, including Elisar von Kupffer's *Lieblingminne und Männerliebe in der Weltliteratur* (The love of favorites and the love of friends in world literature), first published by Spohr in 1900. This volume was a direct inspiration for one of the only non-German-language anthologies published in this period, Edward Carpenter's *Ioläus*, which escaped English censorship by using the euphemism of "friendship" and avoiding explicit mention of same-sex love.[58]

Friendship—*Freundschaft*—was a particularly vital theme for much German literature, and one that lent itself easily to the incipient "gay" canon.[59] The seemingly homoerotic language of the German Romantics was especially useful for demonstrating both the trans-historical and particularly the Germanic character of same-sex love. As the literary historian Paul Derks has argued, the German Romantics lived in a golden age (1750–1850) when relationships between men that were potentially sexual were (mis)recognized as mere friendships. Only the scrutiny of scientific and medical study after 1850, Derks argues, created a new visibility that ruined the inconspicuous same-sex sensuality of "romanticism."[60] This peculiar feature of German literature was remarked upon not only by Germans. The Russian and Francophone psychiatrist Marc-André Raffalovich emphasized the special, erotic character of "German friendship" (*"L'amitié allemande"*)—citing the works of Schlegel, Hamman, Gleim, Arnim, and Brentano, among others—in a chapter of his 1896 treatise on homosexuality (*Uranisme et Unisexualité*).[61] Commentary and criticism published in both *Jahrbuch* and *Der Eigene* deduced male eroticism in the works of Goethe, Grillparzer, Hölderlin, Kleist, Platen, and Schiller, as well as the alleged sexual character of many of their same-sex relationships.[62] For example, the recent discovery of a letter from Heinrich von Kleist to his friend Ernst von Pfuel inspired an animated debate in the pages of *Der Eigene* about Kleist's sexual orientation, a discussion that was dutifully recounted in the literary reviews of *Jahrbuch*.[63]

In Berlin's hothouse climate of homosexual rights activism, some of this classical literature was so fervent that it risked censorship. For example, the officials who brought obscenity charges against Adolf Brand and Max Spohr for the May 1903 issue of *Der Eigene* cited—among others—Schiller's poem "Die Freundschaft" as obscene, but without naming Schiller or recognizing, apparently, his authorship.[64]

> Was't not this omnipotent desire,
> That in love's eternal happy fire
> Did *our* hearts unto each other force?
> Friend, upon *thine* arm—delight!
> Venture I to th' spiritual sun so bright
> Joyful on perfection's course.
>
> Happy! happy! *Thee* have I thus found,
> Have from out of millions *thee* wound round,
> And from out of millions, *thou* art *mine*—
> Let the savage chaos come once more,
> Let the atoms in confusion pour,
> For eternity our hearts entwine.
>
> Must I not from out *thy* flaming eyes
> Draw th' reflection of *my* paradise?
> But in *thee* I wonder at myself—

Fairer does th' fair earth to me appear,
In the friend's demeanor shines more clear,
Lovelier the Heaven itself.

Melancholy drops the tearful weight,
Sweetly th' storm of passion to abate,
In the breast of charity;—
Seeks not e'en the tortuous delight,
Friend, within the spirit's sight,
A voluptuous grave impatiently?[65]

The state attorney claimed that "the depicted embraces and kisses between friends, if not a direct glorification of pederasty are doubtless a glorification of pederastic foreplay, which offends popular feelings of shame and morality, as long as Paragraph 175 remains the law."[66] The censors' ignorance of the poem's authorship and their claim that Schiller had glorified "pederastic foreplay" was widely ridiculed in the liberal press. According to literary historian Marita Keilson-Lauritz, mention of the poem was eventually expunged from the formal charge after its correct attribution, signaling the officials' embarrassment. Of course, Spohr was fined two hundred marks all the same, while Brand received a two-month prison sentence.[67]

Hirschfeld's *Jahrbuch* and Brand's *Der Eigene* were also responsible for identifying the inherent "gayness" of many contemporary German works (and in some cases their authors) by reviewing and critiquing them. Austrian writer Robert Musil published *The Confusions of Young Törless (Die Verwirrungen des Zöglings Törleß)* in Vienna in 1906, which was reviewed the following year in Hirschfeld's *Monatsbericht*.[68] Hirschfeld and Brand both established and adhered to fairly specific theories, or perhaps creeds, and did not always embrace work that was later very popular. For example, Thomas Mann's *Death in Venice (Tod in Venedig)*, published in 1912, was virtually ignored by the homosexual press, at least initially. Not until 1914 did *Jahrbuch* finally discuss the novella in a larger review essay by Kurt Hiller, who described Mann's work as "an example of moralistic narrowness," since the protagonist's love for a boy is treated as a "symptom of degeneration" and depicted "nearly the same as cholera."[69] What Hiller was first to identify was an implicit theme in Mann's work, expressive of Mann's repressed homosexuality—explored exhaustively in Hiller's essay by literary scholars and critics—that equated homosexuality with degeneration.[70]

Whether negative or positive, such reviews were not limited to German-language writings. Hirschfeld, Brand, and the Spohr Verlag were instrumental in introducing much foreign-language literature to their German readers and often in providing them with German translations. The 1901 French-language *Dédé,* by Achille Essebac (the pseudonym for and an anagram of the author's surname, Bécasse), was a story of the homoerotic relationship of two schoolboys. The novel was published in German translation by Spohr in 1902, and gained a cult following in Germany.[71] (In the 1920s there was even a Dédé bar in Berlin, named for the novel.) The French-language novel *Escal-Vigor,* by Belgian author Georges Eekhoud, was published in German translation in 1903, likewise by Spohr. In this novel an aristocratic aesthete and artist falls in love with his peasant model and protégé; Eekhoud was brought before a Belgian court on obscenity charges, which only increased the book's popularity in France and soon after in Germany.[72] With its homoerotic overtones, André Gide's *L'Immoraliste* (1902) was reviewed in *Jahrbuch* in 1903; the German translation appeared in 1905.[73] In 1904 Danish author Herman Bang published *Mikaël,* the story of an artist who falls in love with his much younger model "Michael." The novel appeared in German translation with Fischer Verlag in 1906, and was made into a feature-length (silent) film in Germany in the 1920s.[74] Russian author and composer Mikhail Kuzmin published *Wings,* the first Russian novel with an explicitly homosexual theme, in 1906. The book received its first German review in 1907, and a German translation appeared in 1911.[75]

The most notable such publications from the Spohr Verlag were translations of Oscar Wilde's works. Although Wilde's 1895 trial had received considerable German press (and was followed closely by Hirschfeld and others), his writings were all but unknown in Germany before his death in 1900.[76] In 1901 Spohr published the first Wilde work in German, *The Picture of Dorian Gray,* translated by the Hirschfeld associate and SHC member Johannes Gaulke. In 1902 Gaulke published his translation of *The Portrait of Mr. W. H.* with Spohr, and in 1903 *The Happy Prince and*

Other Stories. Another SHC member, Hermann Freiherr von Teschenberg, who had fled his native Austria in the wake of a homosexual scandal
and then made Wilde's acquaintance in London in 1895 before settling
in Berlin, translated several of Wilde's plays—including *The Importance
of Being Ernest, Lady Windermere's Fan, A Woman of No Importance,* and
Salomé (which also served as Richard Strauss's opera libretto)—and
published them with Spohr between 1901 and 1904. Although most of
Spohr's Wilde publications went through multiple editions, the press
was soon faced with competing translations issued by more prominent
German presses, including Fischer, Insel, and Reclam.[77]

Arguably the German-homosexual criticism of many non-German
authors—Oscar Wilde, Walt Whitman, or André Gide—played a significant if not central role in their initial recognition as "queer." The
German reception of Walt Whitman is especially striking. Not only
was it the Berlin activists who "outed" Whitman (followed by the vehement denials of many of his American, English, French, and German
admirers); a debate also unfolded among the Germans about the exact
character of Whitman's sexuality. Was Whitman a "homosexual" who
experienced erotic feelings exclusively for men, or was he a virile "masculinist" figure who potentially loved women but realized his highest
spiritual expression in male friendships, whether erotic or not? Or was it
irresponsible even to speculate about Whitman's sex life?

Although Whitman had been discussed and translated in Germany
since at least the 1870s, it was only in a lengthy character sketch published in *Jahrbuch* in 1905 that his suspect sexuality was first addressed.[78]
The author Eduard Bertz, who studied philosophy in Germany and later
lived in Paris, England, and America before returning to Berlin, had
signed the SHC petition against Paragraph 175 and also served as a member of the SHC board of directors. In his essay Bertz analyzed Whitman's apparent indifference to women and also described his intimate
male friendships. More significantly, perhaps, Bertz dismissed the masculinist credo that sexual intimacy among men (and implicitly bisexuality) was all but ubiquitous. Bertz's analysis, moreover, had a political
motivation: he judged "masculinism" an ineffective strategy for legal
reform: "The small minority that has been persecuted and despised by
the normal majority must first strive to be tolerated by this majority,"

Bertz opined. "Anything beyond this is foolishness and forgets to consider the facts."[79]

Bertz's allegation that Whitman was homosexual most disturbed Whitman's German admirers. Chief among these was Johannes Schlaf, naturalist author and founder of the German "Whitman cult." Like Bertz, Schlaf had signed the SHC petition. But he clearly feared that Bertz's claims would affect Whitman's reputation and rejected them in a pamphlet published the following year. In the debate that followed, Bertz argued even more vehemently that Whitman displayed the signs of congenital homosexuality. Literary historian Walter Grünzweig argues that Schlaf "secured" Whitman's reputation in Germany and that "if Bertz had prevailed, German reception of Whitman would have taken a different and, at least at that time, decidedly more narrow turn."[80] As the most important German editor and translator of Whitman's work, Schlaf was able to undermine Bertz's credibility.[81] American reviews of the Bertz-Schlaf dispute were sharply critical of Bertz. According to the SHC *Monatsbericht,* one of these reviews made the first-ever mention in an American periodical of the German homosexual rights movement.[82]

While Bertz upset the "straight," mainstream Whitman followers, he also annoyed the masculinists for employing a Hirschfeldian paradigm. Writing in response in *Der Eigene,* Herbert Stegemann, a onetime SHC member who made common cause with Brand and then Benedict Friedlaender, questioned Bertz's Hirschfeldian science, arguing that psychology or medicine did not have the objective expertise to assess the "homosexuality" of a literary figure and that only the individual author or poet should be allowed to proclaim (or not) his (or her) sexual preference(s).[83] In another response, Peter Hamecher, who had complicated relationships with both Hirschfeld and Brand, argued that Whitman was without question a representative of "physiological friendship," an expression that aligned him clearly with Brand and Friedlaender, and defined Whitman as a "masculinist," a man who *chose* homosocial or homoerotic relationships, but not a "homosexual" with an inborn sexual orientation.[84]

While the explanatory frameworks of Hirschfeld and the masculinists fostered creative tensions, the groups grew further and further apart, arguably weakening the struggle for legal reform. Brand had attended SHC meetings, at least until his incarceration in 1903, but he clearly lost patience with Hirschfeld's science and more timid strategies. Hirschfeld's theory of sexual intermediacy could more easily accommodate Brand's pragmatic bisexuality, but Brand—who likely never really understood Hirschfeld's theoretical position—rejected Hirschfeld's essentialism as hopelessly emasculating. Brand also promoted a more aggressive approach to legal reform. Beginning in 1903, SHC members debated the efficacy of staging a mass "self-outing," something that Brand strongly endorsed. If a thousand SHC members, many of them public figures or successful professionals or wealthy aristocrats, were to profess publicly their homo- or bisexuality, it would cause a law enforcement crisis. Prosecuting a large number of otherwise respectable citizens would be inconceivable; allowing such a group to flout the law, on the other hand, would render it meaningless. The scheme was debated in SHC meetings on several occasions and ultimately rejected. Along the way, the SHC took baby steps, advising members to begin to "out" themselves to trusted friends and family and encouraging donors to allow their names to be disclosed in SHC publications.[85]

The discussion that surrounded the tactic of "outing," whether third-party or voluntary, appears to have emerged from the Krupp scandal of 1902. Recall that *Vorwärts,* the official, national paper of the Social Democratic Party, had essentially "outed" Krupp by reporting his escapades (with underage boys) on the island of Capri, leading to his official expulsion from Italy. The German press coverage that followed the *Vorwärts* scoop led, in turn, to Krupp's alleged suicide. In a short piece published in Maximilian Harden's weekly *Die Zukunft,* psychiatrist Albert Moll reflected sarcastically on Krupp's demise and its lessons for the homosexual rights movement: "The homosexuals are sometimes reproached for agitating too much. But what should they otherwise do? . . . Perhaps they simply need an uncompromising leader who can lead them to their goal over a mountain of corpses. They need only to name publicly those men whose homosexuality is notorious and can easily be proven."[86] This was a striking and perhaps chilling observation, even if Moll was making it in jest. It also inspired the expression "path over corpses," which was uttered with great frequency in discussions about the utility of "outing."

Brand found the "path over corpses" a particularly appealing tactic, and in 1904 he published a short pamphlet, *Kaplan Dasbach und die Freundesliebe* (Kaplan Dasbach and friend-love), in which he recounted his correspondence and confrontations with Georg Friedrich Dasbach, a Jesuit priest, parliamentarian, and sometime leader of the Catholic Center Party.[87] A native of Cologne, Dasbach was also a central figure in the opposition to the SHC petition and its efforts to reform Paragraph 175. The minutes recorded from SHC meetings mention the repeated efforts that were made to reach out to Dasbach, and on at least one occasion in 1902 Hirschfeld actually met with the politician. Although SHC sources are never explicit, it appears almost certain that the homosexual rights activists believed they had identified one of their own in Dasbach, and therefore a natural ally, or, if in fact an opponent, alternatively, one who might be silenced.[88] The occasion for Brand's particular initiative (and publication) was a *Vorwärts* article claiming that Dasbach had been unsuccessfully blackmailed by an adolescent hustler in Cologne. (This was reminiscent of the report published about Krupp, and incredibly opportunistic, of course, since Dasbach, as a Catholic Center politician, was likewise considered a political and class enemy.) After the boy had demanded one hundred marks, Dasbach reported him to authorities, who identified the boy as a prostitute and a convicted perpetrator of blackmail. The boy received a nine-month prison sentence, and Dasbach appeared to emerge from the scandal with his reputation intact.[89]

After the newspaper report on the blackmail attempt, Brand began sending Dasbach copies of *Der Eigene* and some of his CoS literature, hoping, no doubt, that he had found not only a potential opponent of the anti-sodomy statute but also an advocate for Greek *Freundesliebe,* like himself. It appears that Brand expected Dasbach to find his own theories more compelling than the doctrine of "sexual intermediacy" promoted by the SHC. Dasbach ignored Brand for several months, but finally met with him in July 1904. In the pamphlet, Brand gives a detailed account of this encounter: Brand confronted Dasbach with the rumors of his many Berlin dalliances with male prostitutes; the priest *cum* parliamentarian swore to Brand that he had never experienced sexual attraction to men *or* to women. Brand also claimed to know that Dasbach purchased nude photographs of adolescent boys and young men, including some of Brand's own publications, which Dasbach categorically denied.[90]

Dasbach's explanation of his actions, as recounted by Brand in the pamphlet, gives a remarkably sympathetic portrait of a naive, confused, and sexually repressed man. Admitting to frequent interactions with the Friedrichstraße rent boys in Berlin, Dasbach averred that his intentions had been completely charitable. Before arriving in Berlin, Dasbach claimed, he had never even heard of homosexuality. He was therefore astonished to learn that the capital harbored such a large population of male prostitutes. His aim had been only to make contact with and help these apparently destitute street urchins. (The story might remind us of British prime minister William Gladstone's evening ministration to the female streetwalkers of London.) In any case, Dasbach reiterated his opposition to a reform of the anti-sodomy statute, and threatened Brand with a libel suite, forcing Brand to retract the insinuation that Dasbach had sex with men. Dasbach weathered the potential scandal caused by Brand's publication, which—at least according to Brand—sold in large numbers. Unremarkable, perhaps, was Dasbach's subsequent demise: soon after, he was accused of frequenting a Berlin hotel whose proprietor was convicted of homosexual procurement. All of this was likewise reported in the press.[91] As a result Dasbach was relieved of his position as the leader of the Center Party in 1905, and he died in 1907 under mysterious circumstances. Suicide was suspected.[92]

The competition between Hirschfeld and those who hoped to promote an alternative to his theory of sexual intermediacy led ultimately to a rupture in the movement. This rift was probably inevitable, and therefore Hirschfeld deserves credit for attempting to accommodate views contrary to his own. Routinely the SHC sponsored lectures—including ones delivered by Friedlaender and Bab—and promoted or at least reported on new scholarship that did not conform to SHC doctrine. All the same, Hirschfeld ultimately controlled the theoretical orientation and the practical activities of the SHC, and those who openly countered his positions were ultimately forced to find other avenues for pursuing their own vision of legal, social, and cultural reform.

Brand challenged Hirschfeld openly, of course, and he maintained—with *Der Eigene* and the CoS—an organizational base independent of the SHC. But it was also the case that his literary and aesthetic interests created a niche that actually prevented him from (or allowed him to avoid) competing directly with the SHC. Many active SHC members were also *Der Eigene* subscribers, and some even maintained close ties with Brand, attending his symposia and other events. Brand's volatile temperament made him something of a loose canon, moreover, and his perennial legal and financial difficulties deflated any expectations that even his closest supporters might have harbored.

Hirschfeld's more direct and effective challenge came from Benedict Friedlaender, whose influence was amplified by his inherited wealth. The great surprise, perhaps, was that Friedlaender remained a major financial supporter of the SHC as late as 1905, when his extra donations for "propaganda" were reported in the monthly newsletters.[93] All the same, Friedlaender announced in December 1906 his new Secession movement (Sezession des WHK), a splinter organization that would maintain the SHC moniker but sever any other affiliation. The Secession took inspiration from the writings of a number of masculinists, including Bab, Wille, and, of course, Friedlaender himself, whose *Renaissance des Eros Uranios* (Renaissance of uranian eros) offered something of an official primer on the masculinists' creed.

Friedlaender not only rejected any characterization of same-sex erotic love as an expression of effeminacy; he asserted the precise opposite, namely, that men who loved men were more virile than most. The "virile" men who loved other men—Alexander the Great or Frederick the Great—were often military or political figures who commanded the loyalty of soldiers and subjects. In Friedlaender's view, social and cultural progress required that the super-virile man be allowed to fulfill his destiny as a charismatic leader. Of course, this required the recognition and even valorization of his homoerotic nature. Obstacles to this cultural vanguard included both the "deception of Christianity" (*Pfaffentrug*) and the "reign of women" (*Weiberherrschaft*). As the domain of women, the bourgeois family—and its values—posed an increasing threat to the future. The reformed society that Friedlaender envisioned would be based, in contrast, on the domination of hyper-virile, homophilic supermen. The only role women would be expected to play in this misogynistic dystopia would be as the vessels of biological reproduction.[94]

The masculinists' misogyny was another important point of difference with Hirschfeld and the SHC, which certainly admitted women, even if relatively few were ever directly involved. For Hirschfeld, the biological determinism of same-sex erotic love applied equally to men and women; lesbians experienced their sexuality as a natural feature of personhood no differently than male homosexuals. Hirschfeld also established close ties to left-wing feminists, who, in turn, supported the cause of homosexual emancipation and legal reform. Hirschfeld's closest feminist colleague was Helene Stöcker, who cofounded (with Hirschfeld's support) the progressive League for the Protection of Mothers and Sexual Reform (Bund für Mutterschutz und Sexualreform) in 1905. Under Stöcker's leadership, the group supported women's rights to sexual self-expression and access to information about birth control. Eventually the league lobbied for the decriminalization of abortion.[95]

The masculinists were also marked by their subtle anti-Semitism. This was expressed negatively as a *völkisch* nationalism, an adjective derived from the German word for people (*Volk*). A kind of hyper-nationalism, this ideology emphasized the racial character of "German" identity and was implicitly if not explicitly anti-Semitic. Beginning in the 1920s, the Nazis represented the most extreme of the *völkisch* political parties. In the vein of *völkisch* thinking, Brand and Friedlaender promoted the superiority of the German race, and cited the super-virile homosexual as distinctly or at least especially German. This was a subtle dig at Hirschfeld, of course, and also a way of denigrating the SHC more generally. A huge percentage of the progressive medical establishment, which supported the anti-sodomy petition, was in fact Jewish. Of course, Friedlaender had himself earned a doctorate in zoology, and although he never evinced any sort of Jewish identity, he was sometimes described as a "baptized Jew" (*getaufter Jude*), an obnoxious German expression that elevated "racial" identity above any formal religious affiliation. It appears likely that his grandfather converted to Lutheranism sometime in the nineteenth century.[96]

Friedlaender failed to build an organization that could counter Hirschfeld or the SHC. Stricken with colon cancer, he took his own life in June 1908. Friedlaender's initiative was not without consequences, however; the Secession demoralized many erstwhile SHC supporters, and contributed to the dissolution of the Leipzig and Munich chapters.

The minutes of the Munich subcommittee complained, for example, that as the conflict between Hirschfeld and Friedlaender unfolded it was difficult to take sides. In a lengthy position paper (*Denkschrift*), the Munich members described their relative ambivalence with both positions. The exaggerated praise for the qualities and accomplishments of homosexuals—a central feature in Friedlaender's characterization of the hyper-virile leader—was excessive: "[S]ome brochures present homosexuals as the noblest specimens of humankind, and one cannot blame those who think differently . . . when they condemn writings that depict the honor of humanity as something that rests in homosexual hands and that only same-sex eroticism allows mankind to achieve its spiritual potential." The subcommittee offered sharp criticisms of Hirschfeld as well: "We cannot spare Dr. Hirschfeld the reproach that the alleged sickness of homosexuality has been overemphasized and that the broad depictions of Berlin's cross-dressing and street prostitution in many of his writings have seriously damaged our cause." Reports from throughout 1907 indicated a dwindling Munich membership, and in May 1908 the subcommittee dissolved itself and directed that remaining members pay dues and correspond directly with the Berlin SHC.[97] The activities of the other subcommittees are not well documented. Certainly the absence of a paper trail suggests that groups in Leipzig, Hamburg, Hanover, and southwest Germany were no longer (or barely) active by the date of Friedlaender's death.

The direct and immediate influence of the Secession can best be seen in its negative influence on the SHC, and its ability to thwart and undermine Hirschfeld and his colleagues. Even so, Hirschfeld, arguably, won the day. His definition of homosexuality as an immutable, hardwired personality trait was widely accepted, certainly among an educated German elite that characterized a small percentage of the total population as well as within most social classes in Berlin. As described in the Introduction (page xv), the German-language encyclopedias *Meyers* and *Brockhaus* followed Hirschfeld's position, explaining that male and female homosexuals suffer from an "inborn and perverse feeling," that they could be found in all social classes, and that they likely made up 1.5 to 2 percent of the population—figures taken from Hirschfeld's survey.[98]

The schism created by Friedlaender and Brand within Berlin's early homosexual rights movement was influential in other respects, however. The "masculinist" impulse within the German movement certainly survived Friedlaender's death in 1908. Those who quibbled with Hirschfeld's biological determinism never disappeared, of course; Brand, certainly, remained a prominent if controversial figure throughout the Weimar Republic. Due in part to theoretical differences and the personal rivalries they inspired, the homosexual rights movement of the Weimar Republic was every bit as divided as its prewar precursor. Friedlaender and the masculinists had a powerful influence not only on self-conscious sexual minorities, moreover, but also on political and social theories of homosocial—if not homoerotic—masculine association. Friedlaender's most important intellectual protégé, Hans Blüher, became a prominent and culturally influential proponent of the idea of a German Männerbund (male association)—also modeled to some extent on ancient Greek models—which bonded as a collectivity through homoerotic and even explicitly homosexual ties. The role of homosociality and friend-love would soon be introduced to the social sciences more generally.

CHAPTER FOUR

The Eulenburg Scandal
and the Politics of Outing

They [the Germans] are not satisfied simply being pederasts, like
the rest of the world. They have to invent homosexuality. Where
science goes and finds itself a niche, my God? They study pederasty,
just as they study epigraphy. . . . Pederasts with emphasis,
sodomites with erudition! And in place of men simply making love
together, through vice, they are homosexuals with pedantry. Go to
Berlin, I tell you—see you in Berlin. That is the journey.

—OCTAVE MIRBEAU, "Berlin-Sodome," *La 628–E8* (Paris, 1907)

On November 7, 1906, the German Kaiser William II (1859–1941)
traveled a short distance north of Berlin to the estate of one of his
closest friends, Prince Philipp zu Eulenburg-Hertefeld (1847–1921). The
occasion was unremarkable. The Kaiser often enjoyed yacht cruises or
weeklong hunting parties with a circle of friends, courtiers, and officials.
Some twelve years older than the Kaiser, Eulenburg had befriended William II in 1887 before his ascension to the throne. At the youthful age
of twenty-nine, William II became the German emperor, following the
deaths in 1888 of both his aged grandfather Emperor William I and his
father, Emperor Frederick III, who reigned for just a few months before
succumbing to cancer. In 1900 the Kaiser elevated Eulenburg to the rank
of prince and named him a hereditary peer in the Prussian House of
Lords, an institution modeled on the British House of Lords and created
with the adoption of the Prussian constitution in 1850.[1] Eulenburg's close

friendship with William II endowed him with a special status, enabling him not only to exert significant behind-the-scenes influence but also to forge a network of officials and aristocrats who often escorted and entertained the monarch. So often had Eulenburg accompanied and even hosted the Kaiser, in fact, that the title of his country estate, Lieben-berg, provided the nickname for the Kaiser's circle of close friends: the "Liebenberg Roundtable" (*Tafelrunde*).

The Liebenberg Roundtable had become a veritable institution, though one that was despised and resented. Many political observers, including members of the Kaiser's own government, referred to the group as a "camarilla," a cadre of friends who used their position at court to exercise private political power. These camarilla members, it was thought, abused their friendship with the Kaiser to gain positions for themselves and, even worse, to influence the Kaiser's views on German foreign policy. Eulenburg provoked the greatest ire. He was blamed for encouraging William II to dismiss Chancellor Bismarck in 1890; the appointments of at least two of Bismarck's successors, Georg Leo Graf von Caprivi and Prince Chlodwig von Hohenlohe-Schillingfürst, were ascribed to his machinations. Into the twentieth century, William II had established an increasingly autocratic "personal monarchy," for which he was manifestly ill-suited. For this, too, Eulenburg and his close associates were frequently blamed; their sycophancy and idolization of the feckless Kaiser reinforced many of his worst characteristics. Eulenburg's critics also disliked his apparent "pacifism" and his support for closer diplomatic ties with France, which seemed to influence the Kaiser's foreign policy, at least for a time.[2]

The three-day hunting excursion was attended by a cast of familiar characters. Among the high-ranking ministers and elite courtiers was one prominent Liebenberg regular, Eulenburg's closest friend Kuno von Moltke (1847-1923). Descended from a prominent Prussian lineage that included many generals, Moltke's career as a Prussian officer and a member of the diplomatic corps was assured at his birth. His achievements, however, were conspicuously disappointing; in 1905 the Kaiser appointed Moltke military commander of the city of Berlin, a high-profile though largely honorific position. A more surprising guest at Liebenberg on this occasion was the French ambassador in Berlin,

Raymond Lecomte. Rumors that Lecomte had enjoyed nearly unfettered access to the Kaiser at Liebenberg roiled the German political class, though Lecomte claimed soon after that in his presence the Kaiser discussed only banalities.[3] For Lecomte's apparent access to the Kaiser, Eulenburg was likewise blamed, since he not only hosted the hunting excursion but was also known to socialize with Lecomte. In addition to serving the French Republic, Lecomte had an unsavory reputation; Berlin police commissioner Tresckow labeled him "king of the pederasts."[4] Monitored by the city police, the French ambassador patronized Berlin's homosexual bars and entertainments, and this too was widely discussed among the city's elite.[5]

Because of Lecomte's presence, this particular outing to Liebenberg marked a fateful turning point for Eulenburg, as well as for the Kaiser. Critics had a powerful weapon with which to neutralize the Liebenberg Roundtable, namely the alleged homosexuality of Eulenburg and his friends. Eulenburg himself was married and had five children. All the same, many believed that he had been targeted for blackmail while posted to the German embassy in Vienna; allegedly, Eulenburg left the post in 1902 to avoid the exposure of his homosexual dalliances.[6] His closest associates, Moltke among them, were also suspected of sexual "abnormalities." Members of the Liebenberg Roundtable, including Eulenburg, wrote poetry and composed songs; they were described as "spiritualists" and known to conduct séances. It also became clear that they cultivated a cult of neo-romantic male friendship, and their correspondence was filled with seemingly homoerotic attestations of friendship. Eulenburg himself was often addressed as "Phili" or "Philine," while Moltke enjoyed the nickname "Tutu." Perhaps most damning was the pet name "Liebchen" or "darling," which they used for the Kaiser.[7]

At the center of this incipient scandal was Maximilian Harden (1861–1927), an influential Berlin journalist who edited a weekly news magazine, *Die Zukunft*. In November 1906 Harden published two derisive articles, implying that Moltke, Eulenburg, and the larger group that made up the Kaiser's entourage were homosexual.[8] Harden published a third piece in January, suggesting that Eulenburg had an inappropriate relationship with Raymond Lecomte. Another article in April accused Eulenburg directly of being homosexual and implied that his behavior was treasonous.[9] When William II eventually learned of the offending accusations in May 1907, he banned both Eulenburg and Moltke from his court and demanded that they respond to Harden's slander. The Kaiser's response was clumsy, however, and forced Moltke to bring charges of libel against Harden, creating a public platform for Harden's accusations. The initial trial triggered a concatenation of subsequent trials, which continued into 1909. Of course, accusations of libel prompted a process of extensive legal discovery. Ultimately, not only Eulenburg but also a significant list of Prussian aristocrats and military officers were suspected of having violated the anti-sodomy statute.

The Eulenburg scandal was a catalyst for transforming popular views of the Kaiser and the monarchy. The trials sparked by Harden's brazen accusations discredited not only the Hohenzollern dynasty but also the Prussian aristocracy and officer corps. At least one historian has compared the affair to the loss of legitimacy suffered by the Bourbons and Louis XVI on the eve of the French Revolution in 1789.[10] By exploiting allegations of sexual impropriety, Harden helped to create a powerful dynamic that combined an exuberant popular medium—the German daily and political press—with the new sexology of naming homosexuality. As journalist Frederic William Wile—Berlin correspondent for the London *Daily Mail* and the *New York Times*—wrote in 1914, "[T]he upheaval caused by Harden's revelations was the most stirring victory wrought in the name of public opinion which Modern Germany has yet witnessed."[11] Indeed, journalism at the turn of the twentieth century had become a political tool, which could also be used to "out" prominent figures. The *Berliner Tageblatt* alone—just one of more than twenty-five Berlin dailies—published more than 150 articles about the Eulenburg scandal in the two-year period before May 1909. The Ministry of Justice collected and preserved more than nine hundred German press clippings devoted to the trials.[12] Press coverage outside Germany was no less extravagant: over fifty journalists from France, Sweden, Russia, England, and the Netherlands were present when Eulenburg's trial for perjury opened in the spring of 1908.[13] More than any single event or publication, the Eulenburg scandal broadcast and popularized the notion of a homosexual identity. The panorama of Berlin's gay life publicized by Magnus Hirschfeld in *Berlins drittes Geschlecht* (Berlin's third sex) in 1904 or by Hans Ostwald's *Männliche Prostitution im kaiserlichen Berlin* (Male prostitution in imperial Berlin) in 1906 was now confirmed and given broader exposure by a drumbeat of trial reports in the German and European press.

Born Felix Ernst Witkowski, Maximilian Harden personified the striking contradictions of fin-de-siècle Berlin. As the child of so-called *getaufte Juden*—"baptized Jews"—Harden adopted his new name when embarking on a short-lived career as a stage actor. By the early 1890s, however, Harden had turned to journalism, and in 1892 he began publication of his independent news magazine, *Die Zukunft*, which he produced weekly for more than thirty years (until 1923). Despite subtle and sometimes virulent anti-Semitism, Harden made a brilliant career for himself in the Berlin metropolis. His independent periodical gained him admiration, and notoriety, and he quickly moved in an elite stratum of Berlin literati, publishers, and artists, as well as politicians and statesmen. Harden made Bismarck's acquaintance soon after the chancellor's "retirement," and cultivated the relationship until Bismarck's death in 1898. Assimilating Bismarck's *Realpolitik*, as well as his critique of the new Kaiser and his government, Harden became an ardent German nationalist, a monarchist, and a vigorous critic of William II. Bismarck also shaped Harden's early suspicion of Eulenburg, whose activities Harden monitored in the pages of *Die Zukunft* beginning in the 1890s.[14] Harden's precise motivations for attacking Eulenburg are often debated, though anti-homosexual animus does not seem to figure among them. Despite his hawkish foreign policy views, Harden was never socially conservative, and he supported the legal reform of Paragraph 175.[15]

Although Harden acted independently, he became an ally and accomplice of Eulenburg's other enemies. In January 1906 German foreign minister Friedrich von Holstein hatched a plot to force Eulenburg to leave Berlin and remove himself from the Kaiser's social orbit, a plan he reported in a letter to the German ambassador in Paris, Prince Radolin. Holstein plotted with Chancellor Bernhard von Bülow, and the two together hoped to undermine Eulenburg and the French ambassador Lecomte by launching "a sensational campaign of scandal in the press" based on accusations of "pederasty." Holstein also identified Harden as the journalist who could disseminate the charges and bring Eulenburg down.[16] Using perceived sexual impropriety for political ends was not unprecedented. But the proposed cooperation of Holstein and Harden represented an innovation in imperial Germany. The authority and influence of the popular press—and of public intellectuals such as Harden—and the susceptibility of the ruling emperor to public opinion signaled the growing significance of the so-called fourth estate. The press, as Holstein recognized, had become a powerful tool of influence and manipulation.

The insulting notes that Harden published in November, following the emperor's hunting excursion at Liebenberg, were cryptic and went largely unnoticed. *Die Zukunft* held an important place among the organs of Berlin's political press, however, and was read closely by the political cognoscenti. Eulenburg, for one, took notice and dispatched an intermediary to negotiate with Harden, whose only demand was that Eulenburg leave the German capital permanently. Harden's coercion was successful, initially, and the Kaiser's friend decamped to a Swiss spa resort, supposedly for health reasons. Earlier in 1906, however, William II had nominated Eulenburg to the Order of the Black Eagle, one of the most prestigious Prussian fraternities, and Eulenburg could not resist attending a showy investiture ceremony in January of 1907.[17]

When Harden learned of Eulenburg's return to Berlin, he recommenced with his campaign. On April 13 the journalist published an incendiary editorial whose message was unambiguous. "Look at this Roundtable," Harden quipped. "They don't dream of conflagrations [*Weltbrände*]; for them it's already warm enough." This double entendre, based on the German slang for homosexual, *"warm,"* explained the pacifism of Eulenburg and his friends as the effect of their "queerness."[18] Two weeks later Harden went a step further, calling attention to the recent disclosure of the homosexuality of Prince Friedrich Heinrich, the Kaiser's cousin. "Because of his inherited sexual perversion," Harden wrote, "the Prince was forced to relinquish leadership of the Order of St. John" (another prestigious Prussian association).[19] It was rumored, in fact, that William II had recently banished his cousin from the Berlin court for "immorality." According to Commissioner Treschow, Prince

Frederick Heinrich's particular kink was to prostitute himself in Tiergarten Park disguised as a groom.[20] "Does the chapter of the Black Eagle deserve a milder assessment?" Harden asked, alluding directly to Eulenburg: "There is at least one member whose *vita sexualis* is no healthier than that of the banned Prince."[21]

The Kaiser was unaware of Harden's slander, however, since his own reading was limited to a conservative Berlin daily, *Der Tagesspiegel*. Neither cabinet ministers nor close advisers had the moxie to inform their sovereign, moreover, and Crown Prince Friedrich Wilhelm finally showed his father the offensive materials at the beginning of May. The revelation incensed the Kaiser, who condemned both Eulenburg and Moltke for not confronting Harden sooner. On May 3 Moltke tendered his resignation as city commander. From Eulenburg, William demanded accountability: "If the charges of perverse tendencies are untrue and his conscience is completely free and clear, he must make an unambiguous declaration to me and then confront Harden. Otherwise I expect him to return the Black Eagle decoration and go immediately into foreign exile."[22] A confrontation with Harden might take one of two courses: either dueling (which had been criminalized after German unification) or some sort of legal challenge. Eulenburg took the second route and cleverly denounced himself for violating Paragraph 175 in the sympathetic jurisdiction of his Liebenberg estate. After a cursory investigation and a very short trial, the presiding district attorney determined that there was no evidence of his friend's—that is, Eulenburg's—guilt. Moltke pursued a different strategy, first challenging Harden to a duel, which the journalist declined, and then bringing suit for libel.[23]

The first Moltke-Harden libel trial found a raucous public reception, opening on October 23, 1907, in the Berlin courthouse of Moabit. Since Moltke's resignation as city commander in May, Berlin's daily press had published regular reports on Harden, Eulenburg, and Moltke. Outside the courthouse, crowds identified and then greeted or jeered the protagonists as they entered and left the proceedings.[24] The crush of both German and foreign journalists was nearly overwhelming, and press tickets for the courtroom became difficult to procure. As the promi-

nent *Vossische Zeitung* reported, "Morning trial Moltke-Harden, evenings Caruso. And everyone expects a celebration [*Fest*]. The demand
for admission tickets for the drama in Moabit, whose outcome cannot be
predicted—tragedy or comedy?—is no less than that for the first appearance of the king of tenors [Caruso] in the Berlin Opera House."[25]

Moltke's libel suit turned on the claim that Harden had stated falsely
that he was homosexual. To defend against this charge Harden and his
lawyers needed to demonstrate, presumably, that Moltke had indeed
engaged in some homosexual activity. The journalist took a different
and ingenious tack, however, and undermined Moltke's accusation by
qualifying his own alleged slander. Instead of providing convincing evidence that Moltke had perhaps been in a homosexual relationship or
patronized a male hustler, the defense attempted instead to convince
the judge and jurors that Moltke had a homosexual "orientation." On
the stand Harden argued that his essays never mentioned specific homosexual practices: "I never asserted that Count Moltke was guilty of any
punishable sexual acts. We [the defense] simply intend to prove that the
General belongs to a circle of friends in which different stages of homosexuality are represented. I am convinced and can prove that Moltke has
abnormal sexual feelings."[26]

The first step of Harden's strategy was to explore Moltke's relationship with his ex-wife, Lilly von Elbe—based on her testimony—and
prove Moltke's aversion to the "fairer sex." Moltke had married the
beautiful young widow in 1896 in a ceremony for which the Kaiser himself had served as a witness. The couple divorced in 1899, though the
marriage ended long before that and was likely never consummated.
Harden had learned of the divorce directly from Lilly, who provided
him with sensitive materials from the proceedings in 1902.[27] Moltke's
apparent mistreatment of his young wife had motivated Lilly, who
attended the trial accompanied by her son (from her first marriage) and
her third husband.[28]

Lilly testified that the failure of her second marriage was caused in
part by Moltke's friendship with Eulenburg. In 1895 Eulenburg was
invested as German ambassador in Vienna, and soon after his appointment he managed to have Moltke assigned as his personal aide, a military attaché in the embassy. The men schemed to leave Lilly in Berlin

after the wedding, though she rejected such a separation from her new husband and followed with her young son. Although the newlyweds shared an apartment, Moltke refused to sleep with Lilly and took up quarters in the embassy. When questioned by Lilly, Moltke replied, "[M]y friend Graf Eulenburg wishes it so." Lilly then confronted Eulenburg, who responded, according to Lilly, "[S]et my friend free, give my friend back to me." Moltke was also given to expressing the crudest misogyny. On one occasion, Lilly claimed, her husband had told her, "I don't find you revolting as a human being, but rather as a woman." Lilly's son, Wolf von Kruse, now a young man and army lieutenant, also testified and described a particularly memorable scene. Once, after discovering that Eulenburg had left a handkerchief in the Moltkes' apartment, Kuno, in the presence of his stepson, pressed it "passionately" to his lips, uttering, "[M]y soul, my love!"[29]

Whether the relationship between Moltke and Eulenburg was ever sexual remained moot; what Harden hoped to establish instead was Moltke's inborn sexual orientation. "I differentiate," Harden explained, "following the best science, between abnormal feelings and homosexual tendencies. There is a great distinction whether the orientation is so advanced that it tends to unnatural activities, or whether the affected person only has abnormal feelings, unhealthy feelings that run counter to normality. If I claim that one has such an inner emotional orientation, I do not mean that this sensuality is ever outwardly manifested." It was Moltke's orientation, then, that was homosexual—not necessarily his sexual practices—and this was all that Harden claimed to have implied in his *Zukunft* articles.[30]

This "science" of sexuality had been developed and popularized by Magnus Hirschfeld, so Harden enlisted the sexologist to provide expert testimony. On the stand, Hirschfeld drew a subtle yet sharp distinction between "friendship" and "love." "We understand the homosexual," Hirschfeld opined, "to be someone who feels a genuine love attraction for someone of the same sex. Whether that person engages in homosexual behaviors is irrelevant from a scientific perspective. Just as some heterosexuals live celibate lives, so too can homosexuals express their love in an idealized, platonic manner." Hirschfeld's assessment of Moltke specifically was that the general displayed an "unconscious homosexuality."[31]

Hirschfeld and Lilly von Elbe carried the day, and on October 29 the trial concluded with Harden's acquittal. The judge declared, "The assumption is correct: He has an aversion to the female sex, he has an attraction to the male sex, and he has certain feminine features. These are all characteristics of homosexuality. . . . It must be emphasized here that no one has claimed that Count Moltke is guilty of any homosexual activity. It is viewed only as established: he is homosexual and has not been able to disguise this orientation in the presence of others."[32] The decision was remarkable considering Moltke's social position, and the repercussions were profound. For one, the Kaiser suffered a nervous breakdown. Two days later the Prussian attorney general declared Harden's exoneration a matter of "public interest" and announced an appeal, this time supported by the Prussian state.[33]

Only days after the Moltke-Harden contretemps was declared a matter of "public interest," requiring an appeal and retrial, Chancellor Bülow brought charges of libel against the firebrand publisher and homosexual rights activist Adolf Brand. In September 1907 Brand had published a special issue of his journal (*Die Gemeinschaft der Eigenen*) titled "Prince Bülow and the Repeal of Paragraph 175." Clearly inspired by Harden's attack on Moltke and Eulenburg, Brand claimed that Bülow, an opponent of Eulenburg, was himself homosexual and that he shared an apartment with his lover, who was also his private secretary. Brand also implied that Bülow's nephew, a Prussian diplomat, likewise named Bernhard, had a sexual relationship with Eulenburg's son-in-law Edmund Jarolymek. These relationships had been open secrets, Brand asserted, at least among members of the Scientific-Humanitarian Committee.[34]

Brand craved the attention that Harden had garnered with his comments in *Zukunft*. Hirschfeld's expert assessment that Moltke was "unconsciously" homosexual was especially irksome to Brand, since it profiled Hirschfeld's sexology and his medical diagnosis. In the pamphlet, Brand condemned Hirschfeld for labeling Moltke while failing to mention Bülow as well. Certainly, Brand envied Hirschfeld's public recognition as an expert. But he also resented the inconsistency and apparent hypocrisy of Hirschfeld's position. Recall that Brand and Hirschfeld had quarreled before over the tactic of outing prominent figures. While

Brand agitated for ruthless disclosure, Hirschfeld and his colleagues in the SHC had argued for the rights of individual privacy. "Dr. Hirschfeld, the supposed protector of homosexuals," Brand claimed, "disclosed the homosexuality of Bülow's opponents, despite his earlier position, but neglected then to expose Bülow as well." The implication, of course, was that Brand himself was the more stalwart defender of those persecuted under Paragraph 175. In Brand's estimation, Hirschfeld allowed politics and the vanity of his own pseudoscience to trump the cause of emancipation. If Hirschfeld genuinely embraced Brand's strategy of liberation "over corpses"—a campaign to out prominent figures, such as Georg Dasbach—then he should have exposed Bülow as well. Brand hoped to redress this oversight with his pamphlet, and expected in doing so to hasten the repeal of the anti-sodomy statute.[35]

Brand's trial for libel opened on November 6, barely a week after Harden's acquittal. Harden's success bolstered Brand's hope that his campaign would promote the acceptance of his own model of homo-erotic friendship. At trial, he opined that same-sex love is simply the "ideal, emotional attraction of one friend to another friend." He explained, "I described the Reichskanzler as homosexual in my article. But in doing so I have not reproached him. Since I strive for the elimination of Paragraph 175 and for the social rebirth of friend-love, the last thing I wanted was to insult Prince Bülow by revealing his homosexual proclivities."[36] Brand clearly distanced himself from Hirschfeld's sexology, and suggested a motivation that was dramatically different from Harden's. Homoerotic "friend-love" was shared by many, he believed, including Bülow, Moltke, and Eulenburg. His purpose in revealing the "friend-love" of political elites, therefore, was to promote understanding, empathy, and ultimately legal reform.

Despite his optimism, Brand was found guilty and given an eighteen-month prison sentence, an outcome that Brand blamed on Hirschfeld. For one thing, Hirschfeld, when called to testify as an expert witness, denied having heard rumors that Bülow was homosexual and claimed to be unable to ascertain such an orientation in the chancellor, whether conscious or not. Brand believed he had been abandoned by one of his "co-conspirators," Count Günther von der Schulenburg, who had promised to provide Brand with evidence that would compromise Bülow. Not only did Schulenburg fail to produce the promised materials, but he also fled Germany for the duration of the trial to avoid a subpoena. Brand later claimed that Hirschfeld himself had provided Schulenburg with the materials documenting Bülow's homosexuality. But after Bülow brought Brand to trial, Hirschfeld—according to Brand—refused Schulenberg the incriminating evidence that would have substantiated Brand's claims and thus allowed Brand to suffer the consequences of a guilty verdict. Brand's ultimate downfall was the testimony given by Bülow himself and by a number of his closest friends and colleagues, including Eulenburg.[37]

Eulenburg's appearance was, in fact, the most startling development in the trial, especially since the two men—Bülow and Eulenburg—were barely on speaking terms. Called as a character witness, Eulenburg swore under oath that Bülow was innocent of Brand's allegations. He was unable to resist the temptation to clear his own name, moreover, and stated as well that he himself had never engaged in any homosexual "depravities" (*Schmutzereien*).[38] In a lengthy statement, Eulenburg also explained his view of male-male friendship:

> Concerning the theories that we have heard before from Dr. Hirschfeld, I must comment. All the fine nuances that he has constructed in his system result ultimately in the reality that no person can any longer feel secure not to be viewed as homosexual. I have been an enthusiastic friend in my youth and am proud of having had such good friends! Had I known that after 25–30 years a man would come forward and develop such a system according to which such potential filth in every friendship lurked, I would have truly forsaken the search for friends. The best that we Germans have is friendship, and friendship has always been honored! I have written letters that overwhelm with friendly emotions, and I will not reproach myself for that. As examples we have the letters of our great heroes, such as Goethe, etc., which are also effusive. I have written such letters myself, but they did not contain anything evil, bad, or filthy![39]

If Eulenburg's expansive defense of "friendship" was ill-advised, his categorical denial of ever having engaged in any homosexual acts turned out to be a fatal misstep. By denying any form of same-sex erotic contact, Eulenburg's claim made the precise sexual acts prohibited by Paragraph 175 irrelevant. His testimony ultimately made him vulnerable to the charge of perjury. Harden and his Munich-based lawyer, Max Bernstein, recognized their opening immediately, and began vetting plans for how they might exploit it. The challenge now was to locate any sexual partners or even witnesses who would attest under oath that Eulenburg had at some point in his life participated in a homosexual act. The prince's sworn denials had lowered the bar, and made Harden's work that much easier.[40]

Before continuing the campaign against Eulenburg, Harden faced trial a second time for libeling Moltke. The proceeding began on December 16, 1907, and ended January 3 with Harden's defeat. This time Moltke and his lawyers, with the help of their own expert witnesses, were able to undermine the testimony of Lilly von Elbe by depicting her as an unstable hysteric. Once Moltke's ex-wife had been discredited, the reliability of Hirschfeld's assessment was called into question. Additionally, the sexologist withdrew his earlier diagnosis of "unconscious homosexuality," possibly due to blackmail and the threat of the revelation of some sexual misdeed.[41] But even now Harden and Bernstein continued to lay a trap for Eulenburg. Called as a character witness, Eulenburg swore yet again that he had "never engaged in any depravities." Upon cross-examination, Bernstein pressed the prince to clarify what he meant and asked for a "precise answer." When Eulenburg balked, Bernstein demanded to know if that included "mutual masturbation," which was technically not a crime under Paragraph 175. Eulenburg finally responded by asking Bernstein, in turn, if he himself did not understand that as a depravity. Although Harden was convicted, Bernstein was able to provoke Eulenburg to swear under oath—now for the second time—that he had never engaged in any homosexual practices. Harden received a prison sentence of four months, which he appealed immediately to the imperial court in Leipzig.

It appeared that Harden's attempt had failed, at least for the time being, and that Moltke and Eulenburg both would be spared public disgrace. The Kaiser was jubilant and at the beginning of 1908 prepared for the full rehabilitation of his friends. There was significant collateral damage, however. During the first Moltke-Harden trial, several soldiers, stationed in Potsdam, gave sensational accounts of homosexual orgies and even rape, which took place in an officer's villa located next door to Moltke's rented apartment. Moltke was never implicated in these sexual crimes, though the investigation of his alleged homosexuality exposed a startling characteristic of the Prussian officer corps. On January 22, military officials opened a court martial against Count Johannes von Lynar, a Prussian general, and the Lieutenant Count Wilhelm von Hohenau. Conducted in the military barracks in Moabit, the trial hall was filled with military figures in uniform as well as former retired officers in civilian garb. "One sees the profile of Count Hohenau," according to one newspaper report, "with a massive, projecting brow . . . no sign of a weak, feminine element."[42] Among the thirty-seven witnesses were many soldiers: "The crowd included many sons of Mars," according to one reporter, and "the scene is practically a parade ground."[43] The most important witness, Johannes Bollhardt, repeated his accusation from the first Harden-Moltke trial that Hohenau had raped him anally as Count Lynar looked on.[44] This and many other accusations were ultimately discounted, and Hohenau was acquitted. Some six months later, however, Hohenau was stripped of his title and suspended from service by a military honor court, though allowed ultimately to keep his pension. Lynar fared worse and was given a fifteen-month prison sentence for the abuse of his authority and office and for dishonoring subordinates with inappropriate touching.[45]

In the meantime, Harden and Bernstein hired a private detective, who hunted for witnesses who could testify to having had sex with Eulenburg. This effort netted the Bavarian fisherman Georg Riedel, who had made Eulenburg's acquaintance many years earlier at a spa resort at Starnberg Lake in southwestern Germany, where Eulenburg had regularly vacationed in the 1880s. Eulenburg not only befriended Riedel but eventually hired the young man to serve as his valet, a position he held for nearly five years. During this period the two were allegedly inseparable, not only in Starnberg but also on Eulenburg's Liebenberg estate in Brandenburg. Although reluctant to come forward, Riedel was protected by the statute of limitations since the presumed homosexual acts had happened decades earlier. A second, though less credible, witness, Jakob Ernst, a day laborer with a record for petty theft, came forward about the same time after recognizing Eulenburg's photo in a Bavarian newspaper.[46]

Harden's challenge now was to find a sympathetic court in which to present Riedel's and Ernst's sworn testimony that they had had sexual contact with Eulenburg. Together Harden and Bernstein devised a brilliant strategy. They enlisted a friend, the editor of the Bavarian *Neue Freie Volkszeitung*, Anton Städele, to publish a story claiming that Eulenburg had bribed Harden for one million marks to suppress evidence of his homosexuality—meaning, in effect, that Eulenburg was able to buy off his tormentor Harden. In response to the article, Harden sued Städele for libel. This time the trial was held in a Munich court, in the kingdom of Bavaria, out of reach of the Prussian authorities. Ernst and especially Riedel were perfect witnesses: both were reluctant to testify, but, when pressured by Bernstein, they performed with great credibility. Neither had any apparent ulterior motive, and the statute of limitations shielded them from self-incrimination. On April 21, 1908, Harden and Bernstein were able to prove Eulenburg's homosexual activity based on the sworn testimony of the two star informants. The Munich court was convinced, and Harden won the staged libel trial. Städele was fined for spreading untruths; Harden then reimbursed him for his trouble.[47]

The Munich verdict had dire consequences for Eulenburg. Suspected now of having perjured himself—not once but twice—the prince was immediately subjected to the scrutiny of Prussian officials. On April 30 three police investigators, including Commissioner Tresckow, a forensic physician, and the director of the Berlin State Court, arrived unannounced at the Liebenberg estate, where they questioned Eulenburg into the evening. Eulenburg denied all charges, and even gave Tresckow his "word of honor as a Prussian Prince" that he had never engaged in any homosexual act. (Tresckow reported later that he had never met a bigger liar.)[48] At the beginning of May the Berlin State Court began preliminary investigations that included a formal discovery. On May 7 court officials brought the star witnesses from the Munich trial, the Bavarians Ernst and Riedel, and staged a direct confrontation with the defendant. This was Eulenburg's final opportunity to exonerate himself before formal charges would be filed. Unable to persuade either man to recant his Munich testimony, Eulenburg was arrested the following day. Although his doctor claimed he was too ill to travel, Eulenburg was deemed a flight risk. The court pressured the police to secure the alleged perjurer, even if medical care were required while in custody. As a result, Eulenburg was taken into custody and then transported to the Charité Hospital in Berlin.[49] This resulted in Eulenburg's ultimate alienation from the Kaiser's court, and on May 22 he returned his many decorations, including the one conferred most recently for the Order of the Black Eagle.[50]

A second, more comprehensive search of the Liebenberg castle was conducted the week after Eulenburg's arrest, turning up a packet of books from the Max Spohr Verlag. The titles were all produced by or related to the SHC and the homosexual rights movement. As one press report commented, "This literature is used almost exclusively by medical doctors or others with a personal interest."[51] On the packet was the name Count Edgar Wedel, Eulenburg's old friend and an imperial court official, who denied to the police having owned the books or even knowing what the Max Spohr Verlag was. At trial Eulenburg admitted writing Wedel's name on the packet, adding callously that it would not have harmed Wedel since he was a bachelor anyway. Eulenburg also mentioned that the books had been sent to the house—he had not ordered them himself. For poor Wedel, the unfortunate association with Eulenburg (coupled with Eulenburg's mendacity) cost him his position and career at court. The Kaiser was reported to have said, "Think of it, our Edgar is also such a swine."[52]

The perjury trial commenced on June 29, attended by Kuno von Moltke, Adolf Brand, and Magnus Hirschfeld, as well as dozens of domestic and foreign journalists. Some sixty witnesses were called, many of whom were forced to travel from Bavaria to Berlin for the proceedings. At the outset, Eulenburg maintained his innocence, though he tempered his earlier claim with an important qualification. As Eulenburg now explained, he had never engaged in any *"punishable* depravities," referring, of course, to the specific sex acts of oral or anal copulation forbidden by Paragraph 175. This was truthful, perhaps, but no longer relevant, since the violation of Paragraph 175 was not the charge that Eulenburg faced. Accused of perjury, Eulenburg was now proven guilty, and of witness tampering as well. Even before the Munich trial, Eulenburg had sent a former factotum and confidante, Georg Kistler, to convince Riedel to avoid mentioning any inappropriate contact, including mutual masturbation. Foolishly, Eulenburg had committed these instructions to writing, and his letter was found in Riedel's possession during discovery. His exact formulation was that "[e]verything [that happened] is beyond the statute of limitations."[53]

Additional witnesses who had not been summoned in Munich gave statements that suggested an extended pattern of behavior, discounting the claim that Eulenburg had merely engaged in *youthful* indiscretions and confirming and complementing Riedel's original testimony. The ship steward Karl Trost, who was posted to the imperial yacht *Hohenzollern* from 1896 to 1899, recounted the personal questions posed to him by Eulenburg: Did he have a girlfriend? Did he or other members of the crew visit bordellos? Did he masturbate, and if so, with other members of the crew? Other young men reported similarly inappropriate advances. Franz Dandl, who had worked as a servant in Starnberg, claimed that Eulenburg had placed an arm around his shoulder and then grabbed his thigh while praising him as a "slender beauty." A blue-collar worker in Munich, Nepomuk Schömmer, claimed to have observed Eulenburg through the keyhole of a Munich hotel engaged in sex with another man.[54]

As the days passed, and the list of witnesses lengthened, Eulenburg's health appeared to worsen. On July 13 he collapsed in the courtroom, and his doctor claimed the next day that he was now too weak to be transported from Charité. At this point court officials began to convene hearings in Eulenburg's hospital room. Finally, on the seventeenth, the proceedings were prorogued, pending some improvement in his health. In September the prince was allowed to return to his Liebenberg home after posting a bail of 100,000 marks.[55]

The third and final Moltke-Harden trial took place on April 20, 1909, and ended the same day with a verdict against Harden, who was ordered to pay a fine of six hundred marks plus the court costs for all three trials, a sum amounting to forty thousand marks. Harden appealed, naturally. But by this time everyone involved, including Moltke, felt that the trials should end. After significant negotiation among Harden, Chancellor Bülow, Moltke, the industrial magnate Walther Rathenau, and the Hamburg shipping baron Albert Ballin, a settlement was reached. Moltke was required to recognize Harden's patriotic motives in writing the articles and withdrew his original suit. In turn, Harden withdrew his appeal. Ballin agreed to pay Harden's fines and costs, and was reimbursed discreetly from a fund administered by the imperial government.[56]

On July 7, 1909, the second and last Eulenburg trial began and ended like the first, with Eulenburg's collapse. Until 1919 Eulenburg was examined biannually by court doctors, who always found him too ill to stand trial. For the rest of his life (until 1920)—a long one, indeed, considering his apparently perilously poor health—Eulenburg was effectively exiled. Every year some court-appointed forensic physician visited the prince to determine whether his physical condition might allow a resumption of the trial.[57]

The impact of the Eulenburg scandal extended far beyond the borders of the German Empire. And it was likely French journalists and their readers who drew the greatest pleasure from Prussia's pink peccadilloes. Even before the Eulenburg affair appeared on the front pages of Europe's dailies, in 1904, Oscar Méténier, naturalist author and son of a Parisian police officer, had published a popular study of Berlin's homosexual subculture, *Vertus et vices allemands* (German virtues and vices). Méténier not only reviewed the public bars and restaurants frequented by "inverts" but also conferred with SHC members and the Berlin police taskforce assigned to monitor the homosexual community.[58] Coverage of the Eulenburg trials could only stoke public interest. In 1907 the French author and critic Octave Mirbeau wrote an immensely popular travelogue based on his automobile journey through the Netherlands, Belgium, and Germany. His closing chapter, "Berlin-Sodome," affects mild shock at the "perverse" manners and mores of imperial Berlin, a clear reflection of the unfolding Eulenburg extravaganza.[59] In the same year native Swiss journalist John Grand-Carteret compiled a collection of German and European caricatures related to the Eulenburg affair. "It appears," Grand-Carteret claimed, summarizing the Berlin SHC, "that if one considers the numbers grouping themselves into societies that a new Freemasonry [of homosexuals] is being created."[60] In 1908 French journalists Henri de Weindel and F. P. Fischer produced yet another volume devoted to the "German vice," *L'homosexualité en Allemagne* (Homosexuality in Germany), which reviewed the history of Paragraph 175 and its impact, the vibrant social life of Berlin's homosexuals, the SHC, and, of course, the Eulenburg trials.[61]

The Eulenburg affair was a "cherry" on the cake, according to a recent account by literary historian Laure Murat, which "confirmed with éclat that the third sex had well and truly found a country: Germany."[62] Indeed, soon after the Krupp scandal, sexologists reignited discussion about the incidence of homosexuality within national contexts. Beginning in 1904, French, German, and Russian psychiatrists debated the size and character of French and German homosexual communities in the pages of *Archives d'anthropologie criminelle* (Archives of criminal anthropology), the leading French journal of criminology. Russian psychiatrist Raffalovich, a conservative Catholic who advocated celibacy outside of heterosexual marriage and who viewed sexual orientation as a product of culture, *blamed* the SHC and its political activism for the size and visibility of Berlin's homosexual community. In response, German psychiatrist Paul Näcke (1851–1913), a close collaborator of Hirschfeld, defended the position that sexual orientation was congenital or inborn. Raffalovich responded by accusing Hirschfeld and the SHC of glorifying "inversion" and contributing to its spread.[63]

At the height of the Eulenburg proceedings, French psychiatrist "Dr. Laupts" (Georges Saint-Paul) attacked Näcke in the pages of *Archives,* claiming, "In France, except for the cosmopolitan mileux of the largest cities, . . . homosexuality has been completely exceptional."[64] Laupts was clearly suggesting that any "French" homosexuality was the result of foreign influence. In a subsequent letter published in the same venue, he reiterated that "homosexuality does not exist except as a very rare state of exception throughout French continental territory, meaning non-colonial."[65] Of course, Laupts's 1896 textbook was subtitled "perverse sexualities and the prevention of inversion," and he affirmed his conservative view (and his disregard for the SHC) in a subsequent letter published in *Archives:* "Homosexuality is contagious and spreads in

France and in Germany at the moment when it is studied, discussed, and written about."[66] Another SHC member, Dr. Eugèn Wilhelm (1866–1951), a law professor and German court official in Strasbourg, countered Laupts's assertions and defended Hirschfeld. Wilhelm later lamented the state of French sexology: "In France—it must be averred—that apart from some rare and meritorious exceptions, the men of science have neglected this material [questions related to sexuality]."[67]

For his part, Hirschfeld insisted that homosexuality was not a particularly German phenomenon ("Our scientific interpretation of the essence of homosexuality [is] as a constant biological variant of sexuality),[68] while also acknowledging the influence of the recent "sensational trials" that had given new life to the "old fairy tales" of a "German vice." If the French spoke of the *vice allemande* or an *Eulenburgue,* the Italians now referred to the homosexual as a *"Berlinese,"* and the English spoke of the "German custom."[69] Through Harden's campaign, Eulenburg's name had entered the popular argot to signify homosexual. Eulenburg's particular scandal and the many others that it exposed were firmly identified as German. But Eulenburg and his associates also helped to broadcast and promote the notion of the innate homosexual as a minority figure in the cast of modern sexual personages.

CHAPTER FIVE

Hans Blüher, the Wandervogel Movement, and the Männerbund

What is the explanation for homosexuality in Wilhelmine society?
What is specifically German about it? The two conflicting homosocial attitudes toward homosexuality coexisted in Wilhelmine
Germany: the one discredited homosexuality and supported a pure,
masculine type, and the other, the Männerbund version, allowed
that male-male relationships could have a sexual connotation. This
is the difference, in fact the contrast to all other European societies.
The social (and legal) disdain for homosexuality goes hand in hand
with a pronounced disposition for homoerotic relationship models.

—NICOLAUS SOMBART, *Die deutschen Männer
und ihre Feinde* (1991)

The Eulenburg scandal had a powerful and negative impact on the
SHC and Berlin's homosexual rights movement. However, alongside any damage came significant publicity that broadcast theories of
homosexuality and brought the work of Hirschfeld and his opponents
to public attention. Eulenburg and the Liebenberg Roundtable were
likewise inspiring for theorists of the homoerotic Männerbund, a complex German term that nearly defies translation. Rendered most simply
as "male association," the concept of the Männerbund gained tremendous popular currency in Germany in the first decades of the twentieth
century. Of course, Männerbund has much broader connotations and
might be used to describe phenomena as diverse as the tribal leadership
of an indigenous group, the ruling junta of an autocratic state, a political

party, or simply cultural patriarchy. As a secretive cabal with tremendous political influence and the whiff of homoeroticism, Eulenburg and the Liebenberg Roundtable appeared to be its very embodiment.

The disclosures that emerged from the Harden-Eulenburg-Brand-Bülow trials provided a timely inspiration for Hans Blüher (1888–1955), who observed the unfolding scandals beginning in 1907 as a student in Berlin. Blüher found the Liebenberg Roundtable a perfect manifestation of the Männerbund, and material for the historical sociology that he would develop into the 1920s. Blüher was also inspired by the incipient German youth movement, in which he himself participated. Germany's inaugural all-male youth organization, the Wandervogel (which translates roughly as "hiking bird" or "wandering bird"), formed in 1897 in the Berlin suburb of Steglitz. A member of this original troupe, Blüher chronicled the history of the early Wandervogel, and developed his theory of the Männerbund based in part on his adolescent experiences. This participation in the Wandervogel also brought Blüher in contact with Berlin's homosexual rights movement and the burgeoning sexological literatures of the early twentieth century. In turn, his autobiographical account of the Wandervogel and his sociology of the Männerbund gained him the attention of homosexual activists, psychiatrists, and, by the 1920s, anti-Semitic nationalists. Only the notoriety of his anti-Semitism, which Blüher incorporated into his theory, can explain how such an influential and popular author would have become so obscure after 1945, even in Germany. Since Blüher was an anti-Semite and sometime homosexual rights activist himself, his intellectual biography provides the perfect lens for considering the popularization and influence of this improbable and underappreciated German construct. Blüher's participation in the original Wandervogel and troupe and his autobiographical chronicle of its early evolution make it nearly impossible to disentangle his experiences from the Wandervogel and the concept of the Männerbund as they developed in Berlin at the turn of the century.[1]

Born in 1888, Blüher was raised in a conservative, bourgeois family. His father was a university-educated professional who personified the culture and ideals of Germany's *Bildungsbürgertum*. Both his paternal and maternal lineages included Protestant ministers, jurists, and government officials. His father and grandfather were *Apotheker*, pharmacists, a prestigious vocation that combined university training with the entrepreneurial management of a drugstore. In 1897 Blüher's family moved from Halle to Steglitz, an expanding, middle-class suburb of southwest Berlin, where his father opened an apothecary. Here Blüher attended the *Gymnasium* in preparation for university study.[2]

Steglitz grammar school instructor Herman Hoffmann Fölkersamb formed a study circle at Blüher's school in 1896, and in 1901 it was registered as the Wandervogel, as a formal association (*Verein*). The group sponsored all manner of youth activities—hiking, camping, team sports, and singing—with an emphasis on independence, accountability, and the spirit of adventure. Despite its back-to-nature character, the group also rented and furnished a clubhouse (*Heim*), which created a space free from adult authority. Here members played games, rehearsed dramatic skits, conducted poetry readings, and planned excursions. The clubhouse became a central feature of the many other groups inspired by the original Steglitz association. As a reaction to the stern discipline and rigid authoritarianism of the domestic and educational life of prewar Germany, the Wandervogel movement spread quickly beyond Steglitz and Berlin. By 1910, imperial Germany counted 204 local organizations with nearly 9,000 members. On the eve of the First World War the number of active participants had climbed to 25,000. Another 10,000 adults were associated with the clubs as group leaders and members of advisory boards.[3]

It comes as no surprise that Blüher embraced the Wandervogel youth group after joining as a fourteen-year-old boy in 1902. From his autobiography we know that he relished the homosocial camaraderie of hiking and singing and the charismatic leadership of an adult *Führer*, or leader, all critical elements of his Männerbund theory. The youth group provided a haven free from the repressive control of parents and teachers. Indeed, Blüher's school experience was reminiscent of the protagonist's of Hermann Hesse's 1906 novel, *Beneath the Wheel*, the story of a talented young student who falters under autocratic teachers and parents before drowning, an apparent suicide. Blüher described the "school pedagogy" of his own *Gymnasium* as "pure dressage [*Dressur*]," a mind-numbing training that "raped the youthful disposition."[4] Literary depictions of afflicted German and Austrian youth—from Wedekind's *Spring Awakening* (1891) to *Beneath the Wheel*, or Robert Musil's *The Confusions of Young Törless* (1906)—help to explain the reception and rapid growth of the youth movement.

The Wandervogel leader who inducted Blüher was a young man named Karl Fischer (1881–1941), who had graduated from the Steglitz *Gymnasium* only a few years earlier. Fischer was responsible for developing a rigid club structure based on strict hierarchy. As Blüher described in his autobiography, the initiation ceremony began with a salute: *"Heil."* Following a script he had devised himself, Fischer asked the fourteen-year-old Blüher if he was prepared to swear his allegiance to the name of the Wandervogel as well as his obedience to the troupe leader (Fischer himself). To each question, Blüher answered in the affirmative. Although Blüher found Fischer "hard," "domineering," and " unpleasant," he also admired the discipline and loyalty that Fischer inspired.[5]

Fischer's leadership style was a source of conflict, however, which led to the first significant Wandervogel division in 1903. Blüher was himself the catalyst when disciplined on an excursion by another group leader for "moral transgressions," shorthand for sexual relations with a fellow member. The leader of the outing sent Blüher home early, and then attempted to have him ejected from the troupe. Fischer, who claimed to exercise superior authority, shielded Blüher and prevented his expulsion. In reaction to Fischer's imperiousness, a splinter group formed in 1904, the catalyst for the so-called *"Führer* controversy," creating a division between the Steglitz Wandervogel and the Alt-Wandervogel, the group to which Fischer and Blüher adhered. Fischer's temperament led to renewed conflict, and in 1906 he was finally forced out of this group as well.[6]

In 1907 Blüher received his *Gymnasium* diploma and began studying classical philology, matriculating first at the University of Basel and then transferring to the University of Berlin. He spent a total of sixteen semesters pursuing a doctorate, and finally dropped his studies in 1915 without receiving the degree. Because of color blindness, Blüher was exempted from military service, and he spent the remainder of the war providing nursing care. Though nominally a student *in* Berlin, Blüher was much more a student *of* the city. It was during this period that he first encountered the fledgling homosexual rights movement with its masculinist and sexological factions. He also spent his student years reading the most recent psychiatric literature—scholarship that had not yet penetrated the conservative halls of the German academy— assimilating these to help make sense of his personal experience. Blüher was also an attentive observer of the Eulenburg scandal and the court trials of Moltke, Harden, Bülow, and Brand. Indeed, the homoeroticism of the Liebenberg Roundtable provided what Blüher considered a clear manifestation of the Männerbund.[7]

In 1906 the wealthy estate owner Wilhelm Jansen replaced Karl Fischer as director of the Alt-Wandervogel, and it was Jansen who created the first direct connection between the homosexual rights movement and the youth organization. A member of Hirschfeld's Scientific-Humanitarian Committee, Jansen was listed on SHC newsletters as business manager and contact person for western Germany. Jansen's estate (*Rittergut*) was in Hessen, and he was responsible for organizing SHC events in Frankfurt. Jansen was also affiliated with Adolf Brand and his organization the Community of the Special (CoS). In 1905 Jansen encountered the Alt-Wandervogel by accident and was intrigued to learn more about it. Once involved, he became an aggressive apostle for the Wandervogel organization and helped to found many affiliated clubs in western Germany.[8]

Jansen introduced Blüher in 1907 to Benedict Friedlaender, who represented, along with Brand, the masculinist faction of Berlin's homosexual rights community. Just months before making the young Blüher's acquaintance, in December 1906, Friedlaender had broken openly with Hirschfeld and initiated the Secession movement out of the SHC. Friedlaender was at that point dying of colon cancer, and Blüher visited him regularly until his death in June 1908. This provided Blüher with his introduction to Friedlaender's *Renaissance des Eros,* which he was able to discuss at length with the author. The work had become an inspiration for the masculinists and promoted the notion of the hyper-virile homosexual as an agent of cultural innovation and political leadership.[9]

Blüher was drawn to Jansen, and likewise to Friedlaender (and his theories), because they helped him to sort out and make sense of his own homoerotic feelings. And like Jansen, Friedlaender provided a positive role model of a same-sex-loving man. Since adolescence, Blüher had been sexually involved with other boys, experiences he chronicled with surprising candor in his writings. His affairs began at the Steglitz *Gymnasium,* where Blüher's classmates were sexually active, primarily with one another. "It was a matter of principle that no one touched a prepubescent boy," Blüher explained. "But among those of the same age, erotic relationships were very passionate; we were seized with a fully aroused Eros which swept through us in the darkness."[10] As a fifteen-year-old, Blüher described falling in love with another member of his Wandervogel troupe: "As he stood in front of me, I saw suddenly how beautiful he was, and from that moment forward, I was in flames. I managed to ignite him and break through all of his barriers; he was too princely a human being not to be free to do whatever he pleased, but generally it was the case that I was always attempting to lure him. He was never submerged in the bath of Eros."[11] Blüher had passionate affairs with other boys or young men at least into his very early twenties, though some of his crushes were clearly unrequited.[12]

He first pursued romantic relationships with women in 1908. In a letter to his parents just before publication of his Wandervogel history in 1912, Blüher described his ascendant heterosexuality as the work of fate. "I have a well-founded belief that it was only a question of chance that weighted the scale to fall on this side [the side of heterosexuality]," he wrote; "for years I had had bad luck in the direction of inversion [homosexuality], and much better luck in that of normalcy, and because the one requires a complete effort, there is not much left for the other. And so the other goes to sleep. The experiment to see if I could awake it again would have cost me too much. In the conditions in which I now live, it is no longer possible."[13]

Blüher never tells us what he believed it might have "cost" him to remain "inverted," though his language suggests fear of both the potential legal persecution and the social discrimination suffered by many homosexuals. In the same letter to his parents, Blüher explained further that his girlfriend, Louise, whom he married soon after, had "had a strong, moderating influence, though it was hardly a passionate relationship."[14]

Certainly the fate of Wilhelm Jansen must have been prominent in

Blüher's mind. In 1908 Jansen was demoted as the executive director of the Alt-Wandervogel, and two years later he was excluded entirely from the organization. After succeeding Fischer in 1906, Jansen had turned his manor house in western Germany into a retreat for Wandervogel members. Jansen was also an adherent of the German life reform movement and an avid nudist; in 1907 he built a swimming pool and bathhouse for nude sunbathing, and he also erected a professional photography studio specifically for nude photography. Unguarded about his sexuality, Jansen experienced significant scrutiny throughout his short tenure as the Alt-Wandervogel director. Rumors swirled about his affairs with individual members, confirmed in his correspondence with Blüher.[15] In March 1908 a newspaper article claimed that "a certain Jansen had organized a club of pederasts (*Päderastenclub*) made up of Latin school boys."[16]

This created much unwanted publicity for the youth movement, which was especially sensitive to charges of homosexual conduct following the Eulenburg scandal. As the Alt-Wandervogel organization expanded, it faced not only external pressure but also the scrutiny of new members, or their fathers, who manned the Parents' Council. In a thoroughgoing purge of troupe leaders suspected of "inversion," Jansen was finally forced to sever his affiliation completely in 1910. He was not so easily defeated, however, and he formed a third organization, the Jung-Wandervogel, in 1911. Surviving until 1933, this group quickly gained a reputation for tolerating homosexuals, although relationships between adult leaders and boys were forbidden.[17]

Drawing on personal experience, Blüher published a three-volume history of the Wandervogel movement in 1912. The study garnered significant attention: both Magnus Hirschfeld and Sigmund Freud (in Vienna) were intrigued by Blüher's synthesis; initially the official Wandervogel organization promoted the first two volumes of his study for its fulsome endorsement of their own goals and ideals. The third volume, as we will see, proved to be more problematic. With his autobiographical account, Blüher created a foundation myth for the Alt-Wandervogel by emphasizing the leadership principle and his central role in its realization.

The role of the *Führer*—the leadership principle—in Blüher's retelling, became a central feature not only of the Wandervogel organization but also of the Männerbund. In Blüher's account, both the *Führer* principle—embodied by Fischer—and the same-sex eroticism of male associations were present in the older, purer Alt-Wandervogel group. In this fashion Blüher used personal experiences to fashion central features of his Männerbund sociology.

Thus the three volumes of Blüher's Wandervogel history were based on his personal experience and the fractious internal politics of the youth movement. But Blüher also drew heavily from a recent, influential work, *Altersklassen und Männerbünde* (Age groups and male associations), which he encountered through his friendship with Benedict Friedlaender. The author of *Altersklassen,* Heinrich Schurtz (1863–1903), had completed a doctorate in geography at the University of Leipzig before accepting a position at the Museum of Natural History in Bremen. Published in 1902, his work was based on more than a decade of careful synthesis of ethnographic studies of the non-Western world. One of the first systematic theorists of the Männerbund, Schurtz argued against earlier anthropological claims that primitive human society had been matriarchal. (One example of such a work was Friedrich Engels's *Origins of the Family, Private Property, and the State,* published in 1884.) Generalizing from the "primitive" indigenous cultures of Africa, Asia, the southwest Pacific, and the Americas, Schurtz claimed to have identified a dramatically different origin of human society, namely the Männerbund.

For Schurtz, the battle of the sexes was a given, and it reflected "the nearly unbridgeable opposition" between men and women.[18] The age-old conflict did not simply pit man against woman, however, but, rather, contrasted the masculine Männerbund with the "maternal" institution of the family. This polarity helped to cement the incommensurability of the sexes. It also explained the inherent superiority of men, and the fundamentally masculine engine of all human culture and social evolution. According to Schurtz, the woman was tied to the family through her sexual drives. In contrast, the man experienced an asexual "social drive" that made him a "facilitator" of the growth of "nearly all higher social development."[19]

Schurtz's antifeminism was a common, if unfortunate, reaction to rapid cultural and economic change in the early twentieth century. Not only in Germany but throughout the Western world, industrialization and urbanization had both increased and worsened the life chances and living standards of men and women alike. Factory and sweatshop labor gave employment to rural men and women, drawing a large pool of workers to burgeoning urban centers. But miserable working conditions and poor wages were a source of poverty and extreme degradation. Some women gained new educational opportunities, however, and gradually, by the end of the nineteenth century, began to enter certain white-collar employments—clerking, stenography, shop sales—that had previously been the exclusive domain of men. As differences between the opportunities available to men and women were (very) slowly eroded, social class gained greater significance as the defining feature of modern German society. One of the responses to this dramatic shift, the theory of the Männerbund, was thus born of a profound misogyny.[20]

The agitation for women's suffrage was also a feature of the Western political landscape by 1900. Women achieved the vote in Germany under the Weimar constitution in 1919, after decades of piecemeal reform. Some girls were allowed to attend German Latin schools beginning in the 1890s, and Prussian universities opened their doors to women in 1908. The Social Democratic Party (SPD)—Germany's largest political party—had an explicit platform plank in support of women's suffrage. In the years before 1914, the SPD's electoral successes created a genuine fear among organized antifeminist groups that a socialist government would enfranchise women.[21]

Conflicts about the status of German women resonated within the youth movement, as well. In 1907 a debate erupted on whether or not to admit girls. The oldest troupe in Steglitz had never admitted girls nor allowed the participation of adult women. Like many of the Wandervogel leaders, Blüher's patron and troupe master Karl Fischer was an outspoken misogynist. The all-male Wandervogel gained the attention of German feminists, however, and in 1905 the Berlin author and philosopher Marie Luise Becker petitioned the Alt-Wandervogel governing council to allow girls to join. Her request was summarily rejected. Though short-lived, the Bund der Wanderschwestern (Association of Hiking Sisters) was organized in 1905. Many others agitated, however, to gain girls' admission to one of the two major organizations. At this point, of course, there were practically no mixed-gender associations, regardless of class or age. Middle-class boys and girls were almost always segregated; certainly they never mingled socially without chaperones. Liberals within the youth movement argued not only for girls' rights but also for the benefits of mixed-gender socialization. Conservative opponents claimed that the Wandervogel boys would lose the unique opportunity of masculine development if no longer allowed to interact in an all-male environment. It was believed that "mixed hiking" (*Gemischtwandern*) also threatened to emasculate Wandervogel boys. By 1911 the Steglitz Wandervogel organization began to sponsor girls' clubs, and the Alt-Wandervogel soon followed suit, though the Neu-Wandervogel organization sponsored boys' clubs exclusively. Not until after 1918, however, did the Steglitz Wandervogel allow activities in which both boys and girls could participate.

For Blüher, the social interaction of boys and girls was nonsensical and a positive threat to the Männerbund. Like Schurtz and other contemporary misogynists, Blüher believed that men and women were profoundly different and that masculine characteristics were intrinsically superior to femininity. Blüher had an additional reason to segregate boys and girls, of course, and that was his theory of the role of overt homosexuality in the forging of male associations. While Schurtz described sexuality as a largely feminine characteristic confined to the family and biological reproduction, Blüher conceived the homoerotic Männerbund as a way to accommodate his own homosexuality. He effectively sexualized Schurtz's "social drive" to explain homoeroticism as the binding and creative force of male associations.[22]

The third volume of Blüher's Wandervogel history, *Die deutsche Wandervogelbewegung als erotisches Phänomen: Ein Beitrag zur Erkenntnis der sexuellen Inversion* (The German Wandervogel movement as an erotic phenomenon: A contribution to the discovery of sexual inversion), developed the thesis that homoeroticism and even explicit homosexuality were fundamental and natural features of the youth movement, and by extension, of the Männerbund. The volume was condemned by the Wandervogel board and quickly drew ire from conservative groups. It also made Blüher's reputation as a cultural radical. The reaction to

Blüher's audacious claim, it appears, was an important turning point in his intellectual trajectory. Despite the denunciation by former allies, Blüher remained committed to the phenomenon of homoeroticism as an explanatory factor of the Männerbund and, as such, a supporter of homosexual rights. The condemnation of right-wing critics, which often included character assassination, drove Blüher to declare his own sexual "normalcy," however, and in 1914 he married his girlfriend, Louise, the first of his two wives. Right-wing invective also helped to shape Blüher's theoretical model, which emphasized an implicit patriarchal misogyny and, increasingly, racialist anti-Semitism.[23]

In 1917 and 1919, Blüher published the first two volumes of *Die Rolle der Erotik in der männlichen Gesellschaft* (The role of eroticism in masculine society), which presented his full-blown sociology of state formation. In this work it was the hierarchical *German* Männerbund—still homoerotic—that claimed responsibility for the origin and growth of not only the state but also world culture. The family, the domain of femininity, was neither a creative force nor even a complement to the Männerbund, but rather its rival, with the single function of human procreation. Germany's Jewish minority, in Blüher's analysis, was a foreign and destructive graft on an otherwise vibrant organism that could best be managed with the Zionist-inspired outmigration envisioned by Theodor Herzl.

Although Blüher made anti-Semitism a central feature of his Männerbund formulation, this did not prevent him from reading and assimilating the sexology and psychiatry of the Jewish doctors Magnus Hirschfeld and Sigmund Freud.[24] Following both Hirschfeld and Freud, Blüher believed in a sexuality continuum that ranged from the absolute heterosexual to the complete homosexual. In his account of the "third sex," Hirschfeld argued that there were specific physical attributes of male and female homosexuals, though he later changed his emphasis to psychological characteristics. It was this theory that informed Hirschfeld's diagnosis of Kuno von Moltke as a "homosexual" in the first Moltke-Harden trial. Recall that although Moltke might never have engaged in homosexual practices, according to Hirschfeld, he could still be classified an "unconscious homosexual," whose telltale signs could be read like a book, at least by a trained expert such as Hirschfeld. Despite his focus on the effeminate male homosexual, Hirschfeld actually proposed a nearly infinite number of natural variations, developing a complicated set of physical and psychological markers that allowed for some forty-three million potential combinations. Most famously, Hirschfeld claimed that sexuality or a particular sexual constitution was inborn and established at birth.

In contrast, Freud argued that all infants were fundamentally pansexual (or polymorphous perverse). With his *Three Essays on the Theory of Sexuality* (1905)—another text that Benedict Friedlaender introduced to Blüher—Freud laid out a psychodynamic explanation that emphasized infant and childhood development. The polymorphous perversion of the infant, in Freud's view, was molded through parental relationships and channeled into a normative heterosexuality. The objective in Freud's model, as any good Darwinian would understand, was adult heterosexual coitus, necessary for procreation and social reproduction. For Freud, then, homosexuality reflected a misstep in this psychodynamic process, since sex between two men (or between two women) was not (re)productive. Freud discounted the notion that same-sex erotic desire was somehow hardwired from birth, and he also rejected the emancipatory project of Hirschfeld. Legal reform was not a priority for Freud, since he considered homosexual desire to be fundamentally pathological.

Blüher drew opportunistically from both thinkers. He embraced Freud's theory of an innate bisexuality, which described, for Blüher, the orientation of a vast majority. Of course, this confirmed Blüher's own experience and identity as an adolescent who loved men but eventually married women. Bisexuality also conformed to the theory and actual sexual practice of most of the masculinists, including Friedlaender and Adolf Brand, both of whom had married. Blüher made an exception to Freud's theory of bisexuality with his notion of the *Männerheld,* a word that defies easy translation but might be defined as a super-virile homosexual who eschews all contact with women and loves men exclusively. This reflected the influence of Friedlaender and was modeled on historical military figures, such as Frederick the Great of Prussia.

Blüher parted company with Freud more significantly in his embrace of Hirschfeld's biological determinism. Here Blüher endorsed Hirschfeld's activism and advocacy for legal reform, and supported—unlike Freud—the abolition of anti-sodomy statutes, in both Germany and the Austro-Hungarian Empire. Blüher also rejected any application of degeneration theory for explaining homosexual behavior. Homo-eroticism, including the exclusive homosexuality of the *Männerheld,* or the super-virile homosexual, was not abnormal and was, moreover, an absolute and essential feature of any successful civilization. The *Führer* of a given Männerbund engaged in creative cultural labor. Blüher completely rejected Freud's implicit assessment of homosexuality as the result of a failed psychodynamic development. Homosexuality for Blüher, unlike for Freud, was a positive and absolute good.

But Blüher not only read and applied the theories advanced by Hirschfeld and Freud. He also made personal contact with both men, and used their professional reputations to further his own career. The publication of the first two volumes of Wandervogel history garnered the attention and positive notice of Hirschfeld and the Scientific-Humanitarian Committee. Blüher was invited to attend SHC meetings, which he did, and he also lectured to the group on the Wandervogel phenomenon. In a personal letter, Berlin sexologist Iwan Bloch, a staunch supporter of Hirschfeld and member of the SHC, wrote Blüher that his Wandervogel study was "a commendable contribution to the research on the problem of homosexuality."[25] Hirschfeld himself wrote the laudatory introduction to the third volume of Blüher's Wandervogel history. Of course, Blüher's earlier friendships with Jansen and Friedlaender had helped him to secure the support of the masculinist wing of the homosexual rights movement. The positive reception of his Wandervogel history allowed him, in turn, to ingratiate himself with the sexological faction, namely Hirschfeld and the SHC.

Blüher also initiated a brief correspondence with Freud beginning in 1910. Although Freud never extended patronage, he was intrigued by Blüher's Wandervogel history and offered the young scholar encouraging advice.[26] Freud even appears to have drawn inspiration from Blüher's work for his 1912–13 publication *Totem and Taboo,* one of his most popular studies. Addressing the cultural psychology of primitive communities and the origins of social organization, Freud adopted the Männerbund—using the term *Männerverbände,* or "male associations"—as the primal form of social organization. In Freud's theory, the tribal leader and original patriarch excluded his sons to eliminate their sexual competition. The exiled offspring then formed the "brother clan," assassinated the patriarch, and established a new, more egalitarian society. The "brother clan," in Freud's conception, was an all-male society created through the oedipal slaying of the father, which resulted in the invention of religion, morality, society, and art. Although Freud refused to sign the SHC petition for homosexual emancipation, he was clearly unable to resist the intellectual allure of the Männerbund.

The homoerotic Männerbund captured the attention of Germany's leading scientists of sexuality, emboldening Blüher to elaborate on his theory. In 1913 he published a lengthy three-part study, "The Three Models of Homosexuality," in Hirschfeld's *Jahrbuch*. Hewing to his belief in a near-universal bisexuality, Blüher argued that sexual "inversion" was a pervasive phenomenon and that nearly all men experienced same-sex erotic desire. The *Männerheld* was ascribed a special status, defined by an exclusive and congenital homosexual orientation. Blüher also created a third category for effeminate homosexuals, who lacked the attributes of true masculinity. Only this category, in Blüher's assessment, represented an aberration.[27]

Much of Blüher's analysis undermined Hirschfeld's own theories—so much so that one is astonished that Hirschfeld published the essay. Hirschfeld did take the liberty of editing Blüher's title, however, exchanging the word "Inversion" with "Homosexuality" and editing out several pages. Blüher still embraced Hirschfeld's biological determinism and his emancipatory project. But Blüher's characterization of the effete homosexual as an aberration of nature was highly insulting to Hirschfeld. Blüher also blurred Hirschfeld's all-important distinction between friendship and erotic love. For Blüher, there existed a seamless continuum from one to the other. Hirschfeld maintained, in contrast, that heterosexual men could cultivate close and even affectionate friendships with other men that never aroused sensual desire.[28] In response to Hirschfeld's edits, Blüher published his piece in its entirety with the Spohr Verlag as a seventy-nine-page pamphlet. The word "homosexual" connoted a medical condition or illness, in Blüher's mind, so he restored the title to its original, "The Three Models of Inversion."[29]

This was Blüher's final collaboration with Hirschfeld and the SHC, and they never had any significant interaction again. And while Blüher's theories clashed powerfully with those of Hirschfeld, his endorsement of homoeroticism was too extreme for Freud. Blüher's alienation from both men, however, was also the result of his growing anti-Semitism.

Anti-Semitism was Blüher's defensive response to the criticism he received from the Wandervogel establishment for the third volume of his study. In 1913 Dr. H. Albrecht, a leading member of one of the national Wandervogel umbrella organizations, reviewed Blüher's three volumes and described his theories as "perverse," "monstrous," and "sick." Responding to the third volume, subtitled "Erotic Phenomenon," Albrecht claimed that Blüher had made a sexual orientation (namely, homosexuality) that "was pathological, according to the generally accepted opinion of contemporary social morality," the basis of the youth movement. "The sexually normal," as Albrecht understood Blüher's claim, had no role to play, and instead only the inverts could be true "commanders of youth." Albrecht also faulted Blüher for sending three thousand "sensational, colored brochures" advertising his Wandervogel study to all of the Prussian school directors.[30]

The national Wandervogel umbrella association responded to Blüher's advertisement with its own letter, addressed to "All School Directors." The association rebuked Blüher for his "odd views" and claimed dishonestly that the Alt-Wandervogel directorate had expelled him years earlier. The letter also claimed that they had already removed anyone who "glorified homosexual inclinations."[31] The Alt-Wandervogel directorate, which had excluded Wilhelm Jansen in 1910, responded similarly with its own missive announcing its intention to expel any remaining homosexuals from its ranks and promising that it had already banned Blüher's publications. Only the "homo"-friendly Jung-Wandervogel umbrella committee did not attempt to discredit Blüher. Among the "respectable" Wandervogel groups, however, it was feared that school officials might ban all youth groups as "pederasts' clubs."[32] And since Blüher's three volumes were widely publicized, the damage had potentially been done.

As Blüher's study gained circulation, and notoriety, the furor within the youth movement exploded. Increasingly, Blüher was not only accused of being a homosexual but also labeled "un-German," "mixed-race," "Jewish," or "half-Jewish." These attacks on Blüher coincided with an anti-Semitic radicalization of the youth movement. In June 1913 the *Berliner Tageblatt* reported an incident in the Saxon town of Zittau where a Jewish girl was expelled from the local Wandervogel chapter because she was not considered "German." The article complained that any "German Jew" who otherwise enjoyed all the rights of German citizenship could be rejected as not a "real German" by the Wandervogel. The newspaper also noted that the girl's father and grandfather had both performed military service in the German army.[33]

The "Zittau event" was a catalyst for a broad discussion of the "Jewish question" within the youth movement. The major Wandervogel publication *Wandervogelführerzeitung* (The journal of Wandervogel leadership) devoted its October edition to the relationship between "Jewry" and the Wandervogel movement. Except for one, every contribution to the special issue recommended that Jews be excluded. Typical was an article by the young engineer Dankwart Gerlach, who had joined as a fourteen-year-old in 1904 and now served as a group leader. Gerlach opined,

> The justification that the Wandervogel is a German movement hits the nail on the head. It is unwise, of course, to be vehemently anti-Semitic, since that would incite the daily press like a mob at our throat. . . . I know many Jews of different ages in the Wandervogel, and I have yet to find one who has internalized the Wandervogel ethos. . . . Rather than force an instinctively anti-Semitic German youth to accompany a Jew on an excursion, is it not better perhaps to say to the Jews: we get along better without you, stay away!?[34]

Gerlach's unabashed bigotry was representative, and the so-called "Jewish issue" of the *Wandervogelführerzeitung* turned a subtle and implicit anti-Semitism into an explicit, though informal, policy. Nationwide by 1914 most German-Jewish youth in the Wandervogel had left the organization.[35]

Blüher responded to his critics by asserting his own racial purity and implicitly embracing the anti-Semitism with which he had been vilified. In order to defend his support for male same-sex eroticism, he distinguished increasingly between his own version of masculine friend-love and the homosexuality of the "Jewish" science of sexology. "The fact that I express understanding for a sexual orientation [homosexual] that is different from my own [heterosexual] is not evidence of some shortcoming," Blüher argued. "My racial heritage gives me the security that my own qualities, good and bad, are manifestly German." In another response to his critics, Blüher asserted, "I love German girls with blond hair and plan to procreate my own race. I consider it my most German characteristic that I not allow my dear enemies and fellow Germans to dictate to me how one has to be German." Emphatically proclaiming his heterosexuality, Blüher doubled down, so to speak, maintaining his intellectual commitment to the homoeroticism of the Männerbund, but by defining it as non-Jewish and distinctly German. In June 1913 he published a seven-page essay calling for the abolition of the anti-sodomy statute, Paragraph 175. Here he used anti-Semitic rhetoric, arguing for the legalization of male same-sex love, especially that "middle ground between usual friendship and the love of homosexuals." He argued that the homoerotic was not "essentially a Jewish characteristic" and could easily be combined with a "race-conscious German-ness."[36]

Blüher incorporated his anti-Semitism fully into his two-volume study *Die Rolle der Erotik in der männlichen Gesellschaft*, published during and just after the war, in 1917 and 1919. As a kind of popular historical sociology, Blüher's new work combined an ethnographic review of important Männerbund models, including ancient Greece, with an outline of his overarching thesis: the erotic Männerbund as the historical agent of social organization and culture, consisting of a uniform age cohort hierarchically structured with an explicit *Führer*, or leader. In volume two, Blüher included his version of the history of the Wandervogel, emphasizing that the racially *German*—meaning not Jewish—youth movement was an ideal-typical Männerbund. Reminiscent of German philosopher Georg Wilhelm Friedrich Hegel (1770–1831), who viewed the Prussian state as the telos, or culmination, of world history, Blüher posited that the apotheosis of the Männerbund was the state, and specifically the German state.

Blüher articulated his most strident anti-Semitism when he addressed the "Jewish question" directly in his 1922 publication *Secessio Judaica,* a short (sixty-six pages), racialist screed masquerading as philosophical rumination. Germany today, according to Blüher, "is a battleground of three historical powers . . . the Roman empire of the Catholic Church, Jewry, and the German Reich of the German nation."[37] These three were incommensurable, Blüher asserted: "One cannot be a Jew and a German; one cannot be a Roman [Catholic] and a German. The German idea distinguishes itself without question from the other two, and the German has no choice."[38] Rehearsing traditional anti-Semitic themes—the Jews are a parasitic race, capable only of mimicry, and guilty of greed and economic extortion—Blüher then praised Zionism for its realistic appraisal and response to the "Jewish question," namely withdrawal or secession into a separate Jewish state.[39] In his own mind, Blüher was not bigoted, however, and he considered his anti-Semitism neither hate-filled nor rabble-rousing; it simply reflected an objective appraisal of contemporary "race" relations. As Blüher himself conceived it, his philosophically grounded anti-Semitism was really only a race-conscious understanding and valorization of what it meant to be properly German.

Blüher's reputation and popular reception scaled incredible heights during the Weimar Republic when he became one of the best-selling authors in Germany. His influence on both the left and the right was profound. Writing in 1925, Thomas Mann claimed that "since Blüher, this element [the homoerotic], at least with the manifestation of the youth movement, has become psychologically bound to our consciousness . . . without doubt, the homoerotic today enjoys a certain cultural goodwill."[40] While cultivating *völkisch* and protofascist interlocutors, Blüher remained friends with a number of left-wing Jewish intellectuals, including Martin Buber, Gustav Landauer, and the SHC activist and openly homosexual communist Kurt Hiller. Blüher also established a written correspondence with the former Kaiser William II, who was whiling away his last decades in Dutch exile. The Nazis never warmed to Blüher, despite the sociological model that he supplied for their movement. Indeed, Blüher condemned both Hitler and his anti-Semitism as early as 1933. Kurt Hiller, just after his release from a concentration camp in late 1933, met Blüher in a Berlin café. The former had been brutalized during his internment and was preparing for exile; Blüher apologized profusely for the anti-Semitism of his Weimar publications.[41] After this, Blüher entered an "internal exile" for the duration of the Third Reich. Despite his distance from the Nazi regime, Blüher was unable to reestablish himself after 1945. In the conservative context of the West German Federal Republic, it was likelier that Blüher's endorsement of homoeroticism and not his erstwhile anti-Semitism made him a pariah. He died in relative obscurity in 1954.

Blüher's full-throated embrace of "respectable" anti-Semitism marked his final break with the German left wing. As the prewar herald and champion of the youth movement, Blüher had predictably been aligned with progressive causes such as the life reform movement, which included nudism and dietary reform. By casting his lot with the anti-Semites, however, he alienated the left entirely and embraced what he himself would label the "conservative revolution." Indeed, Blüher was among the first to couple the words "conservative" and "revolution" when describing the extra-parliamentary, right-wing reaction to the new Social Democratic Weimar Republic. The expression became a central concept and virtual synonym for the configuration of old-school conservatives, *völkisch* German nationalists, and, eventually, Nazis, who comprised Weimar's antidemocratic opposition.

Blüher's theory of the homoerotic Männerbund garnered a notoriety that distanced him from many conservative elites, as well as the Nazis, both before and after 1933. However, the Männerbund remained broadly influential and was popularized throughout the Weimar Republic. It was difficult for Blüher and his contemporaries not to view the demobilized troops after November 1918, who formed the Freikorps and other right-wing militia groups, and later the Nazi Party itself, as Männerbund manifestations. Indeed, Blüher's theory provided a sociological model and intellectual substrate for much of the Nazi movement. For Weimar's myriad youth groups, spanning the political spectrum from left to right, the Männerbund was a self-evident reality.

The unbearable irony of Blüher's popular success was how the homoerotic Männerbund disseminated a knowledge of same-sex love, and conditioned its tentative acceptance, despite persistent and often vehement resistance on the part of many conservatives. How could one suppress and punish adolescent homosexual experimentation if it were properly understood, according to Blüher, as healthy and German? And why would one condemn the openly homosexual adult if, as Blüher's model of the *Männerheld* maintained, he might also be a virile nationalist and perhaps a military or political leader? A greater irony still was Blüher's popularization of the "Jewish" sciences of psychiatry and sexology. Via Blüher, even the vehement anti-Semite might internalize an understanding that bisexuality was nearly universal or, conversely, that sexual orientation was hardwired. If mutually exclusive, neither construct could please an old-school conservative. Christian dogma and traditional morality could scarce hold back the tide of sexual modernity. It is difficult, indeed, to imagine the culture of Weimar Germany without considering the Männerbund.

CHAPTER SIX

Weimar Sexual Reform and the Institute for Sexual Science

It was formerly the case that ignorance counted as innocence and reticence about sexual questions was considered holy. Much has changed and today we recognize that in sexual questions ignorance means guilt and our sacred duty is to break the conspiracy of silence. To make cultural progress in this area we cite the words of Francis Bacon, "Knowledge is power."

—MAGNUS HIRSCHFELD, "Opening Speech of the Third International Congress of the World League for Sexual Reform in Wigmore Hall from September 8–14, 1929," in *Die Aufklärung*, 9 (1929)

In March 1919, just months after the November armistice that ended the Great War, Magnus Hirschfeld opened the Institut für Sexualwissenschaft (Institute for Sexual Science) in an opulent villa at the northern edge of Berlin's Tiergarten Park. The first such facility in the world, the institute was supported by the Dr. Magnus-Hirschfeld-Stiftung, a nonprofit foundation with an endowment of thirty thousand marks. Even before the war ended, in May 1918, Hirschfeld gained support for his plan from Berlin's police president, who then promoted the idea to the Prussian minister of the interior. The institute offered medical and psychological counseling on a range of sexual issues to thousands of individuals, including heterosexual men and women, homosexuals, cross-dressers, and intersex individuals. The institute also represented the first attempt to establish "sexology," or sexual science, as a topic of legitimate academic study and research. Nowhere else in the world was there so much as a university department or chair devoted to the subject, much less an entire institute. Hirschfeld's reputation as a sexologist also helped to attract medical doctors and psychiatrists, who visited the institute for research or to participate in seminars and conferences.[1]

The original plan for the institute called for an equal division between medical practice and research. While the practice was expected to be self-supporting through paying clients and patients, research would rely on the funding provided by the endowed foundation. Hirschfeld's ambitious design included research departments of sexual biology, pathology, sociology, and ethnography. The medical and therapeutic practices were to include medical treatment and psychological counseling for a range of problems related to sexuality, venereal disease, and birth control. The institute also opened Germany's first sexual counseling center, the Center of Sexual Counseling for Married Couples, which served as a model for the many clinics opened in the 1920s in Berlin and throughout Germany.

The institute acquired an adjacent property in 1921, which created additional space for the library, an auditorium, and a surgical unit. By this point the entire complex had more than fifty rooms. The basement of the main villa housed the domestic staff and kitchen as well as several offices. The ground floor had reception, waiting, and consultation rooms. Hirschfeld's personal quarters and the museum were housed on the second floor, where the X-ray apparatus and laboratories were likewise located. The adjoining residential house had clinics for patients and a large lecture hall. The library and other records were housed in a separate building in the courtyard.

The institute's formal staff was fairly limited and included several secretaries, domestic help, and Hirschfeld's younger friend and lover Karl Giese (1898–1938), who served as the archivist, librarian, and museum curator. The only salaried medical doctor was Arthur Kronfeld. An endocrinologist, Dr. Arthur Weil, left the institute for the United States in 1923. This was the year of the Great Inflation, which marked a significant turning point, largely by reducing the institute's initial endowment to a few hundred marks. The institute's purchase of the adjoining property just two years earlier proved especially fortuitous, since real estate turned out to be one of the best hedges against complete financial disas-

ter. Another victim of the inflation was the *Jahrbuch für sexuelle Zwischenstufen,* the scholarly journal of sexual science that Hirschfeld had
published with the Spohr Verlag since 1899. The loss of the endowment
meant that Hirschfeld was ultimately forced to give up his dream of supporting scientific research. Without funding, the institute depended on
unpaid interns or PhD students who volunteered their time in exchange
for the opportunity to work there. After 1925, the institute largely for-
sook the pretense of pursuing original research and focused entirely on
medical and psychological practice, its advocacy for legal reform, and its
various campaigns to provide public education on sexuality and birth
control.[2]

The institute's emphasis on public education quickly helped to
broaden its reputation, not only within Germany but throughout the
Western world. One example of this public outreach was the museum
of sexuality, referred to in some sources as the "Hirschfeld Museum."
Geared to titillate and entertain as well as to educate, the museum pre-
sentation followed three themes: variation in sexual orientation (primarily homosexuality), the diversity of sexual drives (illustrated with
examples of fetishism, masochism, and sadism), and an ethnography of
sexual expression from all corners of the world. Much of the display
consisted of wall-mounted charts and photographs. But there were also
banks of cases filled with objects, including Hirschfeld's collection of
phalluses (from around the globe), objects that had belonged to fetish-
ists, and various sex toys.[3]

"Visited this remarkable Institute," reported the English feminist
Dora Russell—second wife of philosopher Bertrand Russell—in 1926,
"where the results of researches into various sex problems and perversions could be seen in records and photographs. We actually met two
people whose sex had been changed by operation."[4] Margaret Sanger,
American founder of Planned Parenthood, described how "this most
extraordinary mansion . . . was furnished sumptuously. On the walls
of the stairway were pictures of homosexuals—men decked out as
women in huge hats, earrings, and feminine make-up; also women in
men's clothing and toppers. Further up the stairs were photographs of
the same individuals" but in their regular clothing, demonstrating their
"normality."[5] New York physician and prominent activist for birth con-

trol Dr. William Robinson published a short account of his visit to the institute in 1925. Like Russell and Sanger, Robinson was struck by the institute's research on homosexuality; he reported an encounter with a male cross-dresser who passed for a woman. But Robinson also recognized the broad, general emphasis on human sexuality and sex reform: "The scope of the Institute is a much wider one, embracing the entire field of sexology. It is an institution absolutely unique in the whole world . . . which I hoped to establish in the United States but which I felt would not thrive on account of our prudish, hypocritical attitude to all questions of sex."[6]

As these laudatory accounts suggest—especially Robinson's—the institute's activities expanded to include the interests of heterosexuals by providing public education and promoting a broad political agenda. This included marital counseling, information on birth control, treatments for venereal disease, and experimental medications for impotence. According to a published report, the institute attracted some 3,500 visitors its very first year, including 1,500 medical doctors and students and another 2,000 "lay" visitors. Of these, some 30 percent "belonged to neither the one nor the other sex but rather to the intersexual variant," meaning homosexuals, lesbians, cross-dressers, and intersex individuals.[7] Although the term is anachronistic, "transgender" persons became a new constituent group served by the institute. With the X-ray, laboratory, and surgical facilities, the institute provided much more than counseling: Hirschfeld and his medical colleagues also pioneered some of the first primitive hormone treatments and sex-reassignment surgeries, effectively creating a nascent science of transsexuality. In addition, the institute housed the office and library of the Scientific-Humanitarian Committee and thus served as an all-purpose political lobby, social club, and clinic for sexual minorities. Becoming a popular tourist destination, the institute was one of the singular institutions that helped to define Weimar Berlin.

The founding of the Weimar Republic inaugurated a period of violent chaos—verging on, if not lurching into, at least episodically, civil war—of profound economic and social dislocation, and of a heady optimism about the prospects of Germany's fledgling democracy. In his New Year's message to SHC members at the beginning of 1919, Hirschfeld wrote, "[T]he great revolution of the last weeks can be greeted only with joy. This new time brings us freedom to speak and to write, and we assume with certainty the emancipation of all those previously oppressed."[8]

One of the great promises of the Weimar Republic was the elimination of all censorship. Although imperial Germany arguably had produced more titles on sexual minorities—scientific, literary, and popular—than the rest of the world combined, censorship had always been a threat for authors, activists, and publishers, including Adolf Brand, Max Spohr, and Hirschfeld. Thus the announcement on November 12, 1918, that "there is no more censorship" was a momentous development that let loose a prodigious outpouring within the arts and sciences, making the Weimar period one of the most creative in German history.[9] Certainly the open discussion of homosexual themes in popular films or the boulevard press illustrated Hirschfeld's claim about the new "freedom to speak and to write."

One of many examples of this was the publication of *Die Freundschaft* (Friendship), the world's first homosexual newspaper sold openly at kiosks. The paper appeared in August 1919, edited by the merchant Karl Schultz (with the support of the SHC). Unlike Hirschfeld's *Jahrbuch* or Adolf Brand's literary journal, *Der Eigene, Die Freundschaft* had a wide and mostly unhindered distribution as well as broad popular appeal. *Die Freundschaft* also helped to establish Berlin's expansive homosexual press, which produced nearly thirty periodical titles throughout the period of the Weimar Republic (see the list provided at the beginning of the bibliography).

The 1920s was also the age of the feature-length film, and Hirschfeld quickly recognized the power of this new medium. Before the end of the First World War, Hirschfeld had begun collaboration with director Richard Oswald to produce *Anders als die Andern* (*Different from the Others*), the first movie to address the social and legal travails of homosexuals. The title was drawn from a novel published in 1904 by Hermann Breuer (using the pseudonym Bill Forster) about the unrequited love of a teacher for his male student. The novel ends with the protagonist's suicide.[10] Although the film depicts the concert violinist Paul Körner falling in love with his student, the plot has little in common with the novel, apart from themes of same-sex erotic love and suicide. Instead the film's central message is the insidious effect of Paragraph 175 on the lives of male homosexuals. The budding romance between Körner and his student is thwarted by family members and the nefarious work of a male prostitute who blackmails the musician. Although the blackmailer is sent to prison for three years, the musician is also found guilty and given a nominal sentence, destroying his career and leading to his suicide. The film also features Hirschfeld as a sympathetic medical doctor who helps to explain both the phenomenon of homosexuality and the injustices of the law.[11]

In addition to Hirschfeld, two other performers, both of whom would find significant success in the 1920s, were cast in central roles. The lead who played Paul Körner, Conrad Veidt (1893–1943), also starred in expressionist films (including *The Cabinet of Dr. Caligari*) and eventually worked in Britain and Hollywood. His most recognizable role was as the Nazi, Major Strasser, in *Casablanca* (1942). Veidt married three times and was by all accounts completely heterosexual. But he was certainly sympathetic to Hirschfeld's cause (as well as an ardent anti-Nazi). Although his role in *Anders* never affected his acting prospects, it shadowed him to some extent. American screenwriter Anita Loos (1889–1981), visiting Weimar Berlin from Hollywood, observed tongue in cheek that "the prettiest girl on the street was Conrad Veidt," since "any Berlin lady of the evening might turn out to be a man."[12] Loos's remark might have also reflected Veidt's following among homosexuals, inspired by his role in *Anders*. His appearances on stage and screen were reported on by journals such as *Die Freundschaft*. He also attended at least one Christmas costume ball meant exclusively for men, according to Christopher Isherwood.[13]

The film's other up-and-coming figure was the bisexual cabaret dancer Anita Berber (1899–1928), who played the sister of Paul Körner's lover. Berber acted in other films, sometimes alongside Veidt, but her notoriety came from her completely nude dance performances, which were outré even in Berlin. With her *garçonne* self-presentation, she embodied the flapper androgyny of the 1920s and was considered an inspiration for the likes of Marlene Dietrich and Greta Garbo. Sadly, her well-known addictions to cocaine, morphine, and opium shortened her career (and her life).[14]

Anders premiered in May 1919 and quickly became a "box-office" success. Within a short period, however, organized protesters began disturbing public screenings. These negative reactions were not spontaneous but, rather, staged disruptions organized by conservative Catholic and Protestant as well as right-wing anti-Semitic groups. The film ultimately spurred formal debate on censorship. While the Weimar constitution of August 1919 assured freedom of expression, it also created certain qualifications specifically for cinema, which were included almost certainly in response to the Hirschfeld-Oswald production. According to the 1919 constitution, films that might be classified as obscene (*Schund und Schmutz*, for example) or deemed dangerous to youth were subject to censorship. Although public screenings were permitted throughout most of northern Germany, the predominantly Catholic southwestern German states banned the film.

In October and November Hirschfeld sponsored screenings at the Institute for Sexual Science for members of the German National Assembly, the Prussian State Assembly, and the federal and Prussian state governments.[15] The effort was in vain, and in May of 1920 German legislators approved a specific censorship law for film. An office in Berlin was now established to review controversial productions. *Anders* was one of the first to be considered and was consigned to a panel of three psychiatrists—Albert Moll, Emil Kraepelin, and Siegfried Placzek—who were public opponents of Hirschfeld and disliked his aggressive advocacy for legal reform. The panel influenced the decision to ban public screenings of *Anders,* which was promulgated in October 1920. The formal determination claimed that the film was biased in its assessment of Paragraph 175 and that it likewise presented a one-sided view of the science, making common cause with the "homosexual party." For these reasons, the panel of psychiatrists argued, the film confused underage viewers about the phenomenon of homosexuality and could function as a recruitment tool. Future screenings of the film would be limited to private audiences and medical professionals. Effectively the only venue where the movie could be viewed was the institute, where it was shown for educational purposes and special events.[16]

Despite the censorship and this apparent defeat, *Anders* helped to establish a peculiar German genre of "enlightenment film" (*Aufklärungs-film*) that was popular throughout the Weimar period. Hirschfeld's collaborator and the director of *Anders,* Richard Oswald, produced what is often considered the first such movie, *Es werde Licht!* (Let there be light!), before the end of the war in 1917. The topic was venereal disease, an especially pressing issue among the mustered troops. No fewer than six enlightenment films are attributed to Oswald, on themes ranging from drug and alcohol abuse to prostitution and abortion. According to one estimate, at least 140 enlightenment films were given theatrical releases by 1933.[17] Hirschfeld continued to dabble in the film business and participated in at least three additional productions, including the 1927 *Gesetze der Liebe: Aus der Mappe eines Sexualforschers* (The laws of love: From the portfolio of a sex researcher), which outlined his own career, the various projects of the institute, and an abbreviated segment from *Anders,* which was ultimately left out to appease censors. Even this measure failed, however, and *Gesetze der Liebe* was ultimately banned in its entirety.

Hirschfeld's involvement in Weimar cinema was limited and, it would appear—considering the censorship of his two most important film projects—of little import. Yet this is misleading. The degree to which sexual minorities and gender ambiguity are depicted in Weimar film demands more careful consideration. For one, the number of films with explicitly homosexual themes or characters is remarkable: *Michael* (1924) was based on the novel by Danish author Herman Bang (1857–1912) about the love affair between a male artist and his male model (published in Danish in 1902 and in German translation in 1904); *Pandora's Box* (1928), based loosely on Frank Wedekind's "Lulu" plays—*Erdgeist* (1895) and *Die Büchse der Pandora* (1904)—was directed by G. W. Pabst and starred the American Louise Brooks; the plot of the 1928 production *Geschlecht in Fesseln: Die Sexualnot der Gefangenen* (*Sex in Chains*) revolved around the love affair of a married man (serving a prison term for murder) with another male prisoner; *Mädchen in Uniform* (1931) told the story of the unconsummated affair between a girl at a Prussian boarding school and her female teacher. These films—by no means a comprehensive list—encountered the scrutiny of censors. But again, the freedom in the 1920s to depict realistic homosexual or lesbian characters, and their relationships, was all but unique to Germany.[18]

Of equal interest—and of far greater number—were the films, usually comedies, that depicted mistaken identities due to cross-dressing. The Ernst Lubitsch film *I Don't Want to Be a Man*, released in 1918 before the end of the war, tells the story of a wealthy young woman who dons men's clothing to escape supervision. At a costume ball, the young woman "passes" successfully, and flirts with her own male tutor, who kisses his charge—believing her to be a boy—on the drunken carriage ride home. The subterfuge is ultimately ended and the young woman and her instructor become a couple. That the pre-Weimar censors permitted a kiss between characters who were both dressed as men is remarkable. The shock of an apparent homosexual encounter is mitigated, however, by humor and the happy heterosexual ending. The list of other films that either involved a cross-dressing character or a significant violation of traditional gender norms is long. A few of the most flagrant would include *Der Geiger von Florenz* (1925–26) and the original 1933 *Viktor und Viktoria* (which starred Julie Andrews in a 1982 remake).

Hirschfeld and the institute had no direct influence on these productions, of course, though one can certainly recognize the Hirschfeldian Zeitgeist. One intriguing anecdote is provided by Hirschfeld's biographer, Charlotte Wolff, who grew up in Berlin in the 1920s. When conducting research on Hirschfeld in west Berlin, Wolff interviewed the cinematographer Hans Casparius, who had had close ties to Hirschfeld, claimed to be his distant relative, and was a frequent visitor to the institute. One of Casparius's credits was his work on G. W. Pabst's film version of Bertolt Brecht's *Threepenny Opera*, released in 1931. Casparius claimed that Pabst and other cinematic luminaries knew and admired Hirschfeld, at least by reputation if not personally, and also acquainted themselves (as did so many) with the transvestite bar Eldorado.[19]

This artistic and cultural freedom heralded by Hirschfeld was accompanied, unfortunately, by a radical nationalist and anti-Semitic reaction. Recall that 1919 was the year that Hans Blüher released the second volume of his *Die Rolle der Erotik in der männlichen Gesellschaft*, with its explicit anti-Semitism and glorification of the nationalist, homoerotic Männerbund. A few years later, in his *Secessio Judaica*, Blüher claimed, "One cannot be a Jew and a German."[20] It was Blüher, in fact, who glorified the right-wing Freikorps—made up of soldiers returning from the Western Front—as the embodiment of his Männerbund and the vanguard of a "conservative revolution." It was the Freikorps, of course, to whom the shaky Social Democratic government turned to suppress communist revolution in Bavaria and elsewhere. Though successful in preserving the republic, the governing Social Democrats fatally poisoned relations with the German communists, making any unified left-wing opposition to the radical right (after 1930) a near impossibility.

Freikorps thugs were almost certainly responsible for disrupting the lectures Hirschfeld delivered in Hamburg in March 1920 by throwing fireworks into the crowded auditorium. Security officers ejected the "protesters," and Hirschfeld was able to complete his talk.[21] In Cologne he was able to speak only with police protection. Engagements in Stettin and Nuremberg were canceled altogether due to threats.[22] Hirschfeld was specifically identified and condemned in anti-Semitic flyers distributed during the unsuccessful Kapp Putsch, the coup attempt in Berlin led by the nationalist Wolfgang Kapp and supported by right-wing elements as well as parts of the military. In October Hirschfeld delivered another lecture, this time in Munich, and, on the way back to his hotel, was assaulted and left bleeding on the pavement. Many German papers announced his death. The *New York Times* reported that "Dr. Magnus Hirschfeld, the well-known expert on sexual science, died in Munich today of injuries inflicted upon him by an anti-Jewish mob."[23] His attackers were never apprehended. It became clear that the radical right, including the fledgling Nazi Party, deliberately identified Hirschfeld in their anti-Semitic rhetoric as the personification of the "Jewish corruption" of Germany. A few days after the attack, Hitler himself commented on Hirschfeld in an appearance at the Munich Hofbräuhaus, castigating the German justice system for granting such a "Jewish swine" the liberty to pervert German culture.[24] Thus the republic's multifaceted political culture not only empowered activism for homosexual emancipation but also permitted violent conservative political reaction.

As an early and abiding focus of Hirschfeld's research, "sexual intermediaries" became one of the institute's chief concerns. The definition of the term had expanded, however, since Hirschfeld first used it in the late nineteenth century to describe primarily male homosexuals and lesbians. Within a short period, the category evolved to include both homo- and heterosexual cross-dressers ("transvestites," as Hirschfeld labeled them), intersex individuals with ambiguous genitalia ("hermaphrodites"), and men or women who identified themselves with the opposite sex (described today as "transgender"). This diverse group comprised "sexual intermediaries," since its many elements all seemed to deviate from the heterosexual norm. Of course, Hirschfeld maintained that these sexual (and gender) variants occurred naturally and were therefore non-pathological. The corollary of this position and Hirschfeld's principal contention was that sexual and gender variation was biologically determined.

What became increasingly clear, however, was that nonnormative sexual orientation—homosexuality—was something completely different from the compulsion to cross-dress. Recall that in 1910 Hirschfeld had published a study, *The Transvestites: The Erotic Drive to Cross-Dress*, that introduced his own neologism and described men and women who wore the clothing of the opposite sex. Cross-dressing had been a puzzling phenomenon, vexing a range of psychiatrists and sexologists from Richard von Krafft-Ebing to Albert Moll, almost all of whom interpreted the practice variously as fetishistic or as a symptom of homosexuality. Hirschfeld's study was the first to give cross-dressing its own appellation and to identify it as something distinct from sexual orientation. He based his analysis on seventeen case studies, and argued that cross-dressers were often heterosexual. Moreover, only a minority of homosexuals had a compulsion to don clothing of the opposite sex. Hirschfeld quickly found a supporter in Havelock Ellis, who was one of the first sexologists to embrace the theory.[25] With this revolutionary "discovery," Hirschfeld began the process of untangling the nineteenth-century conflation of sexual orientation and gender identity.[26]

Before Hirschfeld's "discovery," public cross-dressing was often associated with prostitution and criminal activity. Those detected in public were arrested for "disturbing the peace," and then photographed for the mug shot album of "homosexuals and blackmailers." Newspaper stories of such arrests became increasingly common beginning in the 1890s.[27]

In addition to these reports, popular entertainment at the turn of the century—along with the transvestite balls and clubs of Berlin's homosexual community—helped to inspire and shape Hirschfeld's theory. In cabarets, circuses, and variety theaters, male and female impersonators drew large crowds. These performers took great pride in the verisimilitude of their impersonations, and many befriended Hirschfeld. A few were even featured in his case studies.[28]

Popular interest propelled the publication of several putative memoirs or biographies documenting the lives and experiences of men and women who adopted the gender identity of the opposite sex.[29] One of the first such publications was the autobiography of an Italian man, edited by Émile Zola, which appeared in German translation in 1899.[30] Perhaps the most sensational story was reported in the Berlin press in December 1906.[31] It involved the suicide of a young man, Alfred H., who had "passed" as a South American aristocrat, "Countess Dina Alma de Paradeda." Posing as the fictional countess, Alfred H. had cut an elegant figure in Berlin—attending the homosexual balls in drag—before moving to Breslau, where he became engaged to a (male) teacher. Increasingly fearful of disclosure, Alfred H. finally killed himself in late 1906. The biography was published in 1907 as *Tagebuch einer männlichen Braut* (Diary of a male bride), based allegedly on the young man's diary.[32] Another striking case study appeared that same year, authored by "N. O. Body" ("nobody"). The volume recounted the early life of Karl M. Baer (1884–1956), born with ambiguous genitalia and then raised as a girl. As a young woman, Baer entered therapy with Hirschfeld before adopting a masculine identity and living as a man.[33]

These accounts appear to have increased understanding for the plight of sexual "intermediaries," especially those who faced the dilemma of how to "perform" gender in public. The liberal press in Berlin tended to offer its support. In January 1906 a certain Frau Katz was detained for the seventh time with her hair cropped short and wearing a man's felt hat, but also in a skirt. When the police demanded identification, she provided two official documents that proved her status as a woman. Still unconvinced, one of the officers finally asked, "Are you really a woman?" As the sympathetic newspaper report explained, "[S]he would only appear unsuspicious if allowed to dress as a man. . . . But if she did so, she would then be committing the offense of which she is now suspected, for the seventh time. What should she do?" The best solution, the article explained, was to educate the police: "There are men with the faces of women, and women with the faces of men. If necessary, police officials need to be schooled by Dr. Hirschfeld. Such mistrust as in this case should not be based on ignorance."[34]

In short order Hirschfeld managed to reform the practices of the Berlin police (which appear to have followed the recommendation of this newspaper report). In 1909 Hirschfeld convinced local authorities to issue a so-called transvestite pass (*Transvestitenschein*) to a young woman, allowing her to work and appear in public wearing men's clothing. Such passes would allow both men and women to appear in the garb of the opposite sex and not fear arrest. Again, there was no formal law that banned cross-dressing, but individuals who did not "pass" successfully were vulnerable to police harassment. Now, if accosted by police or another citizen, the cross-dresser could produce the pass as proof of official permission.[35] Although there are no precise figures, it is clear that up until 1933 Hirschfeld and other sympathetic medical doctors petitioned local authorities for and procured dozens of transvestite passes for patients and clients.[36]

In 1912 the *Berliner Tageblatt* described how nineteen-year-old Georg von Zobeltitz, member of an old noble family, formerly with ties to the Hohenzollern court, was arrested for public cross-dressing. "The alleged culprit was soon released," the paper explained, "once it was determined that it was a case not of disorderly conduct but instead of a transvestite." The article explained that "Zobeltitz had been in treatment for an extended period with Dr. Magnus Hirschfeld, had always felt the urge to wear women's clothing, and had learned to fashion his own clothing and hats with tremendous expertise."[37] Within a year, Zobeltitz had acquired a transvestite pass in Potsdam (where he resided), presumably with Hirschfeld's help. When called before a military recruitment commission in Potsdam in 1913, the young man appeared dressed as a woman, presenting proof of his dispensation. The *Berliner Börsen-Courier* explained that "[s]uch cases in which officials, on the basis of medical assessments, grant permission to men and women to wear the clothes of the opposite sex have increased significantly in recent times. The reason for this has less to do with greater frequency of such cases than with a growing awareness of their correct scientific understanding."[38] Though never stating so explicitly, the news reports implied that Zobeltitz was deemed ineligible for military service.[39]

Similar press reports seemed to suggest a growing familiarity with, if not actual acceptance of, public cross-dressing. Another newspaper article from 1912 described a married heterosexual couple who cross-dressed together in public. The husband, a retired official, donned a wig, a dress, jewelry, and makeup, while his wife—who worked as a tailor—wore trousers and a false moustache. The two would patronize restaurants in drag and parade through the streets of their respectable Schöneberg neighborhood. Although neighbors recognized when the two exchanged clothing, "they were never certain if the couple engaged in deliberate mischief or if they both manifested the pathology of transvestitism."[40]

Although Hirschfeld's understanding of "sexual intermediary" expanded and grew more complicated, his belief in the biological basis of sexual and gender variation remained unshaken. His view was reinforced by the contemporary experiments and discoveries of the Austrian physiologist Eugen Steinach (1861–1944), a pioneer in the field of endocrinology. As a director at the Institute for Experimental Biology in Vienna, Steinach used "distortive experimentation" to explore physiological development. This included transplantation experiments. Specifically, Steinach implanted male rats and guinea pigs with the ovaries of their female counterparts; conversely, female rats and guinea pigs received testicular implants. The results observed by Steinach were startling: the male animals appeared to develop female behaviors and physical characteristics, while the female creatures were "masculinized," sometimes mounting other females as if to copulate. Steinach argued that the hormones of these sex glands, what he called "glandular juices"—only later were they named testosterone and estrogen—were responsible for shaping sexual physiology as well as gender identity. He also theorized that an imbalance of the "glandular juices" might account for nonnormative sexual and gender behaviors in humans. This meant, for example, that a homosexual man might be treated with the testicular tissue of a heterosexual.[41] For Hirschfeld, this was solid evidence of the biological basis for sexual behavior, and he cited Steinach's discoveries as irrefutable proof of his own third-sex theory.[42]

Although Steinach reported his formal research in science journals, he also popularized his discoveries in both print and film media.[43] Most successful was *Der Steinachfilm* (The Steinach film)—yet another example of the so-called Weimar "enlightenment film"—which premiered in Berlin in 1923 at the Ufa-Palast Cinema at the Zoo Station. For weeks the seventy-minute documentary sold out multiple daily showings in the 2,100-seat movie theater. It was screened as well in venues throughout Germany and Austria. The film provided background on basic endocrinology, and explained how the "glandular juices" produced in the testes and ovaries were distributed throughout the body. These substances not only formed distinctive masculine and feminine physical characteristics but also entered the brain, shaping typically feminine or masculine sensibilities. Any imbalance of these sex hormones might result in some nonnormative gender or sexual variation. The film also demonstrated how castrated male and female rats implanted with ovaries or testicles would begin to exhibit the sexual behavior and physical form of the opposite sex. The film then profiled an intersex individual with both a penis and breasts, and hypothesized that "hermaphroditism" results from some hormonal anomaly.

Clearly Steinach had assimilated Hirschfeld's theory of sexual intermediaries: the film displayed human subjects to demonstrate the hip, waist, and shoulder proportions of a "normal" man, and those of a "feminized" intermediary. Caused by hormonal imbalance, sexual intermediacy also helped to explain why some men preferred feminine jobs or pastimes (child care and embroidery, for example), while certain women entered masculine domains. The film's most arresting scene showed Steinach performing a surgical procedure; after removing the undescended testicle of a "normal" man, Steinach bisected it and implanted one of the halves into the groin of a homosexual patient. The film's intertitle explained how the secretions from this implant would alter the homosexual's erotic orientation, and essentially make him "straight."[44]

The surgical procedure that Steinach demonstrated in his film was one that had already been used on human subjects in Berlin. Hirschfeld, for one, participated in such procedures—testicular implants—in the institute's surgery in the first years of the Weimar Republic. It seems odd in retrospect that an activist for the rights of homosexuals would have attempted to "fix" their orientation or make them "normal." Hirschfeld was not pursuing a "cure," however, but hoping rather to prove that sexual orientation was determined by sex hormones, which would demonstrate in turn the biological underpinnings of sexual and gender variation. The experimentation failed miserably and was quickly halted. The fate of the test subjects and likewise the source of the implanted testicles remain unknown, moreover, since Hirschfeld never published a detailed account and made only passing mention of these dubious procedures. Although Hirschfeld's cavalier experimentation was not exceptional, the application of Steinach's theories to human subjects illustrates the relatively extreme measures taken by both doctors and their patients.[45]

What Hirschfeld and many others quickly grasped was that if hormone therapy might be used to change sexual orientation or "cure" homosexuals, it might also aid those who hoped to change their biological sex. The 1923 *Steinachfilm* had certainly broadcast the therapeutic potential of sex hormones. But even before this, in 1920, Steinach had published a popular sixty-eight-page pamphlet explaining his research and its applications.[46] The pamphlet was mentioned by one young man who wrote Hirschfeld in 1920—a rare surviving letter preserved at the Kinsey Institute—explaining that he was "more woman than man." This correspondent also described that he had just had the chance to read "the book about artificial rejuvenation and sex change," a clear reference to Steinach. The promise of hormone therapy inspired him to write Hirschfeld: "[W]ould it not perhaps be possible to remove my testicles and in their place insert an ovary, and then in this fashion I could become a complete woman. . . . I trust you completely Herr Dr., and perhaps I could serve science as an important experiment."[47] Included with this missive was a small photograph of the man in drag. As the Berlin PhD student Werner Holz, who worked at the institute, commented in his 1924 dissertation, "a majority of transvestites express the wish to be castrated."[48] For many cross-dressers, apparently, identification with the opposite sex entailed the desire for a complete physical metamorphosis. Simply affecting femininity or masculinity with dress and manners no longer satisfied.

This was indeed a therapeutic frontier. Medical ethics was in its infancy, and decisions about specific surgical procedures were made by individual doctors in response to their patients' wishes. In 1916 the Berlin doctor and psychotherapist Max Marcuse published the case study of a thirty-six-year-old man, "Herr A.," who approached Marcuse for hormone treatment and the removal of his male genitalia. As Marcuse reported, Herr A. had always wanted to be a girl, and as a young man fantasized that his penis and testicles might be "violently removed." Marcuse's patient had learned of Steinach's experiments in the popular press, and hoped that the discovery of sex hormones might offer a practical treatment. In his study, Marcuse explained that the "presence of his penis and testicles caused him [Herr A.] great despair," leading to thoughts of suicide. Although Marcuse availed himself of Hirschfeld's neologism and described Herr A. as a case of *Transvestitismus*, the parallels between Herr A. and most of Hirschfeld's case studies were superficial at best. Marcuse considered Herr A. pathological or mentally ill— a diagnosis Hirschfeld would have likely rejected—and denied the request for surgery. Marcuse was willing to provide a kind of primitive hormone therapy, however, and treated Herr A. with an unspecified "ovarian preparation," which reportedly quieted and comforted the man.[49]

One of the first (primitive) male-to-female sex-reassignment surgeries was undertaken in stages, beginning at the institute in Berlin and then completed in Dresden in 1920–21. The patient was a twenty-three-year-old officer who had attended a military academy and then fought in the First World War. Since childhood, the young man claimed to have felt himself trapped in the wrong body; he pursued a military career in the desperate attempt to demonstrate his masculinity. Not even military service, however, was able to mitigate his feminine feelings, and after the war he fell into a suicidal depression. Hirschfeld's colleague Dr. Arthur Kronfeld began the initial treatment. Refusing to amputate the penis, Kronfeld finally agreed to remove the man's testicles (though not his scrotal sack); Kronfeld justified his decision as a measure to prevent the man from committing suicide. The effect was quite positive, in Kronfeld's report. Castration led to a certain "psychic relaxation and a permanent feeling of harmony and balance." The patient lost secondary sex characteristics, including facial hair, and was able to live and pass more easily as a woman.

The following year, in March 1921, the Dresden gynecologist Dr. Richard Mühsam performed a second surgery on the same patient, implanting an ovary. A month after this, Mühsam refashioned the patient's penis and scrotal sack into a "vagina-like structure" by cutting from the scrotum to the perineum and then "hiding" the penis in the open wound and using the scrotal skin to form something like a labia over it. Mühsam was pleased with his handiwork—the first known attempt to construct a vagina for a man—but the patient, ultimately, was not. By August the former officer returned and reported experiencing erections in his now "hidden" penis. Moreover, he had met and fallen in love with a young woman, given up his cross-dressing, adopted a masculine demeanor, and insisted that Mühsam now undo the surgery. The doctor complied and was able to "restore" the penis and close the "vagina-like structure." The fate of the implanted ovary was never reported, nor its source, though the man lived a productive life, reportedly, completing a medical degree and pursuing a career as a pathologist.[50]

Mühsam also participated in an early female-to-male sex-reassignment procedure. The patient, a painter, had always considered herself a "man in disguise," and underwent a double mastectomy and a hysterectomy in 1912 at the age of thirty-five. In 1921 Mühsam agreed to remove the patient's ovaries as well. Although the painter died in 1924 of tuberculosis, Mühsam claimed that the surgeries, overall, had a salutary effect on the patient's sense of well-being and "spiritual condition."[51] Mühsam published this research in 1926, claiming at this point that he had conducted four testicle implants on three homosexuals and one bisexual. The "Steinach procedure," as Mühsam understood it, required the insertion of half a testicle of a heterosexual man into the patient's stomach muscle (oblique), where the "testicular hormone" (and the testicle itself) would be absorbed. The operation initially induced heterosexual tendencies, Mühsam reported, but had a lasting effect only for the bisexual. These results were ultimately so disappointing that Mühsam, like Hirschfeld and others, abandoned the procedure.[52]

Although there are relatively few detailed case studies, the institute attracted a large number of cross-dressers, many of whom were certainly "total transvestites," as Hirschfeld would label them. In 1926, the gynecologist Ludwig Levy-Lenz joined the institute as a staff member and quickly became the primary surgeon for most sex-reassignment procedures. As Levy-Lenz described, "This task [sex reassignment] fell to me, as surgeon of the Institute, and I was able to find a quite satisfactory solution to the problem of creating an artificial vagina and artificial lips of the vulva. . . . I almost became a 'specialist' in plastic genital operations—a strange calling indeed!" Levy-Lenz also introduced surgical procedures to feminize or masculinize facial features by altering noses, chins, lips, and cheekbones.[53] From other sources it is clear that Levy-Lenz and other institute-affiliated surgeons performed hysterectomies, oophorectomies (removal of the ovaries), and breast-reduction surgeries. The institute developed "ovarian" and "testicular preparations" to be injected as a primitive form of hormone therapy. The institute's X-ray facility was used for depilation or hair removal, though the dangerous and unpleasant side effects included nausea and skin burns. Medical doctors had experimented with paraffin injections to reconstruct breasts for women disfigured in accidents, but this procedure was considered too dangerous to continue and had been halted before the war.[54] Although experimental and, ultimately, dangerous, these sex-reassignment procedures were developed largely in response to the ardent requests of patients. In one case, Levy-Lenz refused to remove the breasts of a sixteen-year-old because of her age. After she mutilated herself with a razor, "in order to necessitate amputation," Levy-Lenz acquiesced and performed the double mastectomy. As Levy-Lenz claimed in his memoirs, "[N]ever have I operated upon more grateful patients."[55]

What Levy-Lenz, Hirschfeld, and others at the institute effectively pioneered was a primitive diagnosis with corresponding treatments for what is now described as gender dysphoria. As historian Rainer Herrn has noted, Hirschfeld used the term *Transsexualismus* but ultimately recurred to his model of "transvestitism."[56] In 1926 Hirschfeld introduced the term "total transvestitism": "We find the strongest form of total transvestitism among those who want to transform not only their sartorial but also their biological appearance. . . . These strive for a complete transformation of their genitalia. . . . This means the elimination of menstruation by removing the ovaries for female transvestites, and for men castration. The number of cases is much greater than one had anticipated before."[57]

Arguably this definition comes close to that of "transsexualism," first used by Dr. Harry Benjamin in the 1950s. Hirschfeld's own theory of sexual intermediacy blurred distinctions between cross-dressing ("transvestitism") and transsexuality ("total transvestitism"), preventing a clear analysis of the phenomenon of transgender identity. However, his early work on cross-dressing and enthusiastic embrace of Steinach's hormonal theory created the essential foundation for the improved terminology and clearer understanding that was to come. In the 1950s Benjamin spearheaded a modern protocol for the medical diagnosis of transsexuality—a condition in which an individual's biological sex conflicts with his or her psychological gender identity—and worked to develop effective sex-reassignment surgeries and hormone treatments, enabling transgender individuals to "transition" from one biological sex to the other.[58]

The influence of the Berlin institute is very direct: Benjamin was born in Berlin, studied medicine in Germany, and met Hirschfeld for the first time around 1907. And it was Hirschfeld, moreover, who introduced Benjamin to the city's homosexual milieu. Although he immigrated to the United States in 1913, Benjamin visited the institute annually throughout the 1920s, and, as a native German speaker, read and closely followed developments in his native capital.[59] For example, Benjamin wrote the introduction for the first English-language treatment of Steinach's theory, which appeared in 1923.[60] Based on the discoveries of Steinach, and the still-somewhat illusive promise of hormone therapy, the institute served as a veritable incubator for the science of transsexuality.

In addition to medical procedures for transgender persons, Hirschfeld and his colleagues offered a range of counseling services geared specifically to homosexual men and women. These sessions typically used Hirschfeld's own special method, "adaptation therapy" (*Adaptionsbehandlung*), which he developed before the war. In his monumental study of 1914, *Homosexualität*, Hirschfeld outlined his approach:

In the first place we reassure the homosexual personality, whether male or female; we explain that they have an innocent, inborn orientation, which is not a misfortune in and of itself but rather experienced as such because of unjust condemnation. Many extremely moral homosexuals, including those who are not abstinent, "suffer far more injustice than they ever inflict." We also emphasize that the unhappiness of being homosexual is often exaggerated, and many are quite content. Homosexuality itself is a burden to no one, even if at present there are many more difficulties, even for a moral person, to becoming a socially useful member of society.[61]

Of greatest importance was befriending others in similar situations, especially those with more experience. A social network of other lesbians and homosexuals was therefore the best hedge against depression and suicide. Hirschfeld and his colleagues actually recommended specific bars and locales for lesbians, homosexual men, and cross-dressers. The institute also attempted to help with the selection of jobs or careers, and sometimes placed patients with appropriate and sympathetic employers. Several cross-dressers, including some who had undergone surgical procedures, found work directly in the institute.

In his protocol for adaptation therapy, Hirschfeld also recommended that patients—especially male homosexuals—be apprised of the dangers of same-sex eroticism: chief among these, police arrest, blackmail, and disease. But his counsel remained generally "sex positive," and he did not emphasize abstinence. Sexual asceticism had its own disadvantages, Hirschfeld believed, including isolation, loneliness, and, potentially, neurosis. Ultimately such decisions needed to be left to the individual, just as individual heterosexuals made choices about friendship, intimacy, and ultimately partnership. Where Hirschfeld differentiated between homosexuals and "straights" was on the question of marriage. Both men and women with same-sex attractions should be strongly discouraged from entering traditional marriages. This might seem self-evident to most. But Hirschfeld felt compelled to counter the advice of some conservative therapists and religious figures who argued that heterosexual marriage could alleviate homosexual desire. Here Hirschfeld made a lone exception for heterosexual transvestites, though he insisted that the transvestite inform his or her partner before entering wedlock. Hirschfeld also rejected "degeneration theory" as an explanation for the etiology of homosexuality (and other sexual peculiarities)—a view espoused by all but the most progressive sexologists. Even Krafft-Ebing abandoned degeneration theory only at the very end of his life, in an essay published in 1901 in Hirschfeld's *Jahrbuch*.[62] Hirschfeld had reframed his position by 1914 when he began to describe homosexuality as a "means to preempt degeneration" by eliminating the chance or opportunity for procreation.[63]

The experiences in therapy of one of Hirschfeld's young patients allow us to consider more closely the application of adaptation theory. As a teenager, Hanns G. lived at the institute for a month in the summer of 1930. The son of a medical doctor who was familiar with Hirschfeld's research, Hanns G. was sent to Berlin for treatment for his manifest homosexuality. As Hanns G. recounted years later, Hirschfeld explained his approach as an attempt to "steel" the youth against all that might threaten him and give him an "awareness of life" to prevent "thoughts of suicide," one of the greatest dangers to young homosexuals. Hanns G. claimed that the putative objective was a "cure." But Hirschfeld's adaptation therapy aimed instead to help the youth accept his sexual orientation and learn how to live with it.

For an entire month, Hanns G. boarded at the institute, where he had formal therapy sessions with Hirschfeld as often as four times a week. An initial orientation consisted of a full sexual history and the careful completion of Hirschfeld's lengthy questionnaire. But adaptation therapy also involved participation in the institute's daily rhythms. Hanns G. met other affluent patients—English men, and some Germans—and also observed the tours of the museum and the erotica collection given by Karl Giese. Afternoon teas were attended by most of the staff, resident patients, and outside friends, including flamboyant cross-dressers who appeared in full drag. Many evenings involved excursions to Berlin's homosexual clubs and bars, where Hanns G. formed his first impressions of the city's vibrant nightlife. A favorite locale was a small pub, Bei Elli, in Skalitzer Straße in the working-class neighborhood of Kreuzberg. Here Hanns G. met young male prostitutes and cross-dressers, as well as blue-collar homosexuals. Hanns G. also attended large costume balls held at the institute, which attracted prominent and open homosexuals.[64]

.   .   .

The Institute for Sexual Science did not limit its services, however, to "sexual intermediaries." In 1919 the Center of Sexual Counseling for Married Couples began welcoming scores of heterosexual women, sometimes accompanied by their husbands or partners, who had pressing questions about sexuality and, most often, about birth control. This was arguably a courageous move, since the Weimar constitution banned advertising for birth control. Although condoms, pessaries, and certain chemical douches were available with a doctor's prescription, the cost for both a medical exam and a contraceptive device was prohibitive for working- and lower-middle-class persons. Therefore the institute sought to make information available to the working poor, whose knowledge and access was the most limited.

Hirschfeld's involvement in feminist and women's health care causes dated to the early twentieth century. He had joined forces with left-wing feminist Helene Stöcker in 1905, when she founded the League for the Protection of Mothers (Bund für Mutterschutz), an organization promoting a wide range of feminist causes, including suffrage and popular access to birth control. Though heterosexual, Stöcker supported homosexual emancipation and the legal reform movement of the SHC; she eventually served as the first woman on its board of directors. When Reichstag lawmakers drafted a new anti-sodomy statute in 1909 that would have additionally criminalized lesbian sexuality, Stöcker and Hirschfeld worked together to defeat the proposed legislation. Stöcker also founded the International Union for the Protection of Mothers and Sexual Reform in 1911.[65] The two activists were thus positioned to spearhead the sex reform movement of the Weimar Republic.

The demographic impact of the First World War was profound, exacerbating tensions between progressive sex reformers and the conservative nationalists who opposed their program, ostensibly for pronatalist reasons. No fewer than 2 million German soldiers had been killed in action, and the new Weimar Republic shed an additional 6.5 million German nationals through the territorial losses dictated by the Versailles Treaty. There were nearly 1 million additional civilian deaths caused by the so-called "hunger blockade" in the last year of the war and the Spanish influenza that swept the world in 1918. Thus Germany's population declined by more than 9 million. A marked "marriage boom" followed the war, but birthrates continued to decline, a trend established around 1900. In 1924 the city of Berlin was reputed to have the lowest birthrate in the entire world.

Despite the pronatalist emphasis of political and religious conservatives, however, Weimar sex reformers were clearly in the ascendancy. For one, the Social Democratic government of the Weimar Republic, which ushered in women's suffrage, was broadly supportive of most feminist causes. Women also enjoyed the backing of the newly formed Kommunistische Partei Deutschlands (Communist Party of Germany), or KPD, which modeled its own policy objectives on those adopted by the Soviet Union. The Russian influence was not insignificant: progressives everywhere, and not just communists, admired the Soviet introduction of no-fault divorce, decriminalization of abortion, easy access to birth control, and elimination of anti-sodomy laws. With the vote, women in Germany not only gained electoral leverage but also participated in the political process by joining special interest groups and even running for public office. Women also entered the professions in ever-greater numbers, especially medicine and education.

Progressive sex reformers such as Hirschfeld and Stöcker hoped to distinguish sexual expression from procreation and allow women (and men) greater erotic fulfillment. It was their objective, as well, that the same right of sexual expression might be established for homosexual men and lesbians. Broadly understood, the philosophical program of the progressive reform movement was "sex positive," and its ambitious goal was to enhance human relationships and improve the quality of life for a new generation. These aims were generally supported, moreover, by Weimar's popular culture as well as the left-wing political leaders of the new republic.

In 1926 the institute began sponsoring public meetings every Monday evening to answer general questions about human sexuality. A box was placed outside the main villa, accessible to passersby, where anyone could deposit an anonymous question, which institute staff members would answer at the weekly meetings. The lion's share of these questions concerned birth control. "What are the disadvantages for a man who more or less regularly uses *coitus interruptus* as a method of birth control?" one participant queried. "The practice is widely used in our province of Schleswig Holstein and is also well-known within my family." Another asked, "Is it safe for a diabetic to carry a pregnancy to term—who decides?" The crucial role of anonymity is clear from many of the questions: "A girl, 26, has been having sex for about two years with a boy who is 25. For protection they use condoms. Since about six months ago the girl no longer experiences satisfaction during sexual intercourse, despite a good relationship with her friend."[66] We do not know with certainty what the responses were to these questions. But they help to illustrate the significant demand for expert information on family planning and birth control. According to Hirschfeld, more than fourteen thousand questions had been submitted by the early 1930s, and overwhelmingly they concerned contraception. With the liberalization of the law banning advertisements for contraception in 1927, public health campaigns for birth control were no longer threatened by legal sanction. The following year the institute published a short pamphlet on methods of contraception, of which some 100,000 copies were distributed by 1932.[67]

Like Stöcker, Hirschfeld hoped to harness the reputation of his own and other German sex reform campaigns to organize and direct an international program. In 1921 he convened in Berlin the first International Congress on Sexual Science, with more than three thousand participants, some of whom traveled from as far away as Tokyo, Peking, Moscow, and San Francisco. A second conference was held in 1928 in Copenhagen, where the World League for Sexual Reform (WLSR) was formally organized. A third conference met in London in 1929, a fourth in Vienna in 1930, and a fifth in Brno, Czechoslovakia, in 1932.[68] Subsequent meetings planned for Paris, Moscow, and the United States were canceled. The ultimate demise of the WLSR was attributed to Hirschfeld's death in 1935 in Nice. As Atina Grossmann has claimed, the institute, which also housed the WLSR offices, was the "world headquarters of the sex reform movement."[69]

Hirschfeld's leadership of the WLSR was part of a broad strategy for effecting the elimination of the anti-sodomy law. For Hirschfeld homosexuals would gain emancipation by following two paths simultaneously: the support of progressive science on human sexuality and the integration of the homosexual political activism with other sex reform movements. We can see how Hirschfeld pursued the latter objective early on by joining forces with Helene Stöcker before the First World War. He promoted the integration of homosexual rights activism and sex reform after 1918 through the activities of the institute. The first of these attempts was not the 1921 Berlin Congress of Sexual Science but rather the formation of a so-called *Aktionskomitee,* or action committee, which sought to bring together the three existing homosexual rights organizations (his own SHC, Adolf Brand's Community of the Special, and a new organization that later adopted the title of League for Human Rights, Bund für Menschenrecht) to fight more effectively for the abolition of Paragraph 175.

An additional initiative came with the formation in 1925 of the Cartel for the Reform of the Sexual Penal Code (Kartell für Reform des Sexualstrafrechts)—a coalition, much respected in legal circles, of organizations calling for changes in German sex crimes legislation and, more generally, in all legal regulations of sexual life. The coalition's participation in this campaign rested on Hirschfeld's basic insight that *isolated* opposition to the anti-sodomy state was doomed to remain ineffective. The search for coalition partners was sparked by the publication of the official draft of a new German penal code in 1925.[70]

At the beginning of 1925 the coalition presented a counter-draft that contained, for the first time, the entire spectrum of proposed reforms (as far as they were relevant to criminal law), which were also formulated within the league. It is no exaggeration to call the coalition a national antecedent to the WLSR, a successful trial run for the combination of demands of the most diverse origins. It seemed logical to attempt this beyond the merely national level. On the one hand, propaganda about the developments in marriage and crime legislation in the Soviet Union was already ubiquitous among leftists in Germany and elsewhere. At the same time, efforts were under way in many western European countries to establish birth control as a fundamental right.

Hirschfeld's effort to link homosexual emancipation with the broader national and international sex reform movements—though arguably a failure—illustrates the salient feature of his life's work and career. Many commentators, admirers, and detractors alike have insisted on distinguishing Hirschfeld's "science," which some deemed quackery, from his political activism. Ludwig Levy-Lenz, who most certainly counted among Hirschfeld's admirers, expressed this truism about Hirschfeld in his memoir. According to Levy-Lenz, "Kraft-Ebing [*sic*] was the father of modern sexual science—M. H. [Magnus Hirschfeld] its obstetrician. It was he who put life and breath into the science of sex of which so little was generally known, and which had hitherto been vegetating in obscurity and he did this by enabling the whole of suffering humanity to share in its achievements."[71]

An encomium indeed, Levy-Lenz's description reduces Hirschfeld to a practitioner, an activist, and perhaps an apostle, though certainly not an effective scientist or theorist—appellations reserved, apparently, for Krafft-Ebing, and perhaps others.

But this assessment fails to recognize Hirschfeld's true genius of combining almost seamlessly his science and activism. Perhaps the motto of the SHC—*"Per scientiam ad justiciam,"* "Through science to justice"—best captures the essence of Hirschfeld's philosophy. Moreover, the work of the Institute for Sexual Science emblematized his impulse to combine theory and practice: the practical effort to ameliorate the lot of sexual intermediaries while developing the first science of transsexuality, and the promotion of sexual freedom supported by the study of human sexuality. We discern this, too, in what might be described as Hirschfeld's "strategic essentialism," namely his commitment to biological determinism as an explanation for homosexuality. His basic conviction—that same-sex desire is an immutable characteristic—was expressed in his first pseudonymous publication on the topic, *Sappho und Sokrates,* published in 1896, and it melded science and politics throughout his career.

CHAPTER SEVEN

Sex Tourism and Male Prostitution in Weimar Berlin

In Berlin, everyone speaks to everyone else, even if not out loud. But everyone knows everything about everyone else at a glance. Rich and poor, professors and students, intellectuals and bartenders all share a common vulgarity. It all comes down to sex. It is a city with no virgins. Not even the kittens and puppies are virgins.

—STEPHEN SPENDER, *The Temple: A Novel* (1988)

How shallow my sophistication may be judged from my surprise, my positive disbelief, when a junior colleague who knew of my inclinations told me that there were places in Germany where boys offered their services for a modest sum. Male tarts? Were there really such things? Was it conceivable?

—T. C. WORSLEY, *Flannelled Fool: A Slice of a Life in the Thirties* (1967)

Berlin meant boys," Christopher Isherwood famously claimed in his autobiographical *Christopher and His Kind*. "Wasn't Berlin's famous 'decadence' largely a commercial 'line,'" Isherwood asked, "which the Berliners had instinctively developed in their competition with Paris? Paris had long since cornered the straight-girl market, so what was left for Berlin to offer its visitors but a masquerade of perversions?" Isherwood's somewhat cynical assessment belied a strong attachment, however, to the open homosexual culture of the German capital, at least as it thrived before the Nazi seizure of power. Invited by poet W. H. Auden, a sometime lover and lifelong friend, Isherwood arrived in Berlin in May 1929, and he lived there episodically until late spring 1933.[1]

Like Auden, Isherwood had many Berlin liaisons, which he pursued in public venues, undisturbed by the local police, or in his favorite locales such as the Kleist Diele or the Cosy Corner, both notorious for their boy prostitution. Berlin's vibrant nightclub culture and cabarets, male prostitution, and indifferent officialdom were some of the elements of the homosexual scene that attracted Isherwood. With his writings, Isherwood made himself not only the foremost English-language chronicler of Weimar Berlin—particularly of the final years before the Nazi seizure of power—but also the city's most famous sex tourist. Isherwood, Auden, and those who made up their circle of English poets, authors, and artists were far from alone. No later than 1920, the open sexual culture of Berlin had been well established, attracting Americans, western Europeans, Scandinavians, and Russians. Not all were "sex tourists" in the narrow sense of the term. Many simply observed and recorded the city's seedier elements without looking for sexual contacts. Yet this voyeuristic impulse to witness and document was inspired by representations of a luridly licentious Berlin and must also be counted as sex tourism. The pervasive prostitution (both male and female), the public cross-dressing, and the easy access to bars and clubs that catered to homosexual men and lesbians were just a few of the features that supported Berlin's sex industry. As Weimar-era cultural critic Siegfried Kracauer argued, modern travel, enabled by industrial technology, "granted access to the beyond," and in Berlin's case, the potential of a utopic sexual world that transcended traditional moralities.[2]

"Male prostitution" also requires qualification, since it subsumes much more than a straightforward commercial transaction for sexual services. Prostitution had always been a feature of almost any same-sex erotic subculture. As such, many same-sex relationships, whether fleeting or long term, involved an element of "prostitution." It is important therefore to consider the broad spectrum of arrangements extending from material dependency to financial remuneration for specific sexual acts. The extremes along this spectrum ranged from committed loving relationships to the briefest of hookups in the Tiergarten Park. Like the prostitute who refuses to kiss her john—considering this an intimacy that should be shared only with a genuine lover—many of the boys and young men who sold themselves for subsistence or perhaps just pocket money experienced disgust or at best indifference when satisfying their patrons. These "prostitutes" differentiated sharply between the sexual services they provided and their personal preferences and love relationships. A large number—as many as a third, in fact—professed to be heterosexual.

Yet others enjoyed the sexual acts they engaged in for pay. For these, prostitution was a source of income when jobs were scarce or a lucrative alternative to more menial labor. Some pursued prostitution hoping to find genuine love, even forging long-term relationships with onetime johns. The men who paid for sex were no less ambivalent, hoping to find and perhaps rescue a youthful partner from the pool of hustlers. Certainly heterosexual prostitution included a similar range of "relationships." But since same-sex erotic love remained nominally illicit, this dynamic among male prostitutes and their clients was that much more pronounced. In effect, the relationship between a street hustler and his john was no more illicit than that of a committed homosexual couple. Indeed, since male prostitution was never specifically criminalized and certain erotic same-sex acts were "illegal," the lines dividing prostitution, opportunistic sex, companionship, and love would remain ambiguous and shifting.

Berlin's homosexual scene after 1918 was itself the critical context for the growth of sex tourism, and relied specifically on a popular, homosexual press with not only a reading public but also advertisers and business supporters. Although failing to eliminate all censorship, as noted before, the Weimar Republic eased laws, permitting far greater freedom for Berlin's press and print media, film industry, arts institutions, and entertainment venues. From 1919 until February 1933, somewhere between twenty-five and thirty separate homosexual German-language journal titles appeared *in* Berlin, some weekly or monthly and others less frequently.[3] These supplemented, of course, Berlin's first homosexual periodicals: Adolf Brand's *Der Eigene* and Hirschfeld's *Jahrbuch*. By contrast, there were practically no such journals published anywhere else in the world until after 1945. Only a few issues of one French-language periodical with significant homosexual content, *Akademos,* were published in Paris in 1909 by the French writer Andre Fersen, who corresponded with both Magnus Hirschfeld and Adolf Brand. The single English-language homosexual periodical appeared in Chicago in 1924, edited by the German-American Henry Gerber, who was stationed in the early 1920s as a soldier in the Rhineland, where he established contacts with homosexual rights activists in Berlin. One German-language Swiss monthly, *Der Kreis* (The circle), was published in Zurich from 1932 to 1967—inspired initially by Berlin's homosexual press and especially the journals of publisher Friedrich Radszuweit.[4]

The homosexual press of Weimar Berlin was therefore truly singular. The first issue of *Die Freundschaft* was sold in the summer of 1919 and monthly thereafter—barring a short hiatus during the hyperinflation of 1923—until February 1933. Arguably the most successful of the Berlin titles, *Die Freundschaft* provided a broad range of features, including news coverage and political commentary. Catering to sexual minorities, a few, including *Der Eigene,* maintained a relatively highbrow literary profile. For a short period beginning in 1927 there was even a transvestite periodical, *Transvestit,* which catered specifically to male and female cross-dressers. The lesbian journals *Die Freundin, Garçonne,* and *Frauen Liebe* published serialized romance novels. Although owned and produced by men, the lesbian journals served their constituents effectively, not only as a mouthpiece for cultural interests but also with the political and social reportage of women journalists, including progressive heterosexual feminists such as Helene Stöcker, the prominent pacifist and advocate for birth control. For example, *Die Freundin* published lesbian opinion polls on a range of issues from abortion to regulated prostitution, and exhorted lesbian readers to vote for gay-friendly parties and candidates in local and national elections.

Certainly the large number of titles reflected the vicissitudes of market demand, and many journals were extremely short-lived. In some cases editors were compelled to change the names of titles to circumvent censors. Most often these ran afoul of the official minders because of nude photography or singles advertisements that were deemed too obvious and therefore culpable of "solicitation." In 1927 a new censorship law was introduced. Although the law targeted primarily nudist and soft-porn publications, it also forced vendors to avoid the open display of homosexual titles. When officials investigated the public sale of potentially offensive periodicals in 1926, they produced photos—preserved now in a Berlin archive—of two of the busiest newspaper kiosks in the city, located at Potsdamer Platz and the Friedrichstraße train terminal, revealing just how openly nudist and homosexual titles were purveyed.[5] Displayed in the photos of the kiosks are not only naked bodies from the covers of nudist periodicals but also several widely distributed homosexual magazines.

Almost all of the journals included advertising. Most common were announcements for same-sex bars, clubs, and cafés. The papers also advertised the goods and services of doctors, dentists, lawyers, private detectives, stationers, haberdashers, barbers, and interior designers. Most appealed directly to homosexual customers, often with an implicit argument—sometimes baldly formulated—that *"friends* patronize *friends."* Certainly for a homosexual man with anal syphilis or a persistent throat rash a gay paper would be the best place to seek the name of an informed and discreet doctor. Those with secrets to keep—and facing blackmail—might find a private detective who investigated extortion threats. Cross-dressers naturally appreciated sympathetic milliners or dressmakers who could tailor for large or awkward sizes. Some business owners—gay, lesbian, or straight—viewed advertising in a gay or lesbian journal as a clever marketing ploy, though it also risked the perception of a self-outing and open membership in the broader homosexual community.

Gay and lesbian publications also included singles ads placed by individuals seeking love relationships. The larger periodicals achieved readerships outside of Berlin and frequently carried notices from all corners of Germany and Austria, as well as German speakers in other parts of Europe. As Fritz H. admitted during a police interrogation in the mid-1930s, he was first drawn to Berlin from his Tyrolean village in 1924 to meet the man with whom he had entered into a correspondence through a singles ad in the Berlin homosexual paper *Eros*. The most popular journals, such as *Die Freundschaft,* boasted subscriptions exceeding ten thousand and an international readership; distribution was as far-flung as North and South America. *Die Freundschaft* also offered its readers, for postage and a small fee, up-to-date urban guides of homosexual and gay-friendly establishments in European and North American cities. In this manner the Berlin journals facilitated the growth of a worldwide, Germanophone community, established not only through personal, face-to-face contact in the urban setting of Berlin but also within the pages of weekly and monthly periodicals.

Many mainstream commercial travel guides, which became increasingly popular throughout the 1920s, alluded to Berlin's sexual peculiarities. However, these references were oblique and likely mistaken for heterosexual prostitution or suggestive cabaret acts, at least by the uninitiated. The homosexual press was more forthcoming. *Die Freundschaft* sponsored the *Internationale Reiseführer* in 1920 (a kind of proto–*Spartacus International Gay Guide,* which is published today), listing not only fifty-four gay and lesbian venues in Berlin but also restaurants and cafés throughout Germany and Europe.[6] Of course, the homosexual press advertised meetings, special social events, and transvestite balls, as well as bars, clubs, restaurants, and cafés.

This remarkable Berlin milieu attracted a large number of foreign visitors, including many homosexuals and some lesbians. Tourists began to trickle into the German capital almost as soon as the war ended in November 1918. The chaos of the early Weimar Republic made Berlin an exciting, if unusually dangerous, destination. The galloping inflation, which began during the last years of the war and only crested at the end of 1923—culminating in currency reform—was also an attraction, since visitors with hard currency could live like royalty. As the lesbian author Djuna Barnes (1892–1982) reported after visiting Berlin in 1921, "It was very nice, things so cheap for us that you felt almost ashamed to be there. Full of buggers from America who bought boys cheap."[7]

The Americans who might have indulged their taste for bargain-basement sex included the modernist artist Marsden Hartley (1877–1943), the author Robert McAlmon (1895–1956), and the Broadway and television actor Harrison Dowd (1897–1964), with whom Barnes cavorted on her visit. Hartley, who had lived in Berlin before the war and had likely fallen in love with a Prussian officer (who seems to have inspired some of Hartley's most exalted and militaristic work—and who, appropriately perhaps, died in combat), was a veritable habitué of 1920s Berlin. According to Hartley's biographer, the artist attended large transvestite costume balls and patronized homosexual bars frequented by male hustlers.[8] As Hartley later recalled, "Life in Berlin then was at the height of heights—that is to the highest pitch of sophistication and abandon. None of us had seen anything quite like the spectacle."[9]

Robert McAlmon was no less inspired. Like so many Americans—including Barnes—McAlmon was based in Paris. A regular of Gertrude Stein's salon, McAlmon is remembered for his memoir *Being Geniuses Together* (1938), which documented the "lost generation" of American expats in interwar Paris. He also published an obscure volume in 1925, *Distinguished Air: Grim Fairy Tales,* describing Berlin's raucous nightlife. In this thinly veiled autobiographical account of his 1923 visit during the Great Inflation, McAlmon depicted a debauched society of pleasure-seeking tourists, mostly western Europeans and Americans, whose hard currency could support all-night parties in bars and dance halls, fueled by cheap and plentiful cocaine, with a supporting cast of penurious Berliners, including cross-dressing drug dealers and prostitutes of both sexes. As one McAlmon character put it, "These boys are all right, but, my god, they must have difficulty in knowing which are their own bodies, and which limbs are their own, after all the gymnastics and promiscuity they've been through."[10]

The American architect Philip Johnson (1906–2005) arrived in Berlin in 1928 to study the Bauhaus and the emerging International Style. As Johnson's biographer Franz Schulze ascertained, Johnson also availed himself of Berlin's male prostitution. "The Americans were the conquerors of old Germany and the young Germans were eager to accommodate them," Johnson reported. "Paris was never that *gastfreundlich*" (hospitable). Unlike most non-German tourists, however, Johnson was a fluent German speaker, claiming later, "I learned it the best way, using 'the horizontal method.' "[11] American artist Grant Wood (1891–1942) also found Berlin revelatory, although his visit served rather to inhibit than to liberate him. After the war, Wood traveled repeatedly to Paris, where he sampled or at least witnessed the sexual hedonism of the 1920s. His 1928 travels in Germany transformed his life, however: the Flemish and German Old Masters of the Pinakothek in Munich were an "aesthetic epiphany," shaping Wood's subsequent style; in contrast, Berlin's openly homosexual culture was an unpleasant, jarring sensory epiphany. The jolt was so great, his biographer suggests, that unlike Isherwood or Auden, Wood retreated not only from Europe but also from the libertinism of urban life, returning to the American Midwest and his native Iowa.[12]

Berlin was a revelation even for other Germans. In his autobiography, *The Turning Point,* Klaus Mann (1906–1949), the homosexual son of writer Thomas Mann, described his first Berlin foray from his native Munich as a seventeen-year-old: "I first came to Berlin in 1923 . . . the inflation was approaching its staggering climax." About the prostitutes on Tauentzienstraße, a famous strip for male and female prostitutes just east of the Kurfürstendamm, Mann wrote,

> One of them brandished a supple cane and leered at me as I passed by. "Good evening Madam," I said. She whispered in my ear: "Want to be my slave? Costs only six billions and a cigarette. A bargain." There were girls who couldn't have been older than 16 or 17. I was told that some of the most handsome and elegant were actually boys in drag. . . . Must look kind of funny, I thought— a boy's body with a pink, lace-trimmed shirt. . . . I was magnetized by the scum. Berlin—the Berlin I perceived or imagined—was gorgeously corrupt. I wanted to stay much longer.[13]

As Mann documents here, the Great Inflation, which wiped out the life savings of the German middle classes, drove many to prostitution and crime. Its cultural implications became a popular preoccupation, and an inspiration for works such as Hans Ostwald's *Moral History of the Inflation.* Not only the salacious but also the practical consequences of the inflation attracted pleasure-seeking tourists, whom Ostwald claimed were popularly described as "guests from Dollarika and from the Dutch Guldenland."[14]

The currency reform that helped to stabilize the republic after 1923 did little to alter Berlin's appeal, such as it was, or its reputation. When young Oxford poet Brian Howard (1905–1958)—the inspiration for Evelyn Waugh's flamboyant homosexual character "Anthony Blanche" in *Brideshead Revisited*—came to Berlin in 1927, he was astonished (disingenuously?) by Berlin's homosexual hedonism. On one of his first nights out alone in Berlin, Howard was compelled to sit at the same table with a German who looked exactly like the family doctor back home: "Fifty, silvery, rather rich-looking, with a dark blue bow tie." The young Howard was pleased to discover that the man spoke English and readily engaged him in discussion. After a short conversation, the German suggested that they move to another locale, a so-called dance palace. Not understanding the character of this second establishment, Howard was jolted to encounter his first homosexual ball. "Presently, the cabaret finished," Howard explained, "and we secured a table by the dancing floor. I remember distinctly the precise moment at which I became sensible of the true nature of my companion and surroundings. . . . [W]hen the band commenced, instantly this enormous floor was convulsed with movement, and I hiccoughed with astonishment to see only men dancing together." Howard soon took his leave—but without the older German gentleman.[15]

The most famous, or perhaps most notorious, Oxbridge graduates (or onetime students) who indulged Berlin's unusual libidinal offerings were members of the literary circle that counted W. H. Auden and Christopher Isherwood as its constitutive members. Both men became apostles for the city's open homosexuality. Although they invited, hosted, and capered with a large group of English visitors, their closest associates remained Stephen Spender (1909–1995), Gabriel Carritt (1908–1999), Alan Bush (1900–1995), John Lehmann (1907–1987), John Layard (1891–1974), and Arthur Calder-Marshall (1908–1992), as well as the artist Rupert Doone (1903–1966). Of course, it was Auden who first moved to Berlin, in October 1928, enticing Isherwood to visit in March 1929. Isherwood was the one who settled in Berlin, however, and ultimately made his name as the chronicler of Weimar.

Like Isherwood, Auden experienced a "coming out" of sorts after his first emotionally satisfying love affairs, prompting him finally to break off his engagement with a young woman in England. Early on, Auden discovered the most popular public cruising areas. In his unpublished "Berlin Journal," he recorded his first, failed attempt to take home a male prostitute from the Passage arcade, whose one entrance extended south from Unter den Linden. Alone one evening, Auden ventured out: "I tried to pick up a boy out in the Passage. He retired to a side passage where there were views to look at through a glass. I looked at the smokes and didn't dare to sneak a look at him. He went away and stood in the middle of the passage, like a faun. I went home. 'You can't be such a coward' I said and set off back again buying cigarettes to make an excuse for a conversation, but he was gone."[16]

In his journal Auden kept a careful tally of relationships—exclusively younger men or boys—the venues where they met, and the precise nature of their sexual encounters.[17] Isherwood followed Auden's example, and his experiences were similar. In a letter to John Layard from January 1930, sent from his rented room at the Institute for Sexual Science, Isherwood mentioned no fewer than eight past and present love interests—Berthold, Otto, Heinz, Pieps, Frantz, the brothers Nowak, and Gunther—all of whom were at least "occasional" prostitutes. "Have also been seeing Frantz, who is much improved," Isherwood reported to Layard. "But we had a row the other day, because I refused to give tischgeld [money for food for the table] to his girl, whom I'd very good naturedly given about ten drinks to at Frantz's suggestion." Prostitution or financial largesse provided Isherwood with his sexual liaisons: "I'm still known as a millionaire, but considered extremely stingy, because I simply cannot afford to give boys more than ten marks, a meal and drinks. I don't know how Wystan [Auden] managed."[18]

Isherwood and Auden were hardly unique. In 1930, Berlin—with a population that by then had increased to 4 million—hosted 280,000 tourists. That same year nearly 40,000 Americans were registered as guests in Berlin hotels. The relaxation of closing hours in 1926 permitted most establishments to remain open around the clock, except from 3 to 6 a.m.; even this restriction was nominal, and the after-hours clubs were always open.[19] The number of gay and lesbian locales in Berlin by this point has been estimated at somewhere between eighty and one hundred. In his 1956 memoir, Gerald Hamilton (1888–1970), the real-life inspiration for Christopher Isherwood's "Mr. Norris," claimed that there were no fewer than "132 homosexual cafes registered as such with the tolerant police."[20] The number that patronized these establishments is impossible to determine, though Magnus Hirschfeld suggested a homosexual population for the city at this time ranging from 50,000 to 100,000.

Certainly this reputation influenced Oxford-educated Maurice Bowra (1898–1971), who visited Berlin on numerous occasions, often with friends. Bowra's contemporary, Cambridge Provost Baron Noel Annan (1916–2000), claimed bluntly, "[Bowra] was the centre of the great homosexual Mafia if you like to call it, of the twenties and thirties."[21] Bowra himself conceded leadership of "The Immoral Front," "the 69th International," or "The Homintern," and anchored a circle of friends— some but not all "like-minded" or homosexual—including John Sparrow, Bob Boothby, Duff Cooper, Christopher Sykes, and Adrian Bishop, who capered with him in Berlin. Bowra had visited Berlin before the war and again in 1922, but he embarked on his first sexual foray in 1928. While negotiating sleeping arrangements with travel companion Sparrow, Bowra asked, "Do we have a room with two beds or two rooms. For the first, it is cheaper. . . . For the second, it might be better if we were to introduce guests late at night. But perhaps one takes them elsewhere?"[22] According to Bowra's biographer, Leslie Mitchell, "Germany was not the only country to offer sexual opportunity, but in Bowra's mind, there seems to have been the clear idea that each country has its own menu fixe. It was Germany for the homosexual and France for the heterosexual."[23] Unlike Auden and Isherwood, Bowra never sustained an erotic relationship and restricted his homosexual dalliances to the German capital, too timid or conservative to risk exposure at home in England.

The English portrait artist Glyn Warren Philpot (1884–1937) visited Berlin in 1931. His encounter with that city's homosexual underworld had a profound spiritual and emotional effect, influencing his adoption of a new style that owed much to international modernism (including the art of George Grosz and Otto Dix). In Berlin Philpot met a young man, Karl Heinz Muller, who was likely his lover and also served as his model for several paintings, including his *St Sebastian* (1932), a common subject of homosexual eroticism, which was never exhibited during Philpot's lifetime. The first London exhibit of Philpot's new work was greeted with overt hostility. The scandal led to a period of acute financial hardship, which undoubtedly contributed to the artist's early death at fifty-three. Tragically, Philpot did not live long enough to see what he regarded as his most ambitious work accepted or approved. His reputation as a portraitist never faltered, though his later pictures remain controversial.[24]

Not only opportunistic or closeted homosexuals were drawn by the spectacles of cross-dressing, same-sex nightclubs, and male prostitution. As so many have suggested, Weimar Berlin attracted curiosity seekers and voyeurs, including the steadfastly heterosexual. If Berlin's reputation was spread largely by word of mouth, a few published sources mentioned the city's alternative charms. One rather unconventional guidebook claimed that "the Cook's Travel Agency takes tourists to these locales as if to a cabinet of curiosities, because this state of affairs [transvestitism] is considered one of the sights of Berlin."[25] The Eldorado was Berlin's most famous transvestite bar and was the one visited most often by slumming straights. As a young man, the author Wolfgang Cordan (1909–1966) worked as a Berlin journalist and described how "the bar differed in no way from the nicer harems of the upper class. Elegant entrance and cloakroom, thank you very much: no tie, no admission, dancing upstairs. Also the blond women in the gold lamé dresses. Only they wore wigs and had artificial breasts." Located in the West End at Nollendorfplatz, the bar became a popular tourist destination for foreign visitors (due in part to Cook's, no doubt), displaying proudly the autographed photos of dignitaries, including celebrities such as the boxer Jack Dempsey, or film stars Rudolph Valentino, Greta Garbo, Charlie Chaplin, and, not surprisingly, Marlene Dietrich.[26]

One of Oxford's "bright young things," David Herbert (1908–1995), a close friend of Paul and Jane Bowles and younger brother of the earl of Pembroke, moved to Berlin in 1927 to enjoy the city's cultural attractions: "The theatre was the best in the world; modern and imaginative, it was far in advance of its counterparts in other capitals." He explained further, "Even after London, which in 1927 had seemed gay enough, life in Berlin was an orgy of fun." The restaurants, bars, and nightclubs, according to Herbert, catered to every conceivable whimsy or taste, upscale, sordid, squalid, and sexual. When relatives visited to assist Herbert's cousin Sidney, hospitalized in Berlin for an operation, the family made an outing to the Eldorado. "My Uncle Geordie was so innocent," Herbert explained, "that he did not realize what was happening all round him, and was deeply shocked at finding a male organ beneath the chiffon dress of the 'girl' sitting on his knee."[27]

The American novelist Sinclair Lewis (1885–1951), who lived in Europe in the 1920s, sent the namesake character from his novel *Dodsworth* (published in 1929) on a Berlin pub crawl. Escorted by hosts, American businessman Sam Dodsworth visits an unnamed transvestite bar: "Here was a mass of delicate young men with the voices of Chorus girls, dancing together and whispering in corners, young men with scarves of violet and rose, wearing bracelets and heavy symbolic rings. And there was girl in lavender chiffon—only from the set of her shoulders Sam was sure that she was a man."[28] French film director Jean Renoir (1894–1979) was a frequent visitor to Berlin during the interwar period and commented on the city's most salient attractions: "[T]he fashionable entertainments in Berlin between the wars were boxing and homosexualism. Sodom and Gomorrah were reborn there. I cannot resist describing an evening at the Grosses Balhaus [*sic*] on the Alexanderplatz. . . . It was huge hall packed with a dense crowd of male and female dancers, but on looking a second time one realized that the 'females' were males in 'drag.' What was disconcerting was their air of respectability." According to Renoir, the city manifested every extreme. "Berlin was the fertile climate in which the best and the worst flourished. The best was the work of painters such as [Bauhaus member] Paul Klee, plays such as those of Bertolt Brecht, films like *The Cabinet of Dr Caligari*. . . . The worst was prostitution, both female and male, which extended even to members of the strict Prussian bourgeoisie."[29]

When Aldous Huxley (1894–1963) first visited Berlin in September 1930, he made the acquaintance of the occultist and drug guru Aleister Crowley (1875–1947), who, according to some accounts, introduced Huxley to mescaline right there in the German capital. Huxley also undertook the requisite tour of the city's famed homosexual haunts, including an unnamed same-sex dance hall. According to his friend Robert Nichols, Huxley admitted later that he had "danced with one of the male prostitutes rather than hurt the fellow's feelings." Nichols had asked Huxley how his party had responded to the importuning young men who approached their table. According to Nichols, Huxley explained, "'I was just a little tipsy when I did it. But I can assure you my dear Bob, a couple of times around that hall and I was sobriety itself. Horror is a wonderful disintoxicant.'"[30] And no doubt the overture of a genuine rent boy conferred an aura of authenticity on Huxley's Berlin experience.

Who were the young men and boys who sold themselves for sex, and why was Berlin such a magnet? Of course, we know that male prostitution had developed almost symbiotically with the city's homosexual milieu. As a traditional garrison town, Berlin had earned a reputation for so-called "soldier" prostitution, mentioned in published sources as early as the late eighteenth century. The most prominent gay cruising sites—the Tiergarten Park, Unter den Linden, and the Passage—were frequented by prostitutes and had been established long before 1900. Berlin's population of male prostitutes ballooned after the First World War, fueled by economic instability and the chaotic demobilization of millions of German soldiers in the weeks following the armistice on November 11, 1918. In September 1921 an internal memo of the Ministry of Public Welfare considered the growth of Berlin's homosexual community and claimed that "the number of male youth, often preadolescents, who sell their sexual services is now estimated at 50,000 for greater Berlin."[31] (This estimate was certainly exaggerated, and a more credible figure of 22,000 was adduced a few years later by the Institute for Sexual Science.)[32] In response, the Prussian minister for public welfare recommended in January 1922 that a general statement about the dangers of male prostitution be issued to public school teachers (at all levels), as well as to the members of the schools' parents' advisory committees, and finally to the staff of juvenile detention homes. The official also recommended establishing a counseling center at the Charité Hospital.[33]

These somewhat feckless recommendations, even where implemented, had little impact, especially in response to the economic hardship that drove both men and women to pursue sex work. The Great

Inflation and later the world economic crash of 1929 conspired to increase the number of boys and young men (in addition to women and girls) who were willing—or compelled—to sell themselves. The ubiquity of male prostitution sustained a public discussion—one that had begun well before the First World War—prompting the Institute for Sexual Science to sponsor a sociological study that was begun in 1926. The study was based on detailed interviews of several hundred male prostitutes and was undertaken by one of Hirschfeld's young colleagues, Richard Linsert (1899–1933). As an active member of the Communist Party, Linsert had joined the institute in 1923. He also worked closely with the Scientific Humanitarian Committee and was elected to its board of directors in 1926. Linsert's methodology was fairly primitive, and he identified his subjects randomly, approaching them in public spaces, often the Tiergarten or the Passage, though also in bars and clubs. The study was never completed, but Linsert published an essay in 1929 that synthesized some of its findings.[34] While the data was presumed lost when the Nazis destroyed the institute in 1933, a typewritten manuscript of one hundred completed questionnaires that Linsert compiled from his estimated three hundred interviews was recently discovered and is now archived by the Magnus Hirschfeld Society in Berlin.[35]

Linsert's questionnaire consisted of thirty questions addressing biography; sexual orientation; "business" details about work venues, "fees," and sexual practices; clashes with police and arrest records; and, finally, personal life, including lovers or spouses. In most cases, Linsert completed the questionnaires himself after conducting lengthy interviews. His descriptions were sometimes unprofessional, including comments about hygiene or dirty underwear, which revealed a lascivious interest if not an actual sexual encounter. In at least one case, Linsert admits to sleeping with his interview subject, Willi M., whom he described as a twenty-five-year-old auto mechanic with a "gripping appearance" and an "intellectual superiority" as both "proletarian and a *Kulturmensch*." Linsert first met Willi M. around 9 p.m. on June 30, 1926, promenading in the Tiergarten Park between the Schiller and Goethe statues. "Sitting on a bench we had lively conversation about social and sexual problems," Linsert tells us, and "Willi M. was very interested in Berlin's homosexual life." Linsert eventually took the young man back to his apartment. Though clearly a prostitute, Willi M. never demanded money from Linsert, nor did Linsert offer to pay him after their tryst, since he feared giving offense. This was their only sexual encounter, moreover, even though Linsert pursued the relationship. The two had brief interactions on several occasions during lectures and other events at the institute, but Willi M. politely deflected Linsert's overtures, and eventually told the would-be sexologist that their initial encounter "was not the right thing." "I mention this case, which deeply upset me," Linsert wrote, "because it demonstrates how a crazy economic and social order can drive a highly competitive and gifted individual to the brink of prostitution. . . . I bitterly regret my sexual indiscretion on that humid summer evening, because it forfeited the friendship of a worthwhile human being."[36]

The ages of those interviewed by Linsert ranged from fourteen to thirty-one, though only ten were under eighteen. The vast majority came directly from Berlin or Brandenburg, seven were from the Rhineland, and four were from southwestern Germany. All were native German speakers, though the three from Silesia also spoke Polish. The overwhelming majority had trained in blue-collar vocations or were unskilled. All but a few were working class with limited education. Not one from the group had attended *Gymnasium,* the elite German secondary education that qualified one for university study. However, the group included eleven sales personnel or other office employees, two actors, two secondary school students, one dancer, one photographer, and one soldier. Some thirty-five of the hundred described themselves as homosexual, twenty-six as bisexual, and thirty-two as heterosexual. Certainly the language is Linsert's, not his subjects', though the labels do correspond to sexual practices and experience. Only one interviewee had ever had a female client, and Linsert described him as bisexual. For those Linsert deemed heterosexual, for example, "non-professional" sexual contact appears to have been exclusively female. There was also a strong correspondence between a subject's presumed orientation and the specific sexual acts engaged in for pay.

The "rates" demanded and received varied tremendously, ranging from as little as fifty pfennig to ten marks and more. (It appears that Isherwood and Auden were quite generous indeed, paying ten marks for a single encounter.) A number of Linsert's respondents, primarily those with girlfriends or female lovers, limited their sexual services to mutual masturbation. However, a majority engaged in most homosexual practices, including oral and anal penetration. Those claiming the greatest remuneration included an "athletic boxer," Hugo G., and Karl W., a competitive swimmer who hoped to represent Germany in international competitions; both reported receiving ten marks or more per sexual act.[37] Others with similarly high earnings included Rudolf L., Albert K., B. Sche., M. P., Karl E., and F. K., whom Linsert described as very good-looking or manicured and well dressed.[38]

Another significant factor in the "price" differentials was the location or venue of solicitation. One of Berlin's particularities was the relatively diffuse character of the homosexual scene, whose bars and clubs were scattered throughout the city. In turn male hustlers plied their trade in most sections of Berlin's vast geography. Linsert counted no fewer than twenty-four separate locations where his interview partners reported picking up johns. He also claimed that through the course of his study he had become aware of some ninety additional sites where one might encounter a male prostitute. These included specific streets and squares in east, west, north, and south Berlin, as well as other outdoor and public venues, such as parks, train stations, and bathrooms. There were also bars or cafés in most sections of the city that catered to male prostitutes and their clients.[39]

The best-paid male prostitutes worked exclusively in west Berlin, where better-heeled patrons, the so-called *Kavaliere* ("cavaliers," or wealthy johns), sought same-sex assignations. These locales were based in the theater and cinema district, which reached from west Berlin's "boulevard of millionaires," the Kurfürstendamm, to Nollendorfplatz. This area expanded dramatically during the Weimar period, and was sometimes described as Berlin's "Broadway."[40] Tauentzienstraße, which extended east from the "Ku'damm," connecting Wittenbergplatz with Nollendorfplatz, was also counted among the more elite cruising areas. The most refined west Berlin bars for male prostitutes included the Kurfürsten Lounge, the Kurfürsten Kasino, the Nürnberger Lounge, the Schloßkonditorei Bellevue, and the Internationale Lounge.

According to a travelogue by French journalist Ambroise Got, the west Berlin bars screened and selected both the male prostitutes and the patrons who were allowed to enter. "Led by a sure guide," Got begins,

"I discover the Kleist-Kasino, in the street of the same name, not far from the Kurfürsten Damm." Got's account was seconded by Linsert's better-paid subjects, who also favored the Kleist Kasino. "No luminous advertising, no loud sign draws it to the attention of the passer-by," Got tells us. "It is an ordinary establishment . . . that is not distinguishable from clubs with women or Likörstuben, the bars that abound in this neighborhood." Got continues,

> It is eleven thirty at night. We enter: the narrow, long room is divided by woodwork, both open and sculpted, into three compartments that have deep recesses like alcoves furnished with circular leather couches. . . . Sheltered by propitious screens placed in abundance at the entrance to the recesses, uni-sexual couples entwine in silence. In the middle of the room, the buffet, leaning against the wall, is besieged by a group of ephebes, sitting high on their stools. They sip cocktails or Swedish punch, looking at one another tenderly; all their moves are studied and nonchalant, their poses, feminine. . . . Establishments haunted by inverts are as plentiful on the east side of Berlin as in the west end and the homosexual scourge wreaks its damage at every level of the population.[41]

The process of introducing hustler and john for a "commercial" transaction is of particular interest in Got's account:

> Next to us, there is a fat man with a ruddy face. . . . He is consulting a booklet that the waiter has brought him by request. On the cover in big calligraphed letters are written the French words 'Je t'aime.' Sneaking a peek I can distinguish a list of names with all sorts of indications. So the fat man, his look sharpened, calls the waiter back, and dictates to him in spotty German—he is Dutch— seemingly fragmentary sentences. . . . The waiter shamelessly and conscientiously plays his role as a go-between and leaves after having noted everything mentally.[42]

The Kleist Kasino, like other west Berlin locales, both profited from and "managed" its patrons' sexual liaisons. And unlike the proletarian central and east Berlin bars, the West End venues actively supported solicitation and screened both the prostitutes and clients who entered their establishments. It becomes clear, moreover, that they did so with police connivance.

The 1926 novel by John Henry Mackay, *Der Puppenjunge* (*The Hustler*), widely noted for its realistic description of Berlin's male prostitution, gave a similar account. The protagonist, a sixteen-year-old from the provinces named Gunther, is befriended by an older and more seasoned male prostitute, who rescues the inexperienced boy from the somewhat tawdry Passage and introduces him to a wealthier class of sexual patrons in the West End. With a better suit of clothing and the introduction provided by his new friend, Gunther is able to find more remunerative "employment." He is also advised to avoid public cruising areas such as the Tiergarten Park or public restrooms, or the shabby bars of east Berlin. After Gunther loses the support of his older friend—who acted as his pimp—the underage boy is no longer allowed into the West End bars. Now Gunther is forced to return to the Passage, and to the Adonis-Diele, one of the proletarian locales in the east.[43]

Wolfgang Cordan offers a revealing description of the Adonis-Diele, located on Alte Jakobstraße: "One must never go too early. Otherwise nothing is going on and one is conspicuous. But also never too late, during the most hectic time. Accordingly I went at 10 o'clock." Inside the smoke-filled "den of iniquity," Cordan claims, turned out to be a typical Berlin *Bierlokal*. "On the right was the bar with its beer taps, and behind it a mirrored wall and colorful liquor bottles." Unlike the Eldorado, Cordan tells us, "there were no photos with expensive autographs. The barkeep was fat and amiable." The back of the establishment, Cordan continues, contained a number of niches with tables and was divided from the front by a screen of hanging artificial flowers. Since the "boys" were only allowed in the back when invited, and it was still too early, they all clustered in the front around the bar. After Cordan and his companion pushed their way past the gaggle of prostitutes, they took their places at a table. The only other customers at this point were four middle-aged men drinking beer and playing skat. "These lower-middle class Berliners with wrinkles of fat, bald heads, and bellies—are they also johns?" Cordan questioned. No, indeed not, as it turned out. They were simply neighborhood shop owners who continued to patronize their old *Stammlokal,* even after the pub had undergone its own peculiar transformation. Known for their tolerant civic attitude, the locals clearly took this sort of thing in stride and were able to coexist with the ambient prostitution.[44]

The contrast between the fashionable West End, or *"Berliner* Broadway," and the neighborhood dive bars of central and east Berlin was especially well analyzed by the Berlin journalist and homosexual rights activist Hans Siemsen (1891–1969). In a short essay published in 1927, Siemsen described Berlin as a sexual laboratory and playground for voyeuristic tourists:

> Especially in literary and pseudo-literary circles, it has become a fashion to "take a stroll through the gay locales." The visitor expects to see shocking dens of vice and highly perverse things. What does he see? Absolutely nothing! In west Berlin some small bars and cafes decorated with red and pink silk lanterns, with names such as "Lounge," "Casino," or "Club." . . . The male prostitutes are out quite early, often by noon, awaiting their johns. They all appear as though they were once pretty. . . . A boy with a steady relationship rarely comes to these locales unless with his friend. Most of them have already had a lengthy career and are in decline. The cavaliers and other johns know almost every boy, and are likewise known to them. But that does not prevent a john from taking up with a prostitute "once again." In North and East Berlin, the locales are simpler, sometimes no more than a *Bouillonkeller* [soup basement]. Among the great misery and wretchedness one also sees some very pretty boys. There are fewer *"Tanten"* ["aunts," or effeminate boys] than in the West. At least a third are "normal," a type that many homosexuals prefer. Much "occasional prostitution": unemployed young workers, idle swastika soldiers, burnt-out reform-school youth, ship's boys, sailors, boys from the provinces, and those who wanted or had to run away from home. The friendship here is more honest, and less costly than in West Berlin. Less fuss, less waffling about the clearly understood business aspect of the matter at hand. What the curious onlooker expects,

the public vice, the sensation—that is missing entirely. There is some cocaine consumption, a few are drunk, with the occasional squabble, a pair of lovebirds cuddling—but in general conduct is uncommonly proper and honorable. Responsible for such decorum is the bartender, who is on good terms with the police and ultimately responsible that everything remains within respectable limits. There is no such thing in all of Berlin as a gay locale that is not known to the police and not under police supervision.[45]

Siemsen's depiction anticipated the preliminary findings of Linsert's study and broadly confirmed other literary and journalistic accounts of male prostitution. While the West End hustlers were better turned out, earned higher fees, and exhibited greater "professionalism," the poorer youth who worked the humble bars and outdoor spaces of central and east Berlin engaged more often in "occasional" prostitution— due primarily to unemployment—and were themselves frequently heterosexual.

An evocative account of the most vulgar prostitution is provided by John Lehmann, a friend of Christopher Isherwood, whose autobiographical novel *In the Purely Pagan Sense* (1976) was inspired in part by his 1932 visit to Berlin. The protagonist was given a tour by his host, William:

One of the first things William did to further my education was to take me on a tour of the homosexual bars and night-clubs. We started with one of the most popular non-smart *Lokals,* the "Cosy Corner." This *Lokal* was a sensational experience for me, a kind of emotional earthquake. . . . The place was filled with attractive boys of any age between sixteen and twenty-one, some fair and curly-haired, some dark and often blue-eyed, and nearly all dressed in extremely short *Lederhosen* which showed off their smooth and sunburnt thighs. Hardly had we found a place, when William told me, in a tone of command rather than of advice: "if you want to pee, it's over there." I went. The lavatory had no cubicles. I was followed in by several boys, who, as if by chance, ranged themselves on either side of me and pulled out their cocks rather to show them off than to relieve nature as I was doing. I don't think a drop fell into the gutter from any of them; I returned to our bench, shaken by this exhibition. . . . William said to me. "Any you fancy?" I shook my head though I knew that any single one of the boys who had followed me would make me happy—if only I knew how to handle him. "Well, there are a couple of boys here I know, who are thoroughly reliable." William said, "I'll call them over." The two were summoned, and ordered to sit on either side of me. I felt rather like a recruit being put through his first bayonet drill. "Don't be shy, but put your hands in their pockets," William commanded, now rather mischievously. I put one hand into the outer *Lederhosen* pocket of the one on my left, and my other into the outer pocket of the one on my right; they were both now snuggling up to me. I had shock of more than surprise when I found that the pockets had been cut off and my hands went straight through to their sex. . . . I did not take either of them home . . . but gave them a few Marks and we continued our pub crawl.[46]

We might question Lehmann's account here—memories embellished with the passage of time—though we know that he was taken to the Cosy Corner by Isherwood in 1932, when he first came to the city from Vienna.

Lehmann, Siemsen, Mackay, Cordan, and Got—as well as Auden and Isherwood—drew sharp distinctions between West End and "non-smart" locales. These observers also recognized that the Berlin police subjected these bars to different rules. Certainly city officials were aware of the nature of all of these establishments—as Siemsen explained—which were left largely unmolested as long as they maintained the prescribed decorum. Indeed, the implicit compact established by Berlin police commissioner Leopold von Meerscheidt-Hüllessem in the late nineteenth century remained the order of the day. But social class and urban geography—which was ultimately also a reflection of class—played significant roles. As the character Gunther in *Der Puppenjunge* discovered, the west Berlin bars *did not* admit underage boys—nor those shabbily dressed—unless accompanied by a trustworthy "guardian" or "chaperone." Because they screened both the prostitutes and their clientele, these establishments appear to have been allowed to flaunt the nominal restrictions placed on pimping and procurement.

By contrast, the east Berlin bars were accessible to all, regardless of age, but also more vulnerable to raids by police or other officials. In *Der Puppenjunge,* Gunther had no trouble entering the working-class dives alone. But he was also arrested in one of these, the Adonis-Diele, during a police raid.[47] Not only the police but also other officials conducted periodic raids on the boy bars of central and east Berlin. Sometimes city social workers trolled the bars for "juvenile delinquents" who had escaped from local orphanages and detention centers. John Layard describes how together with Auden and Isherwood he helped three young hustlers who had escaped from a detention facility. One evening at the Cosy Corner, probably early winter 1929, the landlord warned that "the Gruener [the "greens," or police] are coming," searching for "three escaped borstal boys in the café." Layard, Auden, and Isherwood were asked to surrender their overcoats, which the three boys donned. They then strolled out of the bar and right past the police, who were deceived by their relatively elegant outerwear. Inside the locale, the police "searched every nook and cranny and couldn't find them." Later the Englishmen rendezvoused with the youth at Alexanderplatz to retrieve their topcoats. The six then spent the remainder of the evening together in Auden's quarters.[48]

As the historian Martin Lücke notes, as many as thirty-seven of Linsert's one hundred boys and men who made up his case studies might have spent time in adolescent homes and orphanages.[49] For many, such an experience was a formative introduction to criminal activity and prostitution.[50] From this same group, fifty-nine had never fallen afoul of the law, while fourteen had been convicted and punished for a crime. With the remaining twenty-seven, it was either unclear or unstated. The most common offense was theft.[51] Strikingly, practically none of Linsert's interview partners admitted to engaging in blackmail, which was addressed explicitly in question number 26 of the survey. A single hustler from the group of one hundred had served a two-year jail sentence for blackmail. The vast majority averred that they would never attempt such a thing. Although anti–Paragraph 175 activists still invoked blackmail as a central argument for eliminating the statute, it was clearly no longer the scourge it had been before the Great War. As one male prostitute in *Der Puppenjunge* explained, the "Berlin johns [*Stubben*] were too shrewd to be extorted."[52]

One sensational case that was widely reported in the press offers the rule-proving exception. In December 1926 the twenty-two-year-old street hustler Alois Dämon was sentenced to two years imprisonment after one of his extortion victims committed suicide in October. Dämon, a native of Austria, had left home at the age of sixteen and worked on a ship before coming to Berlin, where he established a significant record of arrests for petty crimes, including solicitation, theft, and assault and battery. Dämon's victim was a thirty-eight-year-old state bureaucrat named Otto Zöhn, who lived with his wife and small child in a small apartment and led "a well-ordered marital life, and did not drink or gamble." Zöhn managed to poison himself by inhaling the gas piped into his apartment for lighting. In his short suicide note he attempted to console his wife—"Dear Ella! Do not be shocked"—explaining that he had "fallen into the hands of extortionists," and that death was his only option. Using the threatening letters found in Zöhn's apartment, the police were able to identify Dämon, who had been known in Berlin since 1924 as a prostitute and investigated once before after another man had accused him of blackmail. Zöhn and Dämon had met in March at the Anhalter train station. Over the course of six months, Zöhn— apparently uncharacteristically—had begun to borrow money from his wife and work colleagues. Although his wife had considered him completely heterosexual, the police suspected that he had had a sexual relationship with the boy.[53]

Other male prostitutes whose "careers" are documented by surviving archival records were most often arrested for loitering or solicitation. The fourteen-year-old Fritz Thomas was arrested in March 1929 for "loitering" in the Passage. Because his own mother was suspected of running a brothel from her apartment, Thomas was eventually sent to an asylum.[54] Kurt Doering had his first sexual encounter as a twenty-year-old when approached by a man in a public restroom in 1930. After this he learned to trade sexual favors for food.[55] Willi Schulz, aged sixteen, was arrested for solicitation in the spring of 1932. It turned out that Schulz had disappeared in January, though his parents had failed to report him missing. Earlier the boy had been banned from school outings because of his sexual escapades. Fearing for the welfare of a younger daughter, Schulz's parents would not allow him to return home and he was sent instead to a juvenile home.[56]

Some youth were reported directly to social service authorities by their own parents. One widowed mother, Frau Steinke, appealed to the guardianship court for help with her nineteen-year-old son, Hans: "I ask that you place my son Hans in a welfare community home. Hans has been making much trouble. He stays out late into the night and then sleeps into the afternoon, only to go out again. Oddly he always has money and somehow ekes out his own living, since I can ill afford to support him. I tell him to look for work, but he threatens me, or at best ignores my advice." Following his investigation, which included a series of home visits, an official of the guardianship court reported,

Hans claims to work as a valet in front of the Charlottenburg opera, but, in fact, he allows men to pick him up there when the theater is closing and only returns in the early morning hours. Opera performances never run past 11:30. He regularly earns as much as 10 Marks in an evening. Ultimately Hans admitted that he not only opens and closes doors for opera patrons, but also leaves with strange men. Hans also explained that he had been seduced by other boys last year, and followed their example. It is clear from his clothing and bearing that he has fostered homosexual contacts. He always irons his shirt and ties and shaves his eyebrows.

Although the court official recommended that Hans be committed to a group home, his fate is unclear.[57]

In 1931, the guardianship court reported on sixteen-year-old Fritz Viert:

The irregularity of his life and his unreliability reflect the influence of homosexual persons. He was approached by strange men in the street who enticed him to engage in homosexual practices. He has regular relations with a special group of men, who can be found in the bars of west Berlin, and he is completely under the influence of those ruined persons. In the bars, he is provided with alcoholic drinks and he smokes a great deal. He also puts on makeup and he powders himself, he dances with the men he knows, and often spends the night in the apartments of the homosexual persons who visit bars.[58]

The court record ends here, and we know even less about Fritz Viert than about Hans Steinke.

One feature of Berlin's nightlife—mentioned in many sources, including Linsert's study of male prostitution—was the widespread use of illicit drugs and especially of cocaine. Not unlike the words "homosexual" or "transvestite," "cocaine" was also a German innovation, first isolated from Peruvian coca leaves and so named by the German PhD student Albert Niemann in the lab of his chemistry professor, Dr. Friedrich Wöhler, at the University of Göttingen in 1859. In the 1870s the German pharmaceutical firm Merck first produced the drug commercially. Cocaine was given initially to morphine addicts, ironically, to counter addiction. Recognized for its numbing qualities, it was also used as a local anesthetic, especially in eye surgeries. Freud became acquainted with the drug in the 1880s, and, somewhat infamously, recommended cocaine to patients while using it himself.[59]

Published medical reports first warned of cocaine's addictive properties in the 1880s, and by the early twentieth century, it was recognized as a powerful and potentially dangerous substance. A Hague Convention in 1911–12 attempted to regulate the distribution of morphine, opium, and cocaine; German drug companies feared limitations on their production, however, and the German government was able to effect a compromise that allowed individual national signatories to "use their best efforts" to control their own pharmaceutical firms. After 1918 the Weimar government became concerned with the diversion of military stockpiles, which created a surge in street-level trafficking. Responding in part to Article 295 of the Treaty of Versailles—which sought to toughen the prewar Hague Convention—the Weimar government issued a regulation in July 1920 that required a specific distribution license, limited to drug manufacturers, wholesalers, pharmacists, and scientific institutions. Popular demand increased illicit trafficking, however, and also the incidence of accidental poisoning. Cocaine sold on the streets was increasingly laced with boric acid or novocaine as well as innocuous fillers. Berlin's university medical clinics claimed that 10 percent of all admissions in 1921 involved cocaine abuse.[60] In 1925, the *New York Times* reported, "Drug Habit Alarms Berlin Police: Cocaine Circulates Like Cigarettes." According to Berlin police, the *Times* claimed, "[d]ope peddlers in Berlin are rivaling American bootleggers for the artfulness with which they have been avoiding detection." Cocaine abuse was especially common "among the prominent residents of Berlin's fashionable West End," the paper reported, and "is considered a fashionable fad." Especially alarming was the "increasing number of drug fiend cases being treated in hospitals."[61]

As Robert McAlmon described in his roman á clef short stories, cocaine could be purchased in Berlin cafés and clubs, often from the barkeep, a bouncer, or a dealer, either behind closed doors or on the street. It was plentiful, and certainly cheap for tourists such as McAlmon, paying with hard currency during the Great Inflation. And, of course, cocaine was the perfect Berlin stimulant—perfect for pub crawls, perfect for all-night clubbing, perfect for sex. As one McAlmon character described,

> Feeling somewhat tired, and potentially sleepy, I was, however, ready to make a night of it, but suggested that if we were to go on we'd better take a sniff of the cocaine we had to liven us up. Getting under an archway entrance, away from the wind, and under the light of a near street lamp, we unfolded the paper containing the cocaine, and cautiously sniffed a little. Feeling no immediate sensation, to be aware whether we'd actually taken any into our nostrils or not, or had blown it away, we sniffed a second time. My nose began soon to feel numbed, and in the back of my throat there was dryness that was mildly disagreeable, while a feeling of nausea was within my stomach. However I felt exhilarated, strong, leapingly light-bodied, and capable of going on without thought of tiredness.[62]

Particularly disturbing for some was the pervasive, public abuse of cocaine not only within the demimonde but also among respectable burghers.[63] In 1927 Brian Howard recorded his first impressions of a "drug fiend," a man who looked like a "retired Prussian General," out with his wife and two young sons in a café in the West End. Unable to grasp what was happening, Howard turned to the café owner: "'What is he doing?' I said . . . the proprietor said, not too quietly, 'He smells hiss coke.' 'What?' I said. 'Hiss coke—he brithss it in.' . . . Presuming that I must be hard of hearing, if not downright dense, the proprietor now bellowed at me, with some asperity, 'CORK-HA-EEN!'"[64] This openness reflected the common representations of cocaine in Weimar popular culture. Fritz Lang's 1922 film *Dr. Mabuse the Gambler* depicts a criminal syndicate in Berlin (run by Mabuse) that—among other illegal operations—manufactures and peddles cocaine.[65] Nicknamed the "Snow Queen" (*Schneekönigin*), Anita Berber (who also happened to play a small uncredited role in *Dr. Mabuse*) was the very face of cocaine consumption (and of many other illicit substances). She confessed openly to her addiction and explained that she had "enflamed nostrils" from the abuse. Her performance "Dances of Depravity, Horror, and Ecstasy" included an episode titled "Kokain," with music by French composer Camille Saint-Saëns.[66] Soon after his arrival in Berlin, Klaus Mann—who later developed his own addictions—met Berber for the first time, and he claimed "it was clear that she had already taken a great deal of cocaine, which she also offered to me."[67] The drug was also featured in popular literature: Otto Rung's *Kokain: Novellen* appeared in 1923; *Cocaina*, the Italian-language novel by Dino Segre, or "Pitigrilli" (1893–1975), was published in 1921. Placed on the Catholic codex of banned books, *Cocaina* appeared in German translation in 1927, when it naturally became a best seller.

It should come as no surprise that German medical science developed a keen interest in the diagnosis and treatment of cocaine addiction. In 1924 two German-Jewish medical doctors, Ernst Joël (1893–1929) and Fritz Fränkel (1892–1944), published *Der Cocainismus*, the first systematic treatment of cocaine addiction. Both men had served as medics in the First World War, where they learned firsthand about morphine addiction. Joël himself had become addicted to morphine during the war, and this is thought to help explain his suicide in 1929. After the armistice Joël and Fränkel founded an addiction clinic in Berlin. Based on their treatment of hundreds of Berlin addicts, the two together published *Cocainismus,* which described the urban culture of cocaine abuse, including cocaine's addictive attributes, withdrawal symptoms, and the most effective methods of treatment. They also included case studies drawn from their practice.[68]

One of the findings of their analysis was an odd connection between cocaine addiction and homosexuality. This association had been emphasized in a 1923 article by Berlin physician Norbert Marx, who published case studies of three men who "acquired" homosexual tendencies under the influence of cocaine.[69] Although such a claim sounds potentially "homophobic," this was not the intention of Joël and Fränkel. Presumably heterosexual, the doctors were unambiguously on the political left, acquaintances if not friends of Hirschfeld, and sympathetic to the cause of homosexual emancipation. Fränkel was a founding member of the German Communist Party in 1919. Joël had been Walter Benjamin's university classmate and, together with Benjamin, a sometime pacifist and antiwar activist. (Benjamin later served as both observer and research subject in the experiments that Fränkel and Joël conducted on the effects of hashish.)[70]

According to Joël and Fränkel, the incidence of homosexuals among cocaine addicts was greater than among alcoholics or morphine addicts, which raised the following questions: "Do male cocaine addicts who sleep with men have a fixed homosexual orientation, or did they acquire a homosexual orientation through their addiction, or, without a homosexual orientation, do they simply have homosexual relations when using cocaine?" The responses of these two scientists hinged on a simple observation about the effects of cocaine. In most men, they argued, significant cocaine abuse caused impotence but without diminishing libido. This had the curious result of influencing apparent heterosexuals—who were potentially bisexual or latently homosexual—to engage in homosexual acts. Of course, cocaine, like any intoxicant, lessened inhibitions, and this helped explain the overrepresentation of inborn homosexuals among the population of addicts, since most homosexuals experienced significant sexual repression. But it was also the divergence of sex drive and sexual capacity that explained the phenomenon.[71] If this seemed dubious, it resonated with other students of addiction. The Zurich psychiatrist and university professor Dr. Hans Maier published a comprehensive textbook, *Der Kokainismus*, in 1926, in which he presented his own case studies of homosexual addicts and endorsed the findings of Joël and Fränkel.[72]

The obvious significance of this unconvincing science was the way it gave expression to a popular perception that cocaine abuse and homosexuality were somehow linked. Consider for example the recollections (and associations) of Berlin street life from the journalist and screenwriter Léo Lania (1896–1961): "Prostitutes, pimps, 'flyin' peddlers. From raincoats to cocaine, from jewels to love—everything on hand, immediate delivery. Boys with painted cheeks and mascara, wearing tight-fitting jackets and pointed shoes."[73] Berlin police superintendent Ernst Engelbrecht was also convinced that homosexual men and lesbians had an intrinsic love of cocaine.[74] And no matter the precise explanation, medical (and government) authorities were certain that cocaine addiction was particularly pronounced among homosexuals. In their monographic study, Joël and Fränkel argued that within an urban environment cocaine abusers develop a kind of community, which supports its members in the struggle to locate dealers and procure the drug. Drawing parallels to homosexual subcultures, they also claimed that cocaine—unlike morphine—stimulates extroversion and sociability, explaining its specific appeal for shy or repressed homosexuals seeking community and contacts.[75] Without really explaining the phenomenon of homosexual addicts, Joël and Fränkel, both "outsiders," provided the pieces that helped to form a larger picture.

Certainly many "insiders" could corroborate their claims. Hans Siemsen confirmed that "cocaine consumption" was common in homosexual establishments.[76] Although his drug of choice was heroin, Klaus Mann—whose introduction to Berlin included the offer of a bump from Anita Berber, after all—also liked to *koks*. In one diary entry from 1932, Mann weighed the relative merits of cocaine and morphine: "The c-effect is not different from the m-effect in principle. Both make one lighter and more industrious. M-effect is more psychological—and much faster—c-effect is more cerebral, less euphoric. An intense sense of levitation when it takes hold." In another entry from later that year, Mann reported, "Big evening with Doris. . . . Seeking C. . . . With transvestites a taxi in the city. . . . To a bar. The right person not there . . . waited for a long time. The old man 'I don't have any of that.' . . . Finally the stuff. To Doris's. Taken."[77]

Cocaine was also commonly used by male prostitutes, as Richard Linsert noted. Among his one hundred case studies, three volunteered information about their drug use. Among these, "Reinhold Sch." was one of the most wretched subjects; Linsert described him as a very attractive young man, who at the age of twenty-four had already begun to appear haggard. He was first introduced to cocaine as an adolescent by an older, wealthy man, who for a time had been his boyfriend. When that relationship ended, "Reinhold Sch." began soliciting johns in West End bars. His income was considerable, and he maintained his appearance and wardrobe. But his drug use increased, and he ultimately became addicted. Compelled to use ever-larger quantities, he sold his clothing, lost his apartment, and found himself homeless. After several arrests for drug possession, "Reinhold Sch." received a two-year prison sentence. Upon his release, he returned to prostitution, but was now reduced to hustling in outdoor spaces, primarily the Tiergarten and in central Berlin.[78] In his monographic study, Hans Maier presented a similar case study of a nineteen-year-old whose cocaine consumption was supported by an older, wealthier "friend." When the relationship ended, the youth supported himself (and his habit) through prostitution. After multiple arrests for possession, however, the young man was sent to an asylum to recover from the effects of acute addiction.[79] Another subject from Linsert's study had a far happier outcome. Herr "B. Sche." counted himself one of the elite and claimed to earn up to four hundred marks a month as a prostitute. He plied his trade in the West End bars, where he likewise developed a cocaine addiction, of which he subsequently cured himself.[80]

It was certainly the more prosperous and better-dressed rent boys—as the preceding case studies suggest—who had access to cocaine. The "fashionable fad," as the *New York Times* described it, was centered in Berlin's West End, home of the theater district and the trendiest bars and cafés. Not surprisingly, therefore, prostitutes with access to these venues were also those who most often encountered the drug and became addicts. All the same, cocaine circulated throughout Berlin. In Mackay's *Der Puppenjunge,* the character "Leo," described as the "tireless cocaine addict," is a fixture at the Adonis-Diele, the proletarian locale in the eastern section of the city.[81] For his study, Linsert also interviewed subjects with fewer resources who consumed or were addicted to cocaine. Identified only as "X.X.," one twenty-year-old was essentially a homeless borstal boy who plied his trade in the Tiergarten and, despite meager earnings, indulged his taste for the drug.[82]

What is clear from these records, including Linsert's unpublished study, is that there existed a large market for male prostitution, which provided young men and boys with a ready source of income. It is also clear that those who sold themselves for sex were primarily working- or lower-class and were compelled by poverty and difficult family backgrounds. The responses that Linsert solicited depict prostitution as an opportunity, and for some, at least, male prostitution gave welcome access to Berlin's homosexual world and temporary income before finding more permanent employment. This attitude is also conveyed in the reports of the guardianship court: city officials treated homosexuality and the Berlin bar scene with relative indifference and complacency. These officials showed greater concern about the availability of easy money, which they felt promoted indolence and the development of bad habits among their youthful charges. Ultimately, young men and boys suffered little of the stigma to which female prostitutes were traditionally subjected.

This was only one significant difference between male and female prostitution. Compared with female prostitution—proverbially the world's oldest profession—male prostitution, at least in the Christian West, was less common, though documented in the largest European cities since the Renaissance. One condition that fostered male prostitution was the presence of some sort of community of same-sex-loving men, coupled with a degree of cultural toleration for—or at least indifference to—homosexuality. The few exceptions might include some of Europe's largest cities, where geography and demography afforded cloak and cover despite legal proscription. One case in point would have been Victorian London, where there was little public awareness or representation of same-sex prostitution, and powerful popular moral censure of homosexuality. This context helps to explain the shock and outrage elicited by the revelations about boy brothels at the trial of Oscar Wilde in 1895.

A reputation for tolerance attracted foreign men, in turn, who helped to create a kind of sex tourism. In Renaissance Italy the cities of Florence, Rome, and Venice were all known destinations for same-sex encounters. After the advent of the Grand Tour in the seventeenth century—inaugurated by Inigo Jones and members of the Whitehall Group of King James I (which included many men who loved other men)—Italy became one of the most important destinations. This was that much more the case in the nineteenth century after the introduction of the Napoleonic Code, which eliminated most remaining anti-sodomy laws. As a result Italy, and specific resorts in particular—Taormina or Capri, for example—become playgrounds for wealthy elites who had been disgraced and forced into exile from England or Germany.

Weimar Berlin might not appear to share any characteristics with Renaissance or modern Italy, especially since same-sex love remained criminalized in Germany. Yet, like Italy, Berlin enjoyed an environment of official indifference, as well as a relative penury, which made travel and extended visits practical for those bearing stronger currencies. It must be emphasized as well that any homosexual relationship remained potentially illicit, at least in Germany. For this reason the stigma of homosexual prostitution was perversely never as great, since any same-sex love was always potentially a crime. Additionally, without the legitimization of bourgeois marriage, homosexual relationships were crudely leavened, at least potentially, by mammon. This also explains why figures such as Auden and Isherwood not only described some of their boyfriends—including those they formally remunerated for sex—as love relationships, but also maintained extended partnerships with sometime male prostitutes. Though unsuccessful, Isherwood devised an elaborate scheme to secure his friend a visa for England after 1933. Ultimately, the boys of Berlin, whether avaricious or not, offered many of the (homo-) sexually repressed their first and perhaps only prospect of discovering the mysteries of love.

CHAPTER EIGHT

Weimar Politics and the Struggle for Legal Reform

We must especially point out that any punishment of homosexuality itself is an error in judgment. Those who made this law were scientific ignoramuses. One could say that it is highly probable that this law would never have been made if the fact that homosexuality is innate [i.e., natural] had been known to legislatures.
—Scientific Humanitarian Committee, Petition to the Reichstag

In October 1929 a Reichstag committee—commissioned to revise the criminal code—voted fifteen to thirteen to eliminate, once and for all, Paragraph 175, the German anti-sodomy statute. This was a momentous and unexpected decision. For the first time since unification, Germany appeared to be on the brink of decriminalizing homosexual relations. The outcome of the vote was that much more surprising, considering the ideological composition of the twenty-eight-member group. While there were fourteen supporters of gay emancipation (including two representatives of the left-liberal German Democratic Party, nine Social Democrats, and three Communists), the remaining fourteen were staunch conservatives, who strenuously opposed any liberalization whatsoever.

Truly remarkable was the position of the committee chairman, Dr. Wilhelm Kahl, a representative of the German People's Party. Kahl and his party were anti-Semitic and suspicious of Weimar democracy, promoting arch-nationalist and socially conservative causes. Yet Kahl, a politician and law professor, was willing to break ranks and cast the deciding vote for reform. In explaining his decision, Kahl argued that the law was ineffective since it caught only a tiny number of its viola- tors, while creating the conditions for the "tragedy of blackmail"; the result was many ruined lives and even suicides. Blackmail was even more common than believed, Kahl claimed, since most victims were afraid to press charges for fear of being arrested. Clearly Kahl remained a social conservative, expressing his disdain for the activists he now sup- ported by arguing that eliminating the statute would "stop the unre- strained agitation and propaganda in favor of homosexuality." Yet he accepted the arguments of Magnus Hirschfeld and other activists that the law was unenforceable, a cause of even greater criminality by spur- ring blackmail, and for these reasons ultimately unjust.[1]

The adoption of these arguments by a leading conservative politician and legal academic marked an unqualified victory for the homosexual rights movement. Since Hirschfeld had first organized the Scientific- Humanitarian Committee in 1897, he and his fellow activists had tire- lessly propagated precisely these claims: while the law enabled the very real criminality of extortion and blackmail, homosexuality was an inborn condition and therefore no offense. During this period, Reich- stag committees charged with revising the legal code had prepared drafts, first in 1908, then eight more times (in 1910, 1911, 1913, 1917, 1919, 1925, 1926, and 1927). But not one of these had included the elimination of the anti-sodomy statute. The decision in October 1929 signaled a leg- islative breakthrough and a long-sought victory.

The apparent success was not Hirschfeld's alone, however. The Wei- mar Republic established after the First World War witnessed an aston- ishing increase in homosexual organizations, fueling the "agitation and propaganda" of which Kahl complained. In addition to Adolf Brand's Community of the Special, a third major group, the Human Rights League, led by the businessman and publisher Friedrich Radszuweit, had emerged as an umbrella organization for a wide range of social, cultural, and political groups that constituted a genuine mass movement. Unlike the smaller and relatively elite organizations formed by Hirschfeld and Brand before 1914, the HRL came to preside over a veritable empire of publications and magazines, social and cultural clubs, and a member- ship that Radszuweit claimed to be in the tens of thousands.

This proliferation after 1918 created remarkable social and cultural resources for homosexual men and women, whose visibility in the Weimar Republic, particularly in Berlin, could escape few contemporary observers. These seemed to be the conditions conducive to legal reform. Yet the reform movement, such as it was, never achieved anything like a uniform program and was riven by faction, rivalry, and an astonishing spectrum of political views. The prewar conflicts between the SHC and the so-called masculinists—both Brand and his supporters and onetime SHC "Secessionists," led by Benedict Friedlaender—were now magnified, expressing the larger, divisive features of Weimar political culture. The advent of a mass homosexual rights movement invited the participation of right-wing nationalists and anti-Semites—often devotees of the writings of Hans Blüher—as well as liberals, Social Democrats, and Communists. And even when united behind the cause of legal reform, activists fought incessantly over specifics. Should a new law equalize the age of consent for heterosexuals and homosexuals? Should homosexual prostitution be criminalized, or more carefully monitored?

Tragically, the political paralysis of the Weimar Republic beginning in 1930 prevented parliamentary action, and the committee's draft revision never came to a vote. The law was not eliminated, nor even liberalized, and instead was made more draconian in 1935 under Nazi rule. Just as the broader homosexual rights movement reflected the variegated politics and culture of the Weimar Republic, its ultimate failure and eventual demise was likewise tied to and emblematic of the fate of Germany's first democratic state.

The hope of finally realizing legal reform at the beginning of the Weimar Republic seemed especially well justified, since Magnus Hirschfeld's political allies, the Social Democrats, had displaced the Kaiser and now headed the new state. In February Hirschfeld wrote the new justice minister, Otto Landsberg, invoking the unprecedented support of SPD chairman August Bebel in 1898: "We trust that you will endeavor to reform the legal code as soon as possible. . . . An emergency law must be introduced to eliminate Paragraph 175, something for which the SHC has fought for years, on legal, biological and ethical grounds. The first such attempt was made by the SPD leader August Bebel, who called for the repeal of the Paragraph directly in the Reichstag. . . . We therefore request a meeting in order to provide a more detailed explanation of our objective."[2]

Landsberg politely demurred, however, responding that he would prefer to meet once Weimar legislators were able to begin a process of comprehensive legal reform.[3] The SHC then turned to Paul Hirsch, SPD minister-president of Prussia (the largest and most powerful federal state in the new republic), who responded likewise that the matter could be addressed only with comprehensive reform.[4] These responses revealed the SPD's lukewarm embrace of homosexual emancipation. But they were also indicative of the relative weakness of the new Weimar state and the existential threats it faced from the radical right.

Despite these disappointing rebuffs, Hirschfeld and SHC members pursued their reform agenda. The new Institut für Sexualwissenschaft, the Institute for Sexual Science—housed in the Tiergarten villa with its adjacent house and additional outbuildings—provided the SHC with office and library spaces and an opulent venue for organizational meetings. On August 30, 1919, the SHC's annual general meeting met in the institute's villa and established a new *Aktionskomitee,* which would direct legal reform efforts with both Adolf Brand's Community of the Special and the newer groups that had formed since the end of the war. In addition to Brand, Hans Kahnert, who had just founded the German Friendship Association, joined the committee. In the following weeks announcements with calls for contributions appeared in the *Jahrbuch, Der Eigene,* and *Die Freundschaft.*[5]

The action committee was initially spearheaded and dominated by the SHC, including Hirschfeld and his SHC colleague, the Jewish and openly homosexual lawyer Kurt Hiller. Under the auspices of the committee, Hirschfeld and the SHC continued to collect signatures for a petition that demanded the repeal of Paragraph 175. One prominent signatory was Gustav Radbruch, who was named federal justice minister in December 1921. Two months later Radbruch met with representatives of the committee, including Hirschfeld, and expressed his support before drafting a reform law that would have eliminated criminal penalties for sexual relations between consenting adult men.[6]

Soon after this, in March, Hirschfeld appeared before the Reichstag to present the petition, which by this point had been signed by a who's who of leading Weimar intellectual and cultural figures, including Albert Einstein, Gerhart Hauptmann, Hermann Hesse, Käthe Kollwitz, Heinrich and Thomas Mann, and the composer Engelbert Humperdinck. Although the petition was also endorsed by leading socialists such as Rudolf Hilferding, and Hermann Müller, who served as chancellor from summer 1921 to spring 1922 (as well as Justice Minister Radbruch), the formal response was disappointing. Instead of agreeing to debate the petition, Reichstag officials responded in December 1922 that they would simply pass it over to the executive branch, which denied Hirschfeld and his allies a public debate or hearing. Despite this defeat, the SHC continued with its campaign to collect signatures and, by 1924, boasted the support of some ten thousand prominent professionals and other public figures. Unfortunately, Radbruch never pursued his initiative, due largely to political instability. By 1925 the right-wing German People's Party—the party of Wilhelm Kahl—controlled the Justice Ministry, and the reform campaign appeared to be stymied.

The prospect of eliminating the anti-sodomy statute in the early 1920s was certainly one factor that motivated the cooperation of the SHC, Adolf Brand, and the Berlin Friendship Association. The greatest energy, arguably, came from the latter (founded by Hans Kahnert in 1919), which promised not only to lobby for legal reform but also to coordinate social events for the homosexual community. Branch associations were soon organized in Dresden, Düsseldorf, Frankfurt, Stuttgart, Hamburg, and Hanover, and in August 1920 the regional chapters formed an umbrella group, the German Friendship Association. The larger organization pledged to fight against Paragraph 175 and offer legal support for members who fell afoul of the law. By 1923, thirty-six local branches in twenty-eight German cities had been organized.[7]

The rapid expansion of the Friendship Associations was a product of the new cultural climate created by the Weimar Republic. The original Berlin chapter registered as a formal *Verein,* or club, in September 1920—a bold step, since it required the submission of a membership list. (In the early twentieth century the SHC had debated and decided against this; they finally registered as a *Verein* in June 1921.)[8] Although there are no surviving club records, the Friendship Associations had a dramatically different membership profile from those of the SHC or Brand's CoS. Members were younger and less fearful of being associated with a homosexual organization. It is also likely that many soldiers returning from the Great War filled their ranks.

Although the clubs engaged politically for legal reform, their stronger attraction was likely the social opportunities they fostered. The branches in Weimar and Hamburg maintained free lending libraries. Berlin had several chapters, including a gay theater troupe, the Theater of Eros, and a Christian worship society, which held Sunday-afternoon services at the Church of the Redeemer. The friendship clubs also sponsored separate lesbian chapters in Berlin, Magdeburg, Munich, and Dresden.[9]

Hirschfeld and the SHC could scarce fail to notice the emergence of what seemed to be a mass movement. In 1922 the committee sent a young law student, Fritz Flato, to the second congress of the German Friendship Association in Munich. Flato had joined the SHC only after the war, probably through an introduction made by Kurt Hiller (whose family had social ties with Flato's).[10] Not finished with his legal training, Flato was only twenty-seven and therefore the perfect age to serve as an SHC representative. In his memoir, Hiller gave a report on Flato's experience: "It was an enormous rendez-vous, apparently, with a noble objective, of course, but a surfeit of dilettantism, parochial cluelessness, and people who were well-meaning but ignorant—exactly what corresponds to a 'movement' based on the masses instead of on biologists, ethnographers, psychologists, jurists, philosophers, literary critics, and authors."[11]

This account certainly betrays Hiller's (and presumably Flato's) snobbish elitism, and, by extension, the general sensibility of the SHC. Since the late nineteenth century, the SHC had lobbied against the anti-sodomy statute by disseminating its sexological research and by attempting to shape the opinions of influential elites: politicians, bureaucrats, professionals, and cultural figures. The motto "Through science to justice" suggested a reliance on elite education and training and did not afford a role for the "common man." Certainly the SHC sponsored countless "popular" events and lectures before 1914, attempting to influence the views of large crowds in beer halls and theaters. But actual membership in the SHC remained an exclusive prerogative for primarily men of means, usually from commercial, professional, and cultural groups. What Flato's account signaled—filtered through Hiller's retelling—was the potential for a genuinely populist movement. Of course, this was predicated on the willingness of large numbers to risk discovery for the sake of a more open and likely more conventional existence. Although the SHC faced real competition for members and financial support, Hirschfeld and his colleagues ultimately embraced the growth of the Friendship Associations, both for what they reflected about Weimar republican culture and for how they might contribute to the struggle for legal reform.

The SHC's more surprising political collaboration in the early 1920s—though very short-lived—was with Adolf Brand and the Community of the Special. Brand's conflicts with Hirschfeld were legion and dated to the early twentieth century. Brand had always despised Hirschfeld's "scientific" analysis based on the study of "sexual intermediaries," and, by contrast, had emphasized "Graecophilic" male-male friendship, especially an idealized relationship between adult men and adolescent or young-adult males. The attention that Hirschfeld seemed to lavish on hermaphrodites, cross-dressers, and effeminate men offended Brand's conception of elite, virile masculinity. Brand also begrudged Hirschfeld the recognition he received as a sexologist and was especially embittered by what he considered Hirschfeld's betrayal during the Eulenburg scandal. Recall that after the sexologist refused in 1907 to attest that Bernhard von Bülow was homosexual, Brand was successfully sued for libel and received an eighteen-month jail term, which he forever blamed on Hirschfeld.

The history of this acrimony makes the rapprochement after 1918 that much more remarkable. At the SHC's general assembly in August 1920, Brand was elected an *Obmann*, a member of the SHC's governing board. At the same gathering Brand agreed that the CoS would make common cause with the SHC (and the Berlin Friendship Association), under the umbrella of the Action Committee, to promote legal reform. And in 1922 Brand participated in the twenty-fifth-anniversary celebrations of the SHC, held in the villa of the Institute for Sexual Science. A possible factor in Brand's new attitude—apart from the general optimism inspired by the founding of the republic—was a general improvement in his own fortunes. For one, he entered a lifelong romantic partnership with Max Miede, twenty-six years his junior, who seemed to help him fulfill and live out his own sexual identity and ideology. It appears that the young man joined Brand (along with Brand's wife and extended family) on the Wilhelmshagen estate just outside of Berlin at the end of or soon after the war.[12]

By November 1919 Brand had resumed editing *Der Eigene,* the first issue published since 1906. With the relaxation of censorship laws, he regularly printed photos of nearly nude boys, adolescents, and young men. In 1921 Brand introduced a special feature, the *Extrapost,* devoted to personal ads. Although censored and fined five thousand marks in 1922 (a relatively modest sum considering the course of the German inflation) for the crime of "solicitation"—the charge was not antihomosexual, since heterosexual publications were similarly censored for personal ads—Brand later resumed publication of the *Extrapost,* but without open distribution at kiosks and newsstands. Brand also published the tabloid *Freundschaft und Freiheit* (Friendship and freedom), modeled on *Die Freundschaft,* in eleven issues in 1921. Later he launched a more successful journal, *Eros,* which included personal ads and appeared from 1927 to 1931. The notices in *Eros* were posted by men from Sweden, Switzerland, Ireland, Russia, England, France, and the United States.[13]

Brand was also able to reinvigorate the CoS, for which he opened a dedicated *Klubhaus* in central Berlin with a calendar of events. Post-inflation (that is, post-1923) membership rates were set at thirty-six marks for basic and sixty marks for the exclusive membership. The less expensive option included a subscription to *Der Eigene* as well as copies of *Rasse und Schönheit* (Race and beauty), an occasional insert of male nudes, as well as free legal advice (concerning Paragraph 175 criminal charges or blackmail threats) and invitations to all social events. The elite membership included additionally the *Extrapost* and the right to place free ads. By 1925, Brand claimed to have established CoS branches, or "Roundtables," in Leipzig, Frankfurt, Breslau, Königsberg, Munich, Hamburg, Dresden, and Cologne.[14]

The ideology of male-male eroticism promoted by Brand and the CoS received a more explicit elaboration now than it had before the war. Here it is tempting to identify the influence of Hans Blüher and his theories. As before, the mutual love of two male friends was considered the most noble relationship. But now the basic bisexuality of all human beings—the Freudian conception likely filtered through Blüher—was more strongly emphasized. Without ambiguity, Brand also identified same-sex erotic love as an absolute good, equal to a merely spiritual relationship (or, for that matter, to heterosexual love), so long as it was part of a committed, loving partnership and did not devolve into mere "animal lust." Brand and the CoS also sanctioned the mentoring friendship—with or without an erotic element—of older and younger men or adolescents. Thus the maturing youth should seek his "highest pleasure, his moral strength, his physical release, and spiritual calm" with another male. Masturbation or self-love was unhealthy and dangerous, sex with female prostitutes risked disease, and premarital heterosexual intercourse was strongly discouraged.[15]

As expected, the CoS maintained its strong opposition to Paragraph 175, which, of course, explained Brand's sometime cooperation with Hirschfeld. Yet to some extent the CoS identified more closely with the right side of Weimar's political spectrum. Here again, it is easy to discern Blüher's influence. The state, it was felt, should not impinge on the private sphere of human sexuality, and this translated into support for a woman's right to abortion. Yet the larger objective in the decriminalization of same-sex love was the regeneration of German society and culture. To that end, the CoS represented an elite vanguard of superior German men who would lead this renewal. Implicit was a strong suspicion of Weimar democracy and Reichstag debate, as well as latent and often explicit anti-Semitism. Germany would benefit most not from the squabbling of democratic institutions but from the autocratic control of a great leader. Blüher's *Führer* principle seemed to provide a model for organizing both personal and public life.[16]

It is hardly surprising that such pronounced philosophical differences (with Hirschfeld and the SHC) would lead to a breach. In April 1923 Brand withdrew the CoS from participation in the Action Committee. He explained the decision by citing the need for national unity: the

French occupation of the Ruhr and the Great Inflation made agitation for legal reform horribly inappropriate.[17]

Brand's nationalism alone, however, could hardly explain his increasingly vulgar, anti-Semitic attacks on Hirschfeld. The critical factor here appears to have been the influence of several young CoS associates. One of these, Ewald Tscheck (1895–1956), a Berlin native, began publishing stories, poems, and essays in *Der Eigene* in 1920. Tscheck was heavily influenced, it appears, by the homoerotic anarchism of John Henry Mackay as well as the masculinist writings of Benedict Friedlaender, Blüher, and Brand himself. He also had a serious flirtation with the fledgling Nazi Party, and possibly joined the Sturmabteilung (SA) in 1924. His introduction to the National Socialists was through Dr. Karl-Günther Heimsoth (1899–1934), who became Ernst Röhm's lover in 1924. (Heimsoth was shot in July 1934 by the Schutzstaffel, the SS, a few days after the assassination of Röhm and some other eighty SA members in the so-called Night of the Long Knives.) Like Tscheck, Heimsoth was influenced by the masculinist wing of the homosexual rights movement, and was a combatant on the Western Front in the last years of the First World War, before beginning his medical studies.[18]

As young, anti-Semitic nationalists, Heimsoth and Tscheck represented the extreme right wing of Germany's homosexual rights activists. They also helped to inspire Brand's intemperate and erratic behavior. In 1925 the two young protofascists collaborated with Brand to publish a special issue of *Der Eigene* that viciously maligned Hirschfeld and the SHC. Titled "Tante Magnesia" (Aunt Magnesia)—a feminizing allusion to "Uncle Magnus" (Hirschfeld)—the special issue included crude and vulgar cartoon caricatures as well as scathing essays, impugning the science, rights activism, and intrinsic "German-ness" of Hirschfeld, the SHC, and its members. In one piece, Brand rehearsed the events of the Eulenburg scandal, ancient history no more, and blamed Hirschfeld for his imprisonment: "The eternal and enormous difference between sexuality and love . . . which was given expression by the two leaders of the movement [Brand and Hirschfeld] demonstrated clearly the elementary conflict between an Oriental and a Nordic sensibility."[19] In other words, Brand's emphasis on masculine friendship expressed his true "Nordic," or German, identity, in opposition to Hirschfeld's effeminate, medicalized "sexuality," which sprang from his "Oriental," or Jewish, nature. In a pamphlet authored by Tscheck—and published by Brand soon after this issue—Tscheck claimed that Hirschfeld, "as a Jew . . . was the most unsuitable leader in the affair of Eros."[20]

Brand's association with Heimsoth and Tscheck was over by the end of the year, however, and he never published material by either author again. Within a short time, moreover, he appears to have recommitted to the challenge of reforming the law. Although he eschewed any future cooperation with Hirschfeld or the SHC, his admiration for the *völkisch* right wing had clearly abated. Incredibly, by 1926 he was admonishing CoS members and the readers of his publications to vote for left-wing parties: "The advocates of Friend-Love should support with money and votes only those political parties that have had the courage to present our demands openly in the Reichstag. . . . No one among our supporters can doubt that it is alone the Social Democrats, the Communists, and the Democrats who have done this. Only they alone might have our votes in the future."[21]

How Brand made such a rapid about-face yet again is difficult to imagine, although his contemporaries were likely unsurprised. In a pithy character sketch, Kurt Hiller described Brand as a "dilettante" with a "shallow intellectual *Niveau*" and inadequate "knowledge." According to Hiller, "Brand exhibited anarchist and German-*völkisch* traits, as well as those of the ultra left and the ultra right, and this made cooperation with him within a movement that hoped to influence public opinion and contemporary legislation nothing but torment."[22] However erratic, naive, or stupid, Brand clearly knew something. He was either scared by the right or understood that parliamentary paths were the only hope for achieving legal reform.

If Brand's tormenting of Hirschfeld and the SHC was a common thread that linked the pre- and postwar periods, Friedrich Radszuweit (1876–1932) was the figure who transcended both men—and their organizations—and truly came to emblematize the flowering of homosexual culture and rights activism in the Weimar Republic. Although a near contemporary of Brand, Radszuweit was more typical of the younger generation that came up (and out) through the 1920s. Though his family background remains murky, Radszuweit was an entrepreneur and businessman and had established a Berlin sweatshop for women's ready-to-wear clothing along with a boutique by about 1901. Nowhere in the prewar period was his name connected with homosexual periodicals or organizations.[23]

Only in 1919 did Radszuweit appear on "the scene" as a fledgling "co-publisher" of *Die Freundschaft* and as chair of one of the Berlin Friendship Associations, the Union of Friends and Girlfriends. By 1922, many of the local Friendship Associations used the name Bund für Menschenrecht, or Human Rights League. Finally, on February 7, 1923, the executive board of the national German Friendship Association, whose governing members included Hans Kahnert (founder of the original Berlin Friendship Association) as well as Radszuweit, adopted the title Human Rights League (HRL). The decision was ratified by the delegates to the annual national convention in Leipzig a month later. With the official name change, the convention affirmed its commitment to the struggle for legal reform, within the framework of the Action Committee, envisioning a division of labor that would leave "artistic propaganda" to the CoS and political lobbying to the SHC. Radszuweit was elected chairman of the national HRL, and his new journal, *Blätter für Menschenrecht* (Paper for human rights), became the official national organ.[24]

This was an important achievement for Radszuweit, and as chairman of the national HRL and publisher of its official journal, he was now positioned to build and consolidate a veritable empire. In this role he integrated his growing publishing concern with rights activism—based on club membership—coupled with the sponsorship of social and cultural events. As soon as Radszuweit attained leadership of the HRL, he worked to distinguish the organization, describing the old Friendship Associations and *Die Freundschaft* as little more than purveyors of "dance-hall culture." If Hirschfeld had leveraged sexology for the cause of homosexual rights and created a seamless continuum from science to activism, Radszuweit now created a near identity between the Weimar "movement" and profit. For Radszuweit, the pursuit of "human rights" went hand in glove with commercial enterprise.[25]

Within Berlin, the HRL sponsored no fewer than five distinct organizations—several of which had been established as Friendship Associations—including the Christian society, a club or "lodge" modeled on the rituals of Freemasonry, the Theater of Eros, a small business association of tavern and shop owners, and a *Damengruppe,* or women's club. The phenomenal growth of the HRL helped to create a reliable national market: according to the statistics published in *Blätter,* there were nationally some 100,000 members organized in more than fifty local clubs by the end of 1924; this number dropped precipitously, but then climbed again to 65,000 by 1927.[26] In the absence of internal HRL records, the accuracy of these figures is impossible to determine. But certainly the ranks of the HRL exceeded almost exponentially those of the SHC or the CoS.

Radszuweit's entrepreneurial savvy was clear from the outset, and his business depended on his publishing interests. He urged members to ignore other periodicals and subscribe exclusively to *Blätter,* whose appeal and circulation he worked assiduously to increase.[27] Appearing fortnightly, the journal published fiction, poetry, and historical profiles of famous homosexuals. It also included an entertainment page with puzzles and word games. The journal quickly developed regular features and sections, including "Auf sapphistischen Pfaden" (On Sapphic paths) for lesbians and periodic reports on science and sexology. In 1924 Radszuweit added a literary supplement, "Die Insel der Einsamen" (Island of the lonely), which he eventually spun off as an independent magazine. That same year Radszuweit began publishing *Die Freundin* (The girlfriend), which targeted both lesbians and transvestites. The journal was surprisingly successful, publishing nude or semi-nude photography, romance stories, poetry, and personal ads (unlike *Blätter*), which were considered less vulnerable to censorship when "soliciting" lesbian as opposed to male homosexual or heterosexual contacts. Published monthly at first, *Die Freundin* began to appear weekly by 1927, and like *Blätter* it survived until March 1933. Radszuweit introduced yet another title, *Das Freundschaftsblatt,* in 1925, with which he hoped to compete directly with *Die Freundschaft.* The new journal was glossier than *Blätter* with lighter fare and higher production values. It appeared monthly and likewise survived until March 1933.

Radszuweit's publications were widely circulated and therefore enormously lucrative. Purveyed from public newsstands and kiosks— alongside the titles with which he competed—they were highly visible and easily available. Even Franz Biberkopf, the hapless protagonist in Alfred Döblin's expressionist 1929 novel, *Berlin Alexanderplatz,* peddled lesbian and homosexual journals while unemployed.[28] Radszuweit reported selling more than fifty thousand copies of single issues of *Blätter* and *Freundschaftsblatt,* though circulation figures are impossible to determine with any certainty. Of course, Radszuweit's newsstand profits were augmented greatly by advertising revenue. Beginning with the first issue of *Die Freundschaft* in 1919, the homosexual press was supported by dozens of bars, clubs, and dance venues, which placed copious advertisements in every issue. Soon small businesses and professionals announced their services as well, including doctors, dentists, lawyers, private detectives, stationers, haberdashers, barbers, and interior designers.

Like any conquering imperialist, Radszuweit left victims in his wake. Initially a casualty himself, Radszuweit was forced from the editorial board of *Die Freundschaft* in 1922. He outmaneuvered his rivals, however, with the renaming—and effective rebranding—of the Friendship Association as the Human Rights League; this represented a veritable coup and gave him his greatest opportunity. Winning the chairmanship of the national HRL allowed him to establish *Blätter für Menschenrecht* as the official organ, displacing *Die Freundschaft,* which had served as the unofficial journal of the old Friendship Associations. One of the losers in this shake-up was Max Danielsen (1885–after 1928), a governing director of the SHC, who coedited *Die Freundschaft* and also held a position on the board of the old German Friendship Association. Once Radszuweit gained control, Danielsen was forced to move on. In 1924 he attempted to reestablish the German Friendship Association and its local affiliates—together with others who resented Radszuweit's growing imperium—as a counterweight to the HRL. The effort failed, and Danielsen founded a new homosexual journal, *Die Fanfare,* with his colleague Curt Neuburger. This title survived only two years, and in 1928 Danielsen founded *Neue Freundschaft,* which was promptly censored and banned, due to a denunciation made by Radszuweit.[29]

In a not dissimilar fashion, Radszuweit effectively "colonized" Berlin's homosexual theater. Begun as an informal reading group in 1919, the Theater of Eros first rehearsed in a workroom at Hirschfeld's institute. This was a short-lived solution, and the fledgling troupe was forced to move periodically thereafter. Not until July 1921 was the company finally able to produce its first play, a stage adaption of the "Uranian" novel *Die Infamen* (The infamous), published by Fritz Geron Pernauhm in 1906. Performances in the Stadttheater in the north Berlin working-class district of Moabit were consistently sold out and became notorious for the passionate kissing of the two male protagonists. The journal *Die Freundschaft* provided both publicity and positive reviews.

In 1923 difficult finances forced the Theater of Eros to seek additional support. By this point the troupe had already produced seventeen different homosexual-themed stage plays in at least seven venues. By folding the company into the HRL, Radszuweit rescued the troupe and also provided the publicity and support of his burgeoning media empire. After he attempted to exercise artistic control, however, the actors broke away and struck out on their own. While Radszuweit appropriated the name and founded his own Theater of Eros, the original organization was too impecunious to continue its work.[30]

Radszuweit also managed to monopolize the legal reform advocacy of the Action Committee. Although the CoS under Brand's direction had exited the "coalition" voluntarily in 1923, the SHC bristled at Radszuweit's domination and felt compelled to leave in 1925, marking the end of any collaborative work among the three organizations. Radszuweit followed the tactics of the SHC in his campaign for legal reform, appealing to elected officials and working to inform the public.

Radszuweit disliked the sexual "ideologies" of both Brand and Hirschfeld, and elaborated an ideological position in the "homosexuality debate" that positioned the HRL somewhere between the two. Like Hirschfeld, the HRL stressed the innate biological nature of homosexuality, as well as its manifestation across time and space, and among all social classes, representing the entire political spectrum from left to right. But by depicting homosexuals as law abiding, and fundamentally middle class, this seemingly ecumenical inclusion ultimately excluded a great many. Radszuweit rejected all stereotypes that depicted homosexuals as disruptive, subcultural, criminal, or effeminate. Prostitutes and their johns, as well as cross-dressers and effeminates, had no place in Radszuweit's vision of homosexual bourgeois respectability. In this connection, Hirschfeld's theory of sexual intermediacy was the subject of particular censure.[31]

But Radszuweit directed his most vehement criticism at Brand and the CoS. Articles published in *Blätter* attacked claims that age-differentiated same-sex relationships were ever appropriate. The notion of "pederasty," as Brand theorized, was based on a naive understanding of adult male sexuality and invited the sexual and emotional abuse of boys and adolescents. Radszuweit was particularly opposed to the claim that human beings shared a fundamental bisexuality, which undermined not only the experience and identity of most homosexuals but also the moral and pragmatic arguments for legal reform. Fundamentally, he thought, homosexual desire was an innate condition that posed no moral or social threat to German society. At the same time, the demand for homosexual emancipation required an explicit commitment to the protection of underage males (and females).[32]

What is revealed in Radszuweit's condemnation of Brand—and his less aggressive criticisms of Hirschfeld—is a belief that homosexuality needed to be presented in the most acceptable light, tamed or domesticated, to find acceptance among a heterosexual majority. This did not signal retreat from the struggle against slander or discrimination. But it did reflect Radszuweit's regard for bourgeois respectability, an attitude conditioned, no doubt, by his own background as a businessman. This is illustrated well by one of the more memorable campaigns of the HRL, namely the public protest of a theater production in the Berlin Komische Oper in July 1927. The theater piece, *Streng Verboten* (Strictly forbidden), included a scene set in the HRL clubhouse Klub der Freunde, which caricatured gay men as swishy and effeminate. In response, a group of HRL members attended and disrupted the performance with jeering. The slander of depicting middle-class homosexuals as less than masculine merited a forceful response, in Radszuweit's estimation, even if it created a public disruption. The protest was savvy indeed. The "Demonstration of Homosexuals" received positive reports in Berlin's liberal press, and the offensive depictions of homosexual men were removed from subsequent performances.[33]

.   .   .

While the three organizations—Hirschfeld's SHC, Brand's CoS, and Rad-szuweit's HRL—remained mutually hostile after 1925, issuing insult and accusation, each continued to pursue legal reform. The HRL remained the most active, compiling petitions and appealing to the Ministry of Justice. At one point Radszuweit even appears to have considered run-ning for federal office. In the pages of *Freundschaftsblatt* in 1926 Radszu-weit proposed a Berlin-based "pan-homosexual" rights party, intended to include nationalists, libertarians, socialists, and communists, as well as lesbians and transvestites. The project was never realized—no par-liamentary candidates were fielded—but it suggested the possibility of creating a cohesive movement among these widely divergent political factions based on the common interest of political reform.[34]

What Radszuweit understood better—or at least considered more astutely—than the others was the tremendous political diversity of the larger homosexual community. In 1926 he conducted an opinion poll among 50,000 members of the national HRL: the results of his analysis, based on some 38,000 responses, were published in January 1927. More than 31,000 respondents claimed to have some formal political affilia-tion. Among these, 16,000 belonged to the Socialist and Communist Parties. Roughly 3,000 belonged to the Catholic Center Party, and the rest—some 12,000—were members of the *völkisch* right wing (meaning both ultranationalist and anti-Semitic); the parties represented in this category included the German Nationalist Party, the German People's Party, and the Nazi Party. What this somewhat sobering statistic indi-cated was that fully 30 percent of the respondents with party affilia-tions were extreme-right nationalists.[35] Although Radszuweit joined and remained a member of the SPD—never expressing the kind of anti-Semitic rhetoric that Brand periodically discharged—he was also pragmatic enough to build a mass organization that attracted members representing proportionately the entire political spectrum.[36]

This strikingly large minority of self-identified right-wing homosexu-als reveals how the First World War helped to catalyze strains of mas-culinist ideology. Some of the demoralized German troops that formed the Freikorps after returning from the front at the end of 1918 also joined the Friendship Associations and then the HRL, able finally to explore the homosocial friendship and same-sex eroticism they had discovered in the trenches. While the new liberal climate of the Weimar Republic permitted a more open homosexual culture, the psychological and socio-logical speculations of Benedict Friedlaender, Adolf Brand, and *especially* Hans Blüher helped these men to make sense of their feelings.

The tragic irony was that so many self-aware homosexuals were affil-iated with political groups that fundamentally rejected them and their cause. The official party responses elicited by Adolf Brand in 1928 on the question of legal reform are especially revealing. The German Com-munist Party was the most steadfast in its support of legal reform, due largely to the fact that the Russian communists had eliminated all anti-homosexual laws and refused to reintroduce them into the first Soviet legal codes. In 1928, KPD leaders responded to Brand as follows: "The Communist Party has taken every appropriate opportunity to stand up for the abolition of Paragraph 175. We remind you only of the most recent discussion on the laws to prevent venereal disease, as well as the committee discussion concerning the reform of criminal law. It goes without saying that we will continue to lead the fiercest battle for the elimination of this paragraph in the future."[37]

This support, however, was often ambivalent. On the one hand, Paragraph 175 represented the suppression of sexual freedom, based on religious teachings. At the same time, orthodox Marxism had always viewed homosexuality as a symptom of bourgeois decadence. In the end, the KPD consistently supported the repeal of Paragraph 175, but rarely discussed the issue of homosexuality. For example, in 1924 party rep-resentatives in the Reichstag proposed the decriminalization of homo-sexual practices for individuals over the age of fourteen. The Reichstag was dissolved soon after this, however, and the proposal never came to a vote; the KPD never raised the issue again.[38]

The bourgeois, left-liberal German Democratic Party also supported the repeal of Paragraph 175 in order to protect individual rights. In response to Brand's solicitation, party leaders wrote, "As can be expected, we are in agreement with the repeal of 175. Even though no decision on this issue has been submitted because our faction in the Reichstag has not yet had the opportunity to take up this question, it is correct to pre-sume that our party representatives will be sufficiently aware to know that it is wrong to suppress a small minority with legal punishments as long as they are not engaging in dangerous behavior."[39]

The National Socialists returned the longest response to Brand's query. They opposed any changes to Paragraph 175, since homosexuality, they argued, diminished the virility of German culture and led to national emasculation. Assuming that any man would indulge homosexual impulses, the Nazis supported the law to enforce the nationalist responsibility to procreate.

> Suprema lex salus populi! Public good before self interest! It is not necessary that you and I live, but it is necessary that the German people endure. And the *Volk* can only do so if it is willing to fight. Thus living means fighting. And it can only fight if it includes people capable of marriage. It can only support these people if it practices discipline, and above all sexual discipline. Free love and licentiousness are obscene. For that reason, we reject this [legal reform], as we reject everything damaging to our people.[40]

The rhetoric of Aryan pro-natalism became the consistent touchstone of Nazi sexual ideology. And it motivated the introduction of a more draconian anti-sodomy law in 1935 after the National Socialists came to power. Yet the many homosexual men who embraced the Nazi cause misapprehended the centrality of Nazi racialist doctrine and how homosexuality appeared to threaten it. Viewing Nazis as the literal embodiment of the homoerotic Männerbund, many were blinded by the homoeroticism of the masculinist ideologues.

Brand did not overlook the Nazi threat, though his political myopia was truly remarkable, and, as Hiller observed, he caused continual torment. In 1928 he began a campaign to discredit Hirschfeld and Radszuweit by sending denunciatory letters to state officials. His opening salvo was a letter addressed to Justice Minister Erich Koch-Weser claiming that neither Radszuweit nor Hirschfeld was morally fit to lead the homosexual rights movement. Radszuweit, according to Brand, was an opportunistic viper who exploited the movement to line his own pockets, while Hirschfeld was a dissolute pervert whose theories undermined German masculinity. With his missive Brand also included copies of two of his publications, *Der Eigene* and *Eros,* both replete with pictures of semi-nude boys, male adolescents, and young adult men. In May 1929 Brand sent another package—with magazines, articles, and CoS literature—to Prussian interior minister Albert Grzesinski. This mailing included a pamphlet outlining the principles of CoS philosophy, including the virtues of age-differentiated love relationships between adult men and male adolescents.[41]

The collapse of the last Weimar coalition at the end of 1929—just months after Kahl cast his committee vote for legal reform—marked the end of a functioning government. The worsening economic depression unleashed by the American stock market crash in October ultimately sealed the fate of the republic. By spring 1930, the new Reichstag election signaled the electoral rise of the Nazis and a bloc of *völkisch* parties led by the German National People's Party. It was not only the prospects for legal reform that had worsened. The economic collapse undermined the ability of the homosexual rights groups to maintain their operations, since their members were no longer able to support them.

Among the three organizations, the CoS had the smallest membership, and Brand himself had only modest resources. By the beginning of 1931 *Der Eigene* had ceased publication. The supplement with personal ads, *Extrapost,* survived for only a few months after that. Brand's more popular periodical, *Eros,* appeared through the end of 1932. But after this the CoS no longer had a literary vehicle. The deepening depression and consequent unemployment made it impossible for many to pay dues or purchase newsstand periodicals. Also significant was the distraction of the tense political situation, including pitched battles between left- and right-wing paramilitary groups in the streets of Berlin.

Since the CoS had often spouted racist, misogynist, and anti-Semitic rhetoric, some of its members were inclined, unsurprisingly, to support the Nazi movement, which appeared to many to be precisely the long-awaited masculinist renewal led by a charismatic *Führer*. Brand complained bitterly of these defections. "Events of last year have thinned the ranks dramatically," he wrote. "The former CoS members have now given their trust and support to the very person who marches at the apex of reaction, and whose own publication has publicly declared that if the [Nazi] Party comes to power, all homosexuals will be strung up from the gallows."[42] Brand appears to have been completely unaware of his own complicity in this development.

Although Brand was forced to halt his publishing before the Nazis even came to power, in January 1933, he did not escape harassment. On five occasions between March and September, Nazis stormed Brand's publishing house in Wilhelmshagen, confiscating photographs, books, journals, and CoS records. He ultimately escaped arrest, however, since he was married and neither Jewish nor a leftist.[43] He nearly survived the war, moreover, perishing only in April 1945 in an Allied bombing raid.

The HRL also suffered membership and revenue losses, and by 1931 published both *Blätter* and *Freundschaftsblatt* less frequently (once every two months) and in smaller editions. Ever the businessman, Radszuweit prepared to make accommodations with the Nazis, and he allegedly wrote Hitler in 1931 requesting protection for right-wing homosexuals. Radszuweit hoped unrealistically that the political profile of his lover, Martin Butzko-Radszuweit, whom he adopted as a son, might help to shield him and the HRL from right-wing persecution. In the 1920s Butzko had been an active member of the Hitler Youth, and he first made Radszuweit's acquaintance when the older man helped extricate Butzko from a brawl with members of a communist youth organization.

Ultimately Radszuweit escaped harassment or worse, but only by succumbing to a heart attack in April 1932. Although Butzko-Radszuweit, who inherited the estate, continued publishing the journals, together with Radszuweit's younger brother, the HRL was all but defunct within months of Radszuweit's death. In February 1933 SA thugs raided and destroyed most of the publishing house, just after publication of the final February/March double issue of *Blätter*.[44]

Although Radszuweit was a savvy opportunist, Hirschfeld—among the three homosexual activists—was the most discerning in his assessment of the Nazis. Subjected as he had been not only to anti-Semitic slander but also to physical violence, Hirschfeld had long perceived the target on his own back. In 1930 he resigned as director of the SHC and embarked on a world tour, never to return to Germany. Though able to escape, Hirschfeld lost a lifetime of labor when Nazis plundered and destroyed his beloved institute in May 1933. He died in France on his sixty-seventh birthday on May 14, 1935.

Epilogue

In many respects, Berlin's queer culture is the city's most essential and distinguishing element—the coagulant and the zest. It was thus in the twenties and in pre-1989 West Berlin, and remains so today.

—NICK PAUMGARTEN, *The New Yorker,* March 24, 2014

On the morning of May 6, 1933, at roughly 9:30 a.m., more than one hundred students, transported in vans, appeared before the Institute for Sexual Science. They were accompanied by a brass band, which serenaded them during the operation. According to eyewitness reports, the institute was empty except for a few staff members. After storming the entrance, the students broke down doors to gain access throughout the building. Systematically, they looted the library, with its twenty thousand volumes, gathering up the works of those authors who had been placed on the Nazis' "black list": Sigmund Freud, Havelock Ellis, Oscar Wilde, Edward Carpenter, Richard von Krafft-Ebing, and, of course, Magnus Hirschfeld. These volumes were carried back to the vans. They also destroyed the display cases and poster boards of the museum, along with portraits hanging on the walls. The institute's collection of some 35,000 photographs, along with works of art, were either strewn on the floor or carted away. At noon the vandals assembled in front of the institute. By this point, the brass band, which continued to perform, had attracted a small crowd, puzzled by the music and the sounds of breaking glass. The leader of the group now made a speech, which was followed by the singing of the "Horst Wessel Song." Carrying a bust of Hirschfeld, the students climbed back in their vans and sped away with their plunder. Later in the afternoon, a second wave appeared, this time members of the SA in uniform. Surveying the destruction and chaos, they gathered up medical files and questionnaires. Three days later, the institute's books and other materials provided some of the fuel for the infamous book burning at the Opernplatz along Unter den Linden.[1]

The physical obliteration of the institute, representing Magnus Hirschfeld's lifework, was devastating, though not surprising. The real shock was how quickly the Nazis struck, a little more than three months after Hitler's appointment as chancellor on January 30. The institute's employees and affiliates were indeed taken off guard, and had not yet secured the most valuable and sensitive materials. Remarkable about this episode, however, was the fact that there was no loss of human life. Although the Nazis had inquired about Hirschfeld's whereabouts, they certainly knew he had already left the country. Many of the institute's staff and affiliates, especially the medical professionals, were Jewish, and some had begun preparations to leave Germany. Among those institute employees who remained behind were several Nazis, who were suspected of spying. A tenant, Helene Helling, had come to the institute in 1930 and then worked as a receptionist. As a Nazi sympathizer she was allowed to remain in the building until 1934, when it was appropriated by the Nazi Party. Another Nazi, Arthur Röser, worked as a maintenance administrator from 1926 until the institute's destruction. Two others, Friedrich Hauptstein and Ewald Lausch, had been lab and doctor's assistants since the mid-1920s. After the raid, both reportedly pledged allegiance to the ideals of the Nazi Party, though it is not clear just how opportunistic they in fact were.[2]

Hirschfeld had embarked on a world tour in November 1930, seemingly able to anticipate the Nazis' rise to power. Traveling to North America, Asia, and the Middle East, he delivered more than 170 lectures. He was feted in New York as the "Einstein of Sex," and he drew crowds everywhere he stopped.[3] Just at the point when he began to receive international accolades, his legacy in Germany—his very life, if he had remained—was being threatened. The trip was a great success, and not only due to the timing.[4] Hirschfeld was back in Europe when the institute was destroyed, but he never returned to Germany. A few days after the destruction, he watched the episode on a newsreel in a Parisian cinema.[5] Until his death in 1935, Hirschfeld lived in France, where he attempted to rebuild his institute from scratch.

There are manifold reasons for why the Nazis pursued Hirschfeld and his colleagues with such fury. Recall that Hirschfeld had been targeted by anti-Semites since soon after the end of the First World War. Throughout the Weimar period he remained a powerful symbol of all that the Nazis detested, as Jew, homosexual, and sexologist. But there were other reasons as well for the Nazis' precipitous attack. The gynecologist Ludwig Levy-Lenz asked precisely this question: "Why was it then . . . that our purely scientific Institute was the first victim which fell to the new regime?" The answer, he claimed, was that "we knew too much." As Levy-Lenz explained, "Our knowledge of such intimate secrets regarding members of the Nazi Party and our other documentary material . . . was the cause of the complete and utter destruction of the Institute for Sexology."[6] There were homosexuals within the Nazi movement, of course, and Lenz's claim is not improbable; unfortunately, he refused to name names. What we can surmise is that the political pluralism of the Weimar homosexual rights movement included a large minority of nationalist and even *völkisch* men and women. Recall the results of Friedrich Radszuweit's 1926 poll to determine the political views of homosexuals: some 30 percent of those questioned identified themselves as right-wing. Certainly Adolf Brand had his own flirtation with *völkisch* nationalists in the 1920s, and his attacks on Hirschfeld were blatantly anti-Semitic. Consider too that the popular Männerbund ideology of the Weimar period helped to assimilate homoeroticism to a nationalist, anti-democratic politics.

Perhaps the best example—or best known, in any case—was Ernst Röhm, a decorated veteran of the war, a member of the Freikorps, and an *alte Kämpfer* ("old fighter") from the Munich beer-hall days of the early Nazi Party.[7] Moreover, Röhm was Hitler's closest friend among the Nazi elite, and the only one with whom he used the informal German address (*du* as opposed to *Sie*). In 1930 Röhm, at Hitler's behest, became leader of the SA, the party's brownshirted militia. In the summer of 1931, however, Röhm was forced to defend himself in two highly publicized trials held in Munich. He had been caught with male prostitutes and was accused of violating the anti-sodomy statute. Through the course of the trials the prosecution managed to produce some of Röhm's private letters and correspondence. The trials also established that Röhm had actually joined the largest of the three homosexual rights organizations, the Human Rights League, in the 1920s. Despite Röhm's scandals, Hitler refused to sack him, and claimed blithely that Röhm's personal life was a private affair.

Of course, the SA provided boots on the ground for the Nazi movement, and after Hitler came to power, they were largely responsible for shoring up Nazi control, at least in the first eighteen months of the regime's rule. The fact that a high-ranking Nazi—at this point Röhm was arguably the second most powerful man in the Third Reich—was openly homosexual did not shield the institute. Nor did it prevent the repression of the homosexual rights movement. The Nazis' "Campaign for a Clean Reich," inaugurated in February 1933, shut down Berlin's homosexual press and closed some fifteen of the most prominent bars. The last publications appeared in March. By summer, the three homosexual rights organizations, including the SHC, had destroyed their membership lists and begun the process of disbanding.[8] Yet these actions were less a singling out of homosexuals than an extension of the more general "coordination," or Gleichschaltung, of German civil society. Most non-Nazi groups during the first months (or in some cases years) of Nazi rule, including those on the right, experienced similar repression or were forced to merge with Nazi organizations. Despite the Gleichschaltung, the vast majority of the estimated eighty to one hundred gay and lesbian bars and clubs in Berlin remained open well into 1935. At this stage the Nazis targeted homosexual men and women only if they were Jewish or leftists.

The fate of Röhm changed all of this, though not because his presence somehow shielded homosexuals, but rather because his murder allowed Heinrich Himmler—Röhm's arch-nemesis among the Nazi elite—free reign to implement a more systematic repression. Röhm's career (and life) came to an abrupt end on July 2, 1934, in the purge of the SA leadership known as the Night of the Long Knives. It was widely rumored that Röhm and many of his associates were discovered in bed with young boys or with each other. The number of those killed is fairly murky, but estimates now hover around eighty-five. Most of the known victims were SA leaders or close Röhm associates. Some had no ties at all to the SA, however, and were simply targeted opportunistically. In a radio address delivered on July 2, Joseph Goebbels, the Nazi minister of propaganda, explained that Hitler had preempted a putsch attempt planned by Röhm and his henchmen. This was a fiction. The real reason was Hitler's need to appease the military, which feared Röhm and his militia. Once Röhm was gone, Hitler was finally able to command the loyalty of the German military and complete the consolidation of his power. Of course, subsequent Nazi propaganda also emphasized Röhm's homosexuality—in addition to his alleged perfidy—and the Nazis' commitment to traditional morality.[9]

Röhm's elimination cleared the way for a more systematic persecution of homosexuals. This campaign was led by Himmler, head of the SS and the ideologue of Nazi homophobia. In 1935 Himmler championed a new, draconian anti-sodomy statute, which criminalized all erotic contact between men. One year later Himmler established the Reich Office to Combat Homosexuality and Abortion. Nazi officials now had the tools to arrest and imprison large numbers of homosexual men on the flimsiest of evidence. This policing reflected Nazi views that male homosexuality was a contagious perversion and that homosexual conduct, like disease, might be cured. The persecution that followed had two major objectives. Nazi officials hoped to curb and redirect the majority of those who had fallen into homosexual "vice" with a variety of treatments, and, if necessary, incarceration. Of these, a small minority of "incorrigibles"—those with "hereditary" conditions who were deemed responsible for "seducing" others— would be exterminated to stop the spread of "infection." During the Third Reich more than 100,000 German men were charged under Paragraph 175, and of these an estimated 5,000 to 15,000 perished in prisons and camps.[10] As Dagmar Herzog has argued, "Many Nazi 'experts' advanced a social constructionist view of sexuality that sexual identity was variable and vulnerable."[11] This was in part an anti-Semitic rebuke of the theories of the "Jewish" Hirschfeld and "his" SHC, but it also persisted long after 1945.

Led by the conservative Christian Democratic Party, the Federal

Republic of West Germany preserved the more draconian Nazi version of Paragraph 175 for a period of twenty years. A reform of West Germany's criminal code with respect to sexual matters, including Paragraph 175, was begun in 1954. The draft that was finally produced in 1962 mimicked the language of early-nineteenth-century medical forensics, and that of the Nazis. According to Herzog the document claimed that homosexual men affected by the law did not suffer an "inborn disposition" and were "overwhelmingly persons who . . . through seduction, habituation, or sexual supersatiation have become addicted to vice or who have turned to same-sex intercourse for purely profit-seeking motive." As such, homosexuality was a remediable and contagious condition, not a fixed sexual orientation, and it threatened "the degeneration of the people and the deterioration of its moral strength."[12] These retrograde generalizations about same-sex eroticism were countered vociferously by progressive West German sexologists and other intellectuals, and the New Left activism of the 1960s effected not only political change but also significant legal reform.[13] In 1969 the Federal Republic decriminalized sexual relations between men over twenty-one. Under pressure from the modern German gay liberation movement, which organized after the New York Stonewall riots of June 1969, the law was reformed again in 1973, when the general age of consent for male same-sex relations was lowered to eighteen.[14]

The German Democratic Republic (East Germany) also criminalized male homosexuality, but stopped prosecuting men over the age of eighteen for same-sex relations after 1957. With the creation of a new East German criminal code in 1968, Paragraph 175 was eliminated entirely. In 1987 East Germany's supreme court ruled that "[h]omosexual persons do not stand outside of socialist society, and are guaranteed the same civil rights as all other citizens." As a consequence of this ruling, a new East German law promulgated in May 1989 established sixteen as the age of consent for both homosexual and heterosexual couples. In 1994, four years after reunification, Paragraph 175 was finally stricken completely from the criminal code of unified Germany, and the legal age of consent was set at fourteen.[15] This equalized age restrictions of homosexual and heterosexual couples, affording a qualified equality under the law and achieving—finally—a primary objective of Karl Heinrich Ulrichs and Magnus Hirschfeld from a century earlier.

Germans are still in the process of recovering their own history. This task is complicated tremendously by the catastrophic destruction of the Nazi era, which abolished institutions, disrupted and scattered networks of friends and activists, and eliminated countless sources. Even those who remained and survived dictatorship and war were compelled to destroy everything—letters, journals, photo albums—that might incriminate them as homosexual. The supreme irony, perhaps, is that the gay pride parades held every summer since the 1970s in Berlin and other major German cities are referred to colloquially as CSD, or "Christopher Street Day," an allusion to the 1969 riots at the Stonewall Inn, the putative birthplace of the "modern homosexual rights movement."

Acknowledgments

This book was conceived years ago, and finished only with the help of many friends and colleagues. I am especially grateful for the intellectual and moral support of Dagmar Herzog, Jonathan Fine, and Richard Wetzell, as well as the great enthusiasm of Gerry Gross and Jill Kneerim. Sarah Watts read and commented on the completed manuscript, and helped me to improve clarity and eliminate infelicities. George Baca was also a valuable critic of my writing and argument. My dissertation advisors, Michael Geyer and John Boyer, are still offering advice (and writing letters)—and have my heartfelt thanks for decades of mentoring. I have also had the support of many Baltimore friends and colleagues, including Uta Larkey, Nelly Lahoud, Ed Larkey, and Peter Jelavich, as well as my cousin John Gingerich. My former student Chelsea Schields read Dutch-language sources for me, and has been an important intellectual interlocutor since I first began studying the history of sexuality. I have also drawn great inspiration from my colleagues in the Goucher College history department—especially Julie Jeffrey and Jean Baker—as well as the many talented students who signed up over the years for my history of sexuality seminars.

In Berlin I benefitted from the scholarship and advice of several historians who have done ground-breaking research on the history of sexuality. These pioneers include Rainer Herrn, Ralf Dose, Günter Grau, and Claudia Schoppmann. At Berlin's Schwules Museum, I relied initially on the expertise of Karl-Heinz Steinle, and, after his departure, that of Jens Dobler. I also had the good luck of meeting Martin Lücke as he was completing and publishing his dissertation on a related subject. Other Berlin friends who have provided tremendous encouragement—and often a place to stay—are Carol Scherer, Dirk Müller, Dirk Ilius, and Christian-Peter Schultz. Nate Halsan spent many hours tracking down book, journal, and newspaper articles for me in the Berlin Staatsbibliothek.

I'm also grateful for residential scholarships at the National Humanities Center and the Center for the Advanced Study in the Behavioral Sciences (CASBS) at Stanford. During these fellowship years, I gained tremendously from the stimulation (and distraction) of the other fellows. In North Carolina it was especially Rachel Weil, Jim Sweet, Sheryl Kroen, and Christopher Browning who kept me both inspired and amused. At CASBS, I enjoyed many rewarding conversations with Rhacel Parreñas, Nancy Whittier, Robert Proctor, Sam Perry, Ted Porter, Allen Isaacman, Enrique Rodrigues-Alegria, and Liz Borgwardt. Lochlann Jain, who was a fellow at CASBS and my neighbor in the Castro, became a great pal, both at Stanford and in the city. Gayle Rubin and Gerard Koskovich were in San Francisco when I lived there, and offered valuable advice as well as help with sources. I exploited fully the generosity of my brother Phil and sister-in-law Kati Andreasson, who allowed me to live with them for several months in Stanford.

My numerous trips to Berlin were funded in part with a John S. Guggenheim Memorial Foundation fellowship, as well as summer research grants from the American Philosophical Society, the German Academic Exchange Service, and Goucher College. A Christopher Isherwood Foundation fellowship from the Huntington Library allowed me to spend two months in Pasadena reading Isherwood's papers and correspondence. I also benefitted from a Phil Zwickler Memorial Research Grant that allowed me to explore the holdings of the Human Sexuality Collection of the Cornell University Library.

Notes

A list of abbreviations used in the notes can be found on page 275.

Introduction

1. New York Public Library, Berg Collection, W. H. Auden, "Berlin Journal," fol. 2r.
2. Carpenter, *W. H. Auden*, quoted from p. 90.
3. Isherwood, *Christopher and His Kind*, p. 16.
4. Zimmermann, *Die Diebe in Berlin oder Darstellung ihres Entstehens, ihrer Organisation, ihrer Verbindungen, ihres Taktik, ihrer Gewohnheiten und ihrer Sprache* (Berlin, 1847; reprint, 1987), p. 163; see also Herzer, *Die Geschichte des § 175* (1990), pp. 30–41.
5. Moll, *Die conträre Sexualempfindung* (Berlin, 1899) 3rd ed., p. 526.
6. Hirschfeld, *Homosexualität des Mannes und des Weibes*, p. 698.
7. Some of the best evidence comes from homoerotic literature of the period. See Stefan Müller. *Ach, nur 'n bisschen Liebe: Männliche Homosexualität in den Romanen deutschsprachiger Autoren in der Zwischenkriegszeit 1919 bis 1939* (Würzburg, 2011), pp. 42–43, 503–04.
8. Herzer, *Magnus Hirschfeld*, p. 14.
9. New York Public Library, "Berlin Journal," fol. 8r.
10. See Kertbeny, *§143 des preussischen Strafgesetzbuches* and *Das Gemeinschädliche des §143*. Kertbeny's identity as the author of these pamphlets was suspected earlier but only confirmed in 1905. See Manfred Herzer biographical introduction in Karl Maria Kertbeny, *Schriften zur Homosexualitätsforschung* (Berlin, 2000), pp. 7–61.
11. Ostwald, *Rinnsteinsprache*, p. 142.
12. Greenberg, *The Construction of Homosexuality;* Crompton, *Homosexuality and Civilization;* or the essays in Herdt, ed., *Third Sex, Third Gender.*
13. Rocke, *Forbidden Friendships.*
14. Berco, *Sexual Hierarchies, Public Status;* Puff, *Sodomy in Reformation Germany and Switzerland 1400–1600.*
15. See Bray, *Homosexuality in Renaissance England*, pp. 16–17, 88–93; Norton, *Mother Clap's Molly House;* Trumbach, "Modern Sodomy," pp. 77–106, and *Sex and the Gender Revolution*, pp. 3–8, 53–59.
16. Van der Meer, "The Persecutions of Sodomites in Eighteenth-Century Amsterdam," pp. 263–310, 286; and L. J. Boon, "Those Damned Sodomites," pp. 237–48.
17. Rey, "Parisian Homosexuals Create a Lifestyle, 1700–1750" and "Police and Sodomy in Eighteenth-Century Paris"; and the essays in Merrick and Ragan, eds., *Homosexuality in Early Modern France.*
18. Valerie Traub has argued that early modern same-sex love between women did not produce a modern lesbian identity but "demonstrate[s] the conditions of emergence *for* such an identity." Perhaps a similar argument might be made for the "mollies" of Enlightenment London. Quoted from Traub, "The Psychomorphology of the Clitoris," p. 85.
19. Foucault, *The History of Sexuality*, vol. 1: *An Introduction*, p. 43. The literature on this

question is voluminous, and I cite sparingly. For the emphatically "constructivist" position on the "medicalization" of homosexuality see Arnold Davidson, "Sex and the Emergence of Sexuality" and "How to Do the History of Psychoanalysis: A Reading of Freud's *Three Essays on the Theory of Sexuality*," *Critical Inquiry* 14 (1987): 252–77. See also the essays in Jan Goldstein, ed., *Foucault and the Writing of History* (Oxford, 1994). David Halperin offers a nuanced reading of Foucault's claim. See "Forgetting Foucault."

20. Rydström, *Sinners and Citizens*, pp. 43–54, 320–21.

21. Healey, *Homosexual Desire in Revolutionary Russia*.

22. See Revenin, *Homosexualité et prostitution masculines à Paris 1870–1918;* Peniston, *Pederasts and Others;* Chauncey, *Gay New York;* Cook, *London and the Culture of Homosexuality, 1885–1914;* Cocks, *Nameless Offences;* and also Abraham, *Metropolitan Lovers.*

23. On the history of Paragraph 175 see Weber, *Der Trieb zum Erzählen;* Mildenberger, *". . . in der Richtung der Homosexualität verdorben": Psychiater, Kriminalpsychologen und Gerichtsmediziner über männliche Homosexualität 1850–1970;* Sommer, *Die Strafbarkeit der Homosexualität von der Kaiserzeit bis zum Nationalsozialismus;* Frank, *Die Strafbarkeit homosexueller Handlungen;* Hutter, *Die gesellschaftliche Kontrolle des homosexuellen Begehrens;* Sievert, *Das Anomale Bestrafen;* and Gollner, *Homosexualität.*

24. *Meyers Großes Konversations-Lexikon*, 16 vols. (Leipzig, 1908), vol. 9, p. 526.

25. *Brockhaus Konversations-Lexikon*, 17 vols. (Leipzig, 1908), vol. 9, p. 315; vol. 10, p. 599; vol. 16, p. 127. Carl Westphal had coined the more cumbersome *conträre Sexualempfindung* (often translated as "sexual inversion") in an 1869 case study, which defined the "pathological reversal" of same-gender sexual attraction. See Westphal, "Die conträre Sexualempfindung."

26. Scott Spector, "The Wrath of the 'Countess Mervida.'"

CHAPTER ONE The German Invention of Homosexuality

1. See John, *Politics and the Law in Late Nineteenth-Century Germany*.

2. See the important scholarship on Ulrichs, including the biographies Kennedy, *Karl Heinrich Ulrichs*, and Sigusch, *Karl Heinrich Ulrichs;* and the essays in Setz, ed., *Die Geschichte der Homosexualitäten und die schwule Identität an der Jahrtausendwende*.

3. Ulrichs's twelve pamphlets are available in English translation, *The Riddle of "Man-Manly" Love*.

4. Ulrichs provides an account of his appearance at the Munich meeting in his sixth pamphlet, "Gladius Furens" ("Raging Sword") in *The Riddle of "Man-Manly" Love*, 1: 261–71.

5. Ibid.

6. Ulrichs has been eulogized by modern gay civil rights activists from around the world. See Setz, ed., *Karl Heinrich Ulrichs zu Ehren* and *Die Geschichte der Homosexualitäten und die schwule Identität an der Jahrtausendwende*.

7. Kennedy, *Karl Heinrich Ulrichs*, p. 1–3.

8. Conze and Kocka, eds., *Bildungsbürgertum im 19. Jahrhundert*.

9. Kennedy, *Karl Heinrich Ulrichs*, p. 3.

10. See Ulrichs's *curriculum vitae* reprinted in Ibid, pp. 262–65.

11. On the Holy Roman Empire see Walker, *German Home Towns*, pp. 11–33.

12. Meinhardt, *Die Universität Göttingen*.

13. Ulrichs's correspondence with his family was first published by Magnus Hirschfeld,

"Vier Breife von Karl Heinrich Ulrichs an seine Verwandten," *JfsZ* 1 (1899), pp. 36–70. They are quoted here from the English translation in Lombardi-Nash, *Sodomites and Urnings*, pp. 2–7.

14. Friedel, *Briefe über die Galanterien von Berlin*.
15. Stieber (anon.), *Die Prostitution in Berlin und ihre Opfer*, pp. 209–10. See also von Schaden, *Berlins Licht- und Schattenseiten*, pp. 72–73.
16. Casper, *Klinische Novellen zur gerichtlichen Medizin nach eigenen Erfahrungen*, pp. 170–71.
17. Kennedy, *Karl Heinrich Ulrichs*, pp. 11–17.
18. Quoted from Ibid., p. 19.
19. Quoted from Hoffschildt, *Olivia*, p. 14.
20. Schildt, "Das Ende einer Karriere," *Capri* 6, no. 4 (1988): 24–33.
21. Kennedy, *Karl Heinrich Ulrichs*, pp. 26–29.
22. On the 1848 revolutions see either of the excellent surveys: Blackbourn, *The Long Nineteenth Century*, or Sheehan, *German History, 1770–1866*.
23. Dobler, "Ulrichs vs. Preußen," pp. 49–126
24. The history of German railways is drawn from several sources including Blackbourn, *The Long Nineteenth Century*; Sheehan, *German History, 1770–1866*; and Roth, *Das Jahrhundert der Eisenbahn*.
25. Roth, *Das Jahrhundert der Eisenbahn*.
26. Kennedy, "Johann Baptist von Schweitzer: The Queer Marx Loved to Hate," *Journal of Homosexuality* 29, no. 2–3 (1995): 69–96.
27. Lombardi-Nash, *Sodomites and Urnings*, pp. 2–7.
28. Ibid., pp. 8–11.
29. Ibid., pp. 18–20.
30. Ibid., p. 12.
31. Ulrichs, *The Riddle of "Man-Manly" Love*, 1: 34–41.
32. Ibid.
33. Ibid., pp. 51–98.
34. Ibid., pp. 119–21, 161.
35. Ibid., pp. 203–6.
36. Ibid., pp. 99–108
37. Ibid.
38. The revised ninth edition of *Handbuch der gerichtlichen Medizin* was published in 1905–07, more than forty years after Casper's death.
39. Casper, "Über Notzucht und Päderastie und deren Ermittlung Seitens des Gerichtsarztes."
40. All direct quotations are taken from ibid., pp. 67–69.
41. Ibid., p. 62.
42. Casper, *Practisches Handbuch der gerichtlichen Medizin*, vol. 2, p. 174.
43. Krafft-Ebing, "Über gewisse Anomalien des Geschlechtstriebs."
44. Ibid., pp. 70–71, 208–09; Oosterhuis, *Stepchildren of Nature*, pp. 47–48, 66–67.
45. Kennedy, "Johann Baptist von Schweitzer," pp. 69–96.
46. Krafft-Ebing, "Die conträre Sexualempfindung," p. 46.
47. Krafft-Ebing, *Psychopathia sexualis*, 6th ed., p. 210.
48. Ibid., 3rd ed., p. 83.
49. Ibid., 5th ed., p. 161.
50. *Meyers Großes Konversations-Lexikon*, 16 vols. (Leipzig, 1908), vol. 9, p. 526. *Brockhaus Konversations-Lexikon*, 17 vols. (Leipzig, 1908), vol. 9, p. 315; vol. 10, p. 599; vol. 16, p. 127.

51. The Victorian-era, English homosexual-rights activists John Addington Symonds and Edward Carpenter used the expression "Uranian love," as did a group of Cambridge classicists, sometimes dubbed the "Uranian poets," who wrote Greek-inspired pederastic poetry. See Edward Perry Warren, *A Defence of Uranian Love*, ed. Michael Matthew Kaylor (Kansas City, 2009). Although Symonds and Carpenter almost certainly adopted the term from Ulrichs and from the German sexological literature that cited him, Michael Matthew Kaylor disputes that the Uranian poets were influenced by Ulrichs and argues instead that, as Classical scholars, they coined the expression independently. See Kaylor, *Secreted Desires: The Major Uranians* (Brno, 2006), 13.

52. Hull, *Sexuality, State, and Civil Society in Germany, 1700–1815*, pp. 345–50.

53. Sommer, *Die Strafbarkeit der Homosexualität*, pp. 31–58.

54. Ulrichs, *Großdeutsches Programm und Lösung des großdeutschen Problems*.

55. Kennedy, *Karl Heinrich Ulrichs*, pp. 99–106.

56. Dobler, "Ulrichs vs. Preußen."

57. From the sixth pamphlet, "Gladius Furens"; see Ulrichs, *The Riddle of "Man-Manly" Love*, 1: 266.

58. Kennedy, *Karl Heinrich Ulrichs*, pp. 111–19.

59. Ulrichs, *The Riddle of "Man-Manly" Love*, 1: 269–70.

60. Goschler, *Rudolf Virchow*.

61. Quoted from the Prussian Scientific Deputation's formal position paper, reprinted in Krafft-Ebing, *Der Conträrsexuale vor dem Strafrichter* (Leipzig, 1894), pp. 35–37.

62. Quoted from Kennedy, *Karl Heinrich Ulrichs*, p. 156.

63. Kertbeny was the pen name of Karl Marie Benkert, an ethnic Hungarian born in Vienna, raised in Budapest, but for much of his working life a resident of Berlin, where he published widely on contemporary and cultural topics. His biography is shrouded in mystery, and only in 1905 was he identified as the author of the pamphlets and inventor of the word "homosexuality." The words "homosexual" and "homosexuality" (in English), derived from a Latin root and a Greek prefix, have come to displace most other historical terms used to describe sexual acts or identities related to same-gender love. See the introductory essay by Herzer in Herzer, ed., *Schriften zur Homosexualitätsforschung*, pp. 7–61.

64. The best account of the Zastrow affair and its influence on Ulrichs's campaign is Dobler, *Zwischen Duldwigspolitik und Verbrechensbekämpfung*, pp. 127–39.

65. Ibid., p. 138.

66. Ulrichs, *The Riddle of "Man-Manly" Love*, 2: 476.

67. Dobler, *Zwischen Duldwigspolitik und Verbrechensbekämpfung*, p. 138.

68. John, *Politics and the Law in Late Nineteenth-Century Germany*.

69. Ulrichs, *The Riddle of "Man-Manly" Love*, 2: 627–88.

70. Kennedy, *Karl Heinrich Ulrichs*, pp. 220–51.

CHAPTER TWO Policing Homosexuality in Berlin

1. Abends von acht bis morgens vier
   Ziehn durch die Friedrichstraße wir.
   So gehn wir nun seit ein'gen Jahren
   Arm in Arm stets auf den Strich,
   In dufter Schale wir stets waren,
   Denn sonst geht das Geschäft ja nich.

Denn erstens muß ein Pupenjunge
Chik und elegant stets gehn;
Und zweitens muß er mit der Zunge
Gar zu bedächtig nicht umgehen;
Und drittens, will er mal was erben,
Muß er auch mal 'nen Kerl hochnehmen

Translated by the author with the help of the following reference work: Hans Ostwald, *Rinnsteinsprache: Lexikon der Gauner-Dirnen-und Landstreichersprache* (Berlin, 1906).

2. *BBZ*, 1 December 1885 (no. 561).
3. Detailed trial records are published in Karsch-Haack, *Erotische Großstadtbilder als Kulturphänomene*, pp. 56–71. See also the reports in *BBZ*, 1 December 1885 (no. 561); *BTb*, 1 December 1885 (no. 609); and *NdAZ*, 1 December 1885 (no. 562).
4. Karsch-Haack, *Erotische Großstadtbilder als Kulturphänomene*, pp. 63–64.
5. Ibid., p. 67.
6. Ibid., p. 70.
7. *NdAZ*, 1 December 1885 (no. 562), p. 2; Karsch-Haack, *Erotische Großstadtbilder als Kulturphänomene*, pp. 69–70.
8. Friedländer, "Aus dem homosexuellen Leben Alt-Berlins," p. 55.
9. Ibid., pp. 45–63. Friedländer drew from his own experience, direct and anecdotal, but also relied on two censored publications that are no longer extant: *Die Geheimnisse der Berliner Passage* (1877), and *Die Männerfreunde von Berlin* (1880). Magnus Hirschfeld discusses *Männerfreunde* in *Berlins drittes Geschlecht*, p. 145, and Iwan Bloch mentions *Geheimnisse* in *The Sexual Life of Our Time*, p. 290.
10. One of Richthofen's underlings, Hans von Tresckow, who directed the Homosexuellen Dezernat after Hüllessem in 1900, claimed in his best-selling memoir that Richthofen was not only gay but also secretly monitored by his own men. *Von Fürsten und anderen Sterblichen*, p. 55.
11. *BIZ*, 2 December 1893 (no. 7), p. 2.
12. Otto (anon.), *Die Verbrecherwelt von Berlin*, p. 174.
13. Ibid., pp. 175–77.
14. Large, *Berlin*, pp. 9–10.
15. Adams, *The Education of Henry Adams*, p. 77.
16. Hamilton, *My Yesterdays*, p. 13.
17. Brunn, *Metropolis Berlin*, pp. 34–35.
18. Vizetelly, *Berlin Under the New Empire*, 1: 181.
19. Edinburgh official James Pollard lauded the Berlin City Council in a series of newspaper essays later published as *A Study in Municipal Government*.
20. Twain, *The Complete Essays of Mark Twain*, pp. 87–89. For the travel literature comparing Berlin and Chicago see Jazbinsek and Thies, eds., *Embleme der Moderne*. In 1903 Berlin sociologist and university professor Georg Simmel published his seminal essay "The Metropolis and Mental Life," which fittingly provided inspiration for the American school of urban sociology at the University of Chicago.
21. Craig, *Germany*, pp. 38–60.
22. Richie, *Faust's Metropolis*, pp. 142–52.
23. Hall, *Cities in Civilization*, p. 377.
24. Richie, *Faust's Metropolis*, pp. 144–45.
25. Werner Hegemann, *Das steinerne Berlin: Geschichte der größten Mietskasernenstadt der Welt* (Berlin, 1930).
26. Bebel, *Aus meinem Leben*, vol. 2, p. 125.

27. LAB, A Rep. 000-02-01: no. 2020, fol. 55; no. 2022, fols. 3r–v.

28. Pollard, *A Study in Municipal Government*, pp. 35–39; Goschler, *Rudolf Virchow*.

29. Huard, *Berlin comme je l'ai vue*, p. 30.

30. Read and Fisher, *Berlin*, p. 128; Large, *Berlin*, p. 26.

31. While Berlin's constabulary was reorganized several times throughout the nineteenth century, its basic structure had been established by 1850 and remained largely unaltered up to 1933. See the excellent study by Jens Dobler, *Zwischen Duldwigspolitik und Verbrechensbekämpfung*, (Frankfurt, 2008).

32. Fosdick, *European Police Systems*, p. 27.

33. The best accounts come from French observers intrigued by the reputation of Berlin's homosexual community. In his 1904 study, Oscar Méténier offered his French readers a brief description of the Berlin task force assigned to monitoring the homosexual community: see *Vertus et Vices allemands*, pp. 112–13. Two French journalists, Henri de Weindel and F. P. Fischer, published a more extensive study in 1908 that periodized the development of Berlin's policing policies. See *L'Homosexualité en Allemagne*, pp. 81–96. See also Ostwald, *Männliche Prostitution*, p. 18.

34. Dobler, *Zwischen Duldungspolitik und Verbrechensbekämpfung*, pp. 35–36.

35. Paul Lindenberg, "Das Berliner Criminalmuseum und das Verbrecheralbum," *Leipziger Illustrierte Zeitung*, 25 May 1895 (no. 2708), pp. 611–13; Dobler, *Zwischen Duldungspolitik und Verbrechensbekämpfung*, pp. 150–52.

36. See the essays in Jane Caplan, ed., *Documenting Individual Identity*, and especially Jane Caplan, "'This or That Particular Person': Protocols of Identification in Nineteenth Century Europe," pp. 63–98.

37. Dobler, *Zwischen Duldwigspolitik und Verbrechensbekämpfung*, pp. 219–37.

38. During the 1869 trial of the alleged sexual deviant Carl von Zastrow, who was convicted of raping and mutilating a young boy, Berlin press reports mentioned the *Päderastenlist* maintained by the police.

39. Ibid., pp. 146–56.

40. Quoted from *The Cloister* (New York, 1969), pp. 12–13. Michael Meyer dates the Berlin ball to February 23, 1893; see *Strindberg: A Biography* (Oxford, 1985), p. 245.

41. Moll's subtitle, *Mit Benutzung amtlichen Materials* (With the use of official documents), indicated his access to official police documents from the Berlin police headquarters, for which he explicitly thanked Hüllessem. See *Die conträre Sexualempfindung*, pp. vii–viii. The work was published in a third edition by 1899. Moll completed his medical degree under Rudolf Virchow at the University of Berlin. At the beginning of the twentieth century, he was considered a leading German psychiatrist. See Sigusch, ed., *Geschichte der Sexualwissenschaft*, p. 209.

42. Krafft-Ebing, *Psychopathia sexualis*, p. 428.

43. Dobler, *Zwischen Duldungspolitik und Verbrechensbekämpfung*, pp. 249–56.

44. The titles are too numerous to review here, but of particular note are the fifty volumes in Hans Ostwald's "Großstadt-Dokumente," devoted primarily to Berlin's seamy underbelly and published between 1904 and 1908. See Thies, *Ethnograph des dunklen Berlin*.

45. In the book's foreword, Moll thanked Glaser—identifying him by the pseudonym "N. N."—as an *"Urning"* and expert. See *Die conträre Sexualempfindung*, pp. vii–viii, and Friedländer, "Aus dem homosexuellen Lebens Alt-Berlins," pp. 61–62.

46. Joux, *Die Enterbten des Liebesglückes*, pp. 99–100, 123–24, 173, 178–79, 204, 221–26. See also Lehmstedt, *Bücher für das "dritte Geschlecht,"* pp. 47–50.

47. Hirschfeld, *Die Homosexualität des Mannes und des Weibes*, pp. 682–83.

48. Flexner, *Prostitution in Europe*, p. 31.
49. Friedländer, "Aus dem homosexuellen Leben Alt-Berlins," p. 56.
50. Although Hannemann gave up the address in 1912, he opened a second bar in a new location in 1913, and had moved again by 1919 to a third venue, which he ran until at least 1928. *Die Fanfare* 39 (1924), and Anon., *Das perverse Berlin*, p. 130.
51. Anon., *Das perverse Berlin*, pp. 133–34.
52. Anon., *Das perverse Berlin*, p. 133–34; Dobler, *Zwischen Duldungspolitik*, pp. 373–74.
53. Anon., *Das perverse Berlin*, p. 139.
54. Ostwald, *Männliche Prostitution*, p. 85.
55. Anon., *Das perverse Berlin*, pp. 35–36.
56. *Kleine Presse*, 15 October 1905 (no. 243).
57. Anon., *Das perverse Berlin*, pp. 112–14.
58. Szittya, *Das Kuriositäten-Kabinett* (Constance, 1923), p. 67.
59. Friedländer, "Aus dem homosexuellen Leben Alt-Berlins," p. 64; Dobler, *Zwischen Duldungspolitik*, pp. 373–74.
60. See Ulrichs, *Memnon* (Leipzig, 1868), pp. 77–78.
61. See Friedländer, "Aus dem homosexuellen Leben Alt-Berlins," pp. 45–63.
62. Otto, *Die Verbrecherwelt von Berlin*, p. 175; Moll, *Conträre Sexualempfindung*, p. 84; Lindenberg, *Berliner Polizei und Verbrechertum*, pp. 105–06; Joux, *Die Enterbten des Liebesglückes*, p. 183; Hirschfeld, *Berlins drittes Geschlecht*, pp. 103–11; Ostwald, *Männliche Prostitution*, pp. 9–12.
63. "Polizei-Verordnung über öffentliche Lustbarkeiten," *Ministerial-Blatt für die gesammte innere Verwaltung in den Königlich Preußischen Staate* 45, no. 8 (1884): 213; Friedrich Retzlaff, *Vorschriften über den Geschäftsbetrieb der Immobilien-Makler, Trödler, Gesindevermieter und Stellenvermittler, Theater-Agenten . . .* (Recklinghausen, 1906), pp. 39–40.
64. Friedländer, "Aus dem homosexuellen Leben Alt-Berlins," pp. 60–61.
65. Dobler, *Zwischen Duldungspolitik und Verbrechensbekämpfung*, pp. 348–54.
66. Konstantin Grell, "Männliche Prostitution," *Die Kritik: Wochenschaue des öffentlichen Lebens* 2, no. 30 (27 April 1895): 788.
67. The article is reprinted in Ostwald, *Männliche Prostitution*, pp. 65–68.
68. *BMp*, 17 October 1899 (no. 244).
69. Méténier, *Vertus et Vices allemands*, pp. 85–87.
70. Schoenaich (pseudo.), *Mein Damaskus*, p. 76.
71. Friedel, *Briefe über die Galanterien von Berlin*, pp. 171–72.
72. Otto, *Die Verbrecherwelt von Berlin*, pp. 173–76; Hirschfeld, *Die Homosexualität des Mannes und des Weibes*, pp. 696–97.
73. Flexner, *Prostitution in Europe*, 1914), p. 31.
74. Hirschfeld, *Die Homosexualität des Mannes und des Weibes*, p. 698.
75. Hiller, *Leben gegen die Zeit*, vol. 2, pp. 27–28.
76. LAB A Pr. Br. Rep. 030 Nr. 18659—"Benutzung der Wege und Plätze im Tiergarten und Besprengung derselben" (unfol.).
77. A policy adapted from the French and described as "regulationism." See Corbin, *Women for Hire: Prostitution and Sexuality in France After 1850* (Cambridge, 1978).
78. Evans, *Tales from the German Underworld* and "Prostitution, State and Society in Imperial Germany"; Krafft, *Zucht und Unzucht*; Schulte, *Sperrbezirke*; Roos, *Weimar through the Lens of Gender*.
79. See LAB, Pr. Br. Rep 30, tit. 28, no. 731, "Allgemeine Deinstangelegenheiten 1877–1900," which includes the pamphlet "Die Organisation der Berliner Criminal-Polizei," fols. 359r–362v.

80. Hiller, *Leben gegen die Zeit*, pp. 27–28; Hirschfeld, *Die Homosexualität*, pp. 581, 591; Lücke, "Das ekle Geschmeiß," pp. 157–72.

81. *BMp*, 6 January 1904 (no. 4).

82. Ibid.

83. Anon., *Das perverse Berlin*, p. 141.

84. Näcke, "Ein Besuch bei den Homosexuellen in Berlin," pp. 244–63.

85. *Vw*, 20 August 1905 (no. 194).

86. *DW*, 15 May 1905 (no. 134).

87. *Der Montag*, 14 May 1906 (no. 20).

88. Hirschfeld, *Berlins drittes Geschlecht*, p. 66.

89. *TR*, 20 March 1898 (no. 79).

90. McLaren, *Sexual Blackmail*.

91. Dobler, *Zwischen Duldungspolitik*, pp. 210–16.

92. Wilhelm Stieber and Hans Schneikert, *Praktische Lehrbuch der Kriminalpolizei* (Potsdam, 1921), p. 31.

93. Tresckow, *Von Fürsten und anderen Sterblichen*, pp. 114–16.

94. See *Vw*, 30 October 1902 (no. 254), and 15 November 1902 (no. 268); Tresckow's account is in *Von Fürsten und anderen Sterblichen*, pp. 126–29. The literature on the Krupp family and this scandal is voluminous: consider William Manchester, *The Arms of Krupp, 1587–1968* (Boston, 1964) or Norbert Muhlen, *The Incredible Krupps* (New York, 1959).

95. *BTb*, 29 August 1905 (no. 438); *Die Zeit am Montag*, 11 September 1905 (no. 37).

96. See *Vierteljahrsberichte des Wissenschaftlich-humanitären Komitees* 2, no. 4 (July 1911): 373.

97. *BTb*, 2 November 1904 (no. 258).

98. See *Die Zukunft*, 2 December 1905 (vol. 52), pp. 311–15; 16 December 1905, pp. 410–12. See also Tresckow, *Von Fürsten und anderen Sterblichen*, p. 162; Ostwald, *Männliche Prostitution*, p. 19; *Monatsbericht des Wissenschaftlich-humanitären Komitees* 4, no. 11 (November 1905): 18, note 19; and *JfsZ* 8 (1906): 912–17.

99. The best newspaper reports and commentary on Hasse's case include *NZ*, 4 January 1905 (no. 8); *BMp*, 2 March 1905 (no. 52); *BVZ*, 3 March 1905 (no. 173). The case is also discussed in Ostwald, *Männliche Prostitution*, pp. 21–27.

100. Ackermann's father had served in the Reichstag and also as president of the second chamber of the Saxon Diet. Ackermann himself was a decorated veteran of the Franco-Prussian War, and enjoyed close ties to the Royal Wettin Court in Dresden and to conservative Saxon political elites. His wife's brother, Dr. Otto Mehnert, was president of the second chamber of the Saxon Diet (like Ackermann's father) and privy councilor to the Saxon king. *BVZ*, 22 December 1904 (no. 600); *Vw*, 17 March 1905 (no. 67).

101. *BMp*, 24 November 1904 (no. 276); *TR*, 11 December 1904 (no. 581).

102. *BMp*, 2 October 1906 (no. 230).

103. *BTb*, 16 January 1911 (no. 28).

104. *BVZ*, 24 August 1909 (no. 393).

105. *NdAZ*, 11 November 1904 (no. 266).

106. *NZ*, 9 February 1907 (no. 67).

107. *BVZ*, 5 May 1906 (no. 208); *NdAZ*, 6 May 1906 (no. 105); *BMp*, 5 May 1906 (no. 104).

108. *BTb*, 20 July 1910 (no. 362).

109. *BTb*, 21 January 1908 (no. 36).

110. *BTb*, 21 August 1905 (no. 424); see also the description of Café Kranzler in "Die Kranzlerecke," *Die große Glocke*, 20 March 1907 (no. 12).

111. *Vw*, 7 December 1906 (no 285).

112. *BTb*, 16 December 1913 (no. 637).

113. *BMp*, 2 June 1899 (no. 127).

114. *NZ*, 24 September 1909 (no. 447).

115. *DW*, 23 April 1905 (no. 117); *BLA*, 9 May 1905 (no. 221); *Vw*, 3 June 1905 (no. 128).

116. *DP*, 23 April 1908 (no. 190).

117. *BTb*, 15 January 1909 (no. 25).

118. *Vw*, 11 June 1905 (no. 135).

119. *BBC*, 23 May 1912 (no. 239).

120. *BVZ*, 30 December 1909 (no. 609).

121. *BTb*, 18 May 1913 (no. 246).

122. *BTb*, 2 July 1910 (no. 330).

123. *DW*, 23 April 1905 (no. 117); *BLA*, 9 May 1905 (no. 221); *Vw*, 3 June 1905 (no. 128); *Vw*, 11 June 1905 (no. 135); *BLA*, 9 January 1907 (no. 14); *DTz*, 4 May 1910 (no. 205); *BTb*, 16 January 1911 (no. 28); *BTb*, 11 October 1913 (no. 517).

124. *Vw*, 11 June 1905 (no. 135); *BLA*, 4 April 1908 (no. 175); Tresckow, *Von Fürsten und anderen Sterblichen*, pp. 42, 67–68, 103.

125. *DW*, 23 April 1905 (no. 117).

126. *BLA*, 6 March 1914 (no. 123).

127. Hirschfeld, *Die Homosexualität des Mannes und des Weibes*, p. 897.

128. *Statistisches Jahrbuch der Stadt Berlin*, 1906–12.

129. *Statistisches Jahrbuch der Stadt Berlin*, 1876–1918.

130. Hirschfeld, *Berlins drittes Geschlecht*, p. 133.

131. Ostwald, *Männliche Prostitution*, p. 18.

132. *Die Freundschaft*, January 1920 (no. 2–3). See also Dobler, "Dr. Heinrich Kopp."

133. A second bar, Little Salvator's, a few blocks south of Seeger's Restaurant, was closed by the police in 1892 for attracting male patrons who prostituted themselves in women's clothing. The locale appears to have been targeted as a center for prostitution, however, and not as a homosexual locale per se. See *JfsZ* 2 (1900): 330; 3 (1901): 559. See also Dobler, *Zwischen Duldungspolitik*, pp. 362–63.

134. GStPrK: I. HA Rep. 77, Ministerium des Innern, tit. 423, no. 102, fol. 6.

135. Ibid., fols. 7r–8v.

CHAPTER THREE The First Homosexual Rights Movement
and the Struggle to Shape Identity

1. Hirschfeld provided an account of the meeting in his memoir published in installments in *Die Freundschaft* (1922–23) and reprinted as *Von einst bis jetzt*, p. 54. Jens Dobler argues that Hüllessem might have attended the meeting in *Zwischen Duldungspolitik* (Frankfurt, 2008), p. 246. See also Dobler, "Nicht nur Verfolgung" and "Zum Verhältnis der Sexualwissenschaft und der homosexuellen Emanzipationsbewegung zur Polizei in Berlin," pp. 329–36. For other accounts of the meeting, see Lehmstedt, *Bücher für das "dritte Geschlecht*," pp. 75–77; and Keilson-Lauritz, *Die Geschichte der eigenen Geschichte*, pp. 30–31.

2. Steakley, "Per scientiam ad justitiam."

3. See the biographical sketches of Bloch and Eulenburg in Sigusch and Grau, eds. *Personenlexikon*, 52–61, 148–57.

4. For Hirschfeld's calculations of the number of potential sexual variations, see *Transvestites: The Erotic Drive to Cross-Dress*, pp. 224–27.

5. Keilson-Lauritz, *Die Geschichte der eigenen Geschichte,* pp. 40–60.

6. Krafft-Ebing, *Der Conträrsexuale vor dem Strafrichter,* p. 3.

7. Lehmstedt, *Bücher für das "dritte Geschlecht,"* pp. 117–19.

8. Ibid., pp. 118–25.

9. See the SHC newsletter, *Monatsbericht des Wissenschaftlich-humanitären Komitees* 3, no. 11 (1 November 1904): 7–8.

10. Lehmstedt, *Bücher für das "dritte Geschlecht,"* pp. 77–85.

11. Hirschfeld, *Die Homosexualität des Mannes und des Weibes,* p. 974.

12. Stark, *Banned in Berlin,* pp. 22–35.

13. Lehmstedt, *Bücher für das "dritte Geschlecht,"* p. 147.

14. Spohr published four of Carpenter's works in German translation, including *Homogenic Love* in 1895—see ibid., pp. 58–61, 202–03.

15. Myers, *Censorship and the Control of Print in England and France, 1600–1910,* pp. 245–46.

16. *British Medical Journal* 1 (24 June 1893): 325.

17. Quoted from Ellis's autobiography, *My Life: Autobiography of Havelock Ellis* (Boston, 1939), p. 367.

18. Burnet, "Some Aspects of Neurasthenia."

19. Myers, *Censorship and the Control of Print in England and France, 1600–1910;* Stora-Lamarre, *L'enfer de la IIIe République.*

20. Artieres, "What Criminals Think about Criminology," pp. 363–75.

21. Revenin, *Homosexualité et prostitution masculines à Paris 1870–1918,* pp. 180–89.

22. KI, Hirschfeld Scrapbook, box 2, folder 6, "Monatsbericht Januar 1903"; *Monatsbericht,* 1 March 1906 (no. 3); and 1 November 1906 (no. 11).

23. KI, Hirschfeld Scrapbook, box 3, folder 1, no. 145, "11. Halbjahrs-Konferenz des wissenschaftlich-humanitären Komitees" (ms., 30 pages).

24. Ibid., pp. 3–9.

25. Ibid., pp. 10–11.

26. Ibid., pp. 17–18, 20–21.

27. Ibid., pp. 19–20.

28. Ibid., pp. 21.

29. Ibid., pp. 21–22.

30. Hirschfeld, "Das Ergebnis der statistischen Untersuchungen über den Prozentsatz der Homosexuellen," *JfsZ* 6 (1904): 109–78.

31. See the press clippings reprinted in *Monatsbericht,* 1 January 1905 (no.1).

32. Herzer, *Magnus Hirschfeld,* pp. 56–76.

33. Collections of the various petitions can be found at GStA PK, I. HA Rep. 84a, no. 8097, fols. 119r–120v; BAB R-8071, no. 1; and KI, Hirschfeld Scrapbook, box 1, folder 1, nos. 9, 9a, 9b, 9c, 9d.

34. Kerbs and Reulecke, eds. *Handbuch der deutschen Reformbewegungen 1880–1933.*

35. Kauffeldt and Cepl-Kaufmann, *Berlin-Friedrichshagen.*

36. Bab, *Die Berliner Boheme,* p. 33.

37. See Carlson, *Anarchism in Germany,* and also Fähnders, *Anarchismus und Literatur.*

38. For Mackay's biography, see Solneman, *Der Bahnbrecher John Henry Mackay;* Kennedy, *Anarchist der Liebe;* also Riley, *Germany's Poet-Anarchist John Henry Mackay.*

39. Fähnders, *Anarchismus und Literatur.*

40. LAB, A Pr. Br. Rep. 030, tit. 95 [Vereine], no. 15317, "Bund für Menschenrechte. 1904–1906."

41. Keilson-Lauritz, *Die Geschichte der eigenen Geschichte,* p. 68.

42. Brand offers his own account of this incident in *Der Eigene* 3, no. 8–9: 292. See also Herzer, "Max Spohr, Adolf Brand, Bernhard Zack."

43. The best recent work on German nudism is Möhring, *Marmorleiber: Körperbildung in der deutschen Nacktkultur (1890–1930).*

44. UT HRC: Ives, George. 1.1. Correspondence, General: Brand, Adolf.

45. Keilson-Lauritz, "Adolf Brand und der Eigene."

46. Marchand, *Down from Olympus.*

47. Bab, *Die Gleichgeschlechtliche Liebe (Lieblingsminne).*

48. Keilson-Lauritz, "Benedict Friedlaender und die Anfänge der Sexualwissenschaft."

49. Karl Friedrich Jordan [Max Katte, pseud.], "Der Daseinszweck der Homosexuellen," *JfsZ* 4 (1902): 272–88, qu. 274, 286. The identification of historical figures alleged to be "homosexual" begins no later than with Ulrichs in his pamphlets. It can be found throughout the medical and psychiatric literature, including Krafft-Ebing and Albert Moll, who published an entire volume devoted to the topic: *Berühmte Homosexuelle.*

50. Lucien Römer, "Heinrich der Dritte, König von Frankreich und Polen," *JfsZ* 4 (1902): 573–669.

51. Keilson-Lauritz, *Die Geschichte der eigenen Geschichte,* pp. 277, 356.

52. *JfsZ* 7 (1905): 165. The aphorism Hirschfeld cited was no. 75 in *Beyond Good and Evil,* trans. R. J. Hollingdale (New York, 2003), p. 60.

53. Keilson-Lauritz, *Die Geschichte der eigenen Geschichte,* pp. 70, 78.

54. On the German reception of Nietzsche see Aschheim, *The Nietzsche Legacy in Germany, 1890–1990.* See also the biography of Nietzsche that explores his alleged homosexuality, as well as the rumor that he contracted syphilis in a "homosexual brothel in Genoa," Köhler, *Zarathustra's Secret,* pp. 210–12.

55. *Monatsbericht,* 1 January 1904 (no. 1), p. 8.

56. The "anthology" appeared in the second volume of his larger work on Greek same-sex love: *Eros oder die Männerliebe der Griechen,* vol. 2, pp. 53–150.

57. Frey, *Der Eros und die Kunst,* quoted from p. 317. Although he published additional essays in *JfsZ,* the identity of Ludwig Frey remains a mystery. See Keilson-Lauritz, *Die Geschichte der eigenen Geschichte,* p. 402.

58. Carpenter, *Ioläus.*

59. Consider the "queering" of the German literary canon in the essays in Kuzniar, ed., *Outing Goethe and His Age,* or the work of Robert Tobin, *Warm Brothers.*

60. Derks, *Die Schande der heiligen Päderastie.*

61. Raffalovich, *Uranisme et Unisexualité,* pp. 157–59, 310–54.

62. Karl Friedrich Jordan [Max Katte, pseud.], "Aus dem Leben eines Homosexuellen," *JfsZ* 2 (1900): 295–323. Also Keilson-Lauritzen, *Die Geschichte der eigenen Geschichte,* pp. 277, 288ff.

63. See the essays in *Der Eigene,* including those of Peter Hamecher, "Heinrich von Kleist: Eine Studie," no. 8–9 (1899–1900): 254–60, and "Heinrich von Kleists Liebesleben," no. 1 (1906): 154–65; and Hans Rau, "Heinrich von Kleist: Eine psychologische Studie," no. 2 (1905): 39–47. See also Detering, *Das offene Geheimnis,* pp. 115–20.

64. *Der Eigene* 5 (1903): 313.

65. Translation cited from *Friedrich Schiller: Poet of Freedom,* vol. 3 (Washington, DC, 1990), pp. 6–7.

> Wars nicht dies allmächtige Getriebe,
> Das zum ewgen Jubelbund der Liebe
> *Unsre* Herzen aneinander zwang?
> Freund, an *deinem* Arm—o Wonne!
> Wag auch ich zur großen Geistersonne
> Freudigmutig den Vollendungsgang.

Glücklich! glücklich! *Dich* hab ich gefunden,
Hab aus Millionen *dich* umwunden,
Und aus Millionen *mein* bist du—
Laß das Chaos diese Welt umrütteln,
Durcheinander die Atomen schütteln:
Ewig fliehn sich unsre Herzen zu.

Muß ich nicht aus *deinen* Flammenaugen
Meiner Wollust Widerstrahlen saugen?
Nur in *dir* bestaun ich mich—
Schöner malt sich mir die schöne Erde,
Heller spiegelt in des Freunds Gebärde,
Reizender der Himmel sich.

Schwermut wirft die bange Tränenlasten,
Süßer von des Leidens Sturm zu rasten,
In der Liebe Busen ab;—
Sucht nicht selbst das folternde Entzücken
In des Freunds beredten Strahlenblicken
Ungeduldig ein wollüstges Grab?

66. The judgment was cited in *Vw,* 13 October 1903 (no. 239).

67. Keilson-Lauritz, *Die Geschichte der eigenen Geschichte,* pp. 91–95.

68. *Monatsbericht,* 1 April 1907 (no. 4).

69. *JfsZ* 14 (1914): 338–41.

70. Philip Kitcher critiques this meme in the Thomas Mann reception in his recent *Deaths in Venice,* pp. 26, 38–46.

71. Essebac, *Dédé.*

72. Eekhoud, *Escal-Vigor.*

73. Reviews in *JfsZ* 5 (1902): 1047–55; 7 (1905): 883. The German translation, *Der Immoralist* (Minden, 1905), was completed by Felix P. Greve.

74. Bang, *Michael.*

75. *Monatsbericht,* 1 July 1907 (no. 7), p. 144; Kuzmin, *Flügel.*

76. Spohr capitalized on this interest and published a pamphlet on the trial, *Der Fall Wilde und das Problem der Homosexualität: Ein Prozeß und Interview,* in 1896.

77. Lehmsted, *Bücher für das "dritte Geschlecht,"* pp. 131–40.

78. Eduard Bertz, "Walt Whitman: Ein Charakterbild," *JfsZ* 7 (1905): 153–287. According to Whitman scholar Gay Wilson Allen, Bertz's *Jahrbuch* essay was the very first time that Whitman was described as "homosexual"—see *The New Walt Whitman Handbook,* pp. 23–24.

79. Bertz, "Walt Whitman," p. 192.

80. Grünzweig provides a detailed account of the debate in *Constructing the German Walt Whitman,* quoted from p. 198.

81. Schlaf, *Walt Whitman Homosexueller?*; see also Bertz's response to Schlaf's pamphlet, *Der Yankee-Heiland.*

82. The review author was German-American Georg Sylvester Viereck writing in the July 1906 issue of *Current Literature.* See *Monatsbericht,* 1 September 1906 (no. 9).

83. See the CoS newsletter *Gemeinschaft der Eigenen* 4 (1905), and for Stegemann's biography, Hergemöller, *Mann für Mann,* p. 673.

84. *Gemeinschaft der Eigenen* 1 (1906), and for Hamecher's biography, Hergemöller, *Mann für Mann*, pp. 321–22.

85. *Monatsbericht* (1 February 2005), no. 2.

86. Moll, "Sexuelle Zwischenstufen," *Die Zukunft* 40 (1902): 425–33, quoted from p. 433.

87. Brand, *Kaplan Dasbach und die Freundesliebe.*

88. KI, Hirschfeld Scrapbook, box 2, folder 6, "Monatsbericht Mai 1902."

89. *Vw*, 7 April 1904 (no. 83); also *BMp*, 3 April 1904 (no. 79).

90. Brand, *Kaplan Dasbach und die Freundesliebe*, p. 10.

91. *Vw*, 23 July 1904 (no. 171).

92. See accounts in *Monatsbericht* 5, 6, 8–9, 10, and 11 (1904); 1, 3, 6 (1905). Also Keilson-Lauritz, *Geschichte der eigenen Geschichte*, pp. 97–103; as well as the Dasbach biography by Thoma, *Georg Friedrich Dasbach.*

93. *Monatsbericht*, 1 May 1905 (no. 5).

94. KI, Hirschfeld Scrapbook, box 2, folder 1, no. 40; see also Keilson-Lauritz, "Benedict Friedlaender und die Anfänge der Sexualwissenschaft."

95. Hackett, "Helene Stöcker: Left-Wing Intellectual and Sex Reformer."

96. Hergemöller, *Mann für Mann*, pp. 244–45.

97. KI, Hirschfeld Scrapbook, box 1, folder 2, no. 25.

98. *Meyers Großes Konversations-Lexikon*, 16 vols. (Leipzig, 1908), 9: 526; *Brockhaus Konversations-Lexikon*, 17 vols. (Leipzig, 1908), 9: 315, 10: 599, 16: 127.

CHAPTER FOUR The Eulenburg Scandal and the Politics of Outing

1. Wedler, *Maximilian Harden und die "Zukunft,"* p. 163.

2. Röhl, *Wilhelm II*, p. 592. In addition to Röhl's and other biographies of the Kaiser, several book-length studies treat the Eulenburg scandal more narrowly, including Hull, *The Entourage of Kaiser Wilhelm II, 1888–1918;* Hecht, "Die Harden-Prozesse"; Jungblut, *Famose Kerle;* Domeier, *Der Eulenburg-Skandal;* and Winzen, *Das Ende der Kaiserherrlichkeit.*

3. Consider the gossip recorded in the letters of the Hohenzollern courtier Marie Fürstin Radziwill, *Briefe fom deutschen Kaiserhof 1889–1915*, pp. 288–89.

4. Tresckow, *Von Fürsten und anderen Sterblichen*, p. 168.

5. Ibid., p. 113.

6. Röhl, ed., *Philipp Eulenburgs politische Korrespondenz*, vol. 3: *Krisen, Krieg und Katastrophen: 1895–1921*, p. 1986.

7. Hull, "Kaiser Wilhelm I and the 'Liebenberg Circle,'" pp. 193–220.

8. Maximilian Harden, "Praeludium" and "Dies Irae," *Die Zukunft* 57 (1906): 251–66, 287–302.

9. Maximilian Harden, "Symphonie" and "Roulette," *Die Zukunft* 58 (1907): 157–74; 59 (1907): 118–30.

10. Huber, *Deutsche Verfassungsgeschichte seit 1789*, vol. 4, p. 301.

11. Frederic William Wile, *Men Around the Kaiser: The Makers of Modern Germany* (Indianapolis, 1914), p. 193.

12. GstA PK, I. HA Rep. 84a, nos. 49838–49840.

13. Hecht, "Die Harden-Prozesse," p. 295.

14. Young, *Maximilian Harden;* Weller, *Maximilian Harden und die "Zukunft";* Neumann and Neumann, *Maximilian Harden (1861–1927).*

15. Neumann and Neumann, *Maximilian Harden (1861–1927)*, pp. 21–26. See also the assessment of Hull, *The Entourage of Kaiser Wilhelm II, 1888–1918*, pp. 135–43.

16. Domeier, *Der Eulenburg-Skandal*, pp. 36, 312.

17. Details of Holstein's machinations and his relationship to Harden are provided in Holstein's translated diaries and correspondence: see *The Holstein Papers*, pp. 447–52.

18. *Die Zukunft*, 13 April 1907 (no. 58), p. 44.

19. *Die Zukunft*, 27 April 1907 (no. 58), p. 118.

20. Tresckow, *Von Fürsten und anderen Sterblichen*, p. 125, and also Zedlitz-Trützschler, *Zwölf Jahre am deutschen Kaiserhof*, p. 162.

21. *Die Zukunft*, 27 April 1907, p. 118.

22. Bernhard von Bülow, *Denkwürdigkeiten*, 4 vols. (Berlin, 1930–31), 2: 312.

23. Domeier, *Der Eulenburg-Skandal*, pp. 86–95.

24. *BTb*, 26 October 1907 (no. 545).

25. *VZ*, 23 October 1907 (no. 498). See additional description of the atmosphere of the first days of the trial in *BTb*, 23 October 1907 (no. 540).

26. Harden documented elements of the trials in *Die Zukunft*—see "Prozeß Moltke," 5 October 1907 (vol. 61), pp. 50–51. Detailed trial transcripts are also provided by veteran court reporter Hugo Friedländer, *Interessante Kriminal-Prozesse*, published in twelve volumes from 1911 to 1921. The collection is now available in a digital "republication" from 2001.

27. Weller, *Maximilian Harden*, pp. 168–69.

28. Friedländer, *Interessante Kriminal-Prozesse*, p. 3898.

29. Ibid., pp. 3988–89.

30. Ibid., p. 3990.

31. Ibid., pp. 3991–92.

32. Ibid., pp. 3992–93.

33. Herzer, *Magnus Hirschfeld*, p. 72.

34. "Fürst Bülow und die Abschaffung des § 175," *Die Gemeinschaft der Eigenen*, 10 September 1907, and also reprinted in *Capri* 17 (1994): 17–19.

35. *Capri* 17 (1994): 17–19.

36. Court protocol from *Berliner Neueste Nachrichten*, 6 November 1907 (evening edition).

37. Brand, *Interessante Briefe und Dokumente zur Bülow-Eulenburg-Intrige*.

38. Linsert, *Kabale und Liebe*, p. 471.

39. Brand, *Interessante Briefe und Dokumente*, p. 20.

40. Domeier, *Der Eulenburg-Skandal*, pp. 269–72.

41. Herzer, *Magnus Hirschfeld*, p. 83.

42. *Bild Zeitung am Mittag*, 22 January 1908.

43. Ibid.

44. Holstein, *The Holstein Papers*, vol. 2: 411, 455.

45. *Bild Zeitung am Mittag*, 25 January 1908.

46. Harden later published detailed accounts of the Moltke and Eulenburg trials in *Köpfe*, vol. 3: "Eulenburg," pp. 169–286, and "Moltke wider Harden," pp. 409–508.

47. Harden, *Köpfe*, vol. 3, pp. 233–39.

48. Tresckow, *Von Fürsten und anderen Sterblichen*, p. 205.

49. Domeier, *Der Eulenburg-Skandal*, pp. 272–4.

50. Haller, *Philip Eulenburg*, pp. 421–23.

51. "Wedel und Eulenburg," *Vw*, 7 July 1908.

52. Tresckow, *Von Fürsten und anderen Sterblichen*, p. 143.

53. *BT*, 8 July 1908; *BLa*, 9 July 1908.
54. Friedländer, *Interessante Kriminal-Prozesse*, pp. 4355–57.
55. Ibid., p. 4361.
56. Harden, *Köpfe*, vol. 3, pp. 503–06.
57. Friedländer, *Interessante Kriminal-Prozesse*, p. 4365.
58. Méténier, *Vertus et Vices allemands*, pp. 112–13.
59. See Mirbeau, *La 628-E8*, pp. 407–14. The book went through multiple editions and was reissued as late as 1939.
60. Grand-Carteret, *Derrière "Lui," L'Allemagne et la Caricature européenne en 1907*, p. 63.
61. Weindel and Fischer, *L'Homosexualité en Allemagne*, pp. 81–96.
62. Murat, *La loi du genre*, pp. 272–73.
63. See Raffalovich's initial essay, "Les groupes uranistes a Paris et a Berlin," pp. 926–36; Näcke's response, "Le monde homo-sexuel de Paris," pp. 182–85; Raffalovich's reply to Näcke, "A propos du syndicat des uranistes," pp. 283–86; and Näcke's answer to Raffalovich, "Quelques details sur les homo-sexuels de Paris," pp. 411–14.
64. Saint-Paul, "Note," *Archives d'anthropologie criminelle* 23 (1908): 313–16, quoted from p. 314.
65. Saint-Paul, "Note," *Archives d'anthropologie criminelle* 24 (1909): 693–96, quoted from p. 693.
66. Ibid., p. 694. Laupts's textbook was *Tares et Poisons*, and he reviewed the arguments he made there in "Dégénérescence ou plethora?" In 1910 he issued a revised edition, *L'homosexualité et les types homosexuals* (Paris, 1910).
67. Eugen Wilhelm, "A propos de l'article du Dr. Laupts sur l'homosexualité," *Archives d'anthropologie criminelle* 24 (1909): 198–207; "Publications allemandes sur les questions sexuelles," pp. 301–09, quoted from p. 301.
68. Hirschfeld, *Die Homosexualität des Mannes und des Weibes*, p. 532.
69. Ibid., pp. 22, 561.

CHAPTER FIVE Hans Blüher, the Wandervogel Movement, and the Männerbund

1. Blüher's relative obscurity is clear from the paucity of scholarship on his life and work. An excellent and recent study is the intellectual biography by Claudia Bruns, *Politik des Eros*. See also Geuter, *Homosexualität in der deutschen Jugendbewegung*, pp. 67–117.
2. Blüher provides copious biographical detail in the first volume of his Wandervogel history, *Wandervogel*, and in his autobiography, *Werk und Tage*, which he revised and expanded for a new edition near the end of his life (Munich, 1953).
3. Scholarship on the Wandervogel and the German Youth Movement more generally is extensive. See Laqueur, *Young Germany;* Müller, *Die Jugendbewegung als deutsche Hauptrichtung neukonservativer Reform;* Neuloh and Zilius, *Die Wandervögel;* Geuter, *Homosexualität in der deutschen Jugendbewegung;* Mogge, "Jugendbewegung"; as well as the essay collections Koebner, ed., *"Mit uns zieht die neue Zeit,"* and Joachim H. Knoll, ed., *Typisch deutsch: Die Jugendbewegung* (Leske, 1988). There are also several published source collections edited by Werner Kindt, including *Die Wandervogelzeit* and *Die deutsche Jugendbewegung 1920 bis 1933*.
4. Blüher, *Wandervogel*, vol. 2, pp. 149, 152–54, 162.
5. Blüher, *Werk und Tage: Geschichte eines Denkers* (Munich, 1953), pp. 186–87.
6. Blüher, *Wandervogel*, vol. 1, pp. 97–150; vol. 2, pp. 5–77.

7. Bruns, *Politik des Eros*, pp. 242–66.
8. Ibid., p. 233; Hergemöller, *Mann für Mann*, pp. 395–96.
9. Geuter, *Homosexualität in der deutschen Jugendbewegung*, pp. 49–58; Bruns, *Politik des Eros*, pp. 138–66.
10. Bruns, *Politik des Eros*, p. 219.
11. Ibid., p. 237.
12. Stabi Berlin, Nachlass Blüher, Kasten 1, M. 9; Blüher, *Werk und Tage*, pp. 42–47.
13. Stabi Berlin, Nachlass Blüher, Kasten 10, Blüher to his parents, 21 April 1912.
14. Ibid.
15. Stabi Berlin, Nachlass Blüher, Kasten 10, Blüher to Jansen, 21 July 1910.
16. Geuter, *Homosexualität in der deutschen Jugendbewegung*, pp. 42–43.
17. Ibid., pp. 49–58.
18. Schurtz, *Alterklassen und Männerbünde*, p. 21.
19. Ibid., pp. 17–20.
20. Planert, *Antifeminismus im Kaiserreich*, pp. 118–51.
21. On the women's movement in imperial Germany, see Evans, *The Feminist Movement in Germany*, and Frevert, *Frauen-Geschichte*.
22. Geuter, *Homosexualität in der deutschen Jugendbewegung*, pp. 59–66; Bruns, *Politik des Eros*, pp. 230–34.
23. Bruns, *Politik des Eros*, pp. 350–55.
24. On Blüher's relationships to both Hirschfeld and Freud, see Bruns, *Politik des Eros*, pp. 257–66, 290–98; Geuter, *Homosexualität in der deutschen Jugendbewegung*, pp. 114–17.
25. Bruns, *Politik des Eros*, p. 337, fn. 34.
26. See the Blüher-Freud correspondence in Stabi Berlin, Nachlass Blüher, Kasten 12, six letters from 1910–13.
27. Blüher, "Die drei Grundformen der sexuellen Homosexualität: Eine sexuologische Studie," in *JfSZ* 13 (1913): 139–65, 326–42, 411–44.
28. See the critique in Numa Praetorius [Eugen Wilhelm], "Die Bibliographie der Homosexualität aus dem Jahre 1913," *JfSZ* 14 (1914): 342–53.
29. Blüher, *Die drei Grundformen der sexuellen Inversion (Homosexualität)*.
30. H. Albrecht, "Hans Blüher über die Wandervogelbewegung," *Zeitschrift der Zentralstelle für Volkswohlfahrt* 3, Sonderdruck (March 1913): 1–4.
31. Quoted from the source collection, Kindt, ed., *Die Wandervogelzeit*, p. 251.
32. Bruns, *Politik des Eros*, p. 356.
33. Reprinted in Kindt, ed., *Die Wandervogelzeit*, pp. 253–54.
34. Quoted from Bruns, *Politik des Eros*, pp. 375–76.
35. Alternative German- and Austrian-Jewish youth organizations had been organized by 1900, inspired often by the Zionist project of Theodor Herzl. See Gert Mattenklott, " 'Nicht durch Kampfesmacht und nicht durch Körperkraft . . .': Alternativen jüdischer Jugendbewegung in Deutschland von Anfang bis 1933," in Koebner, ed., *"Mit uns zieht die neue Zeit,"* pp. 338–59.
36. All quotations from Bruns, *Politik des Eros*, pp. 371–73.
37. Blüher, *Secessio Judaica*, p. 15.
38. Ibid., pp. 15–16.
39. Ibid., pp. 21–22.
40. Thomas Mann, *Essays*, vol. 2: *Für das neue Deutschland, 1919–1925*, ed. Hermann Kurzke and Stephan Stachorski (Frankfurt, 1993), pp. 271–73.
41. Hiller, *Leben gegen die Zeit*, p. 117.

CHAPTER SIX Weimar Sexual Reform and the Institute for Sexual Science

1. GStA PK, A Pr. Br. Rep. 030, no. 17625, Dr. Magnus Hirschfeld Stiftung 1919, fols. 1–30v.
2. Ralf Dose and Rainer Herrn are preparing a book-length study of the institute. Most of the minute detail in this chapter comes from the CD-ROM *Institut für Sexualwissenschaft*, which documents a 2002 exhibit mounted by the Magnus-Hirschfeld-Gesellschaft (including Dose and Herrn).
3. D'Alessandro, "Über alles die Liebe."
4. Russell, *The Tamarisk Tree*, p. 219.
5. Sanger, *An Autobiography*, pp. 286–87.
6. Robinson, "The Institute of Sexual Science," p. 393.
7. "Bericht über das erste Tätigkeitsjahr (1. Juli 1919 bis 30. Juni 1920) des Instituts für Sexualwissenschaft," *JbfsZ* 20 (1920): 54–74, quoted from p. 55.
8. Quoted in Eissler, *Arbeiterparteien und Homosexuellenfrage*, p. 34.
9. Theis, "Verdrängung und Travestie," p. 102, fn. 1.
10. Forster, *Anders als die Andern*.
11. The film was believed lost until a significant fragment was discovered in a Russian film archive in the early 1990s and made available on DVD. For a comprehensive review of the film, its history, and its censorship see Steakley, *Anders als die Andern*. See also the valuable discussion in Lücke, *Männlichkeit in Unordnung*, pp. 236–43; as well as the discussion by Dyer, "Weimar—Less and More Like the Others," and by Hohmann, *Sexualforschung und -aufklärung in der Weimarer Republik*, pp. 258–76.
12. Loos, *A Girl Like I*, p. 248.
13. Isherwood, *Christopher and His Kind, 1929–1939*, p. 126.
14. Gordon, *The Seven Addictions and Five Professions of Anita Berber*; Fischer, *Tanz zwischen Rausch und Tod*.
15. "Aus der Bewegung," *JfsZ* 20 (1920–21): 116–17.
16. Steakley, *Anders als die Andern*, pp. 105–7.
17. Hohmann, *Sexualforschung*, pp. 258–76.
18. Kuzniar, *The Queer German Cinema*, and McCormick, *Gender and Sexuality in Weimar Modernity*. For valuable reference see also Brockmann, *A Critical History of German Film*, and Elsaesser, *Weimar Cinema and After*.
19. Wolff, *Magnus Hirschfeld*, pp. 440–44.
20. Blüher, *Secessio Judaica*, p. 15.
21. *Die Freundschaft* 10 (1920).
22. "Aus der Bewegung," p. 127.
23. *New York Times*, 12 October 1920.
24. Adolf Hitler, *Sämtliche Aufzeichnungen 1905–1924*, ed. Eberhard Jäckel (Stuttgart, 1980), p. 248.
25. Ellis, "Sexo-ästhetische Inversion," pp. 136–37.
26. See Herrn, *Schnittmuster des Geschlechts*, for an excellent analysis of Hirschfeld's pivotal contributions. Herrn claims that by 1906 Hirschfeld distinguished clearly between homosexual and heterosexual cross-dressers (pp. 57–61). See also Hirschauer, *Die soziale Konstruktion der Transsexualität*.
27. Some examples include *BBZ*, 7 February 1894 (no. 31); *BMZ*, 22 January 1898 (no. 18).
28. See Dobler, "Der Travestiekünstler Willi Pape alias Voo-Doo," pp. 110–21; there is also a large collection of picture postcards of German performers in the Cor-

nell University Library, MS Collection, no. 7636, "German Transvestite Postcards, 1903–1920."

29. Anon., *Eine Weib?;* anon., "Die Wahrheit über mich," pp. 292–307; Böhme, ed., *Tagebuch einer Verlorenen, von einer Toten.*

30. Anon., *Der Roman eines Konträrsexuellen.* The original French version was published in 1895.

31. For example, *BTb,* 11 December 1906 (no. 628).

32. Anon., *Tagebuch einer männlichen Braut.* The title had appeared in at least three editions by 1909. See the recent edition published in 2010 with the valuable afterword by Jens Dobler (pp. 154–75).

33. N. O. Body, *Aus eines Mannes Mädchenjahren* (Berlin, 1907). Karl Baer was the director of the B'nai B'rith in Berlin before his immigration to Israel in 1938. His identity as "N. O. Body" was established only recently. For a full account see the English edition, *Memoirs of a Man's Maiden Years;* see also Thorson, "Masking/Unmasking Identity in Early Twentieth-Century Germany."

34. *WaM,* 22 January 1906 (no. 4).

35. *BTb,* 30 January 1909 (no. 54).

36. Herrn, *Schnittmuster des Geschlechts,* pp. 68–69.

37. *BTb,* 27 February 1912 (no. 106); see also the lengthy account in *Verzaubert in Nord-Ost,* pp. 58–80.

38. Quoted from *BBC,* 18 March 1913 (no. 129).

39. Reports appeared as well in *BBZ,* 18 March 1913 (no. 129); *DTz,* 18 March 1913 (no. 140); *VZ,* 18 March 1913 (no. 140); *BTb,* 18 March 1913 (no. 140); *BVZ,* 18 March 1913 (no. 129); *KJ,* 22 March 1913 (no. 12).

40. *BLA,* 30 August 1912 (no. 441).

41. Steinach, "Willkürliche Umwandlung von Säugetier-Männchen in Tiere mit ausgeprägt weiblichen Geschlechtscharakteren und weiblicher Psyche" and "Pubertätsdrüsen und Zwitterbildung."

42. Hirschfeld, *Geschlechtskunde,* vol. 1, pp. 564, 584–85.

43. In 1920 Steinach published a short, popular account of his research: *Verjüngung durch experimentelle Neubelebung der alternden Pubertaätsdrüse.*

44. Herrn und Brinckmann, "Von Ratten und Männern."

45. Schmidt, "Helfer und Verfolger."

46. Steinach, *Verjüngung durch experimentelle Neubelebung der alternden Pubertaätsdrüse.*

47. KI, Hirschfeld Scrapbook, box 2, fol. 2, p. 72.

48. Holz, "Kausistischer Beitrag zum sogenannten Transvestitismus," p. 30.

49. Marcuse, "Ein Fall von Geschlechtsumwandlungstrieb."

50. Mühsam, "Chirurgische Eingriffe bei Anomalien des Sexuallebens," pp. 452–53.

51. Ibid., p. 455.

52. Ibid., p. 451.

53. Levy-Lenz, *Memoirs of a Sexologist,* pp. 464, 488, 489.

54. Holz, "Kasuistischer Beitrag"; Kankeleit, "Selbstbeschädigungen und Selbstverstümmelungen der Geschlechtsorgane"; Felix, "Genitalumwandlung an zwei männlichen Transvestiten," pp. 223–26.

55. Levy-Lenz, *Memoirs of a Sexologist,* p. 463.

56. Herrn, *Schnittmuster des Geschlechts,* p. 21.

57. Hirschfeld, *Geschlechtskunde,* vol. 1, p. 592.

58. Benjamin, *The Transsexual Phenomenon;* see also Meyerowitz, *How Sex Changed.*

59. See the interview with Benjamin on the occasion of his one hundredth birthday: "Der transatlantische Pendler," *Sexualmedizin* 14, no. 1 (1985): 44–45.

60. Kammerer, *Rejuvenation and the Prolongation of Human Efficiency.*
61. Hirschfeld, *Die Homosexualität des Mannes und des Weibes,* pp. 441–42.
62. Krafft-Ebing, "Neue Studien auf dem Gebiete der Homosexualität," quoted from pp. 5–6.
63. Hirschfeld, *Die Homosexualität des Mannes und des Weibes,* pp. 439–61.
64. See the interview conducted by Rosa von Praunheim on 13 October 1991 and published in *Capri* 3 (1991): 11–16.
65. Hackett, "Helen Stöcker."
66. BAB, R 8069, no. 3, fols. 14, 32, 66.
67. Hirschfeld and Linsert, *Empfängnisverhütung: Mittel und Methoden,* p. 5; see also Usborne, "Geburtenkontrolle in der Weimarer Republik und Magnus Hirschfelds widersprüchliche Interessen."
68. Arthur Weil, ed. (on behalf of the institute), *Sexualreform und Sexualwissenschaft;* Riese and Leunbach, eds., *Sexual Reform Congress, Copenhagen 1–5;* Haire, ed., *Sexual Reform Congress, London 8–14;* and Steiner, ed., *Sexualnot und Sexualreform.*
69. Grossmann, *Reforming Sex,* p. 135.
70. Kartell für Reform des Sexualstrafrechts, *Sittlichkeit und Strafrecht.*
71. Levy-Lenz, *Memoirs of a Sexologist,* p. 387.

CHAPTER SEVEN   Sex Tourism and Male Prostitution in Weimar Berlin

1. Isherwood, *Christopher and His Kind,* pp. 2–4.
2. Siegfried Krakauer, "Travel and Dance," in *The Mass Ornament: Weimar Essays* (Cambridge, 1995), p. 73.
3. Herzer, ed., *Bibliographie zur Homosexualität;* Uwe Schön, "Die Zeitschriften der Homosexuellenbewegung in Deutschland," typewritten ms. (1987), in SchwMu, Al/2oo/ Schön/1-W.
4. Jackson, *Living in Arcadia,* p. 30; Chauncey, *Gay New York;* Hohmann, ed., *Der Kreis;* and Kennedy, *The Ideal Gay Man.*
5. LAB, A Pr. Br. Rep. 030, tit. 121, no. 16935.
6. The Berlin entry fills pages 7–16 of the sixty-three-page pamphlet, which is reprinted in *Forum: Homosexualität und Literatur* 14 (1998).
7. Quoted from Herring, *Djuna,* pp. 97–98.
8. Ludington, *Marsden Hartley,* p. 160. See also Weinberg, *Speaking for Vice,* pp. 141–62.
9. Hartley, *Somehow a Past.*
10. McAlmon, *Distinguished Air,* p. 37.
11. Quoted from Schulze, *Philip Johnson,* pp. 54, 61.
12. Evans, *Grant Wood,* pp. 64–76.
13. Mann, *The Turning Point,* pp. 87–88.
14. Ostwald, *Sittengeschichte der Inflation,* p. 126.
15. Quoted from Howard's journal published in *Brian Howard,* p. 235.
16. NYPL Berg, W. H. Auden, "Berlin Journal."
17. Ibid.
18. UCSD MSCL, MSS84, John Layard Papers, box 1, fol. 15, Isherwood to Layard, 5 January 1930.
19. Koshar, *German Travel Cultures,* pp. 82–86.
20. Hamilton, *Mr. Norris and I,* p. 129–30.
21. Quoted from Mitchell, *Maurice Bowra,* p. 123.

22. Quoted from ibid., p. 137.

23. Ibid., p. 137.

24. Delaney, *Glyn Philpot*, pp. 120–24; Aldrich, *Colonialism and Homosexuality*, pp. 157–59.

25. Moreck, *Führer durch das "lasterhafte" Berlin*, p. 132.

26. Cordan, *Die Matte*, pp. 87–88.

27. Herbert, *Second Son*, quoted from pp. 37, 38, 39.

28. Lewis, *Dodsworth*, (New York, 1929), p. 239.

29. Renoir, *My Life and My Films*, pp. 95, 96.

30. Sybille Bedford, *Aldous Huxley: A Biography* (Chicago, 1973), p. 241.

31. GStA PK, I. HA Rep. 77, tit. 435, no. 6, "Die polizeilichen Massregeln gegen die zum öffentlichen Ärgernis gereichenten Unsittlichkeiten 1815–1930," fol. 70a.

32. Linsert, "Der Strichjunge," p. 34.

33. GStA PK, I. HA Rep. 77, tit. 435, no. 6.

34. Linsert, "Der Strichjunge."

35. Magnus Hirschfeld Gesellschaft, "Linsert Enquete" (ms.), 276 pp. For a report on the "Linsert Enquete" see Dose, "Gay Studies am Institut für Sexualwissenschaft?" See also the important study by historian Martin Lücke, *Männlichkeit in Unordnung.*

36. MHG, LE, no. 16.

37. MHG, LE, nos. 21, 56.

38. MHG, LE, nos. 59, 83, 85, 86, 88, 89.

39. Linsert, "Der Strichjunge," pp. 58–59.

40. Kiaulehn, *Berlin*, p. 578.

41. Got, *L'Allemagne a nu*, pp. 107–08.

42. Ibid., p. 109.

43. Mackay, *The Hustler*, pp. 52–55.

44. Cordan, *Die Matte.*

45. Siemsen appended the essay as an afterword to his 1927 novelization of a same-sex love affair, *Verbotene Liebe.* See Siemsen, *Schriften*, pp. 247–48.

46. Lehmann, *In the Purely Pagan Sense*, pp. 44–45.

47. Mackay, *The Hustler*, p. 243.

48. UCSD MSCL, MSS84 (John Layard Papers), box 59, fol. 6, Autobiography (typewritten ms.), pp. 203–04.

49. Lücke, *Männlichkeit in Unordnung*, pp. 150–232.

50. Both "W. H." and "X. X." reported that they had their first homosexual encounters and learned about prostitution in detention facilities—see MHG, "Linsert Enquete" (ms.), nos. 90, 98.

51. Linsert, "Der Strichjunge," pp. 44–45.

52. Mackay, *The Hustler*, p. 192.

53. LAB, A Rep. 359-01, no. 1012.

54. LAB, A Rep. 350, no. 14157.

55. LAB, A Rep. 358-02, no. 20888.

56. LAB, A Rep. 350, no. 14169.

57. LAB, A Rep. 342, no. 5905.

58. LAB, A Rep. 342, no. 5968.

59. Gay, *Freud*, pp. 42–45.

60. For the history of cocaine, see Friman, "Germany and the Transformations of Cocaine, 1860–1920," and also Stephens, *Germans on Drugs.*

61. *NYT*, 16 August 1925.

62. McAlmon, *Distinguished Air*, pp. 37–38. Drugs seem to have been especially perva-

sive in the period leading up to the Great Inflation of 1923. See English journalist Gerald Hamilton, who first came to Berlin in 1921: *As Young as Sophocles*, pp. 180–81.

63. Scheuer, "Rauschgifte—Kokain"; Frank, "Rauschgiftseuche."

64. Howard's "Berlin Journal," excerpted in *Brian Howard*, pp. 237–38.

65. Elsaesser, *Weimar Cinema and After*, pp. 156–88.

66. Gordon, *The Seven Addictions and Five Professions of Anita Berber*, p. 177.

67. Quoted from Pieper, ed., *Nazis on Speed*, vol. 1, p. 36.

68. Joël and Fränkel, *Der Cocainismus*. See also the account of both doctors in Friedrich, *Before the Deluge*, p. 344.

69. Marx, "Beiträge zur Psychologie der Kokainomanie," p. 550.

70. Benjamin's notes on his hashish trips were published posthumously with an introduction that quoted from a Joël essay. See Benjamin, *On Hashish*.

71. Joël and Fränkel, "Kokainismus und Homosexualität."

72. Maier, *Der Kokainismus*, pp. 97–100. See also Scheuer, "Rauschgifte—Kokain."

73. Lania, *Today We Are Brothers*, p. 214.

74. Engelbrecht and Heller, *Berliner Razzien*, pp. 12–16. See also Weka, *Stätten der Berliner Prostitution*, pp. 90–91.

75. Joël and Fränkel, *Cocainismus*, pp. 28–29, and "Kokainismus und Homosexualität," p. 1564.

76. Siemsen, *Schriften*, p. 248.

77. *Tagebücher*, 6 vols. (Munich, 1989–91), vol. 1, pp. 32, 88.

78. MHG, "Linsert Enquete" (ms.), subject no. 35.

79. Maier, *Kokainismus*, pp. 169–70.

80. MHG, "Linsert Enquete" (ms.), subject no. 85.

81. Mackay, *The Hustler*, p. 89.

82. MHG, "Linsert Enquete" (ms.), subject no. 98.

CHAPTER EIGHT Weimar Politics and the Struggle for Legal Reform

1. BAB, R30071/5776, 49, "Bericht über die Verhandlung im Strafrechtsausschuß," fols. 7–8.

2. BAB, R3001/5774, fols. 120–21.

3. Ibid., fol. 122.

4. Sievert, *Das Anomale Bestrafen*, p. 49.

5. *JfsZ* 20 (1920–21): 107–08.

6. *JfsZ* 22 (1922): 60.

7. *Blätter für Menschenrecht* 1 (15 February 1923): p. 4.

8. SHC, *Tätigkeit und Zweck des Wissenschaftlich-humanitären Komitees* (Berlin, 1924), p. 12.

9. See the "Ortsgruppen" reports in *Blätter für Menschenrecht* 1 (15 February 1923): 4; 12 (28 July 1923): 4; 17 (1 October 1923): 4.

10. Hiller, *Leben gegen die Zeit (Logos)*, p. 233.

11. Hiller, *Leben gegen die Zeit (Eros)*, p. 87.

12. Hergemöller, *Mann für Mann*, p. 511.

13. *Eros* 4, 5, 6 (1930).

14. *Satzung der GdE* (Berlin, 1925), in UT HRC, British Sexological Society Papers, Misc. 2, ALS, ITLS.

15. Ibid.

16. Ibid.
17. Willy Bremer, "Homoerotik und Politik," *Blätter für Menschenrecht* 14 (1 September 1923): 2.
18. Hergemöller, *Mann für Mann*, pp. 331–35, 695–96.
19. Brand, "Gegen die Propaganda der Homosexualität," in *Der Eigene* 10, no. 9 (1925): 405–13, quoted from p. 407.
20. Waldecke, *Das Wissenschaftlich-humanitäre Komitee*, p. 12.
21. Brand, "Volksentscheid und Reichstagswahlen," *Der Eigene* 11 (1926): 80.
22. Hiller, "Persönliches über Magnus Hirschfeld," *Der Kreis* 16, no. 5 (1948): 4.
23. Paul Weber, "Zum 50. Geburtstag Friedrich Radszuweits," *Das Freundschaftsblatt* 4, no. 16 (1926): 1–2.
24. See monthly reports in *Blätter für Menschenrecht* 1 (15 February 1923): 2; 3 (15 March 1923): 2; and 5 (15 April 1923): 2–3.
25. Friedrich Radszuweit, "Unsere Stunde ist gekommen," *Blätter für Menschenrecht* 1, no. 1 (15 February 1923): 1; 1, no. 7 (15 May 1923).
26. Friedrich Radszuweit, "Unsere Bewegung: Rückblick und Ausblick," *Blätter für Menschenrecht* 7, no. 1 (January 1929): 1–2.
27. Friedrich Radszuweit, "Wenn zwei dasselbe tun . . . ," *Blätter für Menschenrecht* 6 (1 April 1923): 5.
28. Döblin, *Berlin Alexanderplatz*, pp. 84–85.
29. Freunde eines Schwulen Museums, *Goodbye to Berlin—100 Jahre Schwulenbewegung* (exhibition catalog), pp. 95–100, 126.
30. Senelick, "The Homosexual Theatre Movement in the Weimar Republic."
31. See the essays authored by Radszuweit: "Sieg oder Niderlage," *Blätter für Menschenrecht* 3, no. 9 (September 1925): 4–5; "W.h.K. und die männliche Prostitution," *Blätter für Menschenrecht* 7, no. 8 (August 1929): 1–3; "Aus der Bewegung," *Blätter für Menschenrecht* 5, no. 12 (December, 1927): 4–5.
32. See "Von der 'männlichen Kultur' und den Schwarmgeistern" [unsigned], *Blätter für Menschenrecht* 2, no. 6 (21 March 1924): 1–2; K. F. Jordan, "Der 'mann-männliche Eros' und die Soziabilität," *Blätter für Menschenrecht* 2, no. 31 (12 September 1924): 1–2; A. B., "Warum bekämpfen die 'Deutschnational' die homosexuelle Bewegung?," *Blätter für Menschenrecht* 4–5 (May 1926): 3–6.
33. See *BLA* 356 (1927); *BVA* 344 (1927); *Blätter für Menschenrecht* 1 (26 July 1927): 4; (exhibition catalog), *Schwulenbewegung*, Freunde eines Schwulen Museums, *Goodbye to Berlin—100 Jahre*, p. 103.
34. *Das Freundschaftsblatt* 2 (14 January 1927).
35. *Das Freundschaftsblatt* 5, no. 1 (7 January 1927): 1–2.
36. Sievert, *Das Anomale Bestrafen*.
37. BAB, R30071/5774, 468, "Anträge auf Beseitigung."
38. Eissler, *Arbeiterparteien und Homosexuellenfrage*, pp. 48, 70.
39. "Anträge auf Beseitigung."
40. Ibid.
41. BAB, R3001/5774, fol. 511.
42. *Eros* 6, no. 3 (1932): 1.
43. See Brand's letters to the British Sexological Society, dated November 1933 and February 1934, in UT HRC, Misc. 2 ALS.
44. Hergemöller, *Mann für Mann*, pp. 171–72.

Epilogue

1. See the eyewitness account in Grau, ed., *Hidden Holocaust?*, pp. 31–33.
2. Wolff, *Magnus Hirschfeld*.
3. An article in the *New York American* announced Hirschfeld's arrival in the United States, "Greatest Expert on Love to Study Romance in US" (16 November 1930).
4. See his travel chronicle, *Weltreise eines Sexualforschers* (1933).
5. Hirschfeld, "Autobiographical Sketch," in Victor Robinson, ed., *Encyclopaedia Sexualis* (New York, 1936), pp. 317–21.
6. Levy-Lenz, *Memoirs*, pp. 429, 430, 442.
7. See the Röhm biography, Eleanor Hancock, *Ernst Röhm: Hitler's SA Chief of Staff* (Basingstoke, 2008); also "Ernst Röhm" in Hergemöller, *Mann für Mann*, pp. 589–90; Herrn, *Anders Bewegt*.
8. See the essays by Manfred Herzer and Andreas Sternweiler in Herzer, ed., *100 Jahre Schwulenbewegung*, pp. 155–68.
9. Zur Nieden, "Aufstieg und Fall des virilen Männerhelden."
10. Lautmann, *Seminar*, p. 333; Richard Plant, *The Pink Triangle: The Nazi War Against Homosexuals* (New York, 1986), p. 154; Burkhard Jellonnek, *Homosexuelle unter dem Hakenkreuz* (Paderborn, 1990), pp. 80–139; Burkhard Jellonnek and Rüdiger Lautmann, eds., *Nationalsozialistischer Terror gegen Homosexuelle* (Paderborn, 2002); Andreas Pretzel and Gabriele Roßbach, *Wegen der zu erwartenden hohen Strafe* (Berlin, 2000).
11. Herzog, *Sex after Fascism*, p. 34.
12. Ibid., quoted from p. 130.
13. Ibid., 152–62.
14. Hans-Georg Stümke and Rudi Finkler, *Rosa Winkel, Rosa Listen: Homosexuelle und "Gesundes Volksempfinden" von Auschwitz bis Heute* (Hamburg, 1981), pp. 352–55.
15. Schulz, *Paragraph 175. (abgewickelt)*.

Sources and Bibliography

Abbreviations

NEWSPAPERS AND JOURNALS

Berliner Börsen-Courier	BBC
Berliner Börsen-Zeitung	BBZ
Berliner Illustrierte Zeitung	BIZ
Berliner Lokal-Anzeiger	BLA
Berliner Morgenpost	BMp
Berliner Tageblatt	BTb
Berliner Volks-Zeitung	BVZ
Deutsche Tageszeitung	DTz
Deutsche Warte	DW
Deutsche Zeitung	DZ
Jahrbuch für sexuelle Zwischenstufen	JfsZ
Das Kleine Journal	KJ
Mitteilungen der Magnus-Hirschfeld-Gesellschaft	MdMHG
Der Montag	DM
National-Zeitung	NZ
Norddeutsche Allgemeine Zeitung	NdAZ
Die Post	DP
Tägliche Rundschau	TR
Vorwärts	Vw
Vossische Zeitung	VZ
Welt am Montag	WaM

MUSEUMS, LIBRARIES, ARCHIVES

Bundesarchiv Berlin	BAB
Cornell Sexuality Collection	CSC
Geheim Staatsarchiv Preuss. Kulturbesitz	GStA PK
Huntington Library	HL
Kinsey Institute	KI
Landesarchiv Berlin	LAB
Magnus-Hirschfeld-Gesellschaft Bibliothek	MHG
NYPL, Berg MS collection	NYPL Berg
Schwules Museum	SchwMu
San Francisco Gay Archive	SFGA
Staatsbibliothek Berlin	Stabi Berlin
Univ. CA San Diego	
Mandeville Special Collections Library	UCSD MSCL
Univ. TX Harry Ransom Center	UT HRC

Homosexual and Lesbian Periodicals Published in Berlin*

Agathon. Published by Paul Steegemann. 1917–18.
Bel Ami. Published by Charles Grieger. 1932–33.
Blätter für Menschenrecht. Published by Friedrich Radszuweit. 1923–33.
Blätter idealer Frauenfreundschaften. Published by Selli Engler. 1924–27.
Das Dritte Geschlecht. Published by Friedrich Radszuweit. 1930–33.
Die Ehelosen und Eheverbundenen. Published by Tiedt. 1926–28.
Der Eigene. Published by Adolf Brand. 1896–31.
Eros. Published by Adolf Brand. 1927–31.
Extrapost des Eigenen. Published by Adolf Brand. 1911–12.
Die Fanfare. Published by Ernst Wolfgang, Curt Neuburger, and Max Danielsen. 1924–26.
Frauen-Liebe und -Leben. Published by Käthe André and Carl Bergmann. 1926–30.
Der Freund. Published by Karl Schultz. 1919.
Die Freundin. Published by Friedrich Radszuweit. 1924–33.
Die Freundschaft. Published by Karl Schultz, Georg Plock, and Georg Krabbenhöft. 1919–33.
Freundschaft und Freiheit. Published by Adolf Brand. 1921.
Freundschaftsblatt. Published by Friedrich Radszuweit. 1925–33.
Der Führer. Published by Lokalinhaber-Klub "Berlin." 1922.
Garçonne. Published by Carl Bergmann. 1930–32.
Gemeinschaft der Eigenen. Published by Adolf Brand. 1904–26.
Der Hellasbote. Published by Hans Kahnert. 1923–24.
Die Insel der Einsamen. Published by Friedrich Radszuweit. 1923–33.
Ledige Frauen. Published by Bruno Balz and Friedrich Radszuweit. 1924–29.
Menschenrecht. Published by Friedrich Radszuweit. 1928–29.
Mitteilungen des Wissenschaftlich-humanitäres Komitee. Published by Magnus Hirschfeld and SHC. 1902–33.
Neue Freundschaft. Published by Max H. Danelsen and Carl Bergmann. 1928.
Der Strom. Published by Karl Schultz. 1921–22.
Uranos. Published by Karl Schultz. 1921–22.

Memoirs, Diaries, First-Person Accounts, Correspondence

Adams, Henry. *The Education of Henry Adams: An Autobiography.* Boston, 1918.
Anon. *Der Roman eines Konträrsexuellen: Eine Autobiographie.* Ed. Émile Zola. Paris, 1895. Trans. Wilhelm Thal. 1899. Reprint. Berlin, 1991.
Anon. "Die Wahrheit über mich: Selbstbiographie einer Konträrsexuellen." *JfsZ* 3 (1901): 292–307.
Bebel, August. *Aus meinem Leben.* 3 vols. Berlin, 1910–46.
Benjamin, Walter. *On Hashish.* Ed. Marcus Boon. Cambridge, 2006.
Bismarck, Otto von. *Gedanken und Erinnerungen.* Berlin, 1898.
Blüher, Hans. *Werk und Tage.* Jena, 1920. New revised edition. Munich, 1953.

---

*Sources: Herzer, ed., *Bibliographie zur Homosexualität,* and Uwe Schön, "Die Zeitschriften der Homosexuellenbewegung in Deutschland," typewritten ms. (1987), in SchwuMu, Al/200/ Schön/1-W.

Body, N. O. [Karl M. Baer]. *Memoirs of a Man's Maiden Years.* Trans. Deborah Simon. 1907. Reprint. Philadelphia, 2006.

Böhme, Margarete, ed. *Tagebuch einer Verlorenen, von einer Toten.* Berlin, 1905.

Bülow, Bernhard von. *Denkwürdigkeiten.* 4 vols. Berlin, 1930–31.

Cordan, Wolfgang. *Die Matte: Autobiografische Aufzeichnungen.* Hamburg, 2003.

Friedländer, Hugo [Hugländer, F., pseud.] "Aus dem homosexuellen Leben Alt-Berlins." *JfsZ* 14 (1914): 45–63.

Friedrich, Otto. *Before the Deluge.* New York, 1972.

Gidlow, Elsa. *Elsa: I Come with My Songs, the Autobiography of Elsa Gidlow.* San Francisco, 1986.

Got, Ambroise. *L'Allemagne a nu.* Paris, 1923.

Hamilton, Gerald. *As Young as Sophocles.* London, 1937.

———. *Mr. Norris and I: An Autobiographical Sketch.* London, 1956.

Hamilton, Lord Frederick. *My Yesterdays.* New York, 1930.

Harden, Maximilian. *Köpfe.* 3 vols. Berlin, 1910–13.

Hartley, Marsden. *Somehow a Past: The Autobiography of Marsden Hartley.* Cambridge, 1997.

Herbert, David. *Second Son: An Autobiogrpaphy.* London, 1972.

Hiller, Kurt. *Leben gegen die Zeit.* 2 vols. Hamburg, 1969–73.

Hirschfeld, Magnus. *Von einst bis jetzt.* 1923. Berlin, 1986.

———. *Weltreise eines Sexualforschers.* 1933.

———. *Magnus Hirschfeld: Testament,* heft II. Ed. Ralf Dose. Berlin, 2013.

Holstein, Friedrich von. *The Holstein Papers,* vol. 4: *Correspondence 1897–1909.* Ed. Norman Rich and M. H. Fisher. Cambridge, 1963.

Homann, Walter [anon.]. *Tagebuch einer männlichen Braut: Die Geschichte eines Doppelwesens.* 1907. Reprint. Berlin, 1996.

Howard, Brian. *Brian Howard: Portrait of a Failure.* Ed. Marie-Jaqueline Lancaster. Devon, 2005.

Huard, Charles. *Berlin comme je l'ai vue.* Paris, 1907.

Isherwood, Christopher. *Christopher and His Kind, 1929–1939.* New York, 1976.

Kessler, Count Harry. *Berlin in Lights: The Diaries of Count Harry Kessler (1918–1937).* New York, 1999.

———. *Journey to the Abyss: The Diaries of Count Harry Kessler, 1880–1918.* Ed. and trans. Laird M. Easton. New York, 2011.

Kiaulehn, Walther. *Berlin: Schicksal einer Weltstadt.* Munich, 1958.

Lange, Friedrich C. *Gross-Berliner Tagebuch 1920–1933.* Berlin, 1951.

Lania, Leo. *Today We Are Brothers: The Biography of a Generation.* Boston, 1942.

Levy-Lenz, Ludwig. *Memoirs of a Sexologist: Discretion and Indiscretion.* New York, 1951.

Loos, Anita. *A Girl Like I.* New York, 1966.

Mackay, John Henry. *Autiobiographical Writings.* Ed. and trans. Hubert Kennedy. Bloomington, IN, 2000.

Mann, Klaus. *The Turning Point: Thirty-five Years in This Century.* New York, 1942.

Méténier, Oscar. *Les Berlinois chez eux: Vertus et Vices allemands.* Paris, 1905.

Mirbeau, Octave. *La 628-E8.* Paris, 1907.

Moll, Albert. *Ein Leben als Arzt der Seele: Erinnerungen.* Dresden, 1936.

Pachter, Henry. *Weimar Etudes.* New York, 1982.

PEM [Paul Markus]. *Heimweh nach dem Kurfürstendamm.* Berlin, 1952.

Podjukl, Otto [Joux, Otto de, pseud.]. *Die Enterblen des Liebesglücks.* Leipzig, 1893.

Radziwill, Marie Fürstin. *Briefe vom deutschen Kaiserhof 1889–1915.* Berlin, 1936.

Renoir, Jean. *My Life and My Films*. Trans. Norman Denny. New York, 1974.

Riess, Curt. *Das waren Zeiten*. Vienna, 1977.

Röhl, John C. G., ed. *Philipp Eulenburgs politische Korrespondenz*, vol. 3: *Krisen, Krieg und Katastrophen: 1895–1921*. Boppard am Rhein, 1983.

Roth, Joseph. *What I Saw: Reports from Berlin 1920–1933*. Trans. Michael Hofmann. New York, 2003.

Russell, Dora. *The Tamarisk Tree: My Quest for Liberty and Love*. London, 1977.

Sanger, Margaret. *An Autobiography*. New York, 1971.

Schoenaich, Paul Freiherr von [Paul von Hoverbeck]. *Mein Damaskus: Erlebnisse und Bekenntnisse*. Hamburg, 1926.

Siemsen, Hans. *Schriften: Verboten Liebe und andere Geschichten*. Essen, 1986.

Spender, Stephen. *World Within World: The Autobiography of Stephen Spender*. Rochester, 1951.

Sziytta, Emil. *Das Kuriositäten-Kabinett: Begegnungen mit seltsamen Begebenheiten, Landstreichern, Verbrechern, Artisten, religiös Wahnsinnigen, sexuellen Merkwürdigkeiten, Sozialdemokraten, Syndikalisten, Kommunisten, Anarchisten, Politikern u. Künstlern*. Constance, 1923.

Tresckow, Hans von. *Von Fürsten und anderen Sterblichen: Erinnerungen eines Kriminalkommissars*. Berlin, 1922.

Twain, Mark. *The Complete Essays of Mark Twain*. New York, 1963.

Weindel, Henri de, and F. P. Fischer. *L'Homosexualité en Allemagne: Étude documentaire et anecdotique*. Paris, 1908.

Wolff, Charlotte. *Hindsight: An Autobiography*. London, 1980.

Zedlitz-Trützschler, Robert. *Zwölf Jahre am deutschen Kaiserhof*. Berlin, 1924.

Zuckmayer, Carl. *A Part of Myself: Portrait of an Epoch*. New York, 1970.

Zweig, Stefan. *The World of Yesterday*. New York, 1943.

Contemporary Homoerotic Literature

Anon. *Liebchen: Ein Roman unter Männern*. 1908. Reprint. Berlin, 1995.

Bang, Herman. *Michael*. 1904. Trans. Julia Koppel. Berlin, 1906.

Döblin, Alfred. *Die beide Freundinnen und ihr Giftmord*. 1924. Reprint. Hamburg, 1978.

———. *Berlin Alexanderplatz*. 1929. Trans. Eugen Jolas. New York, 1961.

Eekhoud, Georges. *Escal-Vigor*. Paris, 1899. Trans. Richard Meienreis. Leipzig, 1903.

Essebac, Achille. *Dédé*. Paris, 1901. Trans. Georg Herbert. Leipzig, 1902.

Flex, Walter. *Der Wanderer zwischen beiden Welten*. 1917. Reprint. Kiel, 1984.

Forster, Bill [Hermann Breuer]. *Anders als die Andern*. 1904. Reprint. Hamburg, 2009.

Gide, André. *Der Immoralist*. 1902. Trans. Felix P. Greve. Minden, 1905.

Granand. *Das erotische Komödiengärtlein*. 1920. Reprint. Hamburg, 1993.

Grünewald, Alfred. *Reseda: Novelle und andere Prosa*. Hamburg, 2013.

Homunkulus. *Zwischen den Geschlechtern: Roman einer geächteten Leidenschaft*. 1919. Reprint. Hamburg, 2012.

Isherwood, Christopher. *Goodbye to Berlin*. 1939. Reprint. New York, 1977.

Kästner, Erich. *Fabian*. 1931. Trans. Cyrus Brooks. New York, 1990.

Koebner, F. W. *Cocain: Mondaine und demimondaine Skizzen*. Berlin, 1921.

Kuzmin, Mikhail. *Flügel*. 1906. Trans. Georg Müller. Munich, 1911.

Lampel, Peter Martin. *Verratene Jungen*. Frankfurt, 1929.

Lawrence, D. H. *The Prussian Officer*. 1914. Reprint. New York, 1995.

Layard, John. *In the Purely Pagan Sense*. London, 1976.

Linden, Karl Friedrich von. *Die Süßen: Ein Berliner Roman*. 1909. Reprint. Hamburg, 2007.

Mackay, John Henry [Sagitta, pseud.]. *Die Bücher der namenlosen Liebe von Sagitta*. Paris, 1913. Trans. Hubert Kennedy. Amsterdam, 1988.

———. *The Hustler*. 1926. Trans. Hubert Kennedy. Boston, 1985.

Mann, Klaus. *The Pious Dance*. 1925. Trans. Laurence Senelick. New York, 1987.

———. *Treffpunkt im Unendlichen*. 1932. Reprint. Hamburg, 1981.

McAlmon, Robert. *Distinguished Air: Grim Fairy Tales*. Paris, 1925.

Ménalkas. *Erna: Jeune Fille de Berlin*. Paris, 1932.

Musil, Robert. *The Confusions of Young Törless*. 1906. Trans. Shaun Whiteside. New York, 2001.

Pernauhm, Fritz Geron. *Der junge Kurt*. 1904. Reprint. Hamburg, 2010.

———. *Die Infamen*. 1906. Reprint. Hamburg, 2010.

Popert, Hermann. *Helmut Harringa: Eine Geschichte aus unsrer Zeit*. Dresden, 1913.

Radszuweit, Friedrich. *Männer zu verkaufen: Ein Wirklichkeitsroman aus der Welt der männlichen Erpresser und Prostituierten*. 1930. Reprint. Hamburg, 2012.

Rausch, Albert H. *Eros Anadyomenos*. Stuttgart, 1927.

Sagitta. *See* Mackay, John Henry.

Schwarzenbach, Annemarie. *Freunde um Bernhard*. 1931. Reprint. Basel, 1993.

Siber, Jules. *Seelen-Wanderung*. 1906. Reprint. Hamburg, 2011.

Siemsen, Hans. *Schriften: Verbotene Liebe und andere Geschichten*. 1913–27. Essen, 1986.

Spender, Stephen. *The Temple*. New York, 1976.

Süskind, W. E. *Jugend*. Berlin, 1929.

Thieß, Frank. *Abschied vom Paradies: Ein Roman unter Kindern*. Stuttgart, 1927.

Vogel, Bruno. *Alf*. 1929. Trans. Samuel B. Johnson. London, 1992.

———. *Ein junger Rebell: Erzählungen und Skizzen aus der Weimarer Republik*. Berlin, 1986.

Wassermann, Jakob. *Der Fall Maurizius*. Berlin, 1929.

———. *Etzel Andergast*. Berlin, 1931.

Wiese, Leopold von. *Kindheit: Erinnerungen aus Meinen Kadettenjahren*. Hanover, 1924.

Wilbrandt, Adolf. *Fridolin's Mystical Marriage*. 1875. Trans. Clara Bell. New York, 1888.

Wildenbruch, Ernst von. *Das edle Blut*. New York, 1906.

Zarek, Otto. *Begierde: Roman einer Weltstadtjugend*. Berlin, 1930.

Zweig, Stefan. *Episode in the Early Life of Privy Councillor D*. In *Conflicts: Three Tales by Stefan Zweig*. 1926. Trans. Eden and Cedar Paul. New York, 1927.

Contemporary Medical, Psychiatric, and Sexological Literature

Adler, Alfred. *Das Problem der Homosexualität und sexueller Perversionen*. Leipzig, 1930.

Anon. *Eine Weib? Psychologisch-biographische Studie über eine Konträrsexuelle*. Leipzig, 1897.

Benjamin, Harry. *The Transsexual Phenomenon*. New York, 1966.

Bloch, Iwan. *The Sexual Life of Our Time*. New York, 1937.

Blüher, Hans. *Die drei Grundformen der sexuellen Inversion (Homosexualität): Eine sexuologische Studie*. Leipzig, 1913.

Burnet, James. "Some Aspects of Neurasthenia." *Medical Times and Hospital Gazette* 3 (February 1906): 58–59.

Casper, Johann Ludwig. "Über Notzucht und Päderastie und deren Ermittlung Seitens des Gerichtsartzes." *Vierteljahrsschrift für gerichtliche und öffentliche Medizin* 1 (1852): 21–78.

———. *Practisches Handbuch der gerichtlichen Medizin*. 2 vols. Berlin, 1858–60.

———. *Klinische Novellen zur gerichtlichen Medizin nach eigenen Erfahrungen*. Berlin, 1863.

Dr. Laupts. *See* Saint-Paul, Georges.

Ellis, Havelock. "Sexo-ästhetische Inversion." *Zeitschrift für Psychotherapie und Medizinische Psychologie* 5 (1914): 134–62.

Ellis, Havelock, and J. A. Symonds. *Sexual Inversion*. 1897. Reprint. Philadelphia, 1901.

Felix, Abraham. "Genitalumwandlung an zwei männlichen Transvestiten." *Zeitschrift für Sexualwissenschaft* 18 (1931): 223–26.

Flexner, Abraham. *Prostitution in Europe*. New York, 1914.

Hadermann, Josef. *Practische Anweisung zu solchen gerichtlich-medizinischen Unterweisungen, welche lebende Personen betreffen: Für Ärzte und Rechtsgelehrte*. Erlangen, 1840.

Haire, Norman, ed. *Sexual Reform Congress, London 8–14. IX. 1929, WLSR, World League for Sexual Reform, Proceedings of the Third Congress*. London, 1930.

Hirschfeld, Magnus. *Sappho und Sokrates: Wie erklärt sich die Liebe der Männer und Frauen zu Personen des eigenen Geschlechts?*. Leipzig, 1896.

———. *§ 175 des Reichsstrafgesetzbuchs: Die homosexuelle Frage im Urteile der Zeitgenossen*. Leipzig, 1898.

———. *Der urnische Mensch*. Leipzig, 1903.

———. "Das Ergebnis der statistischen Untersuchungen über den Prozentsatz der Homosexuellen." *JfsZ* 6 (1904): 109–178.

———. *Transvestites: The Erotic Drive to Cross-Dress*. 1910. Trans. Michael Lombardi-Nash. New York, 1991.

———. *Die Homosexualität des Mannes und des Weibes*. Berlin, 1914.

———. *Geschlechtskunde auf Grund dreißigjähriger Forschung und Erfahrung*. 5 vols. Stuttgart, 1926–30.

Hirschfeld, Magnus, and Richard Linsert. *Empfängnisverhütung: Mittel und Methoden*. Berlin, 1928.

Holz, Werner. "Kausistischer Beitrag zum sogenannten Transvestitismus." PhD diss. University of Berlin, 1924.

Jäger, Gustav. *Entdeckung der Seele*. 3rd ed. Leipzig, 1884.

Joël, Ernst, and Fritz Fränkel. *Der Cocainismus*. Berlin, 1924.

———. "Kokainismus und Homosexualität." *Deutsche medizinische Wochenschrift* 38 (1925): 1562–65.

Kammerer, Paul. *Rejuvenation and the Prolongation of Human Efficiency: Experiences with the Steinach-Operation on Man and Animals*. New York, 1923.

Kankeleit, Otto. "Selbstbeschädigungen und Selbstverstümmelungen der Geschlechtsorgane." *Zeitschrift für die gesamte Neurologie und Psychiatrie* 107 (1927): 414–81.

Kartell für Reform des Sexualstrafrechts. *Sittlichkeit und Strafrecht: Gegenentwurf zu den Strafbestimmungen des amtlichen Entwurfs eines algemeinen deutschen Strafgesetzbuches über geschlechtliche und mit dem Geschlechtsleben im Zusammenhang stehende Handlunge (Abschnitte 17, 18, 21, 22, 23) nebst Begründung*. Berlin, 1927.

Krafft-Ebing, Richard von. "Über gewisse Anomalien des Geschlechtstriebs . . ." *Archiv für Psychiatrie und Nervenkrankheiten* 7 (1877): 291–312.

———. "Die conträre Sexualempfindung vor dem Forum." *Jahrbücher für Psychiatrie und forensische Psychologie* 6 (1885): 34–47.

———. *Psychopathia sexualis*. 3rd, 5th, 6th, and 9th eds. Stuttgart, 1888, 1890, 1891, 1894.

———. *Der Conträrsexuale vor dem Strafrichter: De sodomia ratione sexus punienda. De lege lata et de lege ferenda. Eine Denkschrift*. Leipzig, 1894.

———. "Neue Studien auf dem Gebiete der Homosexualität." *JfsZ* 3 (1901): 1–36.

Linsert, Richard. "Der Strichjunge: Eine Darstellung von 100 Lebensläufen männlicher Prostituierter." In Richard Linsert, ed., *§ 297 "Unzucht zwischen Männern"? Ein Beitrag zur Strafgesetzreform*. Berlin, 1929.

Maier, Hans W. *Der Kokainismus: Geschichte, Pathologie, medizinische und behördliche Bekämpfung*. Leipzig, 1925.

Marcuse, Max. "Ein Fall von Geschlechtsumwandlungstrieb." *Zeitschrift für Psychotherapie und medizinische Psychologie* 6 (1916): 176–92.

Marx, Norbert. "Beiträge zur Psychologie der Kakainomanie." *Zeitschrift für die gesammte Neurologie und Psychiatrie* 80 (1923): 550.

Mende, L. J. K. *Ausführliches Handbuch der gerichtlichen Medizin für Gesetzgeber, Rechtsgelehrte, Ärzte und Wundärzte*. 5 vols. Leipzig, 1819–32.

Moll, Albert. *Die conträre Sexualempfindung: Mit Benutzung amtlichen Materials*. Berlin, 1891.

Mühsam, Richard. "Chirurgische Eingriffe bei Anomalien des Sexuallebens." *Therapie der Gegenwart* 67 (1926): 451–55.

Näcke, Paul. "Le monde homo-sexuel de Paris." *Archives d'anthropologie criminelle* 20 (1905): 182–85.

———. "Quelques details sur les homo-sexuels de Paris." *Archives d'anthropologie criminelle* 20 (1905): 411–14.

Parent-Duchatelet, Alexandre. *La Prostitution a Paris au XIX siècle*. 1836. Paris, 1981.

Raffalovich, Marc-André. *Uranisme et Unisexualité: Étude sur différentes manifestations de l'instinct sexuel*. Paris, 1896.

Riese, H., and J. H. Leunbach, eds. *Sexual Reform Congress, Copenhagen 1–5. VII. 1928, WLSR, World League for Sexual Reform, Proceedings of the Second Congress*. Copenhagen and Leipzig, 1929.

Robinson, William. "The Institute of Sexual Science." *Medical Critic and Guide* 25, no. 10 (1925): 391–96.

Saint-Paul, Georges [Dr. Laupts, pseud.]. *Tares et Poisons: perversion et perversité sexuelles; une enquête médicale sur l'inversion. . . . La guérison et la prophylaxie de l'inversion*. Paris, 1896.

———. "Les groupes uranistes a Paris et a Berlin." *Archives d'anthropologie criminelle* 19 (1904): 926–36.

———. "A propos du syndicat des uranistes." *Archives d'anthropologie criminelle* 20 (1905): 283–86.

———. "Dégénérescence ou plethora?" *Archives d'anthropologie criminelle* 23 (1908): 731–48.

———. *L'homosexualité et les types homosexuals*. Paris, 1910.

Scheuer, Oskar. "Rauschgifte—Kokain." In Leo Schidrowitz, ed., *Sittengeschichte des Lasters*, 163–84. Vienna, 1927.

Steinach, Eugen. "Willkürliche Umwandlung von Säugetier-Männchen in Tiere mit ausgeprägt weiblichen Geschlechtscharakteren und weiblicher Psyche." *Pflüg Archiv für die gesammte Physiologie des Menschen und der Tiere* 144 (1912): 71–108.

———. "Pubertätsdrüsen und Zwitterbildung." *Archiv für Entwicklungsmechanik* 42 (1916): 307–32.

———. *Verjüngung durch experimentelle Neubelebung der alternden Pubertätsdrüse*. Berlin, 1920.

Steiner, Herbert, ed. *Sexualnot und Sexualreform: Verhandlungen der Weltliga für Sexualreform. IV. Kongress abgehalten zu Wien vom 16. bis 23. September 1930*. Vienna, 1931.

Weil, Arthur, ed. *Sexualreform und Sexualwissenschaft: Vorträge gehalten auf der I. Internationalen Tagung für Sexualreform auf sexualwissenschaftlicher Grundlage in Berlin*. Stuttgart, 1922.

Westphal, Carl. "Die conträre Sexualempfindung: Symptom eines neuropathischen (psychopathischen) Zustandes." *Archiv für Psychiatrie und Nervenkrankheiten* 2 (1869): 73–108.

Contemporary Printed Sources and Published Source Collections

Anon. *Das perverse Berlin: Kulturkritsche Gänge.* Berlin, 1908.

Bab, Julius. *Die Gleichgeschlechtliche Liebe (Lieblingsminne): Ein Wort über ihr Wesen und ihre Bedeutung.* Berlin, 1903.

———. *Die Berliner Boheme.* Berlin, 1904.

Bertz, Eduard. *Der Yankee-Heiland: Ein Beitrag zur modernen Religionsgeschichte.* Dresden, 1906.

Blüher, Hans. *Die deutsche Wandervogelbewegung als erotisches Phänomen: Ein Beitrag zur Erkenntnis der sexuellen Inversion, m. e. Vorwort v. Dr. med. Magnus Hirschfeld.* Berlin, 1912.

———. *Wandervogel: Geschichte einer Jugendbewegung.* 2 vols. Berlin, 1912.

———. *Die Rolle der Erotik in der männlichen Gesellschaft.* 2 vols. Jena, 1917–19.

———. *Secessio Judaica: Philosophische Grundlegung der historischen Situation des Judentums und der antisemitischen Bewegung.* Berlin, 1922.

Brand, Adolf. *Kaplan Dasbach und die Freundesliebe.* Charlottenburg, 1904.

———[Franz Schwarzer, pseud.]. *Interessante Briefe und Dokumente zur Bülow-Eulenburg-Intrige.* Berlin, 1909.

———. *Die Bedeutung der Freundesliebe für Führer und Völker.* Berlin, 1923.

Carpenter, Edward. *Ioläus: An Anthology of Friendship.* London, 1902.

Chancellor, John. *How to Be Happy in Berlin.* London, 1929.

De Leeuw, Hendrik. *Sinful Cities of the Western World.* New York, 1934.

Documents of the Homosexual Rights Movement in Germany, 1836–1927. New York, 1975.

Engelbrecht, Ernst, and Leo Heller. *Berliner Razzien.* Berlin, 1924.

———. *Kinder der Nacht.* Berlin, 1925.

Flexner, Abraham. *Prostitution in Europe.* New York, 1914.

Fosdick, Raymond. *European Police Systems.* New York, 1915.

Frank, Ladislaus. "Rauschgiftseuche." In Magnus Hirschfeld, ed., *Sittengeschichte der Nachkriegszeit,* 352–57. Berlin, 1931.

Frey, Ludwig [pseud.]. *Der Eros und die Kunst: Ethischen Studien.* Leipzig, 1896.

Friedel, Johann. *Briefe über die Galanterien von Berlin.* Gotha, 1782.

Friedlaender, Benedict. *Die Renaissance des Eros Uranios: Die physiologische Freundschaft, ein normaler Grundtrieb des Menschen und eine Frage der männlichen Gesellungsfreiheit in naturwissenschaftlicher, naturrechtlicher, culturgeschichtlicher und sittenkritischer Beleuchtung.* Berlin, 1904.

———. *Denkschrift verfasst für die Freunde und Fondszeichner des Wissenschaftlich-Humanitären Komitees.* Berlin, 1907.

Friedländer, Hugo. *Interessante Kriminal-Prozesse: Ein Pitaval des Kaiserreichs.* 12 vols. Berlin, 1911–21.

Friedländer, Hugo [Hugländer, F., pseud.]. "Aus dem homosexuellen Leben Alt-Berlins." *JfsZ* 14 (1914): 45–63.

Grand-Carteret, John. *Derrière "Lui," L'Allemagne et la Caricature européenne en 1907.* Paris, 1907.

Guérin, Daniel. *The Brown Plague.* Trans. Robert Schwartzwald. Durham, 1994.

Haeberle, Erwin J., ed. *Anfänge der Sexualwissenschaft: Historische Dokumente.* Berlin, 1983.

Haller, Johannes. *Philip Eulenburg: The Kaiser's Friend.* London, 1930.

Heller, Leo. *So siehstse' aus Berlin!* Munich, 1927.

Hergesheimer, Joseph. *Berlin.* New York, 1932.

Herzer, Manfred, ed. *Schriften zur Homosexualitätsforschung.* Berlin, 2000.

Hiller, Kurt. *§ 175: Die Schmach des Jahrhunderts.* Berlin, 1922.

Hirschfeld, Magnus. *Berlins drittes Geschlecht.* Leipzig, 1904.

Hirschfeld, Magnus, ed. *Sittengeschichte des Weltkrieges 1914–1918.* Leipzig, 1929.

———. *Sittengeschichte der Nachkriegszeit 1918–1930.* Leipzig, 1932.

Hoeniger, Franz. *Berliner Gerichte.* Leipzig, 1906

Hößli, Heinrich. *Eros oder die Männerliebe der Griechen.* 2 vols. St. Gallen, 1836–38.

Huber, Ernst Rudolf. *Deutsche Verfassungsgeschichte seit 1789.* 8 vols. Stuttgart, 1957–90.

Joux, Otto de [Otto Rudolf Podjukl]. *Die hellenische Liebe in der Gegenwart.* Leipzig, 1896.

———. *Die Enterbten des Liebesglückes oder das dritte Geschlecht.* 2nd ed. Leipzig, 1897.

Karsch-Haack, Ferdinand. *Erotische Großstadtbilder als Kulturphänomene.* Berlin, 1926.

Kennen Sie Berlin? Stettin, 1929.

Kertbeny, Karl Maria. *§143 des preussischen Strafgesetzbuches vom 14. April 1851 und seine Aufrechterhaltung als §152 im Entwürfe eines Strafgesetzbuches für den Norddeutschen Bund.* Leipzig, 1869. Republished in Manfred Herzer, ed., *Schriften zur Homosexualitätsforschung,* 63–150. Berlin, 2000.

———. *Das Gemeinschädliche des §143 des preussischen Strafgesetzbuches vom 14. April 1851 und daher seine notwendige Tilgung als §152 im Entwürfe eines Strafgesetzbuches für den Norddeutschen Bund.* Leipzig, 1869. Republished in Manfred Herzer, ed., *Schriften zur Homosexualitätsforschung,* 151–229. Berlin, 2000.

Kindt, Werner, ed. *Die Wandervogelzeit: Quellenschriften zur deutschen Jugendbewegung 1896–1919.* Cologne, 1968.

———. *Die deutsche Jugendbewegung 1920 bis 1933: Die bündische Zeit.* Düsseldorf, 1974.

Kracauer, Siegfried. *Berliner Nebeneinander: Ausgewählte Feuilletons 1930–33.* Zurich, 1996.

Kuppfer, Elisar von. *Lieblingminne und Männerliebe in der Weltliteratur.* Leipzig, 1900.

Lessing, Theodor. *Haarmann: The Story of a Werewolf.* 1925. Reprinted in Theodor Lessing, Karl Berg, and George God, eds., *Monsters of Weimar: The Stories of Fritz Haarmann and Peter Kurten.* London, 1993.

Lindenberg, Paul. *Berliner Polizei und Verbrechertum.* Leipzig, 1892.

Linsert, Richard. *Kabale und Liebe: Über Politik und Geschlechtsleben.* Berlin, 1931.

Moll, Albert. *Berühmte Homosexuelle.* Wiesbaden, 1910.

Moreck, Curt. *Sittengeschichte des Kinos.* Dresden, 1926.

———. *Kultur- und Sittengeschichte der neuesten Zeit: Das Genussleben des modernen Menschen.* Dresden, 1929.

———. *Führer durch das "lasterhafte" Berlin.* Leipzig, 1931.

———. *Erotik in der menschlichen Gesellschaft der Gegenwart.* Censored. N.d.

Näcke, Paul. "Ein Besuch bei den Homosexuellen in Berlin." *Archiv für Kriminal-anthropologie und Kriminalistik* 15(1904): 244–63.

Ostwald, Hans. *Männliche Prostitution.* Leipzig, 1906.

———. *Rinnsteinsprache: Lexikon der Gauner- Dirnen- und Landstreichersprache.* Berlin, 1906.

———. *Sittengeschichte der Inflation: Ein Kulturdokument aus den Jahren des Marktsturzes.* Berlin, 1931.

Otto, Gustav [anon.]. *Die Verbrecherwelt von Berlin.* Berlin, 1886.

Pollard, James. *A Study in Municipal Government: The Corporation of Berlin.* Edinburgh, 1893.

Polzer, Walter. *Sexuell-Perverse.* Leipzig, 1930.

Salardenne, Roger. *Hauptstädte des Lasters.* Berlin, 1931.

Satyr [pseud.]. *Lebeweltnächte der Friedrichstadt.* Leipzig, 1906.

Schaden, Adolph von. *Berlins Licht- und Schattenseiten.* Dessau, 1822.

Schidrowitz, Leo, ed. *Sittengeschichte des Lasters.* Vienna, 1927.

Schlaf, Johannes. *Walt Whitman Homosexueller? Kritische Revision einer Whitman-Abhandlung von Dr. Eduard Bertz.* Minden, 1906.

Schurtz, Heinrich. *Alterklassen und Männerbünde: Eine der Darstellung der Grundformen der Gesellschaft.* Berlin, 1902.

Schwarzer, Franz. *See* Brand, Adolf.

Setz, Wolfram, ed. *Karl Heinrich Ulrichs zu Ehren: Materialien zu Leben und Werk.* Berlin, 2000.

———. *Neue Funde und Studien zu Karl Heinrich Ulrichs.* Hamburg, 2004.

Stieber, Wilhelm [anon.]. *Die Prostitution in Berlin und ihre Opfer: In historischer, sittlicher, medizinischer und polizeilicher Beziehung beleuchtet.* Berlin, 1846.

Szatmari, Eugen. *Das Buch von Berlin: Was nicht im "Baedeker" steht.* Berlin, 1927.

Tscheck, Ewald. *See* Waldecke, St. Ch.

Ulrichs, Karl Heinrich. *Großdeutsches Programm und Lösung des großdeutschen Problems.* Frankfurt, 1862.

———. *The Riddle of "Man-Manly" Love: The Pioneering Work on Male Homosexuality.* Trans. Michael A. Lombardi-Nash. 2 vols. Buffalo, NY, 1994.

Vizetelly, Henry. *Berlin Under the New Empire.* 2 vols. London, 1879.

Waldecke, St. Ch. [Ewald Tscheck]. *Das Wissenschaftlich-humanitäre Komitee: Warum ist es zu bekämpfen und sein Wirken schädlich für das deutsche Volk?* Berlin, 1925.

Weka. *Stätten der Berliner Prostitution.* Berlin, 1930.

Wel, Conrad. *Das verbotene Buch.* Hannover, 1929.

Werthauer, J. *Sittlichkeitsdelikte der Großstadt.* Leipzig, 1907.

Wilhelm, Eugen. "Publications allemandes sur les questions sexuelles." *Archives d'anthropologie criminelle* 27 (1912): 301–09.

Zimmermann, C. W. *Die Diebe in Berlin oder Darstellung ihres Entstehens, ihrer Organisation, ihrer Verbindungen, ihres Taktik, ihrer Gewohnheiten und ihrer Sprache.* 1847. Reprint. Berlin, 1987.

Secondary Sources

Abraham, Julie. *Metropolitan Lovers: The Homosexuality of Cities.* Minneapolis, 2008.

Aldrich, Robert. *Colonialism and Homosexuality.* Routledge, 2002.

Allen, Gay Wilson. *The New Walt Whitman Handbook.* New York, 1975.

Aronson, Theo. *Prince Eddy and the Homosexual Underworld.* London, 1994.

Aschheim, Steven. *The Nietzsche Legacy in Germany, 1890–1990.* Berkeley, 1992.

Bauer, Heike. *English Literary Sexology: Translations of Inversion, 1860–1930.* Basingstoke, 2009.

Baumann, Imanuel. *Dem Verbrechen auf der Spur: Eine Geschichte der Kriminologie und Kriminalpolitik in Deutschland 1880 bis 1980.* Göttingen, 2006.

Baumgardt, Manfred. "Das Institut für Sexualwissenschaft (1919–1933)." In Rüdiger Lautmann, ed., *Homosexualität: Handbuch der Theorie- und Forschungsgeschichte,* 117–23. Frankfurt, 1993.

Baumont, Maurice. *L'Affaire Eulenburg et les Origines de la Premiere Guerre mondiale*. Paris, 1933.

Beachy, Robert. "The German Invention of Homosexuality." *Journal of Modern History* 82, no. 4 (2010): 801–38.

———. "To Police *and* Protect: The Surveillance of Homosexuality in Imperial Berlin." In Scott Spector, Helmut Puff, and Dagmar Herzog, eds., *After the History of Sexuality*, 109–23. New York, 2012.

Becker, Peter. *Verderbnis und Entartung. Eine Geschichte der Kriminologie des 19. Jahrhunderts als Diskurs und Praxis*. Göttingen, 2002.

Belach, Helga, and Wolfgang Jacobsen, eds. *Richard Oswald: Regisseur und Produzent*. Munich, 1990.

Berco, Cristian. *Sexual Hierarchies, Public Status: Men, Sodomy, and Society in Spain's Golden Age*. Toronto, 2007.

Bischof, Gunter, Anton Pelinka, and Dagmar Herzog, eds. *Sexuality in Austria*. New Brunswick, 2006.

Blackbourn, David. *The Long Nineteenth Century: A History of Germany, 1780–1918*. Oxford, 1998.

Boon, L. J. "Those Damned Sodomites: Public Images of Sodomy in the Eighteenth Century Netherlands." In Kent Gerard and Gert Hekma, eds., *The Pursuit of Sodomy: Male Homosexuality in Renaissance and Enlightenment Europe*, 237–48. New York, 1989.

Boyer, Debra. "Male Prostitution and Homosexual Identity." *Journal of Homosexuality* 17, nos. 1–2 (1989): 151–84.

Bray, Alan. *Homosexuality in Renaissance England*. New York, 1982.

Bridenthal, Renate, Atina Grossmann, and Marion Kaplan, eds. *When Biology Became Destiny: Women in Weimar and Nazi Germany*. New York, 1984.

Brockmann, Stephen. *A Critical History of German Film*. Rochester, 2010.

Brunn, Gerhard. *Metropolis Berlin*. Berlin, 1992.

Bruns, Claudia. *Politik des Eros: Der Männerbund in Wissenschaft, Politik und Jugendkultur*. Cologne, 2008.

Bruns, Claudia, and Walter Tilmann, eds. *Von Lust und Schmerz: Eine historische Anthropologie der Sexualität*. Vienna, 2004.

Caplan, Jane, ed. *Documenting Individual Identity: The Development of State Practices in the Modern World*. Princeton, 2001.

Cardon, Patrick. *Discours littéraires et scientifiques fin-de-siècle: Autour de Marc-André Raffalovich*. Paris, 2008.

Carlson, Andrew R. *Anarchism in Germany: The Early Movement*. Metuchen, 1972.

Carpenter, Humphrey. *W. H. Auden: A Biography*. Boston, 1981.

Chauncey, George. *Gay New York: Gender, Urban Culture, and the Making of the Gay Male World, 1890–1940*. New York, 1994.

Cocks, H. G. *Nameless Offences: Homosexual Desire in the 19th Century*. London, 2003.

Conze, Werner, and Jürgen Kocka, eds. *Bildungsbürgertum im 19. Jahrhundert*. Stuttgart, 1985.

Cook, Matt. *London and the Culture of Homosexuality, 1885–1914*. Cambridge, 2008.

Corbin, Alain. *Woman for Hire: Prostitution and Sexuality in France after 1850*. Trans. Alan Sheridan. Cambridge, MA, 1978.

Craig, Gordon. *Germany, 1866–1945*. Oxford, 1980.

Crompton, Louis. *Homosexuality and Civilization*. Cambridge, 2003.

D'Alessandro, Stephanie. "'Über alles die Liebe': The History of Sexual Imagery in the Art and Culture of the Weimar Republic." PhD diss. University of Chicago, 1997.

Davidson, Arnold. "Sex and the Emergence of Sexuality." *Critical Inquiry* 14 (1987): 16–48.

Davis, Whitney. *Queer Beauty: Sexuality and Aesthetics from Winckelmann to Freud and Beyond*. New York, 2010.

Delaney, G. P. *Glyn Philpot: His Life and Art*. Aldershot, 1999.

Derks, Paul. *Die Schande der heiligen Päderastie: Homosexualität und Öffentlichkeit in der deutschen Literatur, 1750–1850*. Berlin, 1990.

Detering, Heinrich. *Das offene Geheimnis: Zur literarischen Produktivität eines Tabus von Winckelmann bis zu Thomas Mann*. Göttingen, 1994.

Dickinson, Edward. "Policing Sex in Germany 1882–1918." *Journal of the History of Sexuality* 16, no. 2 (2007): 204–50.

Dickinson, Edward, and Richard Wetzell. "The Historiography of Sexuality in Modern Germany." *German History* 23, no. 3 (2005): 291–305.

Dinges, Martin, ed. *Männer—Macht—Körper: Hegemoniale Männlichkeiten vom Mittelalter bis Heute*. Frankfurt, 2005.

Dobler, Jens. "Leopold von Meerscheidt-Hüllessem (1849–1900)." *Archiv für Polizeigeschichte* 9 (1998): 73–79.

———. "Zum Verhältnis der Sexualwissenschaft und der homosexuellen Emanzipationsbewegung zur Polizei in Berlin." In Ursula Ferdinand et al., eds., *Verqueere Wissenschaft? Zum Verhältnis von Sexualwissenschaft und Sexualreformbewegung in Geschichte und Gegenwart*, 329–36. Münster, 1998.

———. "Nicht nur Verfolgung—auch Erfolge: Zusammenarbeit zwischen Schwulenbewegung und Polizei in der Kaiserzeit und in der Weimarer Republik." *Comparativ* 9, no. 1 (1999): 48–60.

———. "Dr. Heinrich Kopp (1871–1941)." *Archiv für Polizeigeschichte* 11, no. 1 (2000): 2–7.

———. "Zensur von Büchern und Zeitschriften mit homosexueller Thematik in der Weimarer Republik." *Invertito* 2 (2000): 85–104.

———. "Die Zensur unzüchtiger Schriften 1871 bis 1933." *Archiv für Polizeigeschichte* 14, no. 40 (2003): 34–45.

———. *Von anderen Ufern: Geschichte der Berliner Lesben und Schwulen in Kreuzberg und Friedrichshain*. Berlin, 2003.

———. "Der Travestiekünstler Willi Pape alias Voo-Doo." *Invertito* 6 (2004): 110–21.

———. "Ulrichs vs. Preußen." In Wolfram Setz, ed., *Neue Funde und Studien zu Karl Heinrich Ulrichs*, 49–126. Hamburg, 2004.

———. *Zwischen Duldungspolitik und Verbrechensbekämpfung: Homosexuellenverfolgung durch die Berliner Polizei von 1848 bis 1933*. Frankfurt, 2008.

Dobler, Jens, ed. *Schwule, Lesben, Polizei: Vom Zwangsverhältnis zur Zweck-Ehe?* Berlin, 1996.

Domeier, Norman. *Der Eulenburg-Skandal: Eine politische Kulturgeschichte des Kaiserreichs*. Frankfurt, 2008.

Dose, Ralf. "Gay Studies am Institut für Sexualwissenschaft? Über ein unbekanntes Manuskript Richard Linserts zur männlichen Prostitution." *MdMHG* 24–25 (1997): 123–38.

———. *Magnus Hirschfeld: Deutscher—Jude—Weltbürger*. Berlin, 2005.

Duberman, Martin, et al., eds. *Hidden from History: Reclaiming the Gay and Lesbian Past*. New York, 1990.

Dudink, Stefan, Karen Hagemann, and John Tosh, eds. *Masculinities in Politics and War: Gendering Modern History*. Manchester, 2004.

Dyer, Richard. "Weimar—Less and More Like the Others." In Richard Dyer, *Now You See It: Studies on Lesbian and Gay Film*, 7–46. New York, 1990.

Eder, Franz. *Kultur der Begierde: Eine Geschichte der Sexualität*. Munich, 2002.

Eissler, W. U. *Arbeiterparteien und Homosexuellenfrage: Zur Sexualpolitik von SPD und KPD in der Weimarer Republik.* Berlin, 1980.

Elsaesser, Thomas. *Weimar Cinema and After.* London, 2000.

Evans, R. Tripp. *Grant Wood: A Life.* New York, 2010.

Evans, Richard J. *The Feminist Movement in Germany: 1894–1933.* London, 1976.

———. "Prostitution, State and Society in Imperial German." *Past and Present* 70 (1976): 106–29.

———. "Polizei, Politik und Gesellschaft in Deutschland 1700–1933." *Geschichte und Gesellschaft* 22, no. 4 (1996): 609–28.

———. *Tales from the German Underworld: Crime and Punishment in the Nineteenth Century.* New Haven, 1998.

———. *The Coming of the Third Reich.* New York, 2003.

Fähnders, Walter. *Anarchismus und Literatur: Ein vergessenes Kapitel deutscher Literaturgeschichte zwischen 1890 und 1910.* Stuttgart, 1987.

Fischer, Lothar. *Tanz zwischen Rausch und Tod: Anita Berber, 1918–1928 in Berlin.* Berlin, 1996.

Foucault, Michel. *The History of Sexuality,* vol. 1: *An Introduction.* Trans. Alan Sheridan. New York, 1978.

Fout, John. "Sexual Politics in Wilhelmine Germany: The Male Gender Crisis, Moral Purity, and Homophobia." In John Fout, ed., *Forbidden History: The State, Society, and the Regulation of Sexuality in Modern Europe,* 259–92. Chicago, 1990.

Frank, Orlik Andreas. *Die Strafbarkeit homosexueller Handlungen.* Aachen, 1997.

Freunde eines Schwulen Museums in Berlin e. V. *Eldorado: Homosexuelle Frauen und Männer in Berlin 1850–1950—Geschichte, Alltag und Kultur.* Exhibition Catalog. Berlin, 1984.

———. *Die Geschichte des § 175: Strafrecht gegen Homosexuelle.* Exhibition Catalog. Berlin, 1990.

———. *Goodbye to Berlin—100 Jahre Schwulenbewegung.* Exhibition Catalog. Berlin, 1997.

Frevert, Uta. *Frauen-Geschichte: Zwischen bürgerlichen Verbesserung und neuen Weiblichkeit.* Frankfurt, 1986.

Friman, H. Richard. "Germany and the Transformations of Cocaine, 1860–1920." In Paul Gootenberg, ed., *Cocaine: Global Histories,* 83–104. London, 1991.

Galassi, Silviana. *Kriminologie im deutschen Kaiserreich: Geschichte einer gebrochenen Verwissenschaftlichung.* Stuttgart, 2004.

Gay, Peter. *Weimar Culture: The Outsider as Insider.* New York, 1970.

———. *Freud.* New York, 1998.

Gerard, Kent, and Gert Hekma, eds. *The Pursuit of Sodomy: Male Homosexuality in Renaissance and Enlightenment Europe.* New York, 1989.

Geuter, Ulfried. *Homosexualität in der deutschen Jugendbewegung: Jungenfreundschaft und Sexualität im Diskurs von Jugendbewegung, Psychoanalyse und Jugendpsychologie am Beginn des 20. Jahrhunderts.* Frankfurt, 1994.

Gilfoyle, Timothy J. "Prostitution in History: From Parables of Pornography to Modernity." *American Historical Review* 104, no. 1 (1999): 117–41.

Gollner, Günther. *Homosexualität: Ideologiekritik und Entmythologisierung einer Gesetzgebung.* Berlin, 1974.

Gordon, Mel. *Voluptuous Panic: The Erotic World of Weimar Berlin.* Los Angeles, 2000.

———. *The Seven Addictions and Five Professions of Anita Berber.* Los Angeles, 2006.

Goschler, Constantin. *Rudolf Virchow: Mediziner, Anthropologe, Politiker.* Cologne, 2002.

Grau, Günter, ed. *Hidden Holocaust? Gay and Lesbian Persecution in Germany 1933–45.* London, 1995.

Greenberg, David F. *The Construction of Homosexuality*. Chicago, 1988.

Grenz, Sabine, and Martin Lücke, eds. *Verhandlungen im Zwielicht: Momente der Prostitution in Geschichte und Gegenwart*. Bielefeld, 2006.

Grossmann, Atina. *Reforming Sex: The German Movement for Birth Control and Abortion Reform, 1920–1950*. Oxford, 1995.

Grumbach, Detlef, ed. *Die Linke und das Laster: Schwule Emanzipation und linke Vorurteile*. Hamburg, 1995.

Grünzweig, Walter. *Constructing the German Walt Whitman*. Iowa City, 1995.

Hackett, Amy. "Helene Stöcker: Left-Wing Intellectual and Sex Reformer." In Renate Bridenthal, ed., *When Biology Became Destiny*, 109–30. New York, 1984.

Haeberle, Erwin J. "Justitias zweischneidiges Schwert—Magnus Hirschfeld als Gutachter in der Eulenburg-Affäre." In Klaus Beier, ed., *Sexualität zwischen Medizin und Recht*, 520. Stuttgart, 1991.

Hall, Peter. *Cities in Civilization*. New York, 1998.

Halperin, David. "Forgetting Foucault." *Representations* 63 (1998): 93–120.

Harris, Victoria. *Selling Sex in the Reich: Prostitutes in German Society, 1914–1945*. Oxford, 2010.

Hartmann, Ilya. *Prostitution, Kuppelei, Zuhälterei: Reformdiskussion und Gesetzgebung seit 1870*. Berlin, 2006.

Healey, Dan. *Homosexual Desire in Revolutionary Russia: The Regulation of Sexual Gender and Dissent*. Chicago, 2001.

Hecht, Karsten. "Die Harden-Prozesse: Strafverfahren, Öffentlichkeit und Politik im Kaiserreich." PhD diss. University of Munich, 1997.

Heidel, Ulf, Stefan Micheler, and Elisabeth Tuider, eds. *Jenseits der Geschlechtergrenzen: Sexualitäten, Identitäten und Körper in Perspektiven von Queer Studies*. Hamburg, 2001.

Herdt, Gilbert, ed. *Third Sex, Third Gender: Beyond Sexual Dimorphism in Culture and History*. New York, 1996.

Hergemöller, Bernd-Ulrich. *Mann für Mann: Biografisches Lexikon zur Geschichte von Freundesliebe und mann-männlicher Sexualität im deutschen Sprachraum*. Hamburg, 1998.

———. "Hans Blühers Männerwelten: Fragmente, Widersprüche, Perspektiven." *Invertito* 2 (2000): 58–84.

Herring, Phillip. *Djuna: The Life and Work of Djuna Barnes*. New York, 1995.

Herrn, Rainer. *Anders Bewegt: 100 Jahre Schwulenbewegung in Deutschland*. Hamburg, 1999.

———. "Vom Traum zum Trauma: Das Institut für Sexualwissenschaft." In Elke Kotowski and Julius Schoeps, ed., *Magnus Hirschfeld: Ein Leben im Spannungsfeld von Wissenschaft, Politik und Gesellschaft*, 173–99. Berlin, 2004.

———. *Schnittmuster des Geschlechts: Transvestismus und Transsexualität in der frühen Sexualwissenschaft*. Gießen, 2005.

Herrn, Rainer, and Christine N. Brinckmann. "Von Ratten und Männern: Der Steinach-film." *Montage/AV* 14, 1 (2005): 78–102.

Herzer, Manfred. *Bibliographie zur Homosexualität: Verzeichnis des deutschsprachigen nichtbelletristischen Schrifttums zur weiblichen und männlichen Homosexualität aus den Jahren 1466 bis 1975 in chronologischer Reihenfolge*. Berlin, 1982.

———. "Max Spohr, Adolf Brand, Bernhard Zack." *Capri* 1 (1991): 15–30.

———. *Magnus Hirschfeld: Leben und Werk eines jüdischen, schwulen und sozialistischen Sexologen*. 2nd ed. Frankfurt, 2001.

———. "Kertbenys Leben und Sexualitätsstudien." In Manfred Herzer, ed., *Schriften zur Homosexualitätsforschung*, 7–61. Berlin, 2000.

Herzer, Manfred, ed. *100 Jahre Schwulenbewegung: Dokumentation einer Vortragsreihe in der Akademie der Künste*. Berlin, 1998.

Herzog, Dagmar. *Sex after Fascism: Memory and Morality in Twentieth-Century Germany.* Princeton, 2005.

———. *Sexuality in Europe: A Twentieth-Century History.* Cambridge, 2011.

Herzog, Dagmar, ed. *Brutality and Desire: War and Sexuality in Europe's Twentieth Century.* New York, 2009.

Hett, Benjamin Carter. *Death in the Tiergarten: Murder and Criminal Justice in the Kaiser's Berlin.* London, 2004.

Hirschauer, Stefan. *Die soziale Konstruktion der Transsexualität.* Frankfurt, 1993.

Hoffschildt, Rainer. *Olivia: Die bisher geheime Geschichte des Tabus Homosexualität und der Verfolgung der Homoseuellen in Hannover.* Hanover, 1992.

Hohmann, Joachim. *Der unterdrückte Sexus.* Lollar, 1977.

———. *Der heimliche Sexus.* Frankfurt, 1979.

———. *Sexualforschung und -aufklärung in der Weimarer Republik.* Frankfurt, 1985.

Hohmann, Joachim, ed. *Der Kreis.* Frankfurt, 1980.

Houlbrook, Matt. *Queer London: Perils and Pleasures in the Sexual Metropolis, 1918–1957.* Chicago, 2005.

Hull, Isabel. *The Entourage of Kaiser Wilhelm II, 1888–1918.* New York, 1982.

———. "Kaiser Wilhelm II and the 'Liebenberg Circle.'" In John Röhl and Nicolaus Sombart, eds., *Kaiser Wilhelm II, New Interpretations: The Corfu Papers,* 193–220. Cambridge, 1982.

———. "Kaiser Wilhelm II und der 'Liebenberg-Kreis.'" In Rüdiger Lautmann and Angela Taeger, eds., *Männerliebe im alten Deutschland: Sozialgeschichtliche Abhandlungen,* 81–117. Berlin, 1992.

———. *Sexuality, State, and Civil Society in Germany, 1700–1815.* Ithaca, 1996.

Hutter, Jörg. "Die Entstehung des § 175 im Strafgesetzbuch und die Geburt der deutschen Sexualwissenschaft: Eine zufällige Beziehung oder ein Komplott von Psychiatrie und Straf-justiz?" In Rüdiger Lautmann and Angela Taeger, eds., *Männerliebe im alten Deutschland: Sozialgeschichtliche Abhandlungen,* 187–238. Berlin, 1992.

———. *Die gesellschaftliche Kontrolle des homosexuellen Begehrens.* Frankfurt, 1992.

In Het Panhuis, Erwin. *Anders als die Andern: Schwule und Lesben in Köln und Umgebung 1895–1918.* Cologne, 2006.

Jackson, Julian. *Living in Arcadia.* Chicago, 2009.

Jazbinsek, Dietmar, and Ralf Thies, eds. *Embleme der Moderne: Berlin und Chicago in Stadttexten der Jahundertwende.* Berlin, 1999.

Jelavich, Peter. *Berlin Cabaret.* Cambridge, 1993.

———. *Berlin Alexanderplatz: Radio, Film, and the Death of Weimar Culture.* Berkeley, 2006.

Jellonnek, Burkhard, and Rüdiger Lautmann, eds. *Nationalsozialistischer Terror gegen Homosexuelle: Verdrängt und ungesühnt.* Munich, 2002.

John, Michael. *Politics and the Law in Late Nineteenth-Century Germany: The Origins of the Civil Code.* Oxford, 1989.

Jones, James W. *"We of the Third Sex": Literary Representation of Homosexuality in Wilhelmine Germany.* New York, 1990.

Jungblut, Peter. *Famose Kerle: Eulenburg—Eine wilhelminische Affäre.* Hamburg, 2003.

Kauffeldt, Rolf, and Gertrude Cepl-Kaufmann. *Berlin-Friedrichshagen. Literaturhauptstadt um die Jahrhundertwende: Der Friedrichshagener Dichterkreis.* Munich, 1994.

Kaye, Kerwin. "Male Prostitution in the Twentieth Century: Pseudo-Homosexuals, Hoodlum Homosexuals, and Exploited Teens." *Journal of Homosexuality* 46 (2003): 1–77.

Keilson-Lauritz, Marita. *Die Geschichte der eigenen Geschichte: Literatur und Literatur-kritik in den Anfängen der Schwulenbewegung am Beispiel des* Jahrbuch für sexuelle Zwischenstufen *und der Zeitschrift* Der Eigene. Berlin, 1997.

———. "Adolf Brand und der Eigene." In Mark Lehmstedt and Andreas Herzog, eds., *Des Bewegte Buch,* 327–48. Wiesbaden, 1999.

———. "Benedict Friedlaender und die Anfänge der Sexualwissenschaft." *Zeitschrift für Sexualforschung* 18 (2005): 311–31.

Keilson-Lauritz, Marita, and Rolf E. Lang, eds. *Emanzipation hinter der Weltstadt: Adolf Brand und die Gemeinschaft der Eigenen.* Berlin, 2000.

Kennedy, Hubert. *Anarchist der Liebe: John Henry Mackay als Sagitta.* Berlin, 1988.

———. *The Ideal Gay Man: The Story of Der Kreis.* New York, 1999.

———. *Karl Heinrich Ulrichs: Pioneer of the Modern Gay Movement.* Concord, 2005.

Kerbs, Diethart, and Jürgen Reulecke, eds. *Handbuch der deutschen Reformbewegungen 1880–1933.* Wuppertal, 1998.

Kitcher, Philip. *Deaths in Venice: The Cases of Gustav von Aschenbach.* New York, 2013.

Koebner, Thomas, ed. *"Mit uns zieht die neue Zeit": Der Mythos Jugend.* Frankfurt, 1985.

Köhler, Joachim. *Zarathustra's Secret: The Interior Life of Friedrich Nietzsche.* New Haven, 2002.

Koshar, Rudy. *German Travel Cultures.* Oxford, 2000.

Kotowski, Elke, and Julius Schoeps, eds. *Magnus Hirschfeld: Ein Leben im Spannungsfeld von Wissenschaft, Politik und Gesellschaft.* Berlin, 2004.

Krafft, Sybille. *Zucht und Unzucht: Prostitution und Sittenpolizei im München der Jahrhundertwende.* Munich, 1996.

Kühne, Thomas, ed. *Männergeschichte—Geschlechtergeschichte: Männlichkeit im Wandel der Moderne.* Frankfurt, 1996.

Kuzniar, Alice, ed. *Outing Goethe and His Age.* Stanford, 1996.

———. *The Queer German Cinema.* Stanford, 2000.

Laqueur, Walter. *Young Germany: A History of the German Youth Movement.* London, 1962.

Large, David Clay. *Berlin.* New York, 2001.

Lauritsen, John, and David Thorstad. *The Early Homosexual Rights Movement (1864–1935).* New York, 1974.

Lautmann, Rüdiger. *Seminar: Gesellschaft und Homosexualität.* Frankfurt, 1977.

Lautmann, Rüdiger, and Angela Taeger, eds. *Männerliebe im alten Deutschland: Sozialgeschichtliche Abhandlungen.* Berlin, 1992.

Lees, Andrew. *Cities, Sin, and Social Reform in Imperial Germany.* Ann Arbor, 2002.

Lehmstedt, Mark. *Bücher für das "dritte Geschlecht": Der Max Spohr Verlag in Leipzig. Verlagsgeschichte und Bibliographie (1881–1941).* Wiesbaden, 2002.

Lücke, Martin. "Männliche Prostitution in den Debatten um eine Reform des Sexualstrafrechts zu Beginn des 20. Jahrhunderts." *Invertito* 5 (2003): 109–21.

———. "Das ekle Geschmeiß: Mann-männliche Prostitution und hegemoniale Männlichkeit im Kaiserreich." In Martin Dinges, ed., *Männer—Macht—Körper: Hegemoniale Männlichkeiten vom Mittelalter bis Heute,* 157–72. Frankfurt, 2005.

———. *Männlichkeit in Unordnung: Homosexualität und männliche Prostitution in Kaiserreich und Weimarer Republik.* Frankfurt, 2008.

Ludington, Townsend. *Marsden Hartley: The Biography of an American Artist.* Boston, 1992.

Magnus-Hirschfeld-Gesellschaft. *Institut für Sexualwissenschaft.* CD-ROM. Berlin, 2002.

Marchand, Suzanne. *Down from Olympus: Archaeology and Philhellenism in Germany, 1750–1970.* Princeton, 1996.

Matysik, Tracie. *Reforming the Moral Subject: Ethics and Sexuality in Central Europe 1890–1930.* Ithaca, 2008.

McCormick, Richard. *Gender and Sexuality in Weimar Modernity: Film, Literature, and "New Objectivity."* New York, 2001.

McLaren, Angus. *Sexual Blackmail: A Modern History.* Cambridge, 2002.

Meinhardt, Günther. *Die Universität Göttingen: Ihre Entwicklung und Geschichte von 1734–1974.* Northeim, 1977.

Merrick, Jeffrey, ed. *Homosexuality in Modern France.* New York, 1996.

Merrick, Jeffrey, and Bryant Ragan, eds. *Homosexuality in Early Modern France: A Documentary Collection.* Oxford, 2001.

Meyerowitz, Joanne. *How Sex Changed: A History of Transsexuality in the United States.* Cambridge, 2002.

Micheler, Stefan. *Fremdbilder und Selbstbilder der "Anderen": Eine Geschichte Männer begehrender Männer in der Weimarer Republik und in der NS-Zeit.* Konstanz, 2005.

Micheler, Stefan, and Jakob Michelsen. "Von der 'schwulen Ahnengalerie' zur Queer Theory: Geschichtsforschung und Identitätsbildung." In Ulf Heidel, Stefan Micheler, and Elisabeth Tuider, eds., *Jenseits der Geschlechtergrenzen: Sexualitäten, Identitäten und Körper in Perspektiven von Queer Studies,* 127–43. Hamburg, 2001.

Mildenberger, Florian: ". . . in der Richtung der Homosexualität verdorben": Psychiater, *Kriminalpsychologen und Gerichtsmediziner über männliche Homosexualität 1850–1970.* Hamburg, 2002.

Mitchell, Leslie. *Maurice Bowra: A Life.* Oxford, 2009.

Mogge, Winfried. "Jugendbewegung." In Diethart Kerbs and Jürgen Reulecke, eds., *Handbuch der deutschen Reformbewegungen: 1880–1933.* Wuppertal, 1998.

Möhring, Maren. *Marmorleiber: Körperbildung in der deutschen Nacktkultur (1890–1930).* Cologne, 2004.

Mosse, George. *Nationalism and Sexuality: Respectability and Abnormal Sexuality in Modern Europe.* New York, 1985.

Mouton, Michelle. *From Nurturing the Nation to Purifying the Volk: Weimar and Nazi Family Policy, 1918–1945.* Cambridge, 2007.

Müller, Jakob. *Die Jugendbewegung als deutsche Hauptrichtung neukonservativer Reform.* Zurich, 1971.

Murat, Laure. *La loi du genre: Une histoire culturelle du "troisième sexe."* France, 2005.

Myers, Robin. *Censorship and the Control of Print in England and France, 1600–1910.* Winchester, 1992.

Neuloh, Otto, and Wilhelm Zilius. *Die Wandervögel.* Göttingen, 1982.

Neumann, Helga, and Manfred Neumann. *Maximilian Harden (1861–1927): Ein unerschrockener deutsch-judischer Kritiker und Publizist.* Würzburg, 2003.

Noack, Andreas. "Die Prostitutionsdebatte in Sexualwissenschaft und Gefährdetenfürsorge der 20er Jahre vor dem Hintergrund der moralischen Krise der bürgerlichen Gesellschaft." In Christian Niemeyer, Wolfgang Schröer, and Lothar Böhnisch, eds., *Grundlinien historischer Sozialpädagogik: Traditionsbezüge, Reflexionen und übergangene Sozialdiskurse,* 259–72. Weinheim, 1997.

Norton, Rictor. *Mother Clap's Molly House: The Gay Subculture in England 1700–1830.* London, 1992.

Oosterhuis, Harry. *Stepchildren of Nature: Krafft-Ebing, Psychiatry and the Making of Sexual Identity.* Chicago, 2000.

Oosterhuis, Harry, ed. *Homosexuality and Male Bonding in Pre-Nazi Germany.* New York, 1991.

Page, Norman. *Auden and Isherwood: The Berlin Years.* New York, 1998.

Peniston, William. *Pederasts and Others: Urban Culture and Sexual Identity in Nineteenth-Century Paris.* New York, 2004.

Peukert, Detlev J. K. *Grenzen der Sozialdisziplinierung: Aufstieg und Krise der deutschen Jugendfürsorge von 1878 bis 1932.* Cologne, 1986.

———. *The Weimar Republic.* Trans. Richard Deveson. New York, 1989.

Pieper, Werner, ed. *Nazis on Speed: Drogen im 3. Reich.* 2 vols. Löhrbach, 2002.

Planert, Uta. *Antifeminismus im Kaiserreich.* Göttingen, 1998.

Plummer, Kenneth, ed. *The Making of the Modern Homosexual.* London, 1981.

Pretzel, Andreas. "Zur Geschichte der 'Ärztlichen Gesellschaft für Sexualwissenschaft' (1913–1933)—Dokumentation und Forschungsbericht." *MdMHG* 24–25 (1997): 35–122.

———. "'Ich habe eingesehen, daß seine Fortsetzung meiner Arbeit im heutigen Deutschland nicht mehr möglich ist': Aus der letzten Strafakte gegen den Verleger und Schriftsteller Adolf Brand (1874–1945)." *MdMHG* 29–30 (1999): 25–50.

Puff, Helmut. *Sodomy in Reformation Germany and Switzerland 1400–1600.* Chicago, 2003.

Quétel, Claude. *History of Syphilis.* Baltimore, 1990.

Raber, Ralf Jörg. *Wir sind wie wir sind: Ein Jahrhundert homosexuelle Liebe auf Schallplatte und CD.* Hamburg, 2010.

Read, Anthony, and David Fisher. *Berlin: The Biography of a City.* London, 1994.

Revenin, Régis. *Homosexualité et prostitution masculines à Paris 1870–1918.* Paris, 2005.

Rey, Michel. "Parisian Homosexuals Create a Lifestyle, 1700–1750." *Eighteenth-Century Life* 9 (1985): 179–91.

———. "Police and Sodomy in Eighteenth-Century Paris: From Sin to Disorder." In Kent Gerard and Gert Hekma, eds., *The Pursuit of Sodomy: Male Homosexuality in Renaissance and Enlightenment Europe,* 128–46. New York, 1989.

Richie, Alexandra. *Faust's Metropolis: A History of Berlin.* New York, 1998.

Riley, Thomas A. *Germany's Poet-Anarchist John Henry Mackay.* New York, 1972.

Rinke, Günter. *Sozialer Radikalismus und bündische Utopie: Der Fall Peter Martin Lampel.* Frankfurt, 2000.

Rocke, Michael. *Forbidden Friendships: Homosexuality and Male Culture in Renaissance Florence.* New York, 1996.

Röhl, John C. G. "Fürst Philipp zu Eulenburg: Zu einem Lebensbild." In Rüdiger Lautmann and Angela Taeger, eds., *Männerliebe im alten Deutschland: Sozialgeschichtliche Abhandlungen,* 119–40. Berlin, 1992.

———. *Wilhelm II: Der Weg in den Abgrund 1900–1941.* Munich, 2008.

Roos, Juia. *Weimar Through the Lens of Gender: Prostitution Reform, Woman's Emancipation, and German Democracy, 1919–1933.* Ann Arbor, 2010.

Rosario, Vernon A., ed. *Science and Homosexualities.* London, 1997.

Rosenkranz, Bernhard, and Gottfried Lorenz. *Hamburg auf anderen Wegen: Die Geschichte des schwulen Lebens in der Hansestadt.* Hamburg, 2005.

Roth, Ralf. *Das Jahrhundert der Eisenbahn: Die Herrschaft über Raum und Zeit 1800–1914.* Ostfildern, 2005.

Rydström, Jens. *Sinners and Citizens: Bestiality and Homosexuality in Sweden, 1880–1950.* Chicago, 2003.

Schildt, Rudolf [Rainer Hoffschildt]. "Das Ende einer Karriere: Entfernung des Amtsassessors Ulrichs aus dem Staatsdienst wegen widernatürlicher Wollust." *Capri* 6, no. 4 (1988): 24–33.

Schlatter, Christoph. *"Merkwürdigerweise bekam ich Neigung zu Burschen": Selbstbilder und Fremdbilder homosexueller Männer in Schaffhausen 1867 bis 1870.* Zurich, 2002.

Schlör, Joachim. *Nachts in der großen Stadt: Paris, Berlin, London 1840–1930.* Berlin, 1991.

Schmidt, Gunter. "Helfer und Verfolger: Die Rolle von Wissenschaft und Medizin in der Homosexuellenfrage." *MdMHG* 3 (1984): 21–32.

Schoppmann, Claudia. *Der Skorpion: Frauenliebe in der Weimarer Republik.* Berlin, 1984.

Schulte, Regina. *Sperrbezirke: Tugendhaftigkeit und Prostitution in der bürgerlichen Welt.* Frankfurt, 1979.

Schulz, Christian. *Paragraph 175. (abgewickelt): Homosexualität und Strafrecht im Nachkriegsdeutschland—Rechtsprechung, juristische Diskussionen und Reformen seit 1945.* Hamburg, 1994.

Schulze, Franz. *Philip Johnson: Life and Work.* Chicago, 1996.

Scott, Joan Wallach. "Gender: A Useful Category of Historical Analysis." *American Historical Review* 91, no. 5 (1986): 1053–75.

Senelick, Laurence. "The Homosexual Theatre Movement in the Weimar Republic." *Theatre Survey* 49, no. 1 (May 2008): 5–35.

Setz, Wolfram, ed. *Die Geschichte der Homosexualitäten und die schwule Identität an der Jahrtausendwende.* Hamburg, 2000.

Sheehan, James. *German History, 1770–1866.* Oxford, 1993.

Sievert, Hermann. *Das Anomale Bestrafen: Homosexualität Strafrecht und Schwulenbewegung im Kaiserreich und in der Weimarer Republik.* Hamburg, 1984.

Sigusch, Volkmar. "Albert Moll und Magnus Hirschfeld: Über ein problematisches Verhältnis vor dem Hintergrund unveröffentlichter Briefe Molls aus dem Jahr 1934." *Zeitschrift für Sexualforschung* 8, no. 2 (1995): 122–59.

———. *Karl Heinrich Ulrichs: Der erste Schwule der Weltgeschichte.* Berlin, 2000.

Sigusch, Volkmar, ed. *Geschichte der Sexualwissenschaft.* Frankfurt, 2008.

Sigusch, Volkmar, and Günter Grau, eds. *Personenlexikon der Sexual-Forschung.* Frankfurt, 2009.

Solneman, K. H. Z. [Kurt Zube]. *Der Bahnbrecher John Henry Mackay: Sein Leben und Sein Werk.* Freiburg, 1979.

Sommer, Kai. *Die Strafbarkeit der Homosexualität von der Kaiserzeit bis zum Nationalsozialismus: Eine Analyse der Straftatbestände im Strafgesetzbuch und in den Reformentwürfen.* Frankfurt, 1998.

Spector, Scott. "The Wrath of the 'Countess Veriola': Tabloid Exposé and the Emergence of the Homosexual Subject in Vienna 1907." In Gunter Bischof, Anton Pelinka, and Dagmar Herzog, eds., *Sexuality in Austria*, 31–48. New Brunswick, 2006.

Spector, Scott, Helmut Puff, and Dagmar Herzog, eds. *After the History of Sexuality: German Genealogies with and Beyond Foucault.* New York, 2012.

Stark, Gary. *Banned in Berlin: Literary Censorship in Imperial Germany.* New York, 2009.

Steakley, James, ed. *Lesbianism and Feminism in Germany, 1895–1910.* New York, 1975.

———. "Film und Zensur in der Weimarer Republik: Der Fall *Anders als die Andern.*" *Capri: Zeitschrift für schwule Geschichte* 21 (1996): 2–33.

———. "Per scientiam ad justitiam: Magnus Hirschfeld and the Sexual Politics of Innate Homosexuality." In Vernon A. Rosario, ed., *Science and Homosexualities*, 133–54. New York, 1997.

———. *Die Freunde des Kaisers: Die Eulenburg-Affäre im Spiegel zeitgenössischer Karikaturen.* Hamburg, 2004.

———. *Anders als die Andern.* Hamburg, 2007.

Stephens, Robert P. *Germans on Drugs: The Complications of Modernization in Hamburg.* Ann Arbor, 2007.

Stora-Lamarre, Annie. *L'enfer de la IIIe République: Censeurs et Pornographes, 1881–1914.* Paris, 1990.

Stümke, Hans-Georg: *Homosexuelle in Deutschland: Eine politische Geschichte.* Munich, 1989.

Taddeo, Julie Anne. *Lytton Strachey and the Search for Modern Sexual Identity: The Last Eminent Victorian.* New York, 2002.

Tamagne, Florence. *A History of Homosexuality in Europe.* 2 vols. New York, 2004.

Theis, Wolfgang. "Verdrängung und Travestie: Das vage Bild der Homosexualität im deutschen Film (1917–1957)." In Freunde eines Schwulen Museums in Berlin e. V., *Eldorado: Homosexuelle Frauen und Männer in Berlin 1850–1950—Geschichte, Alltag und Kultur,* 102–13. Berlin, 1984.

Theweleit, Klaus. *Male Fantasies.* 2 vols. 1977. Reprint. Minneapolis, 1987–89.

Thies, Ralf. *Ethnograph des dunklen Berlin: Hans Ostwald und die "Großstadt-Dokumente."* Cologne, 2006.

Thies, Ralf, and Dietmar Jazbinsek, eds. *Embleme der Moderne Berlin und Chicago in Stadtexten der Jahrhundertwende.* Berlin, 1999.

Thoma, Hubert. *Georg Friedrich Dasbach: Priester, Publizist, Politiker.* Trier, 1975.

Thorson, Helga. "Masking/Unmasking Identity in Early Twentieth-Century Germany: The Importance of N. O. Body." *Women in German Yearbook* 25 (2009): 149–73.

Timm, Annette F. *The Politics of Fertility in Twentieth-Century Berlin.* Cambridge, 2010.

Tobin, Robert. *Warm Brothers: Queer Theory and the Age of Goethe.* Philadelphia, 2000.

Traub, Valerie. "The Psychomorphology of the Clitoris." *GLQ: A Journal of Lesbian and Gay Studies* 2 (1995): 81–113.

Trumbach, Randolph. *Sex and the Gender Revolution,* vol. 1: *Heterosexuality and the Third Gender in Enlightenment London.* Chicago, 1998.

———. "Modern Sodomy: The Origins of Homosexuality, 1700–1800." In Matt Cook, ed., *A Gay History of Britain,* 77–106. Oxford, 2007.

Usborne, Cornelia. "Geburtenkontrolle in der Weimarer Republik und Magnus Hirschfelds widersprüchliche Interessen." In Elke Kotowski and Julius Schoeps, eds., *Magnus Hirschfeld: Ein Leben im Spannungsfeld von Wissenschaft, Politik und Gesellschaft,* 95–115. Berlin, 2004.

van der Meer, Theo. "The Persecutions of Sodomites in Eighteenth-Century Amsterdam: Changing Perceptions of Sodomy." In Kent Gerard and Gert Hekma, eds., *The Pursuit of Sodomy: Male Homosexuality in Renaissance and Enlightenment Europe,* 263–310. New York, 1989.

Verzaubert in Nord-Ost: Die Geschichte der Berliner Lesben und Schwulen in Prenzlauer Berg, Pankow und Weißensee. Sonntags Club, ed. Berlin, 2009.

Walker, Mack. *German Home Towns: Community, State, and General Estate, 1648–1871.* Ithaca, 1971.

Walkowitz, Judith R. *Prostitution and Victorian Society: Women, Class and the State.* Cambridge, 1980.

Weber, Philippe. *Der Trieb zum Erzählen: Sexualpathologie und Homosexualität, 1852–1914.* Bielefeld, 2008.

Wedler, Uwe. *Maximilian Harden und die "Zukunft."* Bremen, 1970.

Weeks, Jeffrey. "Inverts, Perverts and Mary-Annes: Male Prostitution and the Regulation of Homosexuality in England in the Nineteenth and Early Twentieth Centuries." *Journal of Homosexuality* 6, nos. 1–2 (1980–81): 113–34.

Weinberg, Jonathan. *Speaking for Vice.* New Haven, 1993.

Weitz, Eric D. *Weimar German: Promise and Tragedy.* Princeton, 2007.

Weller, Björn Uwe. *Maximilian Harden und die "Zukunft."* Bremen, 1970.

Wetzell, Richard F. *Inventing the Criminal: A History of German Criminology, 1880–1945.* Chapel Hill, 2000.

Widding, Bernd. "'Ein herber Kultus des Männlichen': Männerbünde um 1900." In Walter Erhart and Britta Herrmann, eds., *Wann ist der Mann ein Mann? Zur Geschichte der Männlichkeit,* 235–48. Stuttgart, 1997.

Winzen, Peter. *Das Ende der Kaiserherrlichkeit: Die Skandalprozesse um die homosexuellen Berater Wilhelms II 1907–1909.* Cologne, 2010.

Wolff, Charlotte. *Magnus Hirschfeld: A Portrait of a Pioneer in Sexology*. London, 1986.

Wünsch, Stefan. "Die Familie Sander: Prostitution, Zuhälterei und Justiz in der späten Weimarer Republik." In Sabine Grenz and Martin Lücke, eds., *Verhandlungen im Zwielicht: Momente der Prostitution in Geschichte und Gegenwart*, 281–99. Beilefeld, 2006.

Young, Harry F. *Maximilian Harden: Censor Germaniae, the Critic in Opposition from Bismarck to the Rise of Nazism*. The Hague, 1959.

zur Nieden, Susanne. "Aufstieg und Fall des virilen Männerhelden: Der Skandal um Ernst Röhm und seine Ermordung." In Susanne zur Nieden, ed., *Homosexualität und Staatsräson: Männlichkeit, Homophobie und Politik in Deutschland 1900–1945*, 147–92. Frankfurt, 2005.

———. "Homophobie und Staatsräson." In Susanne zur Nieden, ed., *Homosexualität und Staatsräson: Männlichkeit, Homophobie und Politik in Deutschland 1900–1945*, 17–51. Frankfurt, 2005.

zur Nieden, Susanne, ed. *Homosexualität und Staatsräson: Männlichkeit, Homophobie und Politik in Deutschland 1900–1945*. Frankfurt, 2005.

Index

Ackermann, Paul, 75
Action Committee (for legal reform), 223,
    226, 231
  CoS withdraws from (1923), 228–9, 234
  division of labor among CoS, SHC, and
    HRL, 231
  SHC withdraws from (1925), 234
adaptation theory, *see* Hirschfeld, Magnus
anarchism, 99–101
  homosexual rights movement, and,
    100–1
  periodicals, 100–1
Annan, Baron Noel, 197
antifeminism, 147
anti-Semitism, xviii, 117, 141, 150, 168–9,
    222, 243
  see also Blüher, Hans and Brand, Adolf
  Männerbund, and, 150
  Wandervogel, and, 141, 155–6
anti-sodomy statute(s), *see also* paragraph
    175
  French Revolution, impact on, 25–6,
    93, 219
    see also Napoleonic Code
  German territories (pre-unification),
    25–6, 38–9
  Germany, imperial (paragraph 175), xv,
    36–9, 82–3
  Germany, Weimar Republic (paragraph
    175), 82–3
  Prussian, xv, 36–9
Association of German Jurists, *see* Ulrichs
Auden, W. H., ix–xii, xix, 188, 194, 195–6,
    197, 202, 209, 219
*Anders als die Andern (Different from the
    Others)*, 164–7
anthropometry, 55

Bab, Edwin, 96, 104, 116
Ballin, Albert, 137
Bang, Herman, 167
Barnes, Djuna, 192
Bebel, August, 51, 90, 94, 98, 222–3
Benjamin, Harry, 178–9
Benjamin, Walter, 215
Berber, Anita, 165–6, 214, 216
Bernstein, Eduard, 98
Berlin
  homosexual bars and venues, x, 34,
    42–7, 59–61, 203–9
  homosexual costume balls, 62–4
  homosexual cruising, 9–10, 65–6, 196,
    200, 203
  homosexual scene, 9–10, 22–3, 58–9, 181,
    189–92
    scientific and ethnographic study of,
      86, 87, 93, 201–3
    tourist destination, as, 198–200
  industry, 49–50
  infrastructure
    housing, 50–1
    public transportation, 52–3,
      65, 99
    sewage and public hygiene, 51–2
  medical profession, 30–1, 37
  population and density, 48
  sex crimes, 32–6
  tourism statistics, 196
  travelogues
    pre-1914, 48–9
    Weimar era, 162–3, 187–8, 192–200,
      203–5
  University of, 9, 143
Bertillon, Alphonse, 55
Bertz, Eduard, 111–12

Bildungsbürgertum, see German educated
    elite
bisexuality, 19, 96–7, 111–12, 151, 159, 165
Bismarck, Otto von, 26, 27–8, 124
Bloch, Iwan, 24, 59, 87, 152
Blüher, Hans, xviii, 99, 119, 140–59, 222,
    237
    see also Männerbund
    antifeminism, and, 149
    anti-Semitism, and, 141, 154, 155–8,
        168–9, 222
    biography, 141–4, 145–6
    Eulenburg scandal, and, 144
    Friedlaender, Benedict, and, 144–5, 152,
        229
    Freud, Sigmund, and, 152–3, 212, 241
    Hirschfeld, Magnus, and, 152, 153–4
    homosexual rights movement, and,
        143–4, 156, 222
    Jansen, Wilhelm, and, 144–5, 152
    marriages, and, 145–6
    military service, and 143–2
    publications, 146–7, 149–50, 154–5, 156,
        157, 168
    sexuality, personal, 143–6
    sexuality, theories of, 150–4
Bölsche, Wilhelm, 100
Bowles, Paul, 198
Bowra, Maurice, 197
Brand, Adolf, xix, 61, 94–5, 108–9, 110, 112,
    144, 151, 164, 185, 190, 221–2, 231,
    239–40
    anarchism, and, 100
    anti-democratic views, and, 228
    antifeminism, and, 116–17
    anti-Semitism, and, 117, 228
    Blüher, Hans, influence of, 228
    Bülow, Bernhard von, 129–32
    biography, 101–2, 103, 227
    Community of the Special (CoS), and,
        xix, 102–3, 144, 185, 221–2, 225,
        227–8
    Dasbach, Georg Friedrich, and, 114–15
    Eigene, Der, and, 61, 100, 101–3, 107,
        108–12, 164, 190, 223, 227
    homosexuality (pederasty), theory of,
        228
    Hirschfeld, Magnus, and, 102, 226,
        238–9

Nietzsche, Friedrich, and, 106
"outing," and, 113–15, 129–32
publications, 227–8
Radszuweit, Friedrich, and, 238–9
Scientific-Humanitarian Committee
    (SHC), and, 94–5, 113, 226–7, 228–30
Stirner, Max, and, 101, 102, 106
Brecht, Bertolt, 199
Brod, Max, 99
Buber, Martin, 157
Bülow, Bernhard von, 124–25, 129–32
Burchard, Ernst, 95, 96,
Bush, Alan, 195

Calder-Marshall, Arthur, 195
canon formation, homosexual
    historical figures, 105–6
    identity, and, 106–7
    literary canon, 106–12
Carpenter, Edward, 92, 107, 241
Carritt, Gabriel, 195
Casper, Johann Ludwig, xv, 6, 9, 22–3, 92
Catholic Center Party (German), 114, 231
censorship, *see also* Germany, censorship
    Britain, 92–3
    France, 93
Chaplin, Charlie, 198
Christopher Street Day (CSD), 247
cinema
    see also censorship, *Anders als die Andern,*
        and Oswald, Richard
    "enlightenment" films, 167
    homosexuality, and, 167–8
cocaine, 212–18
    abuse among homosexuals, 193, 207,
        215–18
    commercial production of, 212
    etymology of, 212
    Freud, Sigmund, and, 212
    treatment for addiction, 214–16
Communist Party of Germany, 183, 201,
    215, 220, 231, 237
    homosexual rights, position, 237
Community of the Special (CoS), *see*
    Brand, Adolf
Cook's Travel Agency, 198
Cordan, Wolfgang, 198, 205–6, 208
Cosy Corner, x, 208, 209
cross-dressing, 87–8

see also *Transvestitenschein*
  periodicals, 190
  police tolerance for, 171–3
  popular culture, in, 171–2
  theories of, 170–71
Crowley, Aleister, 199

Danielsen, Max, 233
Dasbach, Georg Friedrich, and, 114–15
degeneration theory, xii, 152, 180–1
Dehmel, Richard, 99
Dempsey, Jack, 198
Derks, Paul, 107–8
Dietrich, Marlene, 166, 198
Döblin, Alfred, 233
Doone, Rupert, 195
Dowd, Harrison, 193
Dix, Otto, 197

Eekhoud, Georges, 110
Eigene, Der, see Brand, Adolf
Einstein, Albert, 224
Einstein of Sex, 242
Elbe, Lilly von, 127–9
Eldorado, the, 198–9, 205
Ellis, Havelock, 24, 92–3, 170, 241
Engelbrecht, Ernst, 216
Engels, Friedrich, 24, 147
Essebac, Achille, 110
Eulenburg, Albert, 87
Eulenburg Scandal, 120–39
  aftermath of, 68, 140–1, 146, 226, 229
Eulenburg-Hertefeld, Prince Philipp zu,
  120–39
  Moltke, Kuno von, and, 127–9

feminism, 147–9, 182, 183
Fersen, André, 190
Fidus, *see* Höppener, Hugo
Fingerprinting, 55
FKK, see Lebensreform Bewegung
Flato, Fritz, 225
Flexner, Abraham, 59, 65
Forster, Bill, 164
Fosdick, Raymond, 54
Foucault, Michel, xiii–xvi
Fränkel, Fritz, 214–16
Frederick the Great, 105, 151
Freikorps, 158, 169

Freud, Sigmund, 150–4, 212
Freundschaft, Die, 164, 165, 190, 191, 223, 231,
  233, 234
Friedlaender, Benedict, 96–7, 104–5, 112,
  116–19, 144–5, 151, 152
Friedländer, Hugo, 62
Friedrichshagen artists' colony, 99–100

Garbo, Greta, 166, 198
Gaulke, Johannes, 110–11
Gemeinschaft der Eigenen, *see* Brand,
  Adolf (Community of the Special)
Gerber, Henry, 190
German Confederation (1815–66), *see*
  Germany
German educated elite
  (*Bildungsbürgertum*), 7–8, 93, 106,
  141–2
German Federal Republic, *see* Germany
German Friendship Association, 224–5
Germany
  Austro-Prussian War, 27–8
  censorship
    as compared to other countries, 91–4,
    167
    homosexual press, and, 106–7, 164,
    189–90, 190–1, 232–3
    pre-1914 period, 20–21, 91, 102–3, 106,
    108–9
    Weimar Republic, 164, 166, 167, 189,
    191
  Franco-Prussian War, 37–8
  German Confederation (1815–66),
    28, 30
  German Democratic Republic (1949–
    89), 246–7
  German Federal Republic, 158, 245–6
  imperial (1871–1918), 97–8
  nationalism, 26–7, 28, 38
  North German Confederation
    (1867–71), 28, 30, 36
  publishing industry, 20–1
  railway construction, 13–14
  revolution of 1848, 12–13, 26
  unification, 26–8, 38–9
  universities, 6, 8, 9, 208
  Weimar Republic (1919–33), 182–3
  war with Denmark, 26
  Zollverein, 13

Gide, André, 110, 111
Giese, Karl, 86, 161, 181
Gladstone, William, 115
Glaser, Adolf, 58, 85–6, 92
Gloeden, Wilhelm von, 102
Goebbels, Joseph, 245
Got, Ambroise, 203, 208
Göttingen, University of, 8, 212
Great Inflation, 161–2, 192, 193, 194, 200–1,
    213, 229
Greece, ancient, influences in Germany
    pederasty, *see* pederasty, and
        Brand, Adolf
  homoerotic literature, 107
  humanities, the, 104
Grell, Konstantin, 63
Grossmann, Atina, 184
Grosz, Georg, 197
Grünzweig, Walter, 112

Hamecher, Peter, 112
Hamilton, Gerald, 196–7
Hanover, Kingdom of (1814–1866), 27
Harden, Maximilian, xviii, 113, 122–23,
    124–5
  biography of, 124
Hartley, Marsden, 192–3
Hasse, August, 74–5
Hauptmann, Gerhart, 99, 224
Healey, Dan, xiii
Hegel, Georg Wilhelm Friedrich, 41, 156
Heimsoth, Karl-Günther, 229
Herbert, David, 198
Herrn, Rainer, 178
Herzer, Manfred, xi
Herzl, Theodor, 150, *see also* Zionism
Herzog, Dagmar, 245–6
Hesse, Hermann, 99, 142–3, 224
Hilferding, Rudolf, 224
Hille, Peter, 100, 104
Hiller, Kurt, 65, 67, 109–10, 157–8, 223, 225,
    230
Hirschfeld, Magnus, ix–xi, xvii–xviii, 40–1,
    59, 69, 82, 83, 100, 197, 201, 215, 231,
    246
  adaptation therapy, and, 179–81
  anti-Semitic attacks on, 169, 229–30,
    240, 243
  biography, 86–8

Blüher, Hans, and, 152, 153–4
Brand, Adolf, and, 102, 226, 229–30
cross-dressing, theories of, 178–9
Dasbach, Georg Friedrich, and, 114
Eulenburg scandal, and, 123–4
feminism, and, 117, 182
Friedlaender, Benedict, and, 116–18
Harden, Maximilian, and, 128–9
homosexuality (sexual intermediacy),
    theories of, 88, 150–4, 169–70
lesbianism, theories of, 117
Meerscheidt-Hüllessem, Leopold von,
    and, 101
Nietzsche, Friedrich, and 106
Scientific-Humanitarian Committee
    (SHC), 85–8, 226–7, 228–30
statistical study of homosexual
    population, 96–7
Tresckow, Hans von, and, 101
world tour, 242–3
Hitler, Adolf, 157, 169, 244
Himmler, Heinrich, 244–5
Hustler, The (Der Puppenjunge), 100, 205,
    208, 209–10, 217
Hollywood, 165
Holstein, Friedrich von, 124–5
Holzmann, Johannes, 95, 100, 105
homosexual press (Germany), 164, 189–92,
    232–3
  see also Germany, censorship
  advertising in, 191–2, 233
  singles advertisements, and, 191–2
  travel guides, and, 192
Homosexualität des Mannes und des Weibes,
    Die (The Homosexuality of Men and
    Women), 90–1, 179–80
homosexuality
  blackmail, based on, 27–8, 71–80, 221
    Ackermann, 75
    Hasse, August, 74–5
    Krupp, Friedrich Alfred, 72–3
  criminality (perceived), and, xi
  essentialism *vs.* social constructionism,
    xiv–xv, 95–7, 116, 118–19, 128–9
  etymology, xi–xii, 31–2
  Capri, island of, 72, 113
  Florence, renaissance, xii–xiii
  German characteristic, considered as,
    120, 138–9, 156

German encyclopedia definitions, xv,
118–19
Germany and, in early modern period,
xiii
German slang, xi–xii, 18, 58, 63
Google Books project, and, xvi
heterosexual marriage, and, 180
Italy and, 72, 219
Jewish characteristic, considered as,
xviii, 156
London, in eighteenth and nineteenth
century, xiii–xiv, 70, 218
Netherlands, in eighteenth century, xiii
Paris, in eighteenth and nineteenth
century, xiii–xiv, 70
Russia, in nineteenth century, xiii
sodomy, traditional diagnosis of, 5–6, 22
Spain, in early modern, xiii
suicide, as cause of, 4–5, 19, 86–7, 164–5,
171, 221
Sweden, in nineteenth century, xiii
theories of, 88, 95–7, 104–5, 127–9, 150–4,
169–70, 228
see also "third-sex" theory
urban subcultures and, xiii–xiv, 70
Höppener, Hugo (Fidus), 100, 102
Hößli, Heinrich, 107
Hoverbeck, Paul von, 64
Howard, Brian, 195, 214
Hüllessem, *see* Meerscheidt-Hüllessem
Human Rights League (HRL), xix, 185, 231
Blätter für Menschenrecht, as official
periodical, 231
cultural associations, sponsored by,
231–2
German Friendship Association, as
precursor to, 223, 231
membership, growth and profile, 232
Radszuweit, Friedrich, as national
chairman, 231
Humperdinck, Engelbert, 224
Huxley, Aldous, 199–200

Institute for Sexual Science, ix–x, xix,
160–86
descriptions by visitors, ix–x, 162–3
destruction of, 241–3
heterosexuals, services for, 182–4
homosexuals, services for, 179–81

museum, ix, 162, 241
Nazi staff members, 242
research on male prostitution, 201–3
sex reassignment procedures, 173–9
International Congress on Sexual Science,
184
intersexuality, 171, 178–9
Isherwood, Christopher, ix-x, xix, 165,
187–8, 194, 195, 196, 197, 202, 207,
209, 219
Israel, Hermann, 73–4

Jagow, Traugott von, 65
Jansen, Wilhelm, 98–99, 144–6, 152
Jahrbuch für sexuelle Zwischenstufen
(Yearbook for sexual
intermediaries), 89, 107, 108,
109–11, 153, 162, 164, 181, 190, 223
Joël, Ernst, 214–16
Johnson, Philip, 193
Joux, Otto de, *see* Podjukl, Otto
Jugendstil, 102

Kahl, Wilhelm, 220–1, 224
Kapp Putsch, 169
Kautsky, Karl, 98
Keilson-Lauritz, Marita, 109
Kertbeny, Karl Maria, 31
Kinsey Institute, 175
Klee, Paul, 199
Kleist, Heinrich von, 108
Kollwitz, Käthe, 224
Kopp, Heinrich, 83
Kraepelin, Emil, 166
Krafft-Ebing, Richard von, xvii, 23–5, 87,
170, 181, 186, 241
Hirschfeld, Magnus, and, 89,
Psychopathia sexualis, 24–5, 57, 92
Ulrichs, Karl Heinrich, and, 23–4, 92
Kracauer, Siegfried, 188
Kronfeld, Arthur, 161, 176
Krupp, Friedrich Alfred, 72–3, 113
Kupffer, Elisar von, 107
Kuzmin, Mikhail, 110

Layard, John, 195, 196, 209
Landauer, Gustav, 157
Lang, Fritz, 214
Lania, Léo, 216

Lasker-Schüler, Else, 100
Lebensreform Bewegung (life reform movement), 98, 146
    see also Wandervogel
    nudism (*FKK*), 98, 103, 146
    youth movement in Germany, 141, 158
Lecomte, Raymond, 121–23, 124,
Lehmann, John, 207–8
Lehmstedt, Mark, 91
Leistikow, Walter, 98
lesbianism, 117, 165–6
    periodicals, 190, 232
    organizations, 231, 232
Levy-Lenz, Ludwig, 177–8, 186, 243
Lewis, Sinclair, 199
Lex-Heinze (Heinze censorship law), 91, 94
Lieberman, Max, 98
life reform movement, *see Lebensreform Bewegung*
Liliencron, Detlev von, 99
Linsert, Richard, 201–4, 207, 217–18
Loos, Anita, 165
Lücke, Martin, 209
Luther, Martin, 4, 15

Mackay, John Henry (Sagitta, pseud.), 100, 105, 205, 208, 210, 229
    see also *Hustler, The*
Magnus Hirschfeld Society, 201
Maltzan-Wedell, Alfred von, 22–3, 35
Mann, Heinrich, 99, 222
Mann, Klaus, ix, 194, 214, 216–17
Mann, Thomas, 99, 109–10, 157, 222
Männerbund, 140–59, 168
    antifeminism, and, 147–8
    anti-Semitism, and, 150
    definition of, 140–1
    Freikorps, as manifestation of, 169
    homosexuality, and, 149–50
    Nazi Party, as manifestation of, 158, 238
    Schurtz, Heinrich, and, 147
    Wandervogel, as manifestion of, 142–3
Mantegazza, Paolo, 24
Marcuse, Max, 176
Marx, Karl, 24, 41
masculinists, xviii, 101–5, 111–12
    see also Blüher, Hans, and Brand, Adolf, and Friedlaender, Benedict

McAlmon, Robert, 193, 213
McLaren, Angus, 71
Meerscheidt-Hüllessem, Leopold von
    biography, 55–6, 58
    Department of Homosexuals (and Blackmailers), and, 54–5, 71, 83
    Hirschfeld, Magnus, and, 86, 101
    homosexual identity, and, 47, 56–7, 58
    innovative policing, and, 55–6, 70, 83–4, 208
    Krafft-Ebing, Richard von, and, 57–8
    male prostitution, and, 64, 70, 71, 208
    Moll, Albert, and, 57, 58
    mugshot album (*Verbrecheralbum*), and, 55–7, 67, 71, 76–7, 78, 81–2
Méténier, Oscar, 59, 63
Mirbeau, Octave, 59, 120
Moll, Albert, xi, 24, 57, 58, 61, 87, 92, 113, 166, 170
Moltke, Kuno von, 121, 126–9, 150–1
Moltke-Harden libel trial, 126–9, 150–1
Mommsen, Theodor, 104
Mosse, George, 42
Mühler, Heinrich von (Prussian Minister of Culture), 36
Mühsam, Erich, 94–5, 96, 100
Mühsam, Richard, 177
Müller, Hermann, 224
Musil, Robert, 109, 143

Näcke, Paul, 50, 68
Napoleonic Code, 219
Nazi Party, xix, 158, 169, 222, 229, 231
    homosexual rights, position on, 238
Nichols, Robert, 199–200
Nietzsche, Friedrich, 104, 105–6
    homosexuality, alleged, 106
Nordau, Max, 99
North German Confederation (1867–71), *see* Germany
nudism (*FKK*), *see Lebensreform Bewegung*

Ostwald, Hans, 60, 69, 83, 124, 194
Oswald, Richard, 164–5, 167
"outing," as legal reform strategy, 113–14

Pabst, G. W., 166
paragraph 175, *see also* anti-sodomy statute(s)

definition, 46
enforcement, difficulty of, 55, 65–6
Reichstag petition to reform, 94–5
Paumgarten, Nick, 241
pederasty, ancient Greek model of, 102–4, 119
see also Brand, Adolf
Pernauhm, Fritz Geron, 234
Philpot, Glyn Warren, 197–8
Placzek, Siegfried, 166
Podjukl, Otto (pseud. Otto de Joux), 58, 89
policing, in Berlin, 42–84
costume balls, 56–7, 62–4
homosexual establishments, 43–7
male prostitution, 54–5, 64–7, 81–2, 83–4, 218–19
Polizei, tradition of, 53
royal authority, as extension of, 53–4
political party orientation among homosexuals, 236–7, 243
pornography, 102
press
Germany and Berlin, 123–4, 125, 126–7
foreign, 123–4, 126–7
Preußen, Crown Prince Friedrich Wilhelm von, 126
Preußen, Prince Georg von, 34
Preußen, Prince Friedrich Heinrich von, 125–6
prostitution
male, xii–xiv, 42, 62- 114–15, 165
blackmail related to, 74–82, 114, 122, 165, 209–10, tourists, as victims of, 78–9
bars and venues, 68–70, 203–9
criminality, and, 69–70, 79–81
German slang, 62
phenomenon, as, 188–9
pimping and solicitation, and, 68–9, 70, 204–5, 208–9
sex tourism, as magnet for, 79, 187–8, 192–8, 219
soldier, 65, 67, 68, 200
relationship to female prostitution, 66, 70, 189, 218–19
female, 66, 70, 189, 218–19
Prussian Medical Affairs Board, 30–1

Psychopathia sexualis, see Krafft-Ebing, Richard von
Pudor, Heinrich, 103

Radszuweit, Friedrich, 190, 221, 240, 243
biography, 230–1, 235, 240
homosexuality, theory of, 234–5
Human Rights League (HRL), and, 231
pederasty, critique of, 235
periodicals, 231, 232–3, 240
homosexual rights activism, 231, 235–6
Theater of Eros, and, 233–4
Raffalovich, Marc-André, 24, 108
Rathenau, Walther, 137
Renoir, Jean, 199
Richthofen, Bernhard von, 46, 70
Rilke, Rainer Maria, 99
Robinson, William, 162–3
romantic literature, German, 107–9
Röhm, Ernst, 229, 243–5
Römer, Lucien von, 95
Rung, Otto, 214
Russell, Dora, 162
Rydström, Jens, xiii

Sadler-Grün, Willibald von, 61
Saint-Saëns, Camille, 214
Sanger, Margaret, 162
Sappho und Sokrates, 86–7, 90, 186
Schiller, Friedrich, 108–9
Schinkel, Karl Friedrich, 9
Schlaf, Johannes, 112
Schleswig and Holstein, duchies of, 26–7
Schurtz, Heinrich, 147–8
Schutzstaffel (SS), 229
Schweitzer, Johann Baptist von, 14–15, 34
schwul, etymology, xi–xii
Scientific-Humanitarian Committee (SHC), xvii–xviii, xix, 40–1, 61, 86–91, 152, 163, 164, 201, 220
Community of the Special (CoS), and, 226–7, 228–30
membership profile, 225–6
Munich subcommittee, 118
political activism, and, 90–1, 94–5, 113–14, 221, 223–4
popular education (propaganda), 89–91, 93–4
secession movement, within, 116–18
social-scientific research, and, 96–7

Segre, Dino, 214
sex reassignment procedures, see Institute
    for Sexual Science
sexology, as "Jewish" science, 156, 159,
    229–30, 245–6
sexual intermediacy, theory of, see "third-
    sex" theory
Siemsen, Hans, 206–7, 208, 216
Social Democratic Party (German), 51,
    72–3, 90, 97–8, 113, 148, 183, 220,
    222, 231
    homosexual rights, position on, 97–8,
    237
Sombart, Nicolaus, 140
Spender, Stephen, 187, 195
Spohr, Max, 85, 87, 88–91, 106, 107, 110,
    164
Stegemann, Herbert, 112
Stein, Gertrude, 193
Steinach, Eugen, 173–5, 179
Stirner, Max, 100, 101
Stöcker, Helene, 117, 182, 190
Strauss, Richard, 111
Strindberg, August, 56–7, 99
Sturmabteilung (SA), 229, 243–5
suffrage movement, see feminism
Symonds, John Addington, 92
Szittya, Emil, 61

Teschenberg, Hermann Freiherr von,
    111
"third-sex" theory, 88
transsexuality
    see also Institute for Sexual Science
    case studies, 171, 176–8
    definition(s), 178–9
    science of, 163, 173–5
        hormone treatment, 175
        sex-reassignment surgery, 174–9
"transvestitism," see cross-dressing
Transvestiten, Die (The Transvestites), 87–8,
    170
Transvestitenschein, 172–3
Tresckow, Hans von, 59, 72–3, 81–2, 101,
    125–6
Tsheck, Ewald, 229–30

Ulrichs, Karl Heinrich, xvi-xvii, 3–41, 62,
    246
    Association of German Jurists, and the,
        3–5, 28–9
    campaign for legal reform, 3–5, 28–30,
        31, 32, 36–7, 39
    Dioning, definition, 17–18, 39
    education, 6–9
    family background, 6–8
    Italy, residency, 39–41
    Kertbeny, and, 31–2
    Krafft-Ebing, and, 23–5, 92
    Numa Numantius as pseudonym, 4,
        17, 25
    pamphlets, 18–21, 29–30, 37, 38, 39
        distribution and influence, 21, 24–5,
            40–1, 91–2, 93, 107
        re-publication, 41, 89
    Urning, xvii, 28, 29
        definition, 17–18, 31, 39

Valentino, Rudolph, 198
Vanselow, Karl, 103
Veidt, Conrad, 165
Virchow, Rudolf, 30–1, 51, 89

Wandervogel, 98–9
    see also Lebensreform Bewegung
    Alt-Wandervogel, 146, 147, 154–5
        origins, 143
        antifeminism, and, 148–9
        anti-Semitism, and, 155–6
    Blüher, Hans, and, 142–3, 149–50
    definition, 141
    diffusion, 142
    Führer principal, and, 142–3
    homosexuality, and, 149–50,
        154–5
    Jung-Wandervogel, 154
    Männerbund, 142–3
    Neu-Wandervogel, 146, 149, 154–5
    participation of girls, and, 148–9
    Steglitz-Wandervogel, 143
    Wanderschwestern (Association of
        Hiking Sisters), 148–9
Waugh, Evelyn, 195
Wedekind, Frank, 99, 143, 167
Weil, Arthur, 161
Werfel, Franz, 99
Westphal, Carl, xiv, 24, 92
Whitman, Walt, 111–12

Wilde, Oscar, 61, 91, 110–11, 218, 241
Wildenbruch, Ernst von, 99
Wille, Bruno, 100, 116
William II, Emperor of Germany (Kaiser),
    71–2, 73, 222
Winckelmann, Johann, 104
Witkowski, Felix Ernst, *see* Harden,
    Maximilian
Wood, Grant, 193–4
World League for Sexual Reform,
    184, 185

World War I, influence on homosexual
    identity, 236–7
Worsley, T. C., 187

youth movement, see *Lebensreform
    Bewegung*

Zastrow, Carl von, 33–6, 54
Zionism, 157, *see also* Herzl, Theodor
Zukunft, Die, 122–23, 124, 125
Zweig, Stefan, 99

A NOTE ABOUT THE AUTHOR

Robert Beachy was trained as a German historian at the University of Chicago, where he received his PhD in 1998. He is presently associate professor of history at Underwood International College of Yonsei University in Seoul, South Korea.

A NOTE ABOUT THE TYPE

This book was set in Monotype Dante, a typeface designed by Giovanni Mardersteig (1892–1977). Its first use was in an edition of Boccaccio's *Trattatello in laude di Dante* that appeared in 1954. Although modeled on the Aldine type used for Pietro Cardinal Bembo's treatise *De Aetna* in 1495, Dante is a thoroughly modern interpretation of the venerable face.

Composed by North Market Street Graphics, Lancaster, Pennsylvania

Printed and bound by Berryville Graphics, Berryville, Virginia

Designed by Maggie Hinders

BOCA RATON PUBLIC LIBRARY

3 3 6 5 6 3 0 0 8 9 5 0 0

306.766 Bea
Beachy, Robert,
Gay Berlin :birthplace of a modern
 identity /

Nov 2014